Melvin Schwartz Ph.D

Addiction and Brain Damage

Edited by Derek Richter

CROOM HELM LONDON
UNIVERSITY PARK PRESS BALTIMORE

© 1980 Derek Richter
Croom Helm Ltd, 2-10 St John's Road, London SW11

British Library Cataloguing in Publication Data
Addiction: Biochemical Aspects of Dependence and Brain Damage *(Conference)*,
   Oxford, 1979
   Addiction and brain damage.
   1. Brain damage − Congresses
   2. Alcoholism − complication and sequelae − Congresses
   3. Drugs − Physiological effect − Congresses
   4. Drugs − Side effects − Congresses
   I. Title II. Richter, Derek   III. Helping Hand Organisation
   616.8'6   RC386.2

   ISBN 0-7099-0254-9

 Published in North America by
UNIVERSITY PARK PRESS
233 East Redwood Street,
Baltimore, Maryland

ISBN 0-8391-4139-4

Library of Congress Card Number: 80-51464

Typeset by Elephant Productions, London SE22
Printed and bound in Great Britain
by Billing and Sons Limited and Kemp Hall Bindery
Guildford, London, Oxford, Worcester

CONTENTS

PREFACE

Alcoholism and drug addiction are presenting serious problems in many parts of the world today. In a number of countries there is evidence of a steady rise in alcohol consumption in recent years and the rising morbidity rate, together with the increased involvement of young people, is a matter for growing concern. It has long been known that heavy drinking can lead, not only to general physical ill health, but also to conditions such as delirium tremens and dementia involving the brain. Addiction is itself a form of mental disorder and recently there have been a number of reports suggesting that heavy drinking, even at socially acceptable levels, can give rise to brain damage in individuals who are susceptible to the effects of alcohol. However, the nature of the brain damage, and the reasons why some individuals are more vulnerable than others, are still far from clear.

In this situation the Helping Hand Organisation, which was founded by Barry Richards in the UK in 1964, organised an international Symposium on 'Addiction: Biochemical Aspects of Dependence and Brain Damage' at Magdalen College, Oxford in September 1979. During the past fifteen years the Helping Hand Organisation has carried out pioneer work on the treatment and rehabilitation of alcoholics and drug addicts in a chain of residential homes and day centres set up by them in different parts of the country. They have also engaged in research on social and other aspects of addiction. The primary purpose of the 1979 Oxford Symposium was to bring together a group of leading scientists and clinical research workers engaged in the study of addiction in different countries so as to provide an opportunity for them to assess the implications of the recent findings on the biochemical and physiological mechanisms involved in dependence and in the causation of brain damage. The papers given at the Symposium are presented in this volume.

The scientific programme of the Symposium was arranged by Dr G.K. Shaw. We are indebted for their generous financial support for the meeting to Astra Chemicals Ltd, Aspro Nicholas Ltd, Barclay's Bank Ltd, Mr Barry Richards, The Brewer's Society, Mr P. Collins, EMI Medical Ltd, The Jurgens Trust, The Medical Research Council, The Mental Health Foundation, The Rank Group Charity, Roche Products Ltd, Sandoz Products Ltd and The Wellcome Trust.

Derek Richter

PART ONE

BIOCHEMICAL AND PHYSIOLOGICAL MECHANISMS

1 THE EFFECTS OF ALCOHOL ON METABOLIC PROCESSES

Hans Krebs

The chief target organs of ethanol are the nervous system and the liver. From the biochemical point of view the mechanism of action of alcohol on the nervous system is still mysterious in many ways. We are only just beginning to get some understanding of the manner in which ethanol interferes with the function of the nervous system. This applies to the mechanism of acute intoxication as well as to the chronic manifestations such as polyneuritis, the deterioration of personality, delirium tremens and Korsakoff's psychosis.

By contrast, we do have some biochemical information on the mechanism of the effects of alcohol on the liver. Above all, it is clear *why* the liver is one of the major target organs. The liver is the only organ which possesses a highly active enzyme capable of breaking down alcohol. This specific role of the liver in disposing of ingested alcohol was discovered by the Danish physiologist, Einar Lundsgaard (1938). He discovered that alcohol is not metabolised by the eviscerated animal but is readily oxidised by the isolated perfused liver. The specific enzyme responsible for the removal of alcohol is alcohol dehydrogenase, an enzyme which has been crystallised and obtained in a pure form. It brings about the reaction:

$$Ethanol + NAD \longrightarrow acetaldehyde + NADH_2$$

By a further dehydrogenation the acetaldehyde is converted to acetic acid, and the acetic acid can then be completely burned either in the liver or in a variety of other tissues, particularly in cardiac muscle and kidney. Although some alcohol appears in the breath and in the urine, probably more than 90 per cent of ingested alcohol undergoes complete oxidation in the body. The oxidation of alcohol is an effective source of energy, because it is coupled with the synthesis of ATP.

Why should the occurrence of this reaction of alcohol in the liver be harmful and, in cases of chronic alcoholism, eventually lead to liver cirrhosis? There is something special about the location of alcohol dehydrogenase within the liver cell, in that this enzyme is located in the cytosol, in contrast to the majority of dehydrogenases which are

11

located within the mitochondria. The rapid dehydrogenation of alcohol to acetic acid causes a unique kind of upset of the intracellular chemical balance. The rate of conversion of NAD into $NADH_2$ causes a shift in the ratio of the concentrations of NAD and $NADH_2$, primarily in the cytosol where most of the synthetic activities of the liver cells are located (see Krebs, 1968; Krebs *et al.*, 1969). This ratio is of great importance to many metabolic processes because most dehydrogenases share with ethanol the coenzymes NAD and $NADH_2$ and their effectiveness depends on the relative concentrations of NAD and $NADH_2$, i.e. the $NAD/NADH_2$ ratio (referred to as the 'redox state' of the NAD-couple).

The shift caused by alcohol in the redox state of this couple is taken to be a major reason for metabolic disturbances in the liver, showing themselves early in the accumulation of fat in the liver of alocholics and ending in cirrhosis. The acetaldehyde formed by alcohol dehydrogenase has also been suspected of being harmful because aldehydes readily interact with amino groups of proteins. However, as the acetaldehyde is rapidly converted to acetic acid, it is doubtful whether its steady-state concentration rises sufficiently to combine with proteins.

Biochemical studies have thus contributed an explanation of why alcohol is toxic to the liver, but this has not led to new ideas about a cure for liver damage.

One of the secondary effects of alcohol on liver metabolism should be mentioned. Under certain conditions, i.e. when alcohol is taken in the fasting state or when carbohydrate intake is low, hypoglycaemia can develop. The mechanism of hypoglycaemia is as follows: the shift in the redox state of the $NAD/NADH_2$ couple inhibits glucose synthesis in the liver. In the fasting state the sources of glucose are limited. Adequate glucose levels in the blood can be maintained only by the resynthesis of glucose from lactic acid formed during exercise and from protein broken down during starvation. Gluconeogenesis is inhibited by alcohol because the pathway of gluconeogenesis is effective only if the $NAD/NADH_2$ ratio is within the normal range. Gluconeogenesis, like the opposite metabolic process, glycolysis, depends on reactions involving this ratio. Therefore changes in the ratio also upset gluconeogenesis. The liver is the main site of gluconeogenesis.

As for the effects of ethanol on the second major target area, the nervous system, the mechanism of the damaging action must be quite different from that in the liver because of the absence of alcohol dehydrogenase from nervous tissue.

The older biochemical approaches to organ function (based on the study of enzymes and metabolic pathways of degradation and synthesis of cell constituents) which have been successful in the study of liver diseases have provided only limited answers to the problems of brain physiology and brain pathology. We must therefore explore whether other areas of biochemistry might be helpful.

In recent years new, more subtle effects of ethanol on metabolic processes have come to light. Work by Mørland and Bessesen (1977), Mørland (1979), Badawy *et al.* (1979), Rothschild *et al.* (1971, 1975) has shown that ethanol inhibits protein synthesis in the liver and other tissues. Tewari and Noble (1979) have demonstrated inhibitory effects of ethanol on protein synthesis in the brain. The experimental basis of this demonstration is the observation that the incorporation of radioactive amino acids into the tissue protein (which can easily be measured) is inhibited by ethanol. What does this mean?

We know from discoveries made by Schoenheimer and Rittenberg (1938) and Schoenheimer (1942) that many tissue proteins and other macromolecules are not stable; they are constantly being broken down and resynthesised, a phenomenon referred to as the 'dynamic state of body constituents'. This phenomenon is especially marked in the liver, where an explanation can be offered for the significance of this 'turnover'. Most liver proteins are enzymes taking part in metabolic processes. These processes are not always the same but depend upon the nutritional state of the organism and other physiological circumstances. When the diet contains much protein then the liver must degrade the excess and either burn it or convert it into fat or carbohydrate, for the body cannot store much protein. When the diet is low in carbohydrate the liver must synthesise glucose by gluconeogenesis.

When the body is exposed to drugs or poisons, for example barbiturates, enzymes are produced which detoxicate the drugs and poisons. The liver cannot at any one time be equipped with all the enzymes it might need in different physiological situations. For this it would have to be a very much larger organ. The liver deals with variable requirements by removing, through proteolysis, enzymes which it does not need in a given situation and by synthesising, from the amino acids released, the enzymes it requires. Thus the dynamic state of proteins is part of a process, adapting the organism to changing physiological circumstances.

Another function of the continuous protein synthesis/degradation is taken to be the elimination and replacement of faulty material. Tissue proteins may become denatured, for example, by the irreversible oxidation of SH-groups, or faulty protein molecules may arise either from mutations or from errors of the translation and transcription of genes. Thus, the turnover of cell constituents serves to maintain a fully functioning cell (Goldberg and Dice, 1974; Goldberg and St. John, 1976).

If ethanol inhibits the turnover of proteins it means that it inhibits the capacity of the organism to adapt itself and to maintain a state of efficiency. Examples of adaptive enzymes are the enzymes for degradation of tryptophan and tyrosine. These are essential amino acids and when the diet is low in protein they must be preserved and not degraded. The body deals with this by getting rid of the enzymes which degrade tryptophan and tyrosine. It is essential that these amino acids are removed when there is an excess. If they are not removed they may give rise to physiologically active substances in excess, such as tyramine and tryptamine. This adaptation of the enzymes is interfered with by ethanol (Mørland and Bessesen, 1977; Mørland, 1974; Badawy *et al.*, 1979; Rawat, 1974).

While, then, for the liver, the significance of the rapid turnover of some proteins can be understood, we cannot yet be quite sure of an analogous explanation for this turnover of cell constituents in the brain. The fact is that protein synthesis does occur in the brain, though not at the same rate as in the liver, and that in brain, as in liver, ethanol can slow down protein synthesis (see Tewari and Noble, 1979; Lindholm and Khawaja, 1979). Presumably in the brain, as in the liver, protein synthesis is an aspect of adaptation. The brain synthesises biologically active polypeptides such as the opioids and also a number of peptide hormones.

There are two aspects of special interest in the present context. The need for these peptides is not constant. Their quantities must therefore vary with time and this is achieved by a rapid turnover. The need also varies in different parts of the brain. In the past it has been difficult, from the biochemical point of view, to account for the mechanism of action of drugs and of toxic agents on the nervous system because such information as was available did not explain the differential effects of the substances in different areas of the brain, as for example, that anaesthetics affect only those areas connected with consciousness, but leave large portions of the brain in a normally functioning state.

I am very hopeful that the exploration of this new field of biologically active peptides, and of the specific receptor sites (see Snyder, 1979; Kosterlitz, 1976) will add greatly to the understanding of the specific neural function.

Finally, let us look at alcohol or drug dependence generally. Regular intake of a drug, or any 'unphysiological' substance, can cause habituation. It follows from what I have said that habituation is, at the biochemical level, the adjustment of the enzymic equipment of the tissues to the intake of special substances, and that this adjustment or adaptation involves continual protein synthesis. If this adjustment is not readily reversible when the stimulus is withdrawn, then the chemical organisation of the tissues – or of some tissues – becomes unbalanced, and to restore the balance the stimulus must be provided again. In other words, the organism has become addicted, has become drug-dependent. Thus we can translate the phenomenon of addiction into the language and concepts of biochemistry. This does not mean that we can now suggest a cure for drug dependence. Perhaps in the long run useful practical measures concerning the management of drug dependence may emerge. At present, prevention and treatment can be based only on practical experience, not on profound theoretical understanding. It needs no biochemistry to come to the conclusion that we must aim at limiting alcohol intake and we must provide intensive treatment for the rehabilitation of addicts.

Abbreviations

NAD   = nicotinamide adenine dinucleotide
$NADH_2$ = reduced nicotinamide dinucleotide

References

Badawy, A.A.-B., Punjani, N.F. and Evans, M. (1979), *Biochem. J., 178*, 575-80
Goldberg, A.L. and Dice, J.F. (1974), *Ann. Rev. Biochem., 43*, 835-69
Goldberg, A.L. and St. John, A.C. (1976), *Ann. Rev. Biochem., 45*, 797-803
Krebs, H.A. (1968), *Adv. Enzyme Reg., 6*, 467-80
Krebs, H.A., Freedland, R.A., Hems, R. and Stubbs, M. (1969), *Biochem. J., 112*, 117-24
Kosterlitz, H.W. (1976) in *Opiates and Endogenous Opioid Peptides*, Elsevier-North Holland Press, Amsterdam
Lindholm, D.B. and Khawaja, J.A. (1979), *Neuroscience, 4*, 1007-13
Lundsgaard, E. (1938), *Compt. rend. Labor. Carlsberg, Ser. Chim., 22*, 333
Mørland, J. (1974), *Biochem. Pharmacol., 23*, 21-35
——— (1979), *Biochem. Pharmacol., 28*, 423
Mørland, J. and Bessesen, A. (1977), *Biochim. Biophys. Acta, 474*, 312-20
Rawat, A.K. (1974), *J. Neurochem., 22*, 915-22
Rothschild, M.A., Oratz, M. and Schreiber, S.S. (eds.) (1975) *Alcohol and Abnormal Protein Synthesis*, Pergamon Press, Oxford

Rothschild, M.A., Oratz, M., Monzelli, J. and Schreiber, S.S. (1971), *J. Clin. Invest., 50*, 1812-18

Schoenheimer, R. and Rittenberg, D. (1938), *Science, 87*, 221-26

Schoenheimer, R. (1942) in *The Dynamic State of Body Constituents*, Harvard University Press, Cambridge, Mass

Snyder, S.H. (1979), 'Opiate receptors and morphine-like peptides', *Harvey Lecture Series, 73*, 291-314

Tewari, S. and Noble, E.P. (1979) in *Biochemistry and Pharmacology of Ethanol* (eds. E. Majchrowicz and E.P. Noble), Plenum Press, New York and London, 541-8

2 CATECHOLAMINE-DERIVED ALKALOIDS IN DEPENDENCE

Virginia E. Davis, Jesse L. Cashaw and
Kenneth D. McMurtrey

Theories of Ethanol-evoked Formation of Alkaloids

The original premise of ethanol-induced formation of pharmacologically active neuroamine-derived alkaloids (mediated by acetaldehyde, the proximal metabolite of ethanol) in mammalian species was simultaneously and independently advanced by our laboratory (Davis, 1971) and by Cohen (1971a). A common feature of both theories is the Pictet-Spengler condensation (Whaley and Govindachari, 1951) of β-arylethylamines with aldehydes to form Schiff base intermediates. These substances subsequently undergo cyclisation, yielding the tetrahydroisoquinoline alkaloids that may be involved in some aspects of alcoholism.

Cohen and his colleagues proposed that acetaldehyde, derived from ethanol, condenses directly with endogenous catecholamines to form biologically active l-methyltetrahydroisoquinolines (Cohen and Collins, 1970; Cohen, 1971a, b; Cohen, 1976). This laboratory also suggested that l-methyltetrahydroisoquinolines may be formed (Yamanaka *et al.*, 1970).

We further theorised that metabolism of ethanol evokes a more intricate chain of events leading to the production of complex 1-benzyl-tetrahydroisoquinolines as aberrant metabolites of catecholamines (Davis *et al.*, 1970; Davis and Walsh, 1970 (a); Davis, 1971). In this case, ethanol-generated acetaldehyde increases the availability of the dopamine-derived aldehyde for condensation with the parent amine by competitively inhibiting the oxidative disposition of the biogenic aldehyde. The result is an enhanced formation of tetrahydropapaveroline (THP, norlaudanosoline), a pharmacologically active benzyltetra-hydroisoquinoline alkaloid.

Further metabolism of the simple tetrahydroisoquinolines formed by direct condensation of acetaldehyde or formaldehyde with catechol-amines appears to be relatively limited. But in plants, benzyltetra-hydroisoquinoline alkaloids are the biogenic precursors of a diverse array of even more complex alkaloids, including the tetrahydroberberine

Figure 2.1: Biogenesis of Isoquinoline Alkaloids

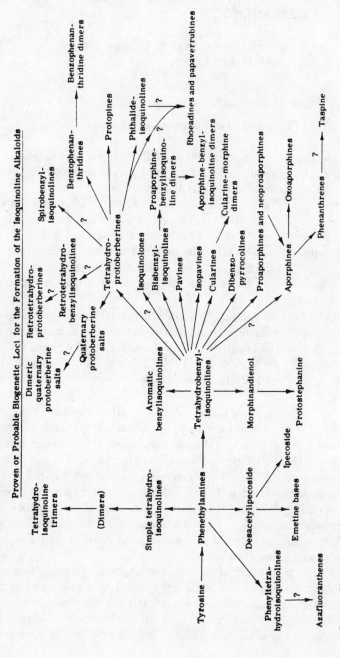

Proven or Probable Biogenetic Loci for the Formation of the Isoquinoline Alkaloids

Source: Shamma, 1972.

(protoberberine), pavine, isopavine, aporphine, morphinane, cularine and protopine groups (Battersby, 1961; Bentley, 1965; Spenser, 1966; Kirby, 1967; Robinson, 1968; Santavy, 1970; Shamma, 1972), as shown in Figure 2.1.

We have proposed that the biosynthesis of complex alkaloids is a capability that is not entirely unique to plants. Certain of these reaction sequences may be evoked in man and animals, as well, which in turn might subserve some of the mechanisms brought into play in the misuse of ethanol and related drugs (Davis *et al.*, 1970; Davis and Walsh, 1970(a); Davis, 1971). The possibility that tetrahydropapaveroline (THP) may follow similar metabolic transformations in mammalian systems is thus an integral part of our hypothesis (see Figure 2.2). The indication in this figure of specific groups of alkaloids (aporphine, morphine and tetrahydroberberine) as emanating from THP is not, however, intended to be an exhaustive and all-inclusive statement of possibilities.

Our hypothesis regarding alcohol-induced alkaloid formation did not arise spontaneously: rather, it was derived from investigations into the effects of ethanol on the metabolism of neurotransmitters in both human subjects and experimental animals. Additionally, they were extended to include other drugs that produce dependence of the alcohol-barbiturate type, e.g. chloral hydrate, paraldehyde and barbiturates.

This is an important consideration for several reasons. Ethanol and related drugs produce a characteristic withdrawal syndrome. Drugs within this class can be substituted for ethanol in preventing or ameliorating alcohol withdrawal symptoms, and these drugs are cross dependent. Finally, the action of these drugs is potentiated when they are taken in combination with ethanol. It thus seems reasonable that common biochemical mechanisms may be responsible for producing the dependence state associated with prolonged and excessive use of ethanol and these pharmacologically equivalent drugs. Although this consideration is usually ignored, studies of the underlying mechanisms in alcohol abuse and dependence should also attempt to resolve the addiction liability of these pharmacologically equivalent drugs.

Common Features of Ethanol and Biogenic Amine Metabolism

It is well known that the primary reaction product of ethanol metabolism is acetaldehyde. It is also generally recognised that the

Figure 2.2: Structural representation of the ethanol-evoked modifications of dopamine metabolism. Known pathways, either *in vitro* or *in vivo*, are indicated by (⟶). The site of inhibition of dopamine metabolism by acetaldehyde, the metabolite of ethanol, is shown by (⟶//⟶). The proposed possible consequence of this inhibition resulting in the formation of diverse classes of complex alkaloids is illustrated by (- - - - →). The formation of tetrahydroprotoberberines in mammalian systems has now been established.

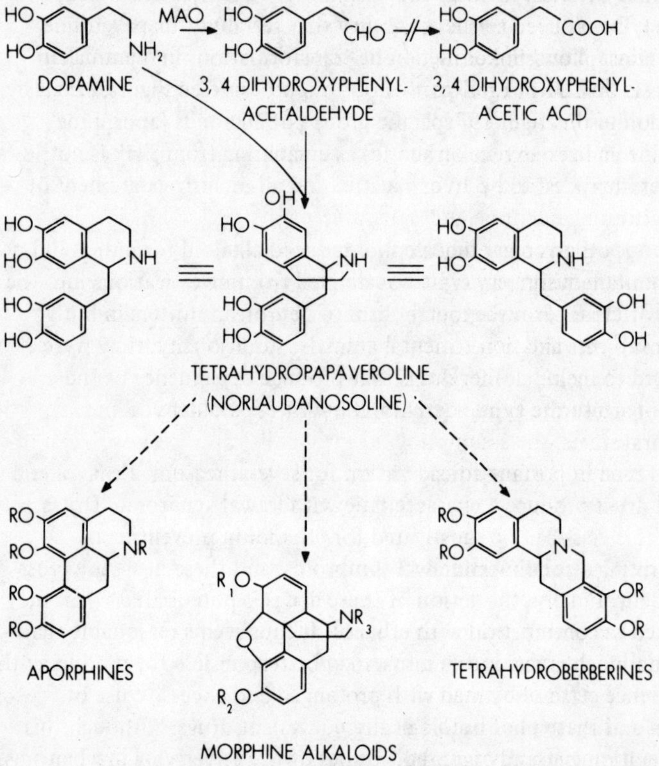

DOPAMINE

3, 4 DIHYDROXYPHENYL-
ACETALDEHYDE

3, 4 DIHYDROXYPHENYL-
ACETIC ACID

TETRAHYDROPAPAVEROLINE
(NORLAUDANOSOLINE)

APORPHINES

MORPHINE ALKALOIDS

TETRAHYDROBERBERINES

	R_1	R_2	R_3
NORMORPHINE	H	H	H
MORPHINE	H	H	CH_3
NORCODEINE	H	CH_3	H
CODEINE	H	CH_3	CH_3

Source: Davis *et al.*, 1970.

major portion of ethanol oxidation is catalysed by NAD-dependent alcohol dehydrogenase (ADH). The ethanol-derived acetaldehyde is oxidised to acetate by NAD^+-linked aldehyde dehydrogenase (ALDH), which has a broad substrate specificity.

Oxidative deamination of biogenic amines such as dopamine, norepinephrine and serotonin by monoamine oxidase results in the formation of the corresponding biogenic aldehydes. The aldehydes derived from these amines may be oxidised to the corresponding acid metabolite by aldehyde dehydrogenase (ALDH) (Deitrich, 1966) or they may be reduced to the alcohol metabolite by alcohol dehydrogenase (Raskin and Sokoloff, 1970) or by NADPH-linked aldehyde reductases (ALDR) (Tabakoff and Erwin, 1970; Ris and von Wartburg, 1973; Anderson *et al.*, 1976). The probability of oxidation or reduction depends to a large extent on the structural characteristics of the amine-derived aldehydes. The β-hydroxylated aldehyde analogs of norepinephrine, normetanephrine and octopamine are primarily reduced to the corresponding glycol metabolites by brain and both oxidised and reduced in the periphery, whereas the primary route of aldehydes without the β-hydroxyl group – such as the aldehydes of dopamine and serotonin – is oxidation to acid metabolites (Rutledge and Jonason, 1967; Breese *et al.*, 1969; Duncan and Sourkes, 1974; Tipton *et al.*, 1977). Because the amine-derived aldehydes and ethanol share common enzyme systems, the assumption is reasonable that the metabolism of ethanol can result in modifications in the catabolism of biogenic amines.

Effect of Alcohol on Amine Metabolism

Evidence has been provided for specific alcohol-induced alterations in the metabolic disposition of neuroamines in man. It was found that ingestion of ethanol by man significantly shifts the metabolism of the aldehyde derivatives of both serotonin (Davis *et al.*, 1967a) and norepinephrine (Davis *et al.*, 1967b, c; Smith and Gitlow, 1967) from an oxidative to a reductive pathway.

Two possible mechanisms may be responsible for the alcohol-evoked modifications in neuroamine metabolism. Decreased availability of NAD^+, with the accompanying increased $NADH:NAD^+$ ratio occurring during the metabolism of ethanol, may divert the metabolism of amine-derived aldehydes from an oxidative to a reductive pathway. Additional evidence indicates that the competitive inhibition of aldehyde dehydrogenase by the primary metabolite of ethanol – namely acetaldehyde — both *in vitro* (Lahti and Majchrowicz, 1967; Lahti and Majchrowicz, 1969) and *in vivo* (Walsh *et al.*, 1970b) plays a major role in the alcohol-induced modifications in amine metabolism. These mechanisms are not necessarily mutually exclusive, but the latter is strongly favoured.

The fact that acetaldehyde is a strong competitive inhibitor of the oxidation of amine-derived aldehydes by aldehyde dehydrogenase is important in this context. For example, the inhibition constant (K_i of 2.6×10^{-6} M) for acetaldehyde in inhibiting the oxidation of 5-hydroxyindoleacetaldehyde by rat brain aldehyde dehydrogenase is low (Lahti and Majchrowicz, 1969). This fact suggests that the oxidation of amine-derived aldehydes may be exquisitely sensitive to inhibition by the acetaldehyde formed during ethanol metabolism, even if the actual concentrations of acetaldehyde are extremely low.

Species Differences

There is a notable species difference in the sensitivity to ethanol-induced modifications in amine metabolism. In the case of human subjects, even moderate doses of ethanol produce dramatic changes in the metabolism of serotonin and norepinephrine (Davis *et al.*, 1967a, b, c; Smith and Gitlow, 1967). In marked contrast, administration of large, even hypnotic, doses of ethanol to rats is relatively ineffective in altering the metabolism of biogenic amines in the periphery; and in this species, administration of large amounts of the ethanol metabolite, acetaldehyde, is required to modify amine metabolism significantly (Walsh *et al.*, 1970b).

The inability of even hypnotic doses of ethanol to shift the metabolism of the norepinephrine-derived aldehyde from an oxidative to a reductive route in the intact rat, in comparison with the marked effect in man, may be related to the fact that the metabolic fate of norepinephrine is different in the two species. In man the major excretion product is the acid metabolite, 3-methoxy-4-hydroxymandelic acid, whereas in the rat the predominant product is the glycol metabolite, 3-methoxy-4-hydroxyphenylglycol. The greater propensity of man, therefore, to oxidise the biogenic aldehyde derivative to the acid metabolite in the periphery may make this pathway more sensitive to competitive inhibition by ethanol-generated acetaldehyde. Furthermore, the affinity of aldehyde dehydrogenase for acetaldehyde may differ markedly in the two species.

The differences in the response of man and rats to ethanol-evoked alterations in biogenic aldehyde metabolism appear to parallel the relative sensitivity of the two species to the pharmacological effects of alcohol. Alcoholism is uniquely a human problem but, because of limitations of techniques for research involving human subjects, certain aspects of biochemical research related to alcoholism must of necessity utilise experimental animals. It is obviously preferable to study the effect of alcohol in a species other than the rat, in a species that would more closely parallel man in his sensitivity to the reinforcing, intoxicating and addicting actions of alcohol. Nevertheless rodents are for economic reasons extensively chosen for such experimentation. Although rodents must often be used in the laboratory, it is important to remain aware of the differences among species in their response to ethanol, and to temper interpretations and extrapolation of any results obtained with experimental animals to man.

Effect of Ethanol and Related Drugs on Formation of Benzyltetrahydroisoquinoline Alkaloids

A pivotal consideration in the metabolism of biogenic amines is the relative propensity of aldehydes derived from specific amines to be further metabolised by the oxidative or the reductive route. Dopamine is an excellent substrate for monoamine oxidase. In contrast to the aldehyde derivative of norepinephrine, the 3,4-dihydroxyphenyl-acetaldehyde generated is preferentially oxidised to 3,4-dihydroxy-phenylacetic acid by aldehyde dehydrogenase (Alivisatos and Tabakoff, 1973), particularly in brain. The aldehyde derivatives of the biogenic amines are highly reactive compounds. Holtz and colleagues (1964) reported that incubation of dopamine with guinea pig liver mitochondria preparations of monoamine oxidase — which lacked the cofactor for further oxidative metabolism of 3,4-dihydroxyphenyl-acetaldehyde formed on deamination of the amine — resulted in the formation of tetrahydropapaveroline. Tetrahydropapaveroline (THP, norlaudanosoline) is the benzyltetrahydroisoquinoline alkaloid produced by the nonenzymatic condensation of 3,4-dihydroxyphenyl-acetaldehyde with the parent amine.

Conditions that interfere with the normal enzymatic disposition of the dopamine-derived aldehyde — for example, a limited cofactor availability or the inhibition of aldehyde dehydrogenase — could be expected to increase the relative proportion of dopamine converted to THP. When this possibility was examined (Walsh *et al.*, 1970a), it was found that the relative formation of THP *in vitro* by rat liver and brain preparations was dependent on the substrate concentration and upon the availability of the aldehyde dehydrogenase cofactor, NAD^+, for further oxidation of the aromatic aldehyde to 3,4-dihydroxyphenyl-acetic acid. Tetrahydropapaveroline was the major metabolite of dopamine in the absence of exogenous coenzyme in both tissues.

Incorporation of the cofactor into incubation mixtures with liver essentially abolished tetrahydropapaveroline production and markedly enhanced the formation of the acid metabolite. With brain preparations, however, the addition of cofactors decreased tetrahydropapaveroline generation and only modestly increased dihydroxyphenylacetic acid formation. Tetrahydropapaveroline remained the major metabolite of dopamine in the brain tissue preparation under all conditions because of the limiting aldehyde dehydrogenase activity in comparison with monoamine oxidase activity in this *in vitro* preparation. Thus the relative amount of dopamine diverted to tetrahydropapaveroline assumed appreciable importance under conditions of limiting aldehyde oxidising capacity.

Ethanol and Acetaldehyde

The effect of ethanol and acetaldehyde on THP formation from labelled dopamine in rat liver and brain preparations was determined in the presence of exogenous NAD^+ (Davis *et al.*, 1970). The cofactor was incorporated to provide unlimited coenzyme for aldehyde dehydro-genase. Ethanol or acetaldehyde suppressed the oxidation of the intermediate aldehyde derivative of dopamine to the corresponding acid, and it concurrently augmented the conversion of dopamine to tetrahydropapaveroline. Competitive inhibition of the oxidation of 3,4-dihydroxyphenylacetaldehyde by acetaldehyde, therefore, facilitated the diversion of the amine-derived aldehyde to the alternative condensation route.

Substantial formation of the direct condensation product of dopamine with acetaldehyde was also observed when rat liver or brain preparations were incubated with ethanol or acetaldehyde (Davis *et al.*, 1970; Yamanaka *et al.*, 1970). The product of this reaction is the simple tetrahydroisoquinoline alkaloid, salsolinol (1-methyl-6,7-dihydroxy-1,2,3,4-tetrahydroisoquinoline).

Ethanol administration increases urinary excretion of catecholamines and stimulates release of these amines from adrenal medullary stores, effects that have been attributed to acetaldehyde derived metabolically from ethanol (Perman, 1958; Duritz and Truitt, 1966; Walsh and Truitt, 1968). Thus, if dopamine is similarly affected and freed from protected storage sites, it may then be more available for alkaloid-forming condensation reactions. Furthermore, the normal oxidative route for disposition of the dopamine-derived aldehyde is also impaired during the metabolism of acetaldehyde.

Chloral Hydrate

The well-established cross dependency and synergy between chloral hydrate and ethanol is of interest in relation to the possible drug-induced formation of amine-derived alkaloids. Incidentally, similar to the changes seen with ethanol, administration of chloral hydrate or paraldehyde to rats decreased the amount of serotonin metabolised in the periphery and excreted as 5-hydroxyindoleacetic acid, and increased 5-hydroxytryptophol excretion (Davis *et al.*, 1969; Huff *et al.*, 1971).

It is noteworthy that chloral hydrate has the potential to modify the disposition of amine-derived aldehydes for two reasons. Chloral hydrate is a potent inhibitor of aldehyde dehydrogenase (Erwin and Deitrich, 1966; Kramer and Deitrich, 1968), and it also competes for the reductive pathway of biogenic aldehyde metabolism (Tabakoff *et al.*, 1974). As with the primary metabolite of ethanol, acetaldehyde, it was found that the presence of chloral hydrate in incubation mixtures of brain stem homogenates supplemented with NAD also markedly decreased formation of 3,4-dihydroxyphenylacetic acid from dopamine and increased the generation of THP (Davis, 1973). Thus, the augmented formation of the alkaloid, THP, as a result of blocking the oxidation of the aldehyde metabolite of dopamine by alcohol, acetaldehyde and chloral hydrate, offers a common pharmacologically-induced aberration of dopamine metabolism.

Barbiturates

There is no evidence that barbiturates and certain tranquillisers chemically unrelated to ethanol inhibit the oxidation of biogenic amine-derived aldehydes. Barbiturates, however, have been shown to be potent inhibitors of the aldehyde reductases of brain (Tabakoff and Erwin, 1970; Erwin *et al.*, 1971; Ris and von Wartburg, 1973; Ris *et al.*, 1975). The aldehyde derivative of norepinephrine, unlike the dopamine-derived aldehyde, is not appreciably oxidised to the corresponding acid by brain aldehyde dehydrogenase. Rather, it is primarily reduced to the glycol by pyridine nucleotide-dependent aldehyde reductases. It is thus conceivable that barbiturate intervention may, to an important extent, evoke aberrant metabolism of the aromatic aldehydes derived from β-hydroxylated phenylethylamines by brain tissue. Consistent with this suggestion are the observations that the primary (i.e., reductive) metabolic pathway of the norepinephrine-derived aldehyde in brain tissue is disrupted by barbiturates. This disruption leads to elevated aldehyde levels and enhanced formation of a putative norepinephrine-derived benzyltetrahydroisoquinoline alkaloid (Davis *et al.*, 1974).

Barbiturates thus are capable of suppressing the reductive disposition of β-hydroxylated phenylacetaldehydes by inhibiting the aldehyde reductases, whereas ethanol, via its metabolite acetaldehyde, affects the metabolic oxidative disposition of phenylethylamine-derived aldehydes by inhibiting aldehyde dehydrogenases. The consequences of these interactions are increased levels of the biogenic aldehydes and a metabolic diversion which result in the formation of aberrant benzyltetrahydroisoquinoline alkaloids derived from the parent amine.

Pharmacological Actions of Tetrahydroisoquinolines

The hypotheses for possible involvement of amine-derived alkaloids in alcoholism generated an explosion of interest in the pharmacology of these compounds. The alkaloids receiving the most attention have been:

(1) 1-(3′,4′-dihydroxybenzyl)-6,7-dihydroxy-1,2,3,4-tetrahydro-isoquinoline (tetrahydropapaveroline, THP, norlaudanosoline) formed by condensation of dopamine with its intermediate aldehyde, 3,4-dihydroxyphenylacetaldehyde;

(2) 1-methyl-6,7-dihydroxy-1,2,3,4-tetrahydroisoquinoline (salsolinol), the condensation product of dopamine and acetaldehyde; and

(3) the condensation products of formaldehyde with the catechol-amines, norepinephrine and dopamine, i.e., 4,6,7-trihydroxy-1,2,3, 4-tetrahydroisoquinoline and 6,7-dihydroxy-1,2,3,4-tetrahydroiso-quinoline, respectively.

Interaction with Aminergic Systems

The tetrahydroisoquinoline alkaloids share molecular geometry with the parent catecholamines. It is not surprising, therefore, that these compounds interact with a variety of aminergic systems. The pharmacological properties of the tetrahydroisoquinoline alkaloids have been the subject of several recent comprehensive reviews (Hirst *et al.*, 1977; Cohen, 1978; Cohen, 1979; Deitrich and Erwin, 1980) and detailed recounting of the enormous body of literature related to this subject is beyond the scope of this presentation. But as an overview, investigations have demonstrated that these alkaloids act as 'false neurotransmitters' and interact with aminergic uptake, storage, transport and metabolism.

It has been reported that the tetrahydroisoquinolines are:

(1) transported into catecholamine neurons, where they are released on stimulation and are able to block the uptake of catecholamines in nerve terminals (Heikkila *et al.*, 1971; Cohen *et al.*, 1972; Greenberg and Cohen, 1972; Cohen, 1973a, b; Greenberg and Cohen, 1973; Locke *et al.*, 1973; Tennyson *et al.*, 1973; Cohen *et al.*, 1974; Mytilineou *et al.*, 1974; Alpers *et al.*, 1975);

(2) inhibitors of monoamine oxidase (Yamanaka 1971; Collins *et al.*, 1973; Cohen and Katz, 1975; Giovine *et al.*, 1976; Katz and Cohen, 1976; Meyerson *et al.*, 1976; Renis *et al.*, 1978);

(3) substrates for and competitive inhibitors of COMT (Collins *et al.*, 1973; Rubinstein and Collins, 1973; Meyerson *et al.*, 1979);

(4) inhibitors of ATP-phosphohydrolases (Meyerson *et al.*, 1978);

(5) either direct agonists or receptor antagonists of amine-sensitive adenylate cyclases (Miller *et al.*, 1974; Sheppard and Burghardt, 1974; Feller *et al.*, 1975; Sheppard *et al.*, 1976; Nimitkitpaisan and Skolnick, 1978; Clement-Cormier *et al.*, 1979);

(6) able to stimulate prolactin secretion by their ability to act as dopamine antagonists (Britton *et al.*, 1979); and

(7) inhibitors of tyrosine hydroxylase (Collins and Weiner, 1977).

Effect of Tetrahydroisoquinolines on Voluntary Consumption of Ethanol

Although evidence of strong interactions of tetrahydroisoquinoline alkaloids with many important neuronal regulatory systems emerged from these investigations, a direct connection between these compounds and alcohol-related behaviour was missing. The direct link was recently furnished by the remarkable findings of Myers and colleagues, which have been described in a series of publications (Melchior and Myers, 1977a, b; Myers and Melchior, 1977; Myers and Oblinger, 1977; Myers, 1978a, b; Melchior, 1979). Because the results are most significant, they can best be summarised by a direct quotation from a review by Myers (1978b):

In a recent series of experiments, the CNS portion of the amine-metabolite theory has been tested directly. In order to stimulate the chronicity of the condensation product's presumed action within the brain during the prolonged ingestion of alcohol, THP has been infused around the clock into the cerebral ventricle of the rat. When animals of the nonalcohol drinking Sprague-Dawley strain are offered alcohol and water in a free-choice paradigm, as THP is infused every 30 min. in a dose as low as 100 pg/μl the rat's volitional intake of 3-9% alcohol suddenly rises (Myers and Melchior, 1977). Surprisingly, when the solution of alcohol is systematically increased in strength to aversive concentrations ranging from 11-30%, the THP-infused rats drink even more alcohol — as much as 13 to 16 g/kg on a given day. Marked ataxia, an elevated blood level, and other intoxication-like symptoms characterize this unusual drinking (Melchior and Myers, 1977a). If the intracerebral applications of THP are cut back to a once per day infusion, thereby reducing drastically the total dose of the TIQ to which the brain is exposed, the rat's normal aversion to alcohol nevertheless disappears. Again, a marked preference develops for the fluid (Myers and Oblinger, 1977), with the rat voluntarily consuming up to 10 g/kg per day of alcohol in concentrations of 15 or 20%.

This powerful pharmacologic effect of incredibly low doses of tetrahydropapaveroline in increasing voluntary alcohol intake appears to be permanent. The exaggerated self-selection of alcohol was found to persist when retesting was carried out one, six and nine months after the chronic infusions of the tetrahydroisoquinoline alkaloid had ceased (Melchior and Myers, 1977a; Melchior, 1979).

Replication of these findings by Deitrich and co-workers (Duncan and Deitrich, 1978; Deitrich and Erwin, 1980) soon followed, with the report that intraventricular infusion of small amounts of tetrahydro-papaveroline increased the rats' preference for ethanol. Additionally, the effect was still present even ten months after infusion of the alkaloid.

This group also stressed another important consideration (Melchior *et al.*, 1978): 'In the chronic infusion of THP, the calculated average level for the lowest effective dose is 0.6 ng/g brain. This suggests that published reports indicating an inability to detect these compounds *in vivo* following the ingestion of ethanol . . . are not sufficiently sensitive to detect levels of the compounds that are physiologically efficacious.' In view of the remarkable potency of tetrahydropapaveroline delivered in picogram quantities into the brain in evoking abnormal drinking, Myers (1978a) also suggested that the endogenous formation of this alkaloid in alcohol-treated animals may be extremely difficult to detect.

Opiate-like Actions

Provocative new information is beginning to emerge suggesting that
the tetrahydroisoquinolines may provide a common mechanism for
some actions of alcohol, opiates and the opiate peptides. This
consideration has been the subject of recent reviews (Blum *et al.*, 1977;
Blum *et al.*, 1978).

One of the first indications of the possible interactions of tetrahydroisoquinolines, alcohol and opiates was the observation of Ross
and co-workers (1974) that ethanol, opiates and salsolinol induced
depletion of brain calcium in acutely treated rats; and that the pre-
treatment of the animals with the narcotic antagonist, naloxone,
blocked the loss of calcium. Salsolinol in the low concentration of only
10^{-8} M, furthermore, inhibited the high affinity binding of calcium to
brain synaptic membranes, and the inhibition was blocked by naloxone
(Ross, 1978). The authors noted that the potency of salsolinol in
blocking calcium binding in brain preparations is similar to the potency
of levorphanol and β-endorphin (Ross, 1978; Ross and Cardenas, 1977).

Furthermore, salsolinol administered intracranially was reported to
augment the analgesia produced by morphine given peripherally (Blum
et al., 1978). Carboxysalsolinol by itself elicited analgesia in a dose
response pattern that could be blocked by naloxone, and it also
increased morphine analgesia in the rat (Marshall *et al.*, 1977).
Salsolinol, tetrahydropapaveroline and the tetrahydroprotoberberine
alkaloids related to tetrahydropapaveroline competed with naloxone
for binding sites in rat brain preparations (Tampier *et al.*, 1977). The
results obtained with salsolinol and tetrahydropapaveroline were
confirmed in another report; the authors (Greenwald *et al.*, 1979) also
noted that the affinity of these alkaloids for receptors decreased in the
presence of high sodium ion concentrations, suggesting that these
alkaloids demonstrate at least partial agonist activity at the opiate
receptor site.

A carboxy derivative of tetrahydropapaveroline (norlaudanosoline
carboxylic acid, NLCA) inhibited naloxone binding by rat brain
preparations and, as is characteristic of opiate agonists, this inhibition
was markedly decreased in the presence of 100 mM NaCl (Lasala *et al.*,
1980). Further approaisal of the opiate-like properties of this
1-benzyltetrahydroisoquinoline alkaloid *in vivo* (Lasala *et al.*, 1980)
was obtained by assays based upon the ability of opiate agonists to
deplete testosterone and luteinising hormone (LH). These assays have
been used to assess structure-activity relationships and to differentiate

between opiate agonists and antagonists (Bruni *et al.*, 1977; Cicero, 1977; Cicero *et al.*, 1977a, b).

Systemic administration of this 1-benzyltetrahydroisoquinoline decreased serum testosterone levels. In addition, the concomitant decrease in serum LH levels resulting from administration of the alkaloid was blocked by simultaneous administration of the opiate antagonist naloxone (Lasala *et al.*, 1980). These responses are characteristic of opiate agonists. In this context, it was suggested that these 1-benzyltetrahydroisoquinolines 'can assume conformations with a juxtaposition of key groups similar to that required for the opiate activity of morphine and methionine-enkephalin', as determined by computer-generated models (Lasala *et al.*, 1980).

New lines of evidence implicating opiate systems in voluntary alcohol administration are also emerging. Suggestions that opiate receptors may be in some way involved in the intense increase in voluntary selection of alcohol observed after intracerebral administration of tetrahydropapaveroline to rats derive from a preliminary report by Lin and Myers (1978). These workers found that, after the increase in alcohol intake evoked by tetrahydropapaveroline was stabilised, systemic administration of naloxone reduced the average intake of alcohol by 53 per cent. Furthermore, Altshuler (1979) recently demonstrated that self-administration of alcohol in rhesus monkeys was significantly decreased by the opiate antagonist, naltrexone. These findings raise the intriguing suggestion that opiate receptor blockade interferes with the voluntary intake of alcohol by experimental animals and implicate endogenous opiate systems in the reinforcing properties of alcohol.

Metabolism of Tetrahydroisoquinoline Alkaloids

A major premise of our hypothesis is that the benzyltetrahydro-isoquinoline alkaloids may be further metabolised by several routes and converted to more complex pharmacologically active alkaloids by mammalian systems (Davis *et al.*, 1970; Davis and Walsh, 1970a; Davis, 1971; Figures 2.1, 2.2). Verification of the formation of tetrahydro-isoquinoline alkaloids could thus be obtained by detection not only of the tetrahydroisoquinolines but also of their metabolites.

Conversion to More Complex Alkaloids

A metabolic possibility for tetrahydropapaveroline and other benzyltetrahydroisoquinolines is the formation of tetrahydroberberine alkaloids through ring coupling mediated by a one carbon unit. The capacity of mammalian systems to effect the biosynthesis of tetrahydroberberine alkaloids has been confirmed by several investigations. Incubation of the soluble supernatant fraction of rat brain or liver with tetrahydropapaveroline and *S*-adenosylmethionine resulted in the formation of tetrahydroberberine alkaloids which were identified as 2,3,10,11-tetrahydroxyberbine, 2,3,9,10-tetrahydroxyberbine and a 2- or 3-monomethylated derivative of a tetrahydroxyberbine. Both brain and liver preparations produced the same ratio of the tetrahydroberberine products and the 2,3,10,11-tetrahydroxy isomer was the major metabolite (Cashaw *et al.*, 1974).

Additionally, the capability of the intact animal to effect the synthesis of the tetracyclic ring system of the tetrahydroberberine alkaloids was demonstrated by identification of four tetrahydroberberines as urinary excretion products in rats after intraperitoneal administration of tetrahydropapaveroline. The 2,3,10,11-isomer was the major tetrahydroberberine alkaloid metabolite excreted. Minor constituents included 2,3,9,10-tetrahydroxyberbine and two *O*-methylated derivatives. The latter were identified as coreximine (2,11-dihydroxy-3,10-dimethoxyberbine) and a 2- or 3-monomethylated berbine derivative. Furthermore, the two isomeric tetrahydroberberine alkaloids (2,3,10,11- and 2,3,9,10-tetrahydroxyberbine) were also identified in the urine of Parkinsonian patients receiving L-dopa therapy (Cashaw *et al.*, 1974).

Prompted by the interest in drug-evoked aberration in biogenic amine metabolism, Kametani and collaborators (1976, 1977) examined the biotransformation of reticuline, 1-(3-hydroxy-4-methoxybenzyl)-2-methyl-6-methoxy-7-hydroxy-1,2,3,4-tetrahydroisoquinoline, in the intact rat and in rat liver supernatant preparations. The conversion of reticuline into coreximine, scoulerine and norreticuline by intact rats or by rat liver preparations in the presence of NADPH was demonstrated by tracer experiments in which radioactive racemic reticuline was used (Kametani *et al.*, 1976).

Further investigations revealed that aerobic incubation of reticuline with liver supernatant preparations supplemented with NADPH, nicotinamide and $MgCl_2$ resulted in the formation of three classes of tetrahydroisoquinoline-derived alkaloids (Kametani *et al.*, 1977). Although significant production was detected with $MgCl_2$ supplementation alone, a substantial increase in biosynthesis of each alkaloid was achieved by the addition of the pyridine nucleotide cofactors. Under the latter conditions, reticuline was metabolised to: tetrahydroberberine alkaloids, coreximine (22.2 per cent) and scoulerine (7.4 per cent); the aporphine alkaloid, isoboldine (3.7 per cent); and the morphinandienone alkaloid, pallidine (2.4 per cent). Biotransformations of reticuline are depicted in Figure 2.3.

In summary, these reports provide substantial support for our original suggestions that mammals, including man, may share some of the capabilities of plants for metabolising 1-benzyltetrahydroisoquinoline alkaloids to an array of even more complex alkaloids (Davis *et al.*, 1970; Davis and Walsh, 1970a; Davis, 1971). Further investigation will be required to elaborate the full potential of animals and man to effect the biosynthesis of various classes of alkaloids derived from the benzyltetrahydroisoquinolines.

Enzymatic O-Methylation

The well-established *O*-methylation pathway for catecholamines, mediated by catechol-*O*-methyltransferase (COMT), is another obvious route for metabolism of the catecholamine-derived alkaloids. The dopamine-derived alkaloids, salsolinol and tetrahydropapaveroline, are excellent substrates for COMT, with maximal velocities three to five times those of norepinephrine and dopamine, respectively. Salsolinol and tetrahydropapaveroline competitively inhibit *O*-methylation of dopamine with respective inhibitor constants (K_i values) of 0.13 and 0.02 mM (Collins *et al.*, 1973). Pyrogallol-sensitive *O*-methylation of tetrahydroisoquinolines, derived by condensation of norepinephrine with acetaldehyde or formaldehyde by rat liver and brain homogenates, has also been observed (Rubinstein and Collins, 1973).

Since the tetrahydroisoquinoline alkaloids are substrates for *O*-methylation, it was useful to delineate the precise pattern of *O*-methylation in order to evaluate their metabolic potential *in vivo*. The specific *O*-methylated products of the optical isomers of tetrahydropapaveroline (THP) and 2,3,10,11-tetrahydroxyberbine obtained on incubation with a COMT preparation were determined by separation and isolation of the products by high performance liquid chromatography. Structural identity was confirmed by synthesis and combined GC/MS. Tetrahydropapaveroline was metabolised primarily to the mono-*O*-methylated 6-*O*-methyl or 7-*O*-methyl product. Notably, the positions of enzymatic *O*-methylation were markedly influenced by the isomeric form of the substrate. Thus, (±)-THP, (+)-THP and (−)-THP were mono-*O*-methylated with a 6:7 position ratio of 2.4, 0.4, and 6.6, respectively. The isomers of

Figure 2.3: Conversion of Reticuline to Aporphine, Morphinandienone and Tetrahydroberberine Alkaloids by Rat Liver Preparations

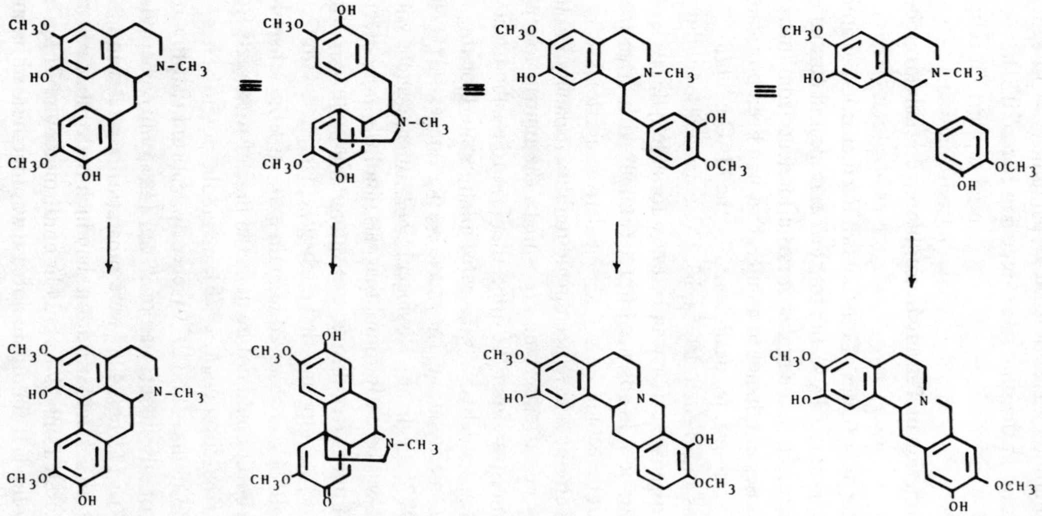

Type:	Aporphine	Morphinandienone	Tetrahydroberberines	
Compound:	Isoboldine	Pallidine	Scoulerine	Cor_eximine
% Yield	3.66	2.35	7.41	22.24

Source: Data from Kametani *et al.*, 1977.

tetrahydroxyberbine were also primarily mono-*O*-methylated, but, in contrast to tetrahydropapaveroline, products mono-*O*-methylated in both rings A and D were formed. The pattern of the mono-*O*-methylation of tetrahydroxyberbines was also markedly influenced by the stereoisomeric form of the substrate (Meyerson *et al.*, 1979).

Endogenous Formation of Tetrahydroisoquinoline Alkaloids

Publication of the hypotheses of ethanol-evoked formation of amine-derived alkaloids prompted a search for their endogenous formation. Salsolinol was detected in the brains of rats after acute administration of intoxicating doses of ethanol to animals that had been pretreated with the COMT inhibitor, pyrogallol, and/or the MAO inhibitor, pargyline (Collins and Bigdeli, 1975a, b). These drugs also inhibit aldehyde dehydrogenase activity and elevate acetaldehyde levels after ethanol administration. In absence of pretreatment with these drugs, salsolinol was not detected.

Several other attempts have been made to detect salsolinol in the brains of mice or rats after chronic exposure of the animals to ethanol without the administration of the drugs that lead to an abnormal accumulation of acetaldehyde or the catecholamines or blocking metabolism via *O*-methylation. They have been unsuccessful (O'Neill and Rahwan, 1977; Riggin and Kissinger, 1977). In agreement with these findings, it was recently found that salsolinol was not detectable in brain tissue of mice after chronic exposure of the animals to ethanol vapours. However, a compound that cochromatographed with *O*-methylated salsolinol was observed in brain extracts from ethanol-treated animals, but it could not be detected in similar extracts from control animals (Hamilton *et al.*, 1978).

Additionally, Collins *et al.* (1979) recently reported that the urinary excretion levels of salsolinol (mean of 29 μg/24 hr) and *O*-methyl-salsolinol (mean of 111 μg/24 hr) were substantially greater in alcoholics admitted for detoxification than in non-alcoholic control subjects who excreted only 1.1 μg/24 hr of salsolinol and 21 μg/24 hr of *O*-methylsalsolinol. It should be noted that procedural differences in the other attempts (Collins and Bigdeli, 1975a, b; O'Neill and Rahwan, 1977; Riggin and Kissinger, 1977) to detect salsolinol precluded isolation of *O*-methylated salsolinol.

Salsolinol and tetrahydropapaveroline have been detected in the urine of Parkinsonian patients receiving L-dopa therapy, and acute ethanol administration appeared to increase urinary levels of these alkaloids (Sandler *et al.*, 1973). Formation of tetrahydropapaveroline was reported by Turner *et al.* (1974) to be 2-15 ng/g brain in rats exposed for eight days to solutions of L-dopa and a peripheral decarboxylase inhibitor in the drinking fluid. In animals given L-dopa and a decarboxylase inhibitor in 10 per cent ethanol as drinking fluid, tetrahydropapaveroline levels were 10-25 ng/g brain. No tetrahydro-papaveroline could be detected in whole brains of control rats or of rats given 10 per cent ethanol for eight days as the sole drinking fluid. Neither the blood levels of ethanol nor the amounts of ethanol consumed, however, were monitored. The relatively brief duration of exposure of the animals to small amounts of ethanol, which can be assumed to be subintoxicating, would not be expected to effect significant modifications in metabolic systems.

Although presently fragmentary, evidence has emerged that catecholamine-derived alkaloids are formed by mammalian systems under conditions that increase the availability of precursors. The absence of a clear definition of the role of ethanol in the formation of these alkaloids may be attributed to several considerations that have not been discussed. First, the initial condensation products may be extremely short-lived intermediates subject to metabolic transformation. Secondly, most studies have focused solely on the detection of salsolinol and tetrahydropapaveroline, the initial condensation products, and have ignored their metabolites. Thirdly, these alkaloids modify alcohol-related behaviour in phenomenally low concentrations, amounts that are beyond the detection limits of previously employed methodology (Melchior *et al.*, 1978; Myers, 1978a).

Benzyltetrahydroisoquinoline alkaloids are obligatory intermediates in the biosynthesis of tetrahydroberberine alkaloids. Our earlier identification of the latter alkaloids as urinary excretion products in Parkinsonian patients receiving L-dopa therapy (Cashaw *et al.*, 1974), therefore, adds substance to the postulate that man not only can form benzyltetrahydroisoquinoline alkaloids but can also convert them to even more complex alkaloids. Since the tetrahydroberberine alkaloids arise biosynthetically from 1-benzyltetrahydroisoquinolines, detection of the former in biological materials is further evidence for the formation of the benzyltetrahydroisoquinoline progenators.

In developing improved methodology for isolating and detecting tetrahydropapaveroline and tetrahydroberberine alkaloids, we found that tetrahydropapaveroline is extremely unstable at low concentrations, whereas the corresponding tetrahydroberberines appear to be less labile. In evaluating the possibility that tetrahydropapaveroline or its tetrahydroberberine metabolites are urinary excretion products in man, therefore, we adopted the strategy of chemically converting endogenous tetrahydropapaveroline to the more stable 2,3,10,11- and 2,3,9,10-tetrahydroxyberberine alkaloids by reaction with formaldehyde before the isolation process and GC/MS analysis.

Combined GC/MS has emerged as a well-accepted technique for conclusive identification of compounds from biological sources. The mass spectra of silylated 2,3,10,11- and 2,3,9,10-tetrahydroxyberbine are identical (Cashaw *et al.*, 1976), containing m/e 587 (molecular ion), m/e 306 (isoquinoline fragment) and m/e 280 (base peak). Although they have identical mass spectra, these two silylated tetrahydroberberines differ in their gas chromatographic retention times (Cashaw *et al.*, 1976).

Mass fragmentograms of silylated extracts of the urine of normal human subjects who were receiving no medication showed peaks in the traces for ions at m/e 280, 306 and 587 at the identical retention time and with the same ratios of 587/280 and 306/280 as the mass fragmentogram of authentic silylated 2,3,10,11-tetrahydroxyberbine. The mass spectrum of the compound with a retention time corresponding to 2,3,10,11-tetrahydroxyberbine proved identical to that of the authentic silylated compound. These results give conclusive evidence for the structure of this compound. Additionally, small peaks in the m/e 280 and 587 fragmentogram traces with the retention time of 2,3,9,10-tetrahydroxyberbine indicated that this compound was also present.

These preliminary data attest to the presence of 2,3,10,11-tetrahydroxyberbine in extracts of normal human urine but at present are solely qualitative, and quantitative assessment will have to await further improvement in isolation and purification techniques. Since the isolation procedure in these preliminary experiments involved conversion of tetrahydropapaveroline to the tetrahydroxyberbines, it is not known if the corresponding alkaloid in normal human urine was tetrahydropapaveroline, or 2,3,10,11-tetrahydroxyberbine, or a mixture of the two. These initial results are too meager for detailed evaluation of the occurrence of tetrahydroisoquinolines and tetrahydroxyberines in human urine, or the possibility of their dietary origin, or the effect of alcohol on the formation of these alkaloids.

Conceptual Considerations

There is an important, but frequently overlooked, consideration related to the endogenous formation of tetrahydroisoquinolines. Although acetaldehyde mediates the formation of both the simple 1-methyltetrahydroisoquinolines and the 1-benzyltetrahydroisoquinolines, there are substantial distinctions in the mechanisms involved. The 1-methyltetrahydroisoquinolines are formed by direct condensation of acetaldehyde with catecholamines. Since acetaldehyde is a reactant, the formation of 1-methyltetrahydroisoquinolines may require relatively high levels of acetaldehyde. In contrast, formation of the 1-benzyltetrahydroisoquinoline, tetrahydropapaveroline, is predicated on the ability of acetaldehyde to inhibit competitively the oxidation of the dopamine-derived aldehyde, which results in an increased availability of the biogenic aldehyde for condensation with the parent amine. Because the K_m value for oxidation of acetaldehyde is substantially less than the K_m value for oxidation of 3,4-dihydroxyphenylacetaldehyde by brain aldehyde dehydrogenase, very low levels of acetaldehyde could inhibit the oxidation of the dopamine-derived aldehyde. The seminal point in the formation of tetrahydropapaveroline is thus not the concentration of acetaldehyde but the metabolism of acetaldehyde.

Evidence of low blood acetaldehyde levels as well as the near absence of acetaldehyde in brains of rats after administration of ethanol has been used to argue against the possibility of tetrahydroisoquinoline formation. A recent report indicates, however, that acetaldehyde is rapidly oxidised by aldehyde dehydrogenase in brains of intact rats. With blood alcohol levels of 200-400 mg per cent and blood acetaldehyde levels of 5-40 μM, brain interstitial fluid levels of acetaldehyde were 7-14 μM. They remained at this level even though no detectable acetaldehyde was found in the whole brain during the metabolism of acutely administered ethanol (Westcott *et al.*, 1979). In this regard it can be noted parenthetically that, to the best of our knowledge, the well-recognised endogenous formation of biogenic aldehydes on deamination of the corresponding amines in brain has never been verified by detection of the aldehydes. Additionally, the possibilities of species differences and the effect of chronicity of alcohol administration on blood and brain acetaldehyde levels have yet to be adequately examined. It is of interest that both alcoholics (Korsten *et al.*, 1975) and nonalcoholic subjects with an alcoholic parent (Schuckit and Rayses, 1979) exhibit significantly elevated concentrations of blood acetaldehyde in comparison with matched controls in response to administration of a fixed dose of ethanol.

The original proposal that aberrant alkaloid metabolites of biogenic amines may play a role in the genesis of alcoholism and the speculations that there may be a connection between alcohol and opiate dependence (Davis *et al.*, 1970; Davis and Walsh, 1970a; Davis, 1971) generated considerable criticism (Davis and Walsh, 1970b; Seevers, 1970). The criticism centered primarily on the lack of cross tolerance and cross dependence between the two classes of drugs. Because in offering the hypothesis it was never the intention to imply that all the diverse effects of alcohol and opiates were equivalent, it was difficult to respond to these criticisms.

Alcohol and opiates do share an addiction liability. With both drugs, use can lead to abuse, which is frequently followed by tolerance and dependence. Although ethanol is widely used by many adults, the critical determinant leading to its abuse by some individuals, with consequent development of tolerance and dependence, i.e. alcoholism, is a most central unresolved problem. Alcohol and opiates share other common characteristics. It has long been noted that production of euphoria (also termed excitement, stimulation, rewarding experience or positive reinforcement) is a common feature of drugs such as alcohol and opiates with dependence liability (Seevers, 1968). It appears in principle, furthermore, that any individual or animal will develop dependence if specific substances are administered in appropriate quantities over a certain period of time. The more potent a dependence-producing substance, and the more rewarding or pleasant its pharmacological effects, the more rapid and stronger is the development of the addiction.

It is possible that the euphoriant, reinforcing or rewarding effects influence and promote ethanol consumption; they may thus be of fundamental relevance to abuse and subsequent development of dependence. In this regard, the exaggerated alcohol selection by animals which have been exposed to minuscule amounts of tetrahydropapaveroline, as well as the implications that endogenous opiate systems are involved in the reinforcing properties of alcohol, suggest a connection between certain actions of alcohol and opiates that may be furnished by the tetrahydroisoquinoline alkaloids.

It might be speculated that the catecholamine-derived alkaloids do not participate directly in alcohol dependence. These alkaloids may instead play a facilitating role in increasing alcohol intake, providing the stimulus for the transition from alcohol use to alcohol abuse; and this latter aspect may be the one that leads to the development of physical dependence. Because of the present finite state of our knowledge, however, we will know this only in retrospect.

Acknowledgement

This work was supported by the Veterans Administration and USPHS Grant AA-00226.

References

Alivisatos, S.G.A. and Tabakoff, B. (1973), 'Formation and metabolism of "biogenic" aldehydes' in *Chemical Modulation of Brain Function* (ed. H.C. Sabelli), Raven Press, New York, 41-66

Alpers, H.S., McLaughlin, B.R., Nix, W.M. and Davis, V.E. (1975), 'Inhibition of catecholamine uptake and retention in synaptosomal preparations by tetrahydroisoquinoline and tetrahydroprotoberberine alkaloids', *Biochem. Pharmacol., 24*, 1391-6

Altshuler, H.L. (1979), 'Behavioral methods for the assessment of alcohol tolerance and dependence', *Drug Alcohol Depend., 4*, 333-46

Anderson, R.A., Meyerson, L.R. and Tabakoff, B. (1976), 'Characteristics of enzymes forming 3-methoxy-4-hydroxyphenylethyleneglycol (MOPEG) in brain', *Neurochem. Res., 1*, 525-40

Battersby, A.R. (1961), 'Alkaloid biosynthesis', *Quart. Rev., 15*, 259-86

Bentley, K.W. (1965), *The Isoquinoline Alkaloids*, Pergamon Press, New York

Blum, K., Hamilton, M.G., Hirst, M. and Wallace, J.E. (1978), 'Putative role of isoquinoline alkaloids in alcoholism: A link to opiates', *Alcoholism: Clin. Exp. Res., 2*, 113-20

Blum, K., Hamilton, M.G. and Wallace, J.E. (1977), 'Alcohol and opiates: A review of common neurochemical and behavioral mechanisms' in *Alcohol and Opiates: Neurochemical and Behavioral Mechanisms* (ed. K. Blum), Academic Press, New York, 203-36

Breese, G.R., Chase, T.N. and Kopin, I.J. (1969), 'Metabolism of ^{3}H-tyramine and ^{3}H-octopamine in rat brain', *Biochem. Pharmacol., 18*, 863-9

Britton, D.R., Rivier, C., Shier, T., Bloom, F. and Vale, W. (1979), 'Dopamine antagonist activity of tetrahydroisoquinolines', *Soc. Neurosci. Abs., 5*, 439

Bruni, J.F., Van Vugt, D., Marshall, S. and Meites, J. (1977), 'Effects of naloxone, morphine and methionine enkephalin on serum prolactin, luteinizing hormone, follicle stimulating hormone and growth hormone', *Life Sci., 21*, 461-6

Cashaw, J.L., McMurtrey, K.D., Brown, H. and Davis, V.E. (1974), 'Identification of catecholamine-derived alkaloids in mammals by gas chromatography and mass spectrometry', *J. Chromatog., 99*, 567-73

Cashaw, J.L., McMurtrey, K.D., Meyerson, L.R. and Davis, V.E. (1976), 'Gas chromatographic-mass spectral characteristics of aporphine and tetrahydroprotoberberine alkaloids', *Anal. Biochem., 74*, 343-53

Cicero, T.J. (1977), 'An *in vivo* assay for the analysis of the biological potency and structure-activity relationships of narcotics: Serum testosterone depletion in the male rat', *J. Pharmacol. Exp. Ther., 202*, 670-5

Cicero, T.J., Badger, T.M., Wilcox, C.E., Bell, R.D. and Meyer, E.R. (1977a),

'Morphine decreases luteinizing hormone by an action on the hypothalamic pituitary axis', *J. Pharmacol. Exp. Ther., 203*, 548-55

Cicero, T.J., Bell, R.D., Meyer, E.R. and Schweitzer, J. (1977b), 'Narcotics and the hypothalamic-pituitary-gonadal axis: Acute effects on luteinizing hormone, testosterone and androgen-dependent systems', *J. Pharmacol. Exp. Ther., 201*, 76-83

Clement-Cormier, Y.C., Meyerson, L.R., Phillips, Y. and Davis, V.E. (1979), 'Dopamine receptor topography, characterization of antagonis requirements of striatal dopamine-sensitive adenylate cyclase using protoberberine alkaloids', *Biochem. Pharmacol., 28*, 3123-9

Cohen, G. (1971a), 'Reactions of catecholamines with acetaldehyde to form tetrahydroisoquinolines' in *Biological Aspects of Alcohol* (eds. M.K. Roach, W.M. McIsaac and P.J. Creaven), University of Texas Press, Austin, Texas, 267-84. (Proceedings of the Third International Symposium on Advances in Mental Science held at the Texas Research Institute of Mental Sciences, Houston, November 1969)

——— (1971b), 'Tetrahydroisoquinoline alkaloids in the adrenal medulla after perfusion with "blood concentrations" of ^{14}C-acetaldehyde', *Biochem. Pharmacol., 20*, 1757-61

——— (1973a), 'Tetrahydroisoquinoline alkaloids: Uptake, storage and secretion by the adrenal medulla and by adrenergic nerves', *Ann. N.Y. Acad. Sci., 215*, 116-19

——— (1973b), 'A role for tetrahydroisoquinoline alkaloids as false adrenergic neurotransmitters in alcoholism' in *Alcohol Intoxication and Withdrawal: Experimental Studies. Advances in Experimental Medicine and Biology, 35* (ed. M.M. Gross), Plenum Press, New York, 33-44

——— (1976), 'Commentary: Alkaloid products in the metabolism of alcohol and biogenic amines', *Biochem. Pharmacol., 25*, 1123-8

——— (1978), 'The synaptic properties of some tetrahydroisoquinoline alkaloids', *Alcoholism: Clin. Exp. Res., 2*, 121-5

——— (1979), 'Interaction of catecholamines with acetaldehyde to form tetrahydroisoquinoline neurotransmitters' in *Membrane Mechanisms of Drugs of Abuse* (eds. C. Sharp and L.G. Abood), Alan R. Liss, Inc., New York, 73-90

Cohen, G. and Collins, M. (1970), 'Alkaloids from catecholamines in adrenal tissue: Possible role in alcoholism', *Science, 167*, 1749-51

Cohen, G., Heikkila, R.E., Dembiec, D., Sang, D., Teitel, S. and Brossi, A. (1974), 'Pharmacologic activity of stereoisomers of 1-substituted 6,7-dihydroxy-1,2,3, 4-tetrahydroisoquinolines: Inhibition of ^{3}H-dopamine accumulation by rat brain slices and lipolytic activity with isolated mouse fat cells', *Eur. J. Pharmacol., 29*, 292-7

Cohen, G. and Katz, S. (1975), '6,7-Dihydroxytetrahydroisoquinoline: Evidence for *in vivo* inhibition of intraneuronal monoamine oxidase', *J. Neurochem., 25*, 719-22

Cohen, G., Mytilineou, C. and Barrett, R. (1972), 'Dopamine-derived tetra-quinoline: Uptake and storage by peripheral sympathetic nerve of the rat', *Science, 175*, 1269-72

Collins, A.C., Cashaw, J.L. and Davis, V.E. (1973), 'Dopamine-derived tetra-hydroisoquinoline alkaloids — Inhibitors of neuroamine metabolism', *Biochem. Pharmacol., 22*, 2337-48

Collins, M.A. and Bigdeli, M.G. (1975a), 'Tetrahydroisoquinolines *in vivo*. I. Rat brain formation of salsolinol, a condensation product of dopamine and acetaldehyde, under certain conditions during ethanol intoxication', *Life Sci., 16*, 585-602

——— (1975b). 'Biosynthesis of tetrahydroisoquinoline alkaloids in brain and other tissues of ethanol-intoxicated rats' in *Alcohol Intoxication and Withdrawal, 2* (ed. M.M. Gross), Plenum Press, New York, 79-91

Collins, M.A., Num, W.P., Borge, G.F., Teas, G. and Goldfarb, C. (1979), 'Dopamine-related tetrahydroisoquinolines: Significant urinary excretion by alcoholics after alcohol consumption', *Science, 206,* 1184-6

Collins, M.A., and Weiner, C.D. (1977), 'Studies on the effects of tetrahydroisoquinoline derivatives of catecholamines and aldehydes on tyrosine hydroxylase' in *Alcohol and Aldehyde Metabolizing Systems* (eds. R.G. Thurman, J.R. Williamson, H.R. Drott and B. Chance), Academic Press, New York, 511-19

Davis, V.E. (1971), 'Alcohol and aberrant metabolism of biogenic amines' in *Biological Aspects of Alcohol* (eds. M.K. Roach, W.M. McIsaac and P.J. Creaven), University of Texas Press, Austin, Texas, 293-312. (Proceedings of the Third International Symposium on Advances in Mental Science held at the Texas Research Institute of Mental Sciences, Houston, November 1969)

Davis, V.E. (1973), 'Neuroamine-derived alkaloids: A possible common denominator in alcoholism and related drug dependencies', *Ann. N.Y. Acad. Sci., 215,* 111-15

Davis, V.E., Brown, H., Huff, J.A. and Cashaw, J.L. (1967a), 'The alteration of serotonin metabolism to 5-hydroxytryptophol by ethanol ingestion in man', *J. Lab. Clin. Med., 69,* 132-40

——— (1967b), 'Ethanol-induced alterations of norepinephrine metabolism in man', *J. Lab. Clin. Med., 69,* 787-99

Davis, V.E., Cashaw, J.L., Huff, J.A., Brown, H. and Nicholas, N. (1967c), 'Alteration of endogenous catecholamine metabolism by ethanol ingestion', *Proc. Soc. Exp. Biol. Med., 125,* 1140-3

Davis, V.E., Cashaw, J.L., McLaughlin, B.R. and Hamlin, T.A. (1974), 'Alteration of norepinephrine metabolism by barbiturates', *Biochem. Pharmacol., 23,* 1877-89

Davis, V.E., Huff, J.A. and Brown, H. (1969), 'Alcohol and biogenic amines' in *Biochemical and Clinical Aspects of Alcohol Metabolism* (ed. V.M. Sardesai), Charles C. Thomas, Springfield, Ill., 95-104

Davis, V.E. and Walsh, M.J. (1970a), 'Alcohol, amines, and alkaloids: A possible biochemical basis for alcohol addiction', *Science, 167,* 1005-7

——— (1970b), 'Morphine and ethanol physical dependence: A critique of a hypothesis', *Science, 170,* 1114-15

Davis, V.E., Walsh, M.J. and Yamanaka, Y. (1970), 'Augmentation of alkaloid formation from dopamine by alcohol and acetaldehyde *in vitro* ', *J. Pharmacol. Exp. Ther., 174,* 401-12

Deitrich, R.A. (1966), 'Tissue and subcellular distribution of mammalian aldehyde-oxidizing capacity', *Biochem. Pharmacol., 15,* 1911-22

Deitrich, R.A. and Erwin, V. (1980), 'Biogenic amine-aldehyde condensation products: Tetrahydroisoquinolines and tryptolines (β-carbolines)', *Ann. Rev. Pharmacol. Toxicol., 20,* 55-80

Duncan, C. and Deitrich, R.A. (1978), 'Role of tetrahydroisoquinolines in ethanol preference', *Fed. Proc., 37,* 420 (Abs.)

Duncan, R.J.S. and Sourkes, T.L. (1974), 'Some enzymatic aspects of the production of oxidized or reduced metabolites of catecholamines and 5-hydroxytryptamine by brain tissue'. *J. Neurochem., 22,* 663-9

Duritz, G. and Truitt, E.B., Jr (1966), 'Importance of acetaldehyde in the action of ethanol on brain norepinephrine and 5-hydroxytryptamine', *Biochem. Pharmacol., 15,* 711-21

Erwin, V.G. and Deitrich, R.A. (1966), 'Brain aldehyde dehydrogenase: Localization, purification and properties', *J. Biol. Chem., 241,* 3533-9

Erwin, V.G., Tabakoff, B. and Bronaugh, R.L. (1971), 'Inhibition of a reduced nicotinamide adenine dinucleotide phosphate-linked aldehyde reductase from bovine brain by barbiturates', *Molec. Pharmacol.*, *7*, 169-76

Feller, D.R., Venkatraman, R. and Miller, D.D. (1975), 'Comparative actions of the trimetoquinol, tetrahydropapaveroline and salsolinol isomers in adrenoceptor systems', *Biochem. Pharmacol.*, *24*, 1356-9

Giovine, A., Renis, M. and Bertolino, A. (1976), '*In vivo* and *in vitro* studies of the effect of tetrahydropapaveroline and salsolinol on COMT and MAO activity in rat brain', *Pharmacology, 14*, 86-94

Greenberg, R.S. and Cohen, G. (1972), 'Tetrahydroisoquinolines and the catecholamine binding granules of the adrenal medulla', *Eur. J. Pharmacol.*, *18*, 291-4

——— (1973), 'Tetrahydroisoquinoline alkaloids: Stimulated secretion from the adrenal medulla', *J. Pharmacol. Exp. Ther.*, *184*, 119-28

Greenwald, J.E., Fertel, R.H., Wong, L.K., Schwarz, R.D. and Bianchine, J.R. (1979), 'Salsolinol and tetrahydropapaveroline bind opiate receptors in the rat brain', *Fed. Proc., 38*, 379 (Abs.)

Hamilton, M.G., Blum, K. and Hirst, M. (1978), 'Identification of an isoquinoline alkaloid after chronic exposure to ethanol', *Alcoholism: Clin. Exp. Res.*, *2*, 133-7

Heikkila, R., Cohen, G. and Dembiec, D. (1971), 'Tetrahydroisoquinoline alkaloids: Uptake by rat brain homogenates and inhibition of catecholamine uptake', *J. Pharmacol. Exp. Ther.*, *179*, 250-8

Hirst, M., Hamilton, M.R. and Marshall, A.M. (1977), 'Pharmacology of isoquinoline alkaloids and ethanol interactions' in *Alcohol and Opiates: Neurochemical and Behavioral Mechanisms* (ed. K. Blum), Academic Press, New York, 167-87

Holtz, P., Stock, K. and Westermann, E. (1964), 'Pharmakologie des Tetrahydropapaverolins und seine Entstehung aus Dopamin', *Naunyn-Schmiedebergs Arch. Pharmakol. Exp. Pathol.*, *248*, 387-405

Huff, J.A., Davis, V.E., Brown, H. and Clay, M.M. (1971), 'The effects of chloral hydrate, paraldehyde and ethanol on the metabolism of ^{14}C-serotonin in the rat', *Biochem. Pharmacol.*, *20*, 476-82

Kametani, T., Takemura, M., Ihara, M., Takahashi, K. and Fukomoto, K. (1976), 'Biotransformation of 1-benzyl-1,2,3,4-tetrahydro-2-methylisoquinolines into tetrahydroprotoberberines with rat liver enzymes', *J. Amer. Chem. Soc., 98*, 1956-9

Kametani, T., Ohta, Y., Takemura, M., Ihara, M. and Fukomoto, K. (1977), 'Biotransformation of reticuline into coreximine, scoulerine, pallidine and isoboldine with rat liver enzyme', *Bioorg. Chem., 6*, 249-56

Katz, S. and Cohen, G. (1976), 'A comparison of 6,7-dihydroxytetrahydroisoquinoline, salsolinol and tetrahydropapaveroline as inhibitors of monoamine oxidase within the adrenergic plexus of the isolated mouse atrium', *Res. Commun. Chem. Pathol. Pharmacol.*, *13*, 217-24

Kirby, G.W. (1967), 'Biosynthesis of the morphine alkaloids', *Science, 155*, 170-3

Korsten, M.A., Matsuzaki, S., Feinman, L. and Lieber, C.S. (1975), 'High blood acetaldehyde levels after ethanol administration: Differences between alcoholic and nonalcoholic subjects', *New Eng. J. Med., 292*, 386-9

Kramer, R.J. and Deitrich, R.A. (1968), 'Isolation and characterization of human liver aldehyde dehydrogenase', *J. Biol. Chem., 213*, 6402-8

Lahti, R.A. and Majchrowicz, E. (1967), 'The effect of acetaldehyde on serotonin metabolism', *Life Sci., 6*, 1399-406

——— (1969), 'Acetaldehyde — An inhibitor of the enzymatic oxidation of

5-hydroxyindoleacetaldehyde', *Biochem. Pharmacol., 18*, 535-8

Lasala, J.M., Cicero, T.J. and Coscia, C.J. (1980). 'Opiate-like effects of norlaudanosolinecarboxylic acids on the hypothalamic-pituitary-gonadal axis', *Biochem. Pharmacol., 29*, 57-61

Lasala, J.M., Coscia, C.J. and Cicero, T.J. (1978), 'Inhibition of catecholamine uptake by naturally-occurring tetrahydroisoquinolines and its possible relevance to both L-dopa chemotherapy in Parkinsonism and to phenylketonuria', *Soc. Neurosci. Abs., 4*, 428

Lin, C. and Myers, R.D. (1978), 'Reversal of THP-induced drinking in the rat by systemic naloxone and morphine', *Alcoholism: Clin. Exp. Res., 2*, 188

Locke, S., Cohen, G. and Dembiec, D. (1973), 'Uptake and accumulation of ^{3}H-6,7-dihydroxytetrahydroisoquinoline by peripheral sympathetic nerves *in vivo*', *J. Pharmacol. Exp. Ther., 187*, 56-67

Marshall, A., Hirst, M. and Blum, K. (1977), 'Morphine analgesia augmentation by and direct analgesia with 3-carboxysalsolinol', *Experientia, 33*, 754-5

Melchior, C.L. (1979), 'Behavioral and biochemical effects of intracerebrally injected alkaloids', *Drug Alcohol Depend., 4*, 347-52

Melchior, C.L., Mueller, A. and Deitrich, R.A. (1978), 'Half-life of tetrahydro-papaveroline and salsolinol following injection into the cerebral ventricle of rats', *Fed. Proc., 37*, 420 (Abs.)

Melchior, C.L. and Myers, R.D. (1977a), 'Preference for alcohol in the rat induced by chronic infusion of tetrahydropapaveroline (THP) in the cerebral ventricle', *Pharmacol. Biochem. Behav., 7*, 19-35

——— (1977b), 'Alcohol drinking induced in the rat after chronic injections of tetrahydropapaveroline (THP), salsolinol or noreleagnine in the brain', in *Alcohol and Aldehyde Metabolizing Systems, 3* (eds. R.G. Thurman, J.R. Williamson, B. Chance and H.R. Drott), Academic Press, New York, 545-54

Meyerson, L.R., Cashaw, J.L., McMurtrey, K.D. and Davis, V.E. (1979), 'Stereo-selective enzymatic O-methylation of tetrahydropapaveroline and tetrahydro-xyberbine alkaloids', *Biochem. Pharmacol., 28*, 1745-52

Meyerson, L.R., McMurtrey, K.D. and Davis, V.E. (1976), 'Neuroamine-derived alkaloids: Substrate-preferred inhibitors of rat brain monamine oxidase *in vitro*', *Biochem. Pharmacol., 25*, 1013-20

——— (1978), 'Isoquinoline alkaloids, inhibitory actions on cation-dependent ATP-phosphohydrolases', *Neurochem. Res., 3*, 239-57

Miller, R., Horn, A. and Iversen, L. (1974), 'Effects of dopamine-like drugs on rat striatal adenyl cyclase have implications for CNS topography', *Nature, 250*, 238-41

Myers, R.D. (1978a), 'Tetrahydroisoquinolines in the brain: The basis of an animal model of alcoholism', *Alcoholism: Clin. Exp. Res., 2*, 145-54

——— (1978b), 'Psychopharmacology of alcohol', *Ann. Rev. Pharmacol. Toxicol., 18*, 125-44

Myers, R.D. and Melchior, C.L. (1977), 'Alcohol drinking: Abnormal intake caused by tetrahydropapaveroline (THP) in brain', *Science, 196*, 554-6

Myers, R.D. and Oblinger, M.M. (1977), 'Alcohol drinking in the rat induced by acute intracerebral infusion of two TIQs and a β-carboline', *Drug Alcohol Depend., 2*, 469-83

Mytilineou, C., Cohen, G. and Barrett, R. (1974), 'Tetrahydroisoquinoline alkaloids: Uptake and release by adrenergic nerves *in vivo*', *Eur. J. Pharmacol., 25*, 390-401

Nimitkitpaisan, Y. and Skolnick, P. (1978), 'Catecholamine receptors and cyclic AMP formation in the central nervous system: Effect of tetrahydroisoquino-line derivatives', *Life Sci., 23*, 375-82

O'Neill, P.J. and Rahwan, R.G. (1977), 'Absence of formation of brain salsolinol in ethanol-dependent mice', *J. Pharmacol. Exp. Ther., 200,* 306-13

Perman, E.S. (1958), 'The effect of acetaldehyde on the secretion of adrenaline and noradrenaline from the suprarenal gland of the cat', *Acta Physiol. Scand., 43,* 71-6

Raskin, N.H. and Sokoloff, L (1970), 'Alcohol dehydrogenase activity in rat brain and liver', *J. Neurochem., 17,* 1677-87

Renis, M., Giovine, A. and Bertolino, A. (1978), 'MAO activity in rat brain stem and cerebral cortex following acute and chronic treatment with ethanol and tetrahydropapaveroline', *Pharmacology, 17,* 1-7

Riggin, R.M. and Kissinger, P.T. (1977), 'Determination of tetrahydroisoquinoline alkaloids in biological materials with high performance liquid chromatography', *Anal. Chem., 49,* 530-2

Ris, M.M., Deitrich, R.A. and von Wartburg, J.P. (1975), 'Inhibition of aldehyde reductase isoenzymes in human and rat brain', *Biochem. Pharmacol., 24,* 1865-9

Ris, M.M., and von Wartburg, J.P. (1973), 'Heterogeneity of NADPH-dependent aldehyde reductase from human and rat brain', *Eur. J. Biochem., 37,* 69-77

Robinson, T. (1968), *The Biochemistry of Alkaloids,* Springer-Verlag, New York, 54-71

Ross, D.H. (1978), 'Inhibition of high affinity calcium binding by salsolinol', *Alcoholism: Clin. Exp. Res., 2,* 139-43

Ross, D.H. and Cardenas, H.L. (1977), 'Levorphanol inhibition of Ca^{++} binding to synaptic membranes *in vitro*', *Life Sci., 20,* 1455-62

Ross, D.H., Medina, M.A. and Cardenas, H.L. (1974), 'Morphine and ethanol: Selective depletion of regional brain calcium', *Science, 186,* 63-5

Rubinstein, J.A. and Collins, M.A. (1973), 'Tetrahydroisoquinoline derived from noradrenalin-aldehyde condensations – Pyrogallol-sensitive O-methylation in rat homogenates', *Biochem. Pharmacol., 22,* 2928-31

Rutledge, C.O. and Jonason, J. (1967), 'Metabolic pathways of dopamine and norepinephrine in rabbit brain *in vitro*', *J. Pharmacol. Exp. Ther., 157,* 493-502

Sandler, M., Carter, S.B., Hunter, K.R. and Stern, G.M. (1973), 'Tetrahydro-isoquinoline alkaloids: *In vivo* metabolites of L-dopa in man', *Nature, 241,* 439-43

Santavy, F. (1970), *The Alkaloids, 12* (ed. R.H.F. Manske), Academic Press, New York

Schuckit, M.A. and Rayses, V. (1979), 'Ethanol ingestion: Differences in blood acetaldehyde concentrations in relatives of alcoholics and controls', *Science, 203,* 54-5

Seevers, M.H. (1968), 'Psychopharmacological elements of drug dependence', *J. Amer. Med. Assoc., 206,* 1263-6

――― (1970), 'Morphine and ethanol physical dependence: A critique of a hypothesis', *Science, 170,* 1113-14

Shamma, M. (1972), *The Isoquinoline Alkaloids: Chemistry and Pharmacology, Organic Chemistry, 25* (eds. A.T. Blomquist and H. Wasserman), Academic Press, New York

Sheppard, H. and Burghardt, C.R. (1974), 'Effect of tetrahydroisoquinoline derivatives on the adenylate cyclases of the caudate nucleus (dopamine-type) and erythrocyte (β-type) of the rat', *Res. Commun. Chem. Pathol. Pharmacol., 8,* 527-34

Sheppard, H., Burghardt, C.R. and Teitel, S. (1976), 'The dopamine-sensitive adenylate cyclase of the rat caudate nucleus. II. A comparison with the isoproterenol-sensitive (beta) adenylate cyclase of the rat erythrocyte for inhibition or stimulation by tetrahydroisoquinolines', *Molec. Pharmacol., 12,*

854-61

Smith, A.A. and Gitlow, S. (1967), 'Effect of disulfiram and ethanol on the catabolism of norepinephrine in man' in *Biochemical Factors in Alcoholism* (ed. R.P. Maickel), Pergamon Press, New York, 53-9

Spenser, I.D. (1966), 'Biosynthesis of the alkaloids related to norlaudanosoline', *Lloydia, 29*, 71-89

Tabakoff, B. and Erwin, V.G. (1970), 'Purification and characterization of a reduced nicotinamide adenine dinucleotide phosphate-linked aldehyde reductase from brain', *J. Biol. Chem., 245*, 3263-8

Tabakoff, B., Vugrincic, C., Anderson, R. and Alivisatos, S.G.A. (1974), 'Reduction of chloral hydrate to trichloroethanol in brain extracts', *Biochem. Pharmacol., 23*, 455-60

Tampier, L., Alpers, H.S. and Davis, V.E. (1977), 'Influence of catecholamine-derived alkaloids and β-adrenergic blocking agents on stereospecific binding of ^{3}H-naloxone', *Res. Commun. Chem. Pathol. Pharmacol., 17*, 731-4

Tennyson, V.M., Cohen, G., Mytilineou, C. and Heikkila, R. (1973), '6,7-Dihydroxytetrahydroisoquinoline: Electron microscopic evidence for uptake into the amine-binding vesicles in sympathetic nerves of rat iris and pineal gland', *Brain Res., 51*, 161-9

Tipton, K.F., Houslay, M.D. and Turner, A.J. (1977), 'Metabolism of aldehydes in brain' in *Essays in Neurochemistry and Neuropharmacology* (eds. M.B.H. Youdin, D.F. Sharman, W. Lovenberg and J.R. Lagnado), John Wiley & Sons, London, *1*, 103-8

Turner, A.J., Baker, K.M., Algeri, S., Frigerio, A. and Garattini, S. (1974), 'Tetrahydropapaveroline: Formation *in vivo* and *in vitro* in rat brain', *Life Sci., 14*, 2247-57

Walsh, M.J., Davis, V.E. and Yamanaka, Y. (1970a), 'Tetrahydropapaveroline: An alkaloid metabolite of dopamine *in vitro*', *J. Pharmacol. Exp. Ther., 174*, 388-400

Walsh, M.J. and Truitt, E.B., Jr (1968), 'Release of ^{3}H-norepinephrine in plasma and urine by ethanol and acetaldehyde in cats and rabbits', *Fed. Proc., 27*, 601 (Abs.)

Walsh, M.J., Truitt, E.B., Jr and Davis, V.E. (1970b), 'Acetaldehyde mediation in the mechanism of ethanol-induced changes in norepinephrine metabolism', *Molec. Pharmacol., 6*, 416-24

Westcott, J.Y., Weiner, H., Myers, R.D. and Shultz, J.W. (1979), 'Acetaldehyde in the rat brain during ethanol metabolism', *Alcoholism: Clin. Exp. Res., 3*, 201

Whaley, W.M. and Govindachari, T.R. (1951), 'The Pictet-Spengler synthesis of tetrahydroisoquinolines and related compounds' in *Organic Reactions* (eds. R. Adams *et al.*) John Wiley & Sons, Inc., New York, *6*, 151-206

Yamanaka, Y. (1971), 'Effect of salsolinol on rat brain and liver monoamine oxidase', *Jap. J. Pharmacol., 21*, 833-6

Yamanaka, Y., Walsh, M.J. and Davis, V.E. (1970), 'Salsolinol, an alkaloid derivative of dopamine formed *in vitro* during alcohol metabolism', *Nature, 227*, 1143-4

3 THE EFFECTS OF ALCOHOL ON THE CELL MEMBRANE: A POSSIBLE BASIS FOR TOLERANCE AND DEPENDENCE

John M. Littleton

Introduction

Ethyl alcohol or ethanol, which is responsible for the great majority of the effects of alcoholic beverages, is a short-chain alcohol, and from its polar hydroxyl group projects a carbon chain only two atoms long. It shares its pharmacological actions with other alcohols which have longer carbon chains, and which tend to be more potent. The simplicity of these molecules and the similarity between their effects and those of general anaesthetics, which also have simple, but dissimilar, structures, suggests that they may act in a simple physicochemical way rather than by influencing specific neurotransmitter receptors (general review see Seeman, 1972). The relationship between lipid solubility and potency of the alcohols and general anaesthetics has led to the hypothesis that these compounds enter the lipid of cell membranes and exert their actions at this site.

This chapter examines the proposition that ethanol causes its pharmacological effects by entering the lipid bilayer at synapses in the brain, and that the synapses respond by altering their lipid composition, a process which leads initially to functional tolerance, and, perhaps, later to physical dependence.

Acute Effects of Ethanol on Membranes

Current hypotheses of cell membrane structure view the membrane as a bilayer of phospholipids with proteins 'floating' on the surfaces of the bilayer or traversing the membrane. An additional component of many membranes of higher organisms is cholesterol, which is probably oriented parallel to the phospholipid molecules on both sides of the bilayer (see Figure 3.1).

One of the most important characteristics of the lipid bilayer is considered to be its 'fluidity'; this is determined by several factors including the packing of the fatty acid chains of the phospholipids, the

Figure 3.1: Organisation of molecules in the cell membrane. The membrane is considered as basically a fluid bilayer. Phospholipids and cholesterol are the main constituents of the bilayer and these lipids influence the activity of neighbouring proteins.

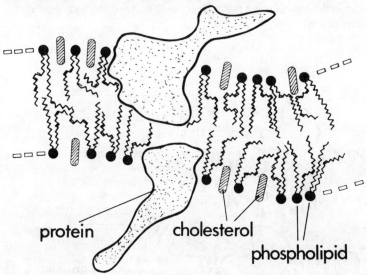

protein   cholesterol

phospholipid

nature and divalent cation binding of the phospholipid head groups, and the ratio of cholesterol to phospholipid molecules in the bilayer. The fluidity of the lipids in the bilayer determines the mobility and to some extent the function of proteins in, or on, the membrane. In general terms, fluidity toward the centre of the bilayer is determined by the degree of unsaturation of the fatty acid side chains (see Cronan and Gelmann, 1975), the more unsaturated the side chains the more fluid is the membrane.

At the bilayer surface, binding of divalent cations, e.g. Ca^{2+}, to the phospholipid head groups reduces the surface fluidity (Chapman, Peel, Kingston and Lilley, 1977) and an increase in ethanol amine head groups relative to choline head groups may have the same effect (Michaelson, Horwitz and Klein, 1974; Seelig, 1978) as may an increase in the cholesterol/phospholipid mole ratio (see Lucy, 1974; Suckling, Blair, Boyd, Craig and Malcolm, 1979). The presence of double bonds in the fatty acid side chains proximal to the head groups can also influence the fluidity relatively close to the membrane surface (see Seelig and Browning, 1977; Seelig and Seelig, 1978).

Figure 3.2: Effects of alcohols on the lipids of the membrane bilayer. The effect of alcohols on the lipid bilayer may be determined by their chain length. Alcohols with a short hydrocarbon chain may be relatively restricted to the membrane surface whereas alcohols with a longer hydrocarbon chain may affect the fluidity of the bilayer at a greater depth.

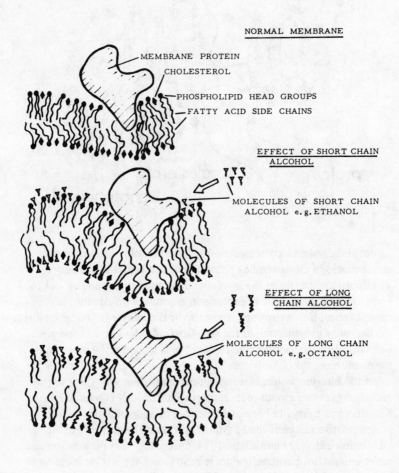

NORMAL MEMBRANE

MEMBRANE PROTEIN

CHOLESTEROL

PHOSPHOLIPID HEAD GROUPS

FATTY ACID SIDE CHAINS

EFFECT OF SHORT CHAIN ALCOHOL

MOLECULES OF SHORT CHAIN ALCOHOL e. g. ETHANOL

EFFECT OF LONG CHAIN ALCOHOL

MOLECULES OF LONG CHAIN ALCOHOL e. g. OCTANOL

Figure 3.3: Hypothetical sphere of influence of ethanol at the membrane surface. It is not known to what extent ethanol can penetrate the membrane. The parts of the lipid molecules near the membrane surface seem most likely to be those affected by ethanol.

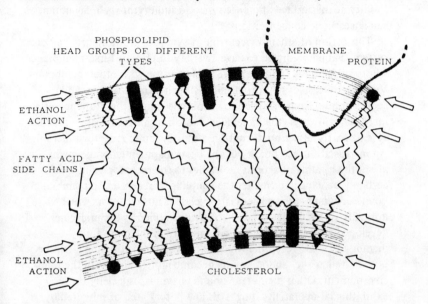

Alcohols and anaesthetics probably enter the lipid portion of the membrane, and the presence of their molecules both expands the membrane and separates the lipid molecules in the membrane (for a review, see Seeman, 1972). This separation of the lipid molecules is thought to allow more movement of the lipids, and hence to increase the fluidity of the membrane. Alcohols, which have a relatively polar hydroxyl group, probably align themselves in the membrane so that the hydroxyl group is restricted to the region of the lipid water interface, and the hydrocarbon chain extends downwards toward the bilayer centre (see Figure 3.2). A short-chain alcohol like ethanol is therefore relatively lipid-insoluble and can only exert its 'fluidising' effect at the surfaces of the bilayer (Figure 3.2). The molecules in the membrane which are influenced by ethanol can therefore include the phospholipid head groups, the proximal parts of the fatty acid side chains, cholesterol molecules, and areas of protein molecules near the lipid-water interface (see Figure 3.3).

There is now considerable evidence, using a variety of physical techniques, that concentrations of ethanol of the same order as those achieved *in vivo* in intoxication, do increase the fluidity of biomembranes close to their surfaces (Chin and Goldstein, 1977a; Vanderkooi, 1979; Johnson, Lee, Cooke and Loh, 1979). The work by Chin and Goldstein in particular establishes that ethanol increases the fluidity at the surface of mouse synaptic and erythrocyte membranes at sub-anaesthetic concentrations.

This action of ethanol, occurring at synapses in the central nervous system, can be predicted to have a variety of effects. First, membranes whose surfaces are fluid are more likely to fuse with other membranes. Vesicular release of neurotransmitters, such as monoamines and acetylcholine, from presynaptic membranes might therefore be initially increased. However, the increase in neurotransmitter release would be at least partly offset by disruption of postsynaptic receptor function. An increased surface fluidity of the postsynaptic membrane might affect the binding of agonist molecules to the receptors, and would certainly be expected to alter the coupling of receptors to membrane-bound enzymes such as adenylate cyclase. Thus receptors which were normally fully coupled might become uncoupled as the molecules developed a greater ability to drift laterally in the more fluid membrane, while receptors which exhibit random coupling might be potentiated as the random events become more frequent in the fluid environment. Other membrane-bound enzymes, especially those exhibiting co-operativity, might also be potentiated or inhibited by ethanol.

Thus the neurochemical effects of this rather simple physico-chemical action of ethanol could in fact be complex. There might initially be increased release of some neurotransmitters, and variable effects on neurotransmitter receptors. The enzymes responsible for neurotransmitter synthesis and receptor responses could also be affected in different ways. As concentrations of ethanol in the brain increased one would expect a generalised disruption of neurotransmission, but this might occur to a greater extent in some synapses than in others. Many changes of this type have been reported in experimental animals after administration of ethanol (see Chapter 6). The result in behavioural terms of all these biochemical changes can only be guessed at, but one might predict that excitation on initial administration of ethanol might be supplanted by confusion, unco-ordination and disruption of normal behaviour patterns, followed by increasing generalised central nervous system depression as concentrations of the drug rise.

It has been argued in this section that a simple physicochemical effect of ethanol on the lipids of central synapses can explain many of the neurochemical and behavioural effects of the drug: but it must be admitted that the mechanism of this physicochemical effect is not firmly established. It should also be stressed that other actions of ethanol, including its metabolism and its effects on the metabolism of body constituents, also play a part in determining the pharmacological profile of the drug. In this chapter, special attention is paid to the effect of alcohol on the lipids of the membranes at the synapse, and this mechanism will be stressed above all other possibilities.

Chronic Effects of Ethanol on Membranes

One of the characteristics of the action of ethanol on all organisms is that its effects tend to be attenuated if administration is continued. This is at least partly due to the development of functional tolerance to ethanol, in which the organism becomes able to function relatively normally at higher and higher concentrations of the drug. Some aspects of functional tolerance at the level of the intact organism have been reviewed recently (Littleton, 1980). If the acute effects of ethanol are due to altered membrane lipid fluidity, it seems logical to consider the possibility that functional tolerance develops because ethanol becomes less able to produce this change. This in turn implies that some change in the membrane must occur to make it resistant to ethanol. This possibility is strengthened by the observations of Chin and Goldstein (1977b) who have shown that cell membranes, from a variety of sites, from mice which were functionally tolerant to ethanol, were resistant to the fluidising effects of ethanol. Johnson, Lee, Cooke and Loh (1979) have recently demonstrated that this resistance to ethanol fluidisation resides in the lipid bilayer of the membrane.

Most organisms have a mechanism by which adaptive changes in membrane fluidity may be accomplished. This is a physiological mechanism necessary to offset the effects of temperature changes on cell membrane function. Hill and Bangham (1975) seem to have been the first to recognise that the mechanism used for adaptation to increased temperature, which increases lipid fluidity, could also explain tolerance to central depressant drugs. There now seems much evidence that this hypothesis is at least partly correct (see below) but it must be recognised that, in the case of ethanol, the drug effects may not be identical to that of increased temperature.

Thus a temperature increase probably affects the fluidity of lipids throughout the membrane, particularly increasing the motion of the fatty acid side chains toward the centre of the bilayer. Ethanol, on the other hand, is probably relatively restricted to the bilayer surfaces, and may have little effect on the fluidity toward the centre of the bilayer. Responses which are an appropriate adaptation to one stimulus need not necessarily be so to the other. This is borne out by the biochemical evidence obtained to date (see below). Evidence has been sought in a variety of organisms and this has an important bearing on the results obtained. Work on 'lower organisms' is therefore considered separately from that performed on mammals. There are similarities in both groups, but the greater complexity of mammalian membranes provides mechanisms for adaptation alternative to those available to simple cells.

Adaptation in Membranes of Lower Organisms

The effect of alteration in temperature on membrane function has been most studied in unicellular organisms and poikilotherms, since homeotherms, by definition, show only very small changes in body temperature under physiological conditions. Many of our concepts of membrane adaptation have therefore been obtained from study of relatively simple cells. It is only comparatively recently that any studies in lower organisms or mammals on membrane adaptation to pharmacological stimuli have appeared in the literature.

Bacteria

Bacteria, and especially strains of *Escherichia coli*, have been much used in studying membrane adaptation. Bacteria have a very simple membrane structure, which consists of a phospholipid bilayer containing phospholipids with relatively little variation in head groups and in fatty acid side chains. Most fatty acids are of 16 and 18 carbon chains, and bacteria contain a very small proportion of polyunsaturated fatty acids in their membranes. There is also less protein, and probably also less complex proteins, than that present in mammalian membranes. Importantly, bacterial membranes contain only small amounts of sterols and usually no cholesterol. Other sterols do not have the same effect as cholesterol in the membrane; the cholesterol molecule seems to be particularly effective in rigidifying the membrane (Suckling, Blair, Boyd, Craig and Malcolm, 1979). This may well have an important bearing on the response of such membranes to fluidising agents. For example, it has been reported (Pang and Miller, 1978) that cannabinols

and barbiturates have diametrically opposite effects on artificial
membranes which contain a high proportion of cholesterol when
compared with membranes which contain little or none.

Bacterial membranes are also largely dependent on lipid sources in
the growth medium for their composition, and probably have rather
different mechanisms for membrane assembly than do mammalian cells.
For these reasons extrapolation from results obtained with bacteria
must be treated cautiously. Cronan and Gelmann (1975) have recently
reviewed adaptation in cell membranes concentrating on bacterial
adaptation.

Temperature adaptation in *E. coli* has been studied by many,
including work by Sinensky (e.g. 1971) which is among the most
complete reports. *E. coli* adapt to a higher temperature in the growth
medium by reducing the proportion of unsaturated fatty acids in their
membrane phospholipids. This is presumed to increase the ability of the
side chains to pack together, and consequently to reduce the intrinsic
fluidity of the membrane. The fluidity increase produced by the
increased temperature in the medium is thus compensated, and normal
membrane function and growth may continue.

Ingram, in 1976, investigated the response of *E. coli* to the presence
of alcohols in the growth medium. From the assumption that alcohols,
like a raised temperature, increase membrane fluidity it would be
predicted that alcohols would elicit the response of reducing
unsaturated fatty acids in bacterial membrane phospholipids. This was
exactly the response which Ingram found with long chain alcohols, but
alcohols with a short hydrocarbon chain, including ethanol, produced
the opposite response. Thus, 2h after placing *E. coli* into a culture
medium containing a high concentration of ethanol, an increase in
unsaturated fatty acids was observed in membrane phospholipids. This
change seemed to share the time course of the resumption of normal
growth rate in the new medium, and subsequent experiments
established that a similar change was produced in response to a
barbiturate (Ingram, Ley and Hoffman, 1978) and that strains of *E. coli*
which could not survive in the ethanol-containing medium were also
unable to alter their membrane phospholipid composition (Ingram,
Buttke and Dickens, 1980). These last experiments suggest that the
mechanism for alteration of membrane phospholipids is genetically
determined, and rests on the function of one of the enzymes of
phospholipid metabolism. As stated previously these are not necessarily
the same as those involved in mammalian metabolism.

These experiments, by Ingram and his group in Florida, establish that *E. coli* adapt to alcohols by altering membrane phospholipid composition. The results are puzzling in that short-chain alcohols produced the opposite effect to that expected. Unless they produce the opposite effect on bacterial membrane fluidity to that produced by long chain alcohols it is difficult to see how both membrane responses could be adaptive. There is no evidence to suggest that this is so, but it remains a possibility. In mammalian membranes there is considerable evidence that short- and long-chain alcohols produce similar effects and that cross tolerance exists (Goldstein, Chin, McComb and Parsons, 1979).

An alternative explanation may be that the changes produced in bacterial membranes by short-chain alcohols are an adaptive response to alteration in fluidity at the membrane surface. Under some conditions the introduction of monounsaturated fatty acids into a phospholipid bilayer can produce greater order of the lipids close to the bilayer surface (Thulborn, Treloar and Sawyer, 1978). This and other possible explanations must be investigated before these interesting results can be fully evaluated.

Tetrahymena

Membrane adaptation has also been investigated in rather more complex unicellular organisms. One of the most commonly used is *Tetrahymena pyriformis* (for a review see Thompson and Nozawa, 1977). The cellular membranes of *Tetrahymena* show much more differentiation and specialisation than those of bacteria. *Tetrahymena* membranes contain rather more unsaturated phospholipids than do those of bacteria and also more protein and sterols, though still no cholesterol. In addition, a high proportion of the membrane lipids are synthesised by the organism rather than simply incorporated from the environment. *Tetrahymena* thus seems a better model than bacteria for mammalian membranes, but it still lacks polyunsaturated phospholipids and cholesterol.

Adaptation to increased environmental temperature by *Tetrahymena* seems to be associated with essentially the same change as that shown by bacteria, that is a reduction in the unsaturated fatty acid side chains of membrane phospholipids (see Thompson and Nozawa, 1977). There is some doubt as to the mechanism by which the change in the membrane occurs. The experiments of Nozawa and Kasai (1978), which show that cycloheximide prevents membrane phospholipid adaptation in *Tetrahymena*, suggest that synthesis of a protein is involved. Subsequent experiments by Skriver and Thompson (1979) put a different interpretation on these findings. The consensus appears to be that a fatty acid desaturase enzyme is the final path by which membrane composition is affected.

Tetrahymena appears to show membrane adaptation to a general anaesthetic, methoxyflurane, by the same mechanism as it does to increased environmental temperature (Nandini-Kishore, Kitajima and Thompson, 1977) arguing that it is the increase in membrane fluidity which is the appropriate stimulus. The effect of ethanol on *Tetrahymena* membranes has recently been reported by the same group (Nandini-Kishore, Mattox, Martin and Thompson, 1979).

As in the case of the bacterial response to ethanol the results are somewhat puzzling. Ethanol *in vitro* was shown by two physical techniques to increase the fluidity of *Tetrahymena* membranes, but the response of *Tetrahymena in vivo* was to increase the content of unsaturated fatty acids of membrane phospholipids in the majority of membrane fractions studied. This, as expected, was associated with a, quite inappropriate, further increase in membrane fluidity. The exception to these results was in the fraction containing mainly ciliary membranes, where a more appropriate reduction in unsaturated fatty acids was seen. Why this should be so, and whether there is any significance in the fact that this 'appropriate' change occurs in what must be assumed to be the most mechanically, and perhaps electrically, active part of the organism, can only be guessed at. It does emphasise that the situation is complex, even in a unicellular organism, and clearly militates against oversimplification in terms of fluidity and adaptation.

Fish

The use of complex poikilotherms such as fish has been common in experiments on membrane temperature adaptation. Goldfish and trout have been most commonly studied. I will discuss temperature adaptation in these species because there seems to me to be an obvious gap in the literature with respect to pharmacological adaptation in fish. Cell membranes of fish are complex and have broadly the same differentiation as that of mammals. They contain polyunsaturated fatty acids, cholesterol and large amounts of complex proteins.

The cell membranes of fish respond to altered temperature in much the same way as that of the lower organisms described earlier. Two illustrations will suffice. Cossins (1977) has described the changes in synaptic membranes in goldfish brain which are associated with altered environmental temperature. At the higher environmental temperature studied, Cossins found a reduction in polyunsaturated fatty acids, particularly in the phosphatidylcholine fraction of synaptic membrane phospholipids. He was unable to find any alteration in cholesterol content of the synaptic membrane. On the other hand Wodtke (1978), who investigated trout liver lipids, found a similar change in phospholipid unsaturation, but also reported an increase in cholesterol content of these membranes. He suggested that the increase in cholesterol content might potentiate the fluidity change associated with reduced phospholipid unsaturation, a situation which may well be relevant to the mammal (see below).

Adaptation to ethanol by fish has been studied, but not at the membrane level. Greizerstein (1977) has demonstrated that goldfish can, very effectively, develop tolerance to the presence of ethanol in their environment. It is clearly desirable, in view of the puzzling results from unicellular organisms, that someone should investigate whether brain membranes from fish alter their lipid composition in response to ethanol.

Membrane Adaptation in Mammals

Mammals are homeotherms and there have, therefore, been relatively few studies on membrane adaptation to temperature change in mammalian species. There are, however, some situations in which mammalian cells are exposed to considerable physiological variations in temperature. Exposed sites, such as the feet and testes, may become considerably colder than the core temperature, and hibernating mammals can show a considerable reduction in core temperature while retaining some normal function. Mammalian cell membranes have a variety of potential mechanisms by which they might adjust fluidity. For example, synaptic membranes of the brain, which one assumes must be the most important site for adaptation to ethanol, contain large amounts of polyunsaturated fatty acids in phospholipids with a variety of head groups; they also contain considerable cholesterol and complex proteins. All are potential sites for adaptation.

Such evidence as exists for mammalian adaptation to temperature suggests that the same mechanisms are available to cell membranes as those of poikilotherms. Thus membrane phospholipids of adipocytes from testes of cold-exposed rats increase their content of unsaturated fatty acids (Cherqui, Cadot, Senault and Portet, 1979) and a similar change has been reported in synaptosomal membranes from brain of hibernating ground squirrels (Goldman, 1975; Goldman and Albers, 1979). The last authors also report a reduction in cholesterol content of brain membranes in these hibernators, but this has not always been found (Blaker and Moscatelli, 1978).

This group also consider a change in unsaturation of ethanolamine plasmalogens to play an important role in brain adaptation in hibernation. The mechanism for these changes in mammalian membrane lipids is unknown, but Goldman (1978) suggests that it may be produced by altered peripheral lipid metabolism, specifically a change in hepatic desaturase activity, which is communicated to the brain via the plasma fatty acid composition. This seems unlikely, mainly because one cannot imagine a brain whose synaptic membranes are at the mercy of minor alterations in plasma fatty acids. This concept seems at variance with the relatively small changes in brain lipids which are induced by major alterations in dietary lipids, for example, essential fatty acid deficiency (Sun, 1972). (At this juncture it should be mentioned that all the changes described here in mammals are in response to a *reduction* in temperature, whereas ethanol-induced adaptation should be more similar to adaptation to *increased* temperature. To my knowledge there are no reports of membrane adaptation to increased temperature in the intact mammal.)

Tissue Culture

One way to overcome the problems inherent in studying membrane lipid adaptation in homeotherms is to study their cells in tissue culture. This approach has been relatively little used to date, but there are two reports which are directly relevant. First Li and Hahn (1978) investigated the relationship between adaptation to increased temperature in the culture medium and adaptation to ethanol. Using cultured Chinese hamster ovary cells they showed that ethanol and increased temperature were additive in their toxicity to the cultured cells, and that cells adapted to increased temperature were also capable of withstanding greater than usual concentrations of ethanol. This paper therefore strongly suggests that ethanol and increased temperature share a similar action at the cellular level and that adaptation to one stimulus is at least partly appropriate to the other.

The other paper of direct relevance has already been mentioned. Ingram, Ley and Hoffman (1978) studied cultured Chinese hamster ovary cells, grown in normal media and media containing ethanol, and compared these with bacterial cells. The mammalian tissue was less able to withstand ethanol, and responded by a reduction in the most polyunsaturated fatty acid present in membrane phospholipids. This would seem to be an appropriate response both to increased temperature and to ethanol-induced fluidisation, but it is difficult to see how it can be reconciled with the bacterial results discussed earlier.

Liver

In the intact mammal the effect of ethanol administration on membrane lipids from a variety of tissues has now been studied. Once again the results are complex and defy any simple explanation. Most of the earlier work is concerned with the effect of chronic administration of ethanol on hepatic phospholipids. Any such effect in the liver is complicated by the role of the liver in ethanol metabolism and the enormous accumulation of lipids, including phospholipid, which occurs during the administration of ethanol (see Griffiths, Abu Murad and Littleton, 1979). Experiments on fatty acid composition of phospholipids from liver without subcellular fractionation therefore give little information on any possible mechanism of adaptation, and indeed we have shown that strain differences in development of ethanol tolerance in mice do not correlate with changes in liver phospholipids (Littleton, Grieve, Griffiths and John, 1979).

Changes in fatty acid composition of mitochondrial phospholipids from liver after chronic administration of ethanol have been reported (Ihrig, French and Morin, 1969). The changes described are a reduction in the most polyunsaturated fatty acid measured, arachidonic acid, at the expense of increased palmitic and linoleic acids. This could represent an adaptation to ethanol, but, in general, one cannot consider the liver a good site to look for membrane adaptation to ethanol because, among other reasons, the altered redox state and relatively high concentrations of acetaldehyde consequent to ethanol metabolism, could considerably complicate the picture.

Cardiovascular system

Cells of the cardiovascular system have also been investigated for their adaptive response to ethanol. Work by Chin and Goldstein (1977b) first established that some membranes from ethanol tolerant mice were resistant to the fluidising effects of ethanol, and this work utilised erythrocyte membranes amongst others (see later). Chin, Parsons and Goldstein (1978) have subsequently suggested that this ethanol resistance may be associated with an increased cholesterol: phospholipid molar ratio in these membranes. This undoutedly occurs;

it is a frequent finding in erythrocytes of the alcoholic patient (see Cooper, 1977), but there it may owe more to disordered lipid metabolism associated with cirrhosis than to any active membrane adaptation.

There are a few reports of alterations in cardiac phospholipids in response to ethanol, and the heart would seem to be a fairly good model for the brain in this respect. Thus a large proportion of caridac membranes undergo continuous electrical changes in life, and the heart contains relatively little stored lipid. Electrical activity may be an important determinant of the adaptive response, since there is strong coupling between membrane fluidity and cation permeability (Pang, Chang and Miller, 1979). It also seems imperative that the heart should have some means of adapting its membrane function in response to agents which affect the physical nature of its membranes. However, the heart is probably influenced directly by circulating plasma lipids, so that any changes observed may be a consequence of this, rather than an adaptive mechanism. As yet no studies of the effect of ethanol on phospholipid composition of different subcellular fractions of heart have been reported, but the effect on total phospholipid composition seems fairly clear-cut.

Reitz, Helsabeck and Mason (1973) investigated the effect of chronic dietary alcohol administration on the rat. They found a highly significant increase in linoleic acid at the expense of the polyunsaturated fatty acids, arachidonic acid and docosahexaenoic acid. These latter fatty acids are the most polyunsaturated found in significant amounts in rat heart phospholipids, and have double bonds close to the membrane surface. A reduction in their amounts could therefore have an adaptive role in the cardiac response to ethanol. We (Littleton, John and Grieve, 1979) have investigated this possibility in the mouse. Here, where the cardiac membrane phospholipids contain greater amounts of polyunsaturated fatty acids than in the rat, the position is essentially the same. After as little as 10 hr of continuous administration of ethanol there is a significant reduction in the most polyunsaturated fatty acid found (docosahexaenoic acid). Later there may also be a reduction in arachidonic acid, but this is variable. Evidence that this may at least be related to an adaptive mechanism is provided by the observations that the time course is of the same order as that with which mice develop tolerance (Grieve and Littleton, 1978), and that the change is strain-dependent (Littleton, Grieve, Griffiths and John, 1980) being shown by those strains of mice which can develop tolerance rapidly, but not by a strain which does not show rapid onset tolerance (Grieve, Griffiths and

Littleton, 1979).

This evidence is not conclusive, and the changes described could be related to increased lipid peroxidation produced by ethanol in the heart (see Abu Murad and Littleton, 1978), to an effect on plasma lipids, or to some toxic effect of ethanol on the myocardium. These last two possibilities seem a little unlikely, since we have not seen changes of this type in plasma lipids (unpublished), and other toxic effects of ethanol on cardiac lipid metabolism are not strain-related in the same way as the change in phospholipid composition described (Griffiths, Abu Murad and Littleton, 1979).

Whatever the mechanism of the change, it could still be adaptive. Peroxidation of membrane lipids can increase the rigidity of the structure (Dobretsov, Borschevskaya, Petrov, Yu and Vladinov, 1977). Despite the objections raised, the changes described in cardiac phospholipid composition in response to ethanol are interesting and deserve further study. The electrical activity and hormonal responsiveness of heart cells and the relative absence of 'inert lipids' (such as stored lipid in the liver or myelin in brain) make the heart an attractive proposition for study of membrane adaptation in the mammal. Evidence to date suggests that cardiac cells respond to ethanol by reducing the proportion of the most polyunsaturated fatty acids in their membrane phospholipids.

Brain

A hypothesis which seeks to explain the development of tolerance to ethanol by an alteration in the lipid composition of cell membranes must clearly demonstrate that such an alteration occurs in brain, preferably at the synapse, in association with the development of tolerance. There are several distinctive aspects of brain lipid metabolism which make such demonstration rather difficult, and interpretation of any changes demonstrated open to question. One of the major problems is simply the depth of ignorance of brain lipid metabolism; the extent to which the brain utilises lipids from the periphery via the blood:brain barrier and the extent of *de novo* synthesis or re-utilisation of existing lipids in the brain is simply unknown, although there is evidence that all occur.

The period at which the brain is most susceptible to altered lipid composition from the periphery is probably early in development, when lipids are being laid down (e.g. Ramsey, 1977). Although it can be shown, that lipids injected into the brain very rapidly become incorporated into membranes of the synapse, endoplasmic reticulum and mitochondria (Sun and Yau, 1976), myelin is not labelled so rapidly. Re-use of membrane fatty acids, such as these from membranes which turn over rapidly, probably makes a large contribution to the economy of brain membranes (Sun and Horrocks, 1973). Thus, although many neuronal membranes in the brain are highly active metabolically and electrically, the brain also contains a high proportion of inert lipid in myelin which although relatively 'inactive' may contribute to a pool that can be re-used in other sites. Until these aspects are understood, the meaning of changes in brain lipid composition is a subject for speculation.

There seems little doubt that neuronal membranes of the mammalian brain are altered by ethanol administration. Chin and Goldstein (1977b) showed that synaptic, microsomal and mitochondrial membranes from ethanol-tolerant mice were resistant to ethanol-induced fluidisation *in vitro*. Myelin membranes from ethanol-tolerant mice did not differ from those of controls. At the synapse, this ethanol resistance is at least partly due to some change in membrane lipids, since Johnson, Lee, Cooke and Loh (1979) showed that membranes re-formed from the extracted synaptosomal lipids of ethanol-tolerant animals exhibited ethanol resistance *in vitro*. There is clear evidence for adaptation to ethanol in lipids of brain membranes, but what form this adaptation takes is still unclear.

Littleton and John (1977) described a change in phospholipid composition of synaptosomes from ethanol-tolerant mice. We described a small reduction in polyunsaturated fatty acids which occurred within 2 hr of continuous administration of ethanol, and which was not much greater after 10 days of administration of the drug. The change was in the most polyunsaturated fatty acids present in significant amounts, which contain double bonds near the membrane surface. The alteration could therefore be an appropriate adaptation to ethanol. It occurs with a time course which is of the right order (Grieve and Littleton, 1978) and has some genetic features in common with rapid onset tolerance (Littleton, Grieve, Griffiths and John, 1979). However, the change observed was very small, even with better subcellular fractionation techniques, which show it confined to the most dense synaptosomal fraction (Littleton, John and Grieve, 1979).

Mitochondria do not seem to show the same alteration, and nor does the fraction containing myelin fragments. Indeed there is a tendency for myelin to show a change in the opposite direction, suggesting that lipids from myelin may be transferred to synaptosomal membranes in response to ethanol administration (see Wirz, 1974, for general discussion). Better subcellular fractionation techniques, for example into pre- and post-synaptic membranes, are required before the extent of the change, and its complexity, can be properly evaluated. The fact that the biochemical changes observed are very small may not mean that they are unimportant. King and Spector (1978) have shown that small alterations in fatty acids of membrane phospholipids of mammalian cells can produce a considerable change in fluidity, and this is directly coupled to cation flux in membranes (Pang, Chang and Miller, 1979).

Another small change in the lipids of membranes at the synapse has also been advanced, by Chin, Parsons and Goldstein (1978), as the mechanism for ethanol resistance of membrances from ethanol-tolerant mice. This is the small increase in the colesterol:phospholipid molar ratio which is associated with tolerance. Cholesterol is thought to rigidify the membrane close to its surface, so that this could be an appropriate response to ethanol. Also, the cholesterol content of the membrane is an important determinant of the membrane's electrical activity (Stephens and Skinitsky, 1977). Moreover, Johnson, Lee, Cooke and Loh (1979) have shown that if cholesterol is removed from mouse synaptosomal membranes the *in vitro* difference in ethanol fluidisation between control and ethanol-tolerant membranes is abolished, and if the same amount of cholesterol is replaced into each set of membranes the difference re-appears.

These results argue strongly that some optimum amount of cholesterol needs to be present in the membrane before the altered lipid composition is *expressed* as ethanol resistance, but that increases or decreases in cholesterol content cannot, by themselves, confer ethanol resistance. Since the only other lipid species which Johnson, Lee, Cooke and Loh (1979) extracted from mouse synaptosomal membranes were phospholipids, their results suggest, by inference, that membrane phospholipid composition is altered. The role of cholesterol in the mammalian membrane may well be to magnify the effect of small adaptive changes in phospholipid composition so that the *status quo* in terms of fluidity is maintained. A similar role for cholesterol in trout liver lipids was suggested, and referred to earlier, by Wodtke (1978).

Very few studies of this sort have been performed in man. Those that have been reported deal mainly with post-mortem material and do not consider the changes in terms of tolerance and dependence. In general terms the changes described are similar to those discussed in animals, but in the human work dietary and toxic effects complicate the picture greatly. Work which is of particular interest is that of

Berghaus *et al.* (1977) on liver lipids, and Lesch, Schmidt and Schmidt (1972; 1973) on brain lipids of alcoholics. There is considerable scope for human investigation in this field.

It is now established that some change in the lipid composition of synaptosomal membranes is associated with the development of functional tolerance to ethanol by the intact mammal. For the last year we have been attempting to investigate the extent to which this relationship could be causal, by altering brain lipid metabolism and evaluating the effect on the subsequent behavioural response to ethanol. This work is now 'in press' and here only the positive results obtained will be discussed.

It has been established that cyclohexamide, an inhibitor of protein synthesis at the stage of formation of the polypeptide chain, can inhibit the temperature-induced adaptation in membrane phospholipids of *Tetrahymena* (Nozawa and Kasai, 1978). We have found (Grieve, Littleton, Jones and John, 1979) that cycloheximide will also prevent the rapid development of functional tolerance to ethanol in mice. Actinomycin D, which inhibits protein synthesis at a different stage, appears not to have this effect.

It is possible to alter the cholesterol content of brain membranes if inhibitors of cholesterol synthesis are given to the mammal early in development (Ramsey, 1977). We have found that one such inhibitor, when given to mice throughout development, lowers synaptosomal cholesterol content (in preparation) and prevents the rapid development of tolerance on subsequent exposure to ethanol (Grieve, Littleton, Jones and John, 1979). Using a similar approach, in which diets containing different proportions of saturated fatty acids are given to mice throughout development, we can obtain small but significant changes in synaptosomal phospholipid composition (in preparation). In these animals a small reduction in polyunsaturated fatty acid composition of synaptosomal phospholipids is associated with resistance to the central depressant effects of ethanol (Littleton, John and Jones, 1980). If, in addition to the diet which lowers the polyunsaturatation of membrane phospholipids, we give the inhibitor of cholesterol synthesis, diazacholesterol, throughout development, the ethanol resistance is prevented (Littleton, John and Jones, 1980).

These results find obvious parallels with the biochemical and biophysical results discussed earlier. They suggest that a small change in the proportion of polyunsaturated fatty acids of phospholipids at the synapse, a change which is associated with ethanol tolerance, can confer resistance to ethanol on the intact organism. However, this change in phospholipid composition is only effective in conferring resistance if the normal amount of cholesterol is present in the synaptic membrane. In those mammalian membranes which are normally low in cholesterol an increase in the proportion of this lipid may be a necessary part of the adaptive process, but, at the synapse, cholesterol appears to play a 'permissive' rather than an 'active' role. We believe these results suggest that a reduction in polyunsaturation of membrane phospholipids is one of the mechanisms used by the mammal to adapt to ethanol. Our evidence suggests that it is also one of the fastest mechanisms, and consideration of other species suggests that it is one of the most primitive. The proposed mechanism is summarised in Figure 3.4.

The Synaptic Membrane in Dependence

In comparison with the work described previously on the relationship between membrane lipid composition and tolerance, information on the synaptic membrane in dependence is virtually non-existent. Work on the relationships between tolerance and dependence is also incomplete, making it necessary for this section to be speculative. A section on dependence is included because the few observations which have been made do point the way to a logical investigation of the molecular basis of physical dependence on ethanol.

Tolerance and Dependence

Hill and Bangham (1975), in their theoretical treatment of central depressant dependence based on membrane fluidity change, make the same assumption that many others have made as to the relation between tolerance and dependence. This assumption is simply that the physical withdrawal syndrome, which characterises physical dependence, represents the exposure of the state of functional tolerance, developed by neurones of the central nervous system during chronic administration of ethanol. On removal of ethanol this neuronal tolerance is no longer appropriate, and functional hyperactivity leading to the withdrawal syndrome is the consequence.

Several predictions flow from this basic hypothesis, which I have discussed in more detail elsewhere (Littleton, 1979a, b). Because neuronal tolerance to ethanol can be instituted very rapidly, whereas more prolonged administration of ethanol is required to produce physical

Figure 3.4: Proposed mechanism for development of tolerance to ethanol at level of the synaptic membrane. Ethanol causes an increase in fluidity at the surface of the normal membrane lipid bilayer. The bilayer responds by reducing the number of double bonds near the surface of the bilayer which offsets the effect of ethanol. An increase in cholesterol content also occurs. Unless the membrane cholesterol content is above a certain critical level, the small change in phospholipid composition is ineffective as an adaptive response to ethanol.

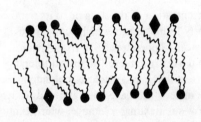

LIPIDS OF
NORMAL MEMBRANE

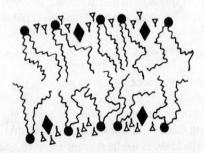

EFFECT OF ETHANOL
ON NORMAL MEMBRANE

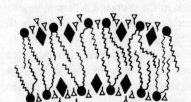

MEMBRANE ADAPTED TO
PRESENCE OF ETHANOL
i.e. TOLERANT

dependence, it is necessary to assume that, under the circumstances of short-term administration of ethanol, neuronal tolerance can be reversed sufficiently rapidly to prevent the occurrence of a withdrawal syndrome. Experiments with inbred strains of mice (Grieve, Griffiths and Littleton, 1979) reinforced the idea that the time course of neuronal adaptation is critical in determining the presence or absence of a withdrawal syndrome. In these experiments, mice which showed slow adaptation (slowly developing functional tolerance) to ethanol were those which had the most severe ethanol withdrawal syndrome, perhaps indicating that they also adapted slowly to the removal of the drug.

These results prompted the idea that physical dependence on ethanol is instituted when the state of neuronal tolerance becomes relatively 'fixed', so that the animal can no longer respond adaptively either to increases in tissue concentration of the drug or to its removal (see Figure 3.5). We have recently found results which support this hypothesis in investigating physically-dependent mice (Rigby and Littleton, 1979). Whereas mice normally achieve functional tolerance rapidly on their first exposure to ethanol, and can lose it equally rapidly if this exposure is brief, mice which have been exposed to the drug for a prolonged period show submaximal tolerance, which cannot be raised rapidly on challenge with higher tissue concentrations of ethanol, and seem to lose this tolerance rather slowly when ethanol is removed. Results which support this slow loss of tolerance on chronic ethanol administration have recently been reported by others (Abu Murad and Thurman, 1979).

Membrane Phospholipids and Dependence

If we now assume that functional tolerance to ethanol is based on an altered phospholipid fatty acid composition at the synaptic membrane, we are able to make some predictions as to the state of the membrane in physical dependence. Some of these predictions seem borne out by such evidence as exists (see below). We have suggested that ethanol tolerance is related to a reduction in the proportion of polyunsaturated fatty acids in synaptic membrane phospholipids. In dependence this change should become 'fixed' so that no further reduction in unsaturation can occur on challenge with higher concentrations of ethanol, and the return to normal lipid composition on removal of ethanol is also inhibited. There seem to be two possibilities which could account for the 'fixing' of tolerance in this way:

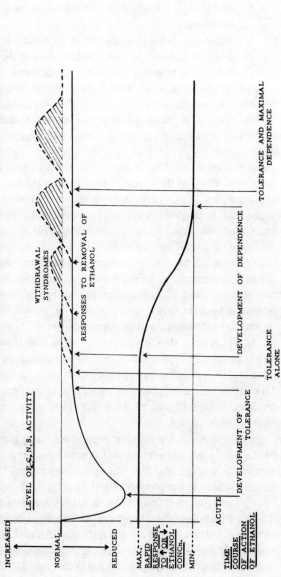

Figure 3.5: Proposed relationship between ethanol tolerance and physical dependence. A stage of ethanol administration exists where tolerance has developed to a maximum, but where the animal is not physically dependent on ethanol. At this stage it is assumed that the central nervous capacity for adaptation is still intact, so that the animal can return its state rapidly to normal on removal of the drug. However, as ethanol administration is continued, this capacity for rapid adaptation is considered to be progressively lost, so that removal of ethanol leads to a progressively greater functional hyperactivity of the nervous system. This leads to a progressively more severe physical withdrawal syndrome.

(1) If phospholipid fatty acid composition is the *only* basis for neuronal tolerance, then dependence may be associated with an inability to alter the fatty acid pattern of phospholipids rapidly. This could be because phospholipid fatty acid turnover is drastically slowed, removing the possibility of rapid change, or because there is some inability to introduce 'new' fatty acids into the membrane.

(2) If mechanisms other than alteration in phospholipid fatty acid composition can also account for tolerance at the neuronal level then all that is required to produce dependence is that, on continued administration of ethanol, the short-term adaptive mechanism (fatty acid composition?) is replaced by some other change, e.g. in phospholipid head groups or membrane proteins, which is slower to occur and cannot be reversed as readily.

There is evidence that these alternatives both exist in different situations. Many of the investigations cited in the last section on tolerance were in fact performed on mice which were also physically dependent on ethanol. Thus physically dependent mice have synaptic membranes which are physically resistant to the *in vitro* fluidising effects of ethanol (Chin and Goldstein, 1977b). In some strains of mice (Littleton and John, 1977; Littleton, Grieve, Griffiths and John, 1980) physical dependence is associated with an alteration in synaptosomal phospholipid fatty acid composition, arguing that, if this change is responsible for the rapid onset of tolerance, it need not be supplanted by another mechanism in dependence. However, in mice of the DBA2 strain, which show slow development of functional tolerance and are highly physically dependent on ethanol, no change in phospholipid fatty acid composition was observed (Littleton, Grieve, Griffiths and John, 1980). This suggests that, at least in this strain, a different, slower mechanism for tolerance exists, which could alone institute the state of physical dependence.

In an attempt to obtain more membrane fractions for analysis we have recently begun to investigate synaptosomal membrances from ethanol-dependent rats. Preliminary findings suggest that, here, there are differences in the proportions of phospholipids with different head groups (unpublished). There is already some work published in Russian which describes changes in phospholipid head groups of brain membranes after chronic administration of ethanol, but it is not clear whether or not these animals were ethanol-dependent (Karagezyan, Amirkhanyan, Amirkhanyan and Aleksandryan, 1975). Much work remains to be done on the lipid composition of synapses in dependence.

In the strains of mice where reduction in polyunsaturation of membrane phospholipids persists into dependence, it is necessary to consider the mechanisms by which this change might become 'fixed'. First there could be a reduction in membrane phospholipid turnover, and evidence exists which suggests that this is a possibility. Thus urethane has been shown to inhibit membrane phospholipid turnover in mammalian brain (Kewitz and Pleul, 1977) and phenethyl alcohol has been reported to reduce phospholipid turnover in bacterial cell membranes (Nunn, 1975). It may be that this is a general property of central depressant drugs, and that it is an intrinsic part of their dependence-producing capacity. This possibility should not be difficult to investigate.

Another explanation depends on the carrier system for fatty acids across cell membranes. In all tissues fatty acid oxidation inside mitochondria depends on their transport into the organelle in combination with carnitine (see Bremer, 1977). It has been suggested (Abdel Latif, Roberts, Karp and Smith, 1973) that carnitine is also necessary for the transfer of fatty acids across the neuronal membrane. It is conceivable that a failure of this mechanism would inhibit the ability of the synapse to incorporate new fatty acids into its membrane. In this connection it is of interest that mitochondria of chronically ethanol-treated rats show 'carnitine-resistance'. That is they require a higher concentration of carnitine *in vitro* to stimulate fatty acid oxidation by mitochondria (Katsumata, 1970). There is also evidence that the enzyme which transports the carnitine:fatty acid combination across membranes, carnitine acyltransferase, is inhibited by chronic ethanol administration (Reitz, 1977).

If all these possibilities are correct, then an increased central nervous system requirement for carnitine could theoretically be the basis for physical dependence on ethanol. This sounds far-fetched, but we have found (Abu Murad, Begg, Griffiths and Littleton, 1977) that increasing the dietary intake of carnitine by mice during the induction of physical dependence on ethanol markedly ameliorates the subsequent physical withdrawal syndrome. Obviously this evidence is very indirect, but it does suggest a role for carnitine, and fatty acid metabolism, in the development of physical dependence on ethanol.

Much remains to be done on the synaptic membrane in dependence. We have concentrated on lipid metabolism but alterations in synaptic proteins and divalent cation binding have also been described (e.g. Noble, Syapin, Vigran and Rosenberg, 1976; Gruber, Dinovo,

Noble and Tewari, 1977; Ross, Kibler and Cardenas, 1977; Michaelis and Myers, 1979). The results which have been obtained have exciting implications for understanding, and controlling, physical dependence on ethanol.

Conclusions

There is evidence which suggests that ethanol exerts the majority of its neurochemical and behavioural effects as a result of a simple physio-chemical action at the surfaces of neuronal membranes. The development of tolerance to ethanol is considered to be due partly to an adaptive alteration in the lipid composition of these membranes. Factors which may have a strong bearing on the appropriateness of the lipid response to ethanol include the electrical activity of the membrane and its cholesterol content. The development of tolerance by this mechanism appears to be genetically determined and may be subject to pharmacological and dietary manipulation. Physical dependence on ethanol at the level of the membrane has not been much studied, but available evidence suggests that some 'fixing' of the membrane composition may convert tolerance to dependence. This could be related to reduced ability to alter phospholipid fatty acid composition, or to the institution of some other, slower, adaptive mechanism. A great deal of work remains to be done before these interrelationships can be understood.

Acknowledgements

Many of these ideas have grown out of discussions with friends and colleagues at King's College and elsewhere. Our own research has been supported by the Medical Council on Alcoholism, the Mental Health Foundation and the Medical Research Council.

References

Abdel Latiff, A.A., Roberts, M.B., Karp, W.B. and Smith, J.P. (1973), 'Metabolism of phosphatidylcholine phosphatidylinositol and palmityl carnitine in synaptosomes from rat brain', *J. Neurochem., 20*, 189-202
Abu Murad, C., Begg, S.J., Griffiths, P.J. and Littleton, J.M. (1977), 'Hepatic triglyceride accumulation and the ethanol physical withdrawal syndrome in

mice', *Br. J. exp. Path., 58*, 606-15

Abu Murad, C. and Littleton, J.M. (1978), 'Cardiac phospholipid composition during continuous administration of ethanol to mice: effects of vitamin E', *Br. J. Pharmacol., 63*, 373-4P

Abu Murad, C. and Thurman, R. (1979), 'A method for investigation of ethanol acute tolerance and dependence', *Fed. Proc., 38*, 378

Berghaus, G. *et al.* (1975), 'Fatty acid pattern of human fat and liver tissues in alcoholics and non-alcoholics: fatty acid pattern as a measure of alcoholism', *Deutsch. Med. Wochenschr., 100*, 1233-8

Blaker, W.D. and Moscatelli, E.A. (1978), 'The effect of hibernation on the lipids of brain myelin and microsomes in the Syrian hamster', *J. Neurochem., 31*, 1513-18

Bremer, J. (1977), 'Carnitine and its role in fatty acid metabolism', *Trends in Biochemical Sciences, 2*, 207-9

Chapman, D., Peel, W.E., Kingston, B. and Lilley, T.H. (1977), 'Lipid phase transitions in model biomembranes. The effect of ions on phosphatidylcholine bilayers', *Biochim. Biophys. Acta., 464*, 260-75

Cherqui, G., Cadot, M., Senault, C. and Portet, R. (1979), 'The lipid composition of plasma membrane and mitochondrial fractions from epididymal adipocytes of cold acclimated rats', *Biochim. Biophys. Acta., 551*, 304-14

Chin, J.H. and Goldstein, D.B. (1977a), 'Effects of low concentrations of ethanol on the fluidity of spin-labelled erythrocyte and brain membranes', *Mol. Pharmac., 13*, 435-41

—— (1977b), 'Drug tolerance in biomembranes: A spin label study of the effects of ethanol', *Science, 196*, 684-5

Chin, J.H., Parsons, L.M. and Goldstein, D.B. (1978), 'Increased cholesterol content of erythrocyte and brain membranes in ethanol-tolerant mice', *Biochim. Biophys. Acta., 513*, 358-63

Cooper, R.A. (1977), 'Abnormalities of cell-membrane fluidity in the pathogenesis of disease', *N. Eng. J. Med., 297*, 371-7

Cossins, A.R. (1977), 'Adaptation of biological membranes to temperature. The effect of temperature acclimation of goldfish upon the viscosity of synaptosomal membranes', *Biochim. Biophys. Acta., 470*, 395-411

Cronan, J.E. and Gelmann, E.P. (1975), 'Physical properties of membrane lipids: biological relevance and regulation', *Bacteriol Rev., 39*, 232-56

Dobretsov, G.E., Borschevskaya, T.A., Petrov, V.A., Yu, A. and Vladimov, V. (1977), 'The increase of phospholipid bilayer rigidity after lipid peroxidation', *FEBS Letts., 84*, 125-8

Goldman, S.S. (1975), 'Cold resistance of the brain during hibernation III. Evidence of a lipid adaptation', *Am. J. Physiol., 228*, 834-8

—— (1978), 'Cold resistance of the brain during hibernation: the role of stearyl CoA desaturase in brain and liver as the source for monoenes', *J. Neurochem., 30*, 397-400

Goldman, S.S. and Albers, R.W. (1979), 'Cold resistance of the brain during hibernation: changes in microviscosity of the membrane and associated lipids', *J. Neurochem., 32*, 1139-42

Goldstein, D.B., Chin, J.H., McComb, J.A. and Parsons, L.M. (1980), 'Chronic effects of alcohols on mouse biomembranes', *Adv. Exp. Med. Biol.*, (in press)

Greizerstein, H. (1977), 'Factors influencing the development of tolerance to ethanol', *Life Sci., 21*, 1249-58

Grieve, S.J., Griffiths, P.J. and Littleton, J.M. (1979), 'Genetic influences on the rate of development of ethanol tolerance and the ethanol physical withdrawal syndrome in mice', *Drug Alc. Dep., 4*, 77-86

Grieve, S.J. and Littleton, J.M. (1978), 'Rapid development of cellular tolerance during continuous administration of ethanol to mice by inhalation', *Br. J. Pharmac., 63*, 375P-6P

Grieve, S.J., Littleton, J.M., Jones, P.A. and John, G.R. (1979), 'Functional tolerance to ethanol in mice; relationship to lipid metabolism', *J. Pharm. Pharmac., 31*, 737-42

Griffiths, P.J., Abu Murad, C. and Littleton, J.M. (1979), 'Ethanol-induced hepatic triglyceride accumulation in mice and genetic differences in the ethanol physical withdrawal syndrome', *Br. J. Addiction, 74*, 37-42

Gruber, B., Dinovo, E.C., Noble, E.P. and Tewari, S. (1977), 'Ethanol-induced conformational changes in rat brain microsomal membranes', *Biochem. Pharmac., 26*, 2181-6

Hill, M.W. and Bangham, A.D. (1975), 'General depressant drug dependency: a biophysical hypothesis', *Adv. Exp. Med. Biol., 59*, 1-9

Ihrig, T.J., French, S.W. and Morin, R.J. (1969), 'Lipid composition of cellular membranes after ethanol feeding', *Fed. Proc., 28*, 626

Ingram, L.O. (1976), 'Adaptation of membrane lipids to alcohols', *J. Bacteriol., 125*, 670-8

Ingram, L.O., Ley, K.D. and Hoffmann, E.M. (1978), 'Drug-induced changes in lipid composition of E. coli and of mammalian cells in culture – ethanol, pentobarbital and chlorpromazine', *Life Sci., 22*, 489-93

Ingram, L.O., Buttke, T.M. and Dickens, B.F. (1980), 'Reversible effects of ethanol on the lipids of E. coli.', *Adv. Exp. Med. Biol.*, in press

Johnson, D.A., Lee, N.M., Cooke, R. and Loh, H.H. (1979), 'Ethanol-induced fluidization of brain lipid bilayers: required presence of cholesterol in membranes for the expression of tolerance', *Mol. Pharmac., 15*, 739-46

Karagezyan, K.G., Amirkhanyan, L.T., Amirkhanyan, O.M. and Aleksandryan, D.V. (1975), 'Inositol containing phospholipids in brain and liver of rats in prolonged alcohol intoxication', *Vop. med. Klin. Mosk., 21*, 269-71

Katsumata, K. (1970), 'Effect of carnitine on the oxidation of palmitate in alcohol-fed liver mitochondria', *J. Vitaminol. (Kyoto), 16*, 249-52

Kewitz, H. and Pleul, O. (1977), 'Inhibition of choline incorporation into brain lipids by urethane, a proposed mechanism of depression of the central nervous system', *Arch. Pharmac., 298*, 205-10

King, M.E. and Spector, A.A. (1978), 'Effect of specific fatty acyl enrichments on membrane physical properties detected with a spin label probe', *J. Biol. Chem., 253*, 6493-501

Lesch, P., Schmidt, E. and Schmidt, F.W. (1972), 'Effects of chronic alcohol abuse on the structural lipids in the human brain. Hepatocerebral degeneration I', *Z. Clin. Chem., 10*, 410

———— (1973), 'Effects of chronic alcohol abuse on the fatty acid composition of major lipids in the human brain. Hepatocerebral degeneration II', *Z. Klin. Chem., 11*, 159

Li, G.C. and Hahn, G.M. (1978), 'Ethanol-induced tolerance to heat and to adriamycin', *Nature, 274*, 699-701

Littleton, J.M. (1979a), 'The assessment of rapid tolerance to ethanol' in *Experimental Handbook of Ethanol Tolerance and Dependence* (eds. Rigter, H. and Crabbe, J.), Elsevier, Amsterdam, in press

———— (1979b), 'Neuropharmacological aspects of ethanol tolerance and dependence', *Adv. Biol. Psychiat., 3*, 75-84

Littleton, J.M., John, G.R. and Grieve, S.J. (1979), 'Alterations in phospholipid composition in ethanol tolerance and dependence', *Alcoholism Clin. Exp. Res., 3*, 50-6

Littleton, J.M., Grieve, S.J., Griffiths, P.J. and John, G.R. (1980), 'Ethanol-induced alteration in membrane phospholipid composition: possible relationship to development of cellular tolerance to ethanol', *Adv. Exp. Med. Biol.*, in press

Littleton, J.M. and John, G. (1977), 'Synaptosomal membrane lipids of mice during continuous exposure to ethanol', *J. Pharm. Pharmac., 29*, 579-80

Littleton, J.M., John G.R. and Jones, P.A. (1980), 'Feeding diets containing different lipids to mice throughout development alters sensitivity and subsequent development of tolerance to ethanol', *Life Sci.*, in press

Lucy, J.A. (1974), 'Lipids and membranes', *FEBS Lett., 40*, 105-11

Michaelis, E.K. and Myers, S.L. (1979), 'Ca^{2+} binding to brain synaptosomes — effects of chronic EtOH intake', *Biochem. Pharm., 28*, 2081-7

Michaelson, D.M., Horwitz, A.F. and Klein, M.P. (1974), 'Head group modulation of membrane fluidity in sonicated phospholipid dispersions', *Biochem., 13*, 2605-11

Nandini-Kishore, S.G., Kitajima, Y. and Thompson, G.A., Jr (1977), 'Membrane fluidising effects of the general anaesthetic, methoxyflurane, elicit an acclimation response to Tetrahymena', *Biochem. Biophys. Acta, 471*, 157-61

Nandini-Kishore, S.G., Mattox, S.M., Martin, C.E. and Thompson, G.A., Jr (1979), 'Membrane changes during growth of Tetrahymena in the presence of ethanol', *Biochim. Biophys. Acta., 551*, 315-27

Noble, E.P., Syapin, P.J., Vigran, R. and Rosenberg, A. (1976), 'Neuraminidase-releasable surface sialic acid of cultured astroblasts exposed to ethanol', *J. Neurochem., 27*, 217-21

Nozawa, Y. and Kasai, R. (1978), 'Mechanism of thermal adaptation of membrane lipids in Tetrahymena pyriformis NT-1. Possible evidence for temperature-mediated induction of palmitoyl-CoA desaturase', *Biochim. Biophys. Acta., 529*, 54-66

Nunn, W.D. (1975), 'The inhibition of phospholipid synthesis in E. coli by phenethyl alcohol', *Biochim. Biophys. Acta., 380*, 403-13

Pang, K-Y., Chang, T-L. and Miller, K.W. (1979), 'On the coupling between anaesthetic induced membrane fluidization and cation permeability in lipid vesicles', *Mol. Pharmac., 15*, 729-38

Pang, K-Y. and Miller, K.W. (1978), 'Cholesterol modulates the effects of membrane perturbers in phospholipid vesicles and biomembranes', *Biochim. Biophys. Acta., 511*, 1-9

Ramsey, R.B. (1977), 'Effect of extended hypocholesterolaemic drug treatment on peripheral and CNS sterol content of the rat', *Lipids, 12*, 841-6

Reitz, R.C. (1977), 'Effect of ethanol on carnitine acyltransferase', *Fed. Proc., 36*, 331

Reitz, R.C., Helsabeck, E. and Mason, D.P. (1973), 'Effects of chronic alcohol ingestion on the fatty acid composition of the heart', *Lipids, 8*, 80-4

Rigby, M. and Littleton, J.M. (1979), 'Experimental observations on the relationship between ethanol tolerance and dependence', *Br. J. Addict., 74*, 363-7

Ross, D.H., Kibler, B.C. and Cardenas, H.L. (1977), 'Modification of glycoprotein residues as Ca^{2+} receptor sites after chronic ethanol exposure', *Drug and Alcohol Dependence, 2*, 305-15

Seelig, A. and Seelig, J. (1978), 'Effect of a single cis bond on the structure of a phospholipid bilayer', *Biochemistry, 16*, 45-50

Seelig, J. (1978), 'Nuclear magnetic resonance and the head group structure of phospholipids in membranes', *Biochim. Biophys. Acta., 515*, 105-40

Seelig, J. and Browning, J.L. (1977), 'General features of phospholipid conformation in membranes', *FEBS Letts., 92*, 41-4

Seeman, P. (1972), 'The membrane actions of anaesthetics and tranquillizers', *Pharm. Rev., 24*, 583-655

Sinensky, M. (1971), 'Temperature control of phospholipid biosynthesis in E. coli', *J. Bacteriol., 106,* 449-55

Skriver, L. and Thompson, G.A., Jr (1979), 'Temperature-induced changes in fatty acid unsaturation of Tetrahymena membranes do not require induced fatty acid desaturase', *Biochim. Biophys. Acta., 572,* 376-81

Stephens, C.L. and Skinitsky (1977), 'Modulation of electrical activity in Aphysia neurones by cholesterol', *Nature, 270,* 267-8

Suckling, K.E., Blair, H.A.F., Boyd, G.S., Craig, I.F. and Malcolm, A.R. (1979), 'The importance of the phospholipid bilayer and the length of the cholesterol molecule in membrane structure', *Biochim. Bioophys. Acta., 551,* 10-21

Sun, G.Y. (1972), 'Effects of a fatty acid deficiency on lipids of whole brain, microsomes and myelin in the rat', *J. Lipid Res., 13,* 56-62

Sun, G.Y. and Horrocks, L.A. (1973), 'Metabolism of palmitic acid in the sub-cellular fractions of mouse brain', *J. Lipid Res., 14,* 206-14

Sun, G.Y. and Yau, T.M. (1976), 'Incorporation of (1-^{14}C) oleic acid and (1-^{14}C) arachidonic acid into lipids in the subcellular fractions of mouse brain', *J. Neurochem., 27,* 87-92

Thompson, G.A., Jr and Nozawa, Y. (1977), 'Tetrahymena: a system for studying dynamic membrane alterations within the eukaryotic cell', *Biochem. Biophys. Acta., 472,* 55-92

Thulborn, K.R., Treloar, F.E. and Sawyer, W.H. (1978), 'A microviscosity barrier in the lipid bilayer due to the presence of phospholipids containing unsaturated acyl chains', *Biochem. Biophys. Res. Commun., 81,* 42-9

Vanderkooi, J. (1979), 'Effect of ethanol on membranes: a fluorescent probe study', *Alcohol. Clin. Exp. Res., 3,* 60-3

Wirz, K.W.A. (1974), 'Transfer of phospholipids between membranes', *Biochim. Biophys. Acta., 344,* 95-117

Wodtke, E. (1978), 'Lipid adaptation in liver mitochondrial membranes of carp acclaimed to different environmental temperatures. Phospholipid composition, fatty acid pattern and cholesterol content', *Biochim. Biophys. Acta., 529,* 280-91

4 METABOLIC ASPECTS OF ETHANOL DEPENDENCE AND TISSUE DAMAGE

Marie E. Bardsley and Keith F. Tipton

Ingestion of ethanol can lead to a variety of biochemical changes some of which are summarised in Figure 4.1. These diverse effects have made it difficult to identify those that are primarily responsible for the phenomena of tolerance, dependence and tissue damage, although there has been no shortage of theories attempting to account for them. It may, however, be possible to eliminate some of the biochemical changes as being of secondary importance and to indicate those areas which would repay further detailed investigation. In this chapter we will first consider some of the problems that have hindered the understanding of the biochemical basis of ethanol-induced dependence and tissue damage and then discuss some of the evidence concerning the possible mechanisms involved.

Figure 4.1: Some Effects of Ethanol

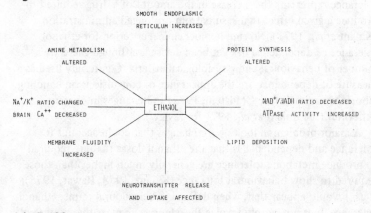

4.1 Problems

Many of the problems affecting studies of the development of ethanol-induced tolerance, dependence and tissue damage in Man have involved the development of suitable criteria for the first two and the choice of satisfactory, standardised animal model systems for use in laboratory studies.

75

4.1.1 Definitions

Although the behavioural sciences have been able to arrive at satisfactory definitions of tolerance and dependence, the situation with biochemical pharmacology is less satisfactory and no simple biochemical change has yet been shown definitely to correlate with the development of either tolerance or dependence. Ethanol differs from other major central nervous system (CNS) depressants in that its primary action does not appear to be a consequence of a direct action of the drug on specific receptors. With the opiates, diazepams and neuroleptics, tolerance can be seen in receptor dose-response curves to the drugs, but no such correlation has been observed in the case of ethanol.

There are two aspects to drug tolerance. Spontaneous or initial tolerance represents the amount of a drug that is necessary to produce a given effect and, as will be discussed later, this aspect of ethanol tolerance has been shown to vary quite widely between animal species and between individuals of the same species, as well as to depend upon the nutritional state of the individual. Such problems can cause wide variability in experimental results, making it difficult to investigate small changes that may occur as a result of ethanol ingestion. Acquired tolerance represents the increase in the amount of a drug required to produce a given effect that results from prolonged administration (Kalant *et al.*, 1971). No simple biochemical criterion for ethanol tolerance or dependence has yet been devised, although there are a number of behavioural and physiological criteria. Commonly used as a measure of dependence are the appearance of convulsions on handling laboratory animals (see Goldstein, 1972) and changes in operant behaviour (see Kalant *et al.*, 1971 for review).

A major problem in looking for changes that could account for tolerance and dependence is that the ethanol doses that are required to produce metabolic tolerance are generally much higher than those required to show behavioural tolerance (Kalant, 1978; Rawat, 1975); thus it would appear that, when defined in behavioural terms, ethanol tolerance does not simply involve the adaptive changes that may result in an increased ability to metabolise it. Studies of the development of tolerance are also complicated by the fact that the time taken for it to develop can depend upon the criterion that is used. With many criteria it may take several days or weeks for tolerance to develop (see Kalant *et al.*, 1971), but Crabbe *et al.* (1979) have reported that a rapidly-reversible tolerance to the hypothermic response to ethanol could be produced by a single injected dose given 24 hours earlier. Such results suggest that there may be a multiplicity of biochemical effects each of which can produce a form of tolerance.

Changes in enzyme levels that arise from chronic ethanol ingestion, which will be discussed later, may add a secondary degree of acquired tolerance due to an increased ability to metabolise the compound. The route of ethanol administration may also affect the extent of this secondary tolerance; for example adaptive changes in the lungs may occur when the ethanol is administered by inhalation (see, e.g. Goldstein, 1975).

4.1.2 Animal Models

The choice of a laboratory animal as a model for investigating the effects of ethanol in man is problematical. Despite the common use of the rat these animals generally do not choose to drink sufficient ethanol to produce liver damage if their diet is adequate (see Lieber *et al.*, 1975). There are, however, alcohol-preferring strains of rat (e.g. ALKO) which have been found to have different patterns of aldehyde dehydrogenase isoenzymes from normal (Berger and Weiner, 1977), a lower total activity of alcohol dehydrogenase (Koivula *et al.*, 1975) and lower steady-state acetaldehyde levels (Eriksson, 1973).

Alcohol dehydrogenase exists as a number of isoenzymes in man and it has been suggested that two of these, the so-called π-isoenzyme (Li *et al.*, 1977) and the 'atypical' isoenzyme (von Wartburg *et al.*, 1974) may be related to variations in spontaneous tolerance (see Li, 1977; Tipton *et al.*, 1978, for reviews). The situation in most laboratory animals is quite different from man in that they possess fewer isoenzymes.

Other animal models are at present less well defined but it appears that considerable differences may exist. The Syrian hamster, for example, has a particularly high preference for ethanol, consistently preferring a 10 per cent ethanol solution to water. Such a level of consumption is considerably higher than that generally accepted by the rat, but it appears to have less effect, both biochemically and behaviourally in the hamster (Harris *et al.*, 1979).

4.1.3 Primary and Secondary Effects

Ethanol is a good source of metabolic energy (see Lieber, 1977, for review) and thus the effects of ethanol consumption in man can be complicated by dietary deficiencies. Studies with laboratory animals can however be carried out under adequate nutritional conditions, which should eliminate complications arising from this source. The lipid deposition that occurs in liver as a result of chronic ethanol consumption, which can ultimately lead to cirrhosis, has been shown to be exacerbated by malnutrition and particularly by lack of essential amino acids in the diet, although a protein-rich diet cannot prevent the development of fatty liver (Lieber and Rubin, 1968). In addition ethanol consumption can have a direct effect on the intestine impairing absorption and giving a secondary cause of malnutrition (see, e.g. Baraona and Lindenbaum, 1977).

The symptoms and pathology of ethanol-induced nerve cell damage in the CNS are similar to those induced by thiamine deficiency (Korsakoff's syndrome) and it has been suggested that ethanol may impair the ability of nerves to use this vitamin. As well as acting as an enzyme cofactor, thiamine may play a role in membrane permeability. It has been proposed that the cyclic interconversion of thiamine di- and tri-phosphates bound to nerve membranes promotes the passage of ions (Itokawa and Cooper, 1970). An adequate thiamine-containing diet will not, however, prevent ethanol-induced neurological damage and it is probable that the similarities to thiamine deficiency may result from a direct effect of ethanol on the membranes affecting their electrical properties (see later) rather than an actual deficiency or an impairment of thiamine function.

The ingestion of ethanol results in a decrease of the $NAD^+:NADH$ ratio in liver which can have important metabolic consequences (see later). It appears that the limiting factor affecting the reoxidation of NADH will depend upon the nutritional state. After starvation the ability of the cellular shuttle systems to transfer reducing equivalents into the motochondria for reoxidation may be the limiting factor, whereas in the fed state it may be the mitochondrial oxidation systems themselves that become limiting (Cederbaum *et al.*, 1977) and thus the extent of the alteration of the $NADH:NAD^+$ ratio will be dependent on dietary state. One of the consequences of the increased $NADH:NAD^+$ ratio is the inhibition of tryptophan pyrrolase, which results in increased concentrations of circulating tryptophan and hence in increased brain 5-hydroxytryptamine (5-HT) levels (Badawy *et al.*, 1979).

Sucrose or glucose also tend to increase the tryptophan and 5-HT levels in the rat (Badawy and Evans, 1976; Evans and Badawy, 1977); and thus the extent, if any, of the elevation of brain 5-HT levels that follows ethanol consumption will depend upon whether the sucrose has been administered to the controls to match the ethanol calories consumed by the experimental animals. The situation is, however, further complicated by the fact that stress will itself result in an elevation of the circulating tryptophan levels.

A final factor which should be borne in mind is that laboratory experiments with animals are usually carried out with pure ethanol, whereas some of the deleterious effects in man may, at least in part, be due to 'impurities' in the alcoholic beverages consumed (see, e.g. Magrinat *et al.*, 1973).

4.1.4 Organ Differences

The major site of ethanol metabolism is the liver (accounting for some 75 per cent of the total – see, e.g. Li, 1977) – and, because of this and the damage to this organ that can result from chronic ethanol consumption, most biochemical studies have concentrated on that organ. The response of the brain to ingested ethanol differs from that of liver and, since the behavioural effects precede many of the biochemical changes, it is important to recognise the different functions of the CNS that may be affected.

Although alcohol dehydrogenase is present in brain (Raskin and Sokoloff, 1970; Duncan *et al.*, 1976) its activity is very low and the contribution that it makes to the total ethanol metabolism in the body is extremely small (Mukherji *et al.*, 1975). Unlike the liver, where ethanol consumption can result in large decreases in the NAD^+ : NADH ratio, there is no significant change in brain (Veloso *et al.*, 1972), although there may be some change in the redox state as reflected by an increased lactate: pyruvate ratio (Rawat and Kuriyama, 1972).

Except at very high concentrations of administered ethanol, the concentrations of acetaldehyde in the brain have been found to be negligible (Eriksson and Sippel, 1977). This absence of acetaldehyde is somewhat surprising since appreciable concentrations of this compound have been found in the cerebro-spinal fluid (CSF) following ingestion of ethanol (Pettersson and Kiessling, 1977). Since there is no known barrier between the CSF and brain tissue (Fernstermacher *et al.*, 1974) the acetaldehyde concentrations in these two compartments might be expected to be similar. The failure to detect this compound in brain might be due to the efficient operation of the brain aldehyde dehydrogenase which has a very low K_m value for acetaldehyde (Duncan and Tipton, 1971), a conclusion which receives support from the observation that the acetaldehyde concentration in the CSF is increased when this enzyme is inhibited (Pettersson and Kiessling, 1977). Another possibility would be the rapid binding of acetaldehyde to, and perhaps reaction with, components in the brain, since a tight-binding interaction between aldehydes and neural membranes has been demonstrated (Alivisatos and Ungar, 1968). These results suggest, however, that the effects of ethanol consumption on the CNS may not be due to interactions of its metabolite acetaldehyde; this aspect will be discussed in more detail in the next section.

4.2 Possible Biochemical Mechanisms

The diverse effects of ethanol have made it difficult to decide which of them may be primarily responsible for the phenomena of tolerance, dependence and tissue damage, and it is probable that no single action can account for all these effects.

4.2.1 Tolerance and Dependence

As discussed earlier, the development of tolerance as assessed behaviourally precedes the adaptive changes in enzyme levels that may allow the more efficient metabolism of ethanol and this section will be devoted to the factors affecting the CNS that might give rise to behavioural tolerance and dependence.

A great deal of speculation has been concerned with the possibility that acetaldehyde rather than ethanol itself is responsible for many of the effects of ethanol (see, e.g. Truitt and Walsh, 1971); however there is now compelling evidence that free acetaldehyde plays no significant role in the central effects of ethanol. This evidence may be summarised as follows:

(1) Acetaldehyde cannot be detected in the brain following ingestion of ethanol under conditions where there are appreciable concentrations in the blood and CSF (see above).

(2) Ethanol ingestion causes characteristic changes in the metabolism of biogenic amines in liver which are due, at least in part, to competitive effects of free acetaldehyde (Turner *et al.*, 1974; Tipton *et al.*, 1977), but such effects cannot be observed in brain.

(3) Inhibition of alcohol dehydrogenase by pyrazole potentiates many of the acute effects of ethanol and delays the onset of withdrawal in alcohol-dependent mice, although it has a convulsant action if administered during withdrawal (Goldstein, 1975). Pyrazole alone has, however, been shown to be able to produce a withdrawal reaction under some conditions (Thurman and Pathman, 1975).

(4) The total liver alcohol dehydrogenase activity is actually lower in

alcohol-preferring strains of rat than normal (Koivula *et al.*, 1975).

(5) The aldehyde dehydrogenase inhibitor disulphiram has no apparent effect on the development of ethanol-dependence or withdrawal (Thurman and Pathman, 1975).

(6) Tertiary butanol, which is not metabolised to the corresponding aldehyde (Wallgren *et al.*, 1973; Thurman and Pathman, 1975), has similar tolerance- and dependence-producing properties to ethanol (Wallgren, 1960; Thurman and Pathman, 1975; McComb and Goldstein, 1979).

Although this evidence would appear to exclude the possibility of free acetaldehyde being involved in the direct effects on the CNS, products of reactions involving acetaldehyde in the periphery, such as tetrahydroisoquinoline alkaloids, which have been shown to be able to cross the blood-brain barrier (Marshall and Hirst, 1976; see also Davis in this book), could add secondary complications to the overall picture. It has also been suggested that ethanol administration results in an elevation of biogenic aldehydes in the brain which could affect sleep patterns (see, e.g. Sabelli and Giardina, 1973) and temperature regulation (McIsaac *et al.*, 1961) and perhaps act as precursors for tetrahydroisoquinoline compound formation. Such an effect is, however, unlikely since an elevation in the concentrations of these aldehydes would be expected to result in alterations in the patterns of biogenic amine metabolites formed (see Tipton *et al.*, 1977; 1978).

The available evidence, therefore, indicates that tolerance and dependence arise primarily from a direct effect of ethanol in the brain. A possible mechanism for this may be the interaction of ethanol with membranes. It has been proposed that the action of anaesthetics is due to their binding to and destabilising the structure of membranes (Seeman, 1972; Allison, 1974), thus interfering with their sodium, potassium and calcium ion-transport processes and hence their electrical properties.

The actions of ethanol *in vitro* have been shown to include fluidisation and expansion of synaptosomal, mitochondrial and erythrocyte membranes (Seeman, 1974; Chin and Goldstein, 1977; Hosein *et al.*, 1977) and inhibition of the changes of sodium and potassium ion levels that result from electrical stimulation (see, e.g. Israel *et al.*, 1975).

The acute effects of short-chain aliphatic alcohols *in vivo* have been shown to correlate with their lipid solubilities (Wallgren, 1960; McComb and Goldstein, 1975; LeBlanc and Kalant, 1975). Chronic treatment with ethanol has been reported to result in a loss of membrane fluidity suggesting a possible mechanism for the development of tolerance (Curran and Seeman, 1977; but see Chin and Goldstein, 1977). In addition McComb and Goldstein (1979) have shown that the potencies of ethanol and tertiary butanol in causing dependence are directly related to their lipid solubilities.

Such an essentially non-specific effect of ethanol would also be expected to affect the activities of membrane bound proteins (Seeman, 1974; Hofmann and Hosein 1978); by analogy to the effects of other anaesthetics (see, e.g. Taussig, 1979), these might be altered *in vitro* under conditions where the membrane interactions were affected.

The inhibitory effect of ethanol on the activity of the mitochondrial sodium-potassium-dependent ATPase, which has been reported to be allosteric (Kalant *et al.*, 1978) and to be relieved in parallel to withdrawal (Roach *et al.*, 1973; Rangaraj and Kalant, 1978), may be related to changes in the structure of the mitochondrial outer-membrane, as has been shown to be the case for the activation of the magnesium-dependent ATPase (Hosein *et al.*, 1977; see also Gordon and Lough, 1972). The activities of these enzymes will, however, be affected by changes in cation availability resulting from the effects of ethanol on membrane permeability. The effects of ethanol in impairing other aspects of mitochondrial function (see, e.g. Bernstein and Penniall, 1978) may also arise directly or indirectly from its effects on membrane structure.

If the primary effect of ethanol is its effect on membranes, this will be modified by a variety of secondary effects that may result from it. For example, ethanol injection has been shown to cause a time-dependent reversible fall in the concentrations of calcium in the brain, which has been attributed to an increased binding to membranes (Ross *et al.*, 1974). Tolerance to this effect was found to develop within 24 hours of the first injection (Ross, 1976) thus resembling the hypothermic effect mentioned earlier.

Interestingly morphine and salsolinol were found to have similar calcium-depleting effects to ethanol, which in all cases were antagonised by the morphine antagonist naloxone (Ross *et al.*, 1974), and cross-tolerance between these drugs could be demonstrated (Ross, 1976). These results suggest that the calcium-depleting effects must be secondary actions of these drugs, since little cross-tolerance has been demonstrated between ethanol and morphine; the withdrawal symptoms from these two drugs are very different and administration of naloxone does not precipitate withdrawal in alcohol-dependent rats

(Goldstein and Judson, 1971). Studies with protein synthesis inhibitors (Ross, 1976; Cox and Osman, 1970) might suggest that this calcium-depleting action principally involves synaptic membranes. This may, however, be complicated by any changes in the redox state of the cells that result from ethanol ingestion, since Lehninger *et al.* (1978) have shown that this influences the ability of mitochondria to accumulate calcium.

The effects of ethanol on the levels of neurotransmitters in the brain are more difficult to assess. It would be tempting to try to ascribe the alterations to the effects of ethanol on nerve membranes, impairing their electrical properties and reducing the levels of calcium ions whose transport is coupled to neurotransmitter release. The situation is, however, more complicated than this as the following brief discussion will show.

All neurotransmitter systems appear to be affected in one way or another by the ingestion and withdrawal from ethanol (see, e.g. Noble and Tewari, 1977; Smith, 1977; Myers, 1978) and, in agreement with the simple theory outlined above, their release from brain tissue appears to be inhibited by ethanol (Israel *et al.*, 1975). There is, however, conflicting evidence on the nature of the changes that occur in the levels of individual neurotransmitters (see, e.g. Noble and Tewari, 1977).

The concentration of acetylcholine in brain is lowered by acute ethanol consumption (Eriksson and Graham, 1973; Israel *et al.*, 1975) but returns to normal on chronic treatment, in a process that may parallel the development of tolerance (Kalant and Grose, 1967; but see Rawat, 1974). In addition the inhibition by ethanol of acetylcholine release from cortical slices may be overcome by high concentrations of potassium ions in the medium (Kalant and Grose, 1967). It has been suggested that changes in acetylcholine levels may be related to ethanol preference (Ho and Kissin, 1975). There appears, however, to be no direct connection between the changes in acetylcholine levels and ethanol dependence since drugs that affect the cholinergic system have no effect on withdrawal (Goldstein, 1975).

Ethanol ingestion, whether acute or chronic, has little effect on the concentrations of noradrenaline and dopamine in the brain (see, e.g. Noble and Tewari, 1977), although it does affect their rates of turnover. The response to a single dose is time-dependent, noradrenaline synthesis being at first stimulated with no significant change in that of dopamine, whereas after several hours the turnover rates of both amines are depressed (Hung and Majchrowicz, 1974).

The mechanisms underlying these effects are still far from clear. Ethanol has been reported to inhibit the release of noradrenaline from brain cortical slices and also to inhibit its re-uptake, but very high concentrations were required to show these effects (see Israel *et al.,* 1975) and they could not be demonstrated *in vivo* when more realistic ethanol doses were used (Thadani and Truitt, 1973).

Chronic ethanol ingestion has been reported to result in a decrease in the rate of turnover of dopamine but an increase in that of noradrenaline, although these did not change during withdrawal (Hunt and Majchrowicz, 1974). A role of catecholamines in the withdrawal process is however indicated by the observation that the symptoms are exacerbated by treatments that stimulate the catecholaminergic system (Collier *et al.*, 1976; Griffiths *et al.*, 1974; Blum and Wallace, 1974; Goldstein, 1973).

The endogenous levels of 5-HT in the brain of alcohol-preferring strains of rats are higher than normal (Ahtee and Eriksson, 1972) and increase on alcohol consumption as do those in normal rats (Badawy *et al.*, 1979). There are, however, disparate reports as to whether the inhibitor of 5-HT synthesis, *p*-chlorophenylalanine (*p*-CPA), affects the alcohol consumption of normal rats (see Myers, 1978).

Studies on 5-HT metabolism show that ethanol decreases the turnover of 5-HT in the brain and it has also been reported to inhibit the transport of the breakdown product, 5-hydroxyindole acetic acid, from the brain (Tabakoff *et al.*, 1975). Rogawski *et al.* (1974) showed that ethanol inhibited tryptophan hydroxylase *in vitro*; this inhibition persisted after solubilisation of the enzyme, indicating that it was not a membrane effect.

Using *p*-CPA and 5,7-dihydroxytryptamine, brain 5-HT levels can be depleted without affecting the acute response to ethanol, although the rate of development of tolerance to ethanol-induced hypothermia and sleep-time was decreased (Frankel *et al.*, 1975). Tryptophan administration accelerated the development of tolerance. On chronic treatment, after the animals have developed physiological tolerance, *p*-CPA does not affect the maintenance of tolerance but does accelerate the loss of tolerance on discontinuing the drug (Frankel *et al.*, 1978).

5-HT is involved in circadian rhythms *via* the hormone melatonin which is synthesised in the pineal gland and several reports suggest that melatonin is involved in preference to alcohol (see, e.g. Geller, 1971).

Using 6-hydroxydopamine to deplete brain catecholamine levels Ritzmann and Tabakoff (1976) appeared to be able to dissociate physiological tolerance to hypothermia and sleep-time from behavioural dependence. Mice injected with 6-hydroxydopamine showed the same severity of withdrawal compared with their ethanol-fed controls. However, on testing tolerance 26 hr after withdrawal, the 6-hydroxydopamine pretreated mice did not show the tolerance seen in the untreated ethanol-fed controls. This can be interpreted in two ways: either that depletion of catecholamines blocks physiological tolerance but not behavioural withdrawal, or that loss of tolerance has been accelerated.

Although ethanol appears to have no consistent effect on the levels of γ-aminobutyric acid (GABA) in brain (see, e.g. Noble and Tewari, 1977) there is evidence that GABA may have a role in modulating the effects of ethanol, since the GABA antagonist, bicuculline, decreases the hyperexcitability associated with ethanol withdrawal; whereas drugs that elevate GABA levels tend to increase it (Goldstein, 1975). These treatments were, however, found to have the opposite effects on ethanol intoxication (Häkkinen and Kulonen, 1976). The putative neurotransmitter glycine may also be implicated in the actions of ethanol since it has been shown to prolong ethanol-induced sleeping time (Blum *et al.*, 1972).

Although confusing and, in some cases, contradictory, these results suggest that a number of factors may be involved in the response of neurotransmitters to ethanol and that further work will be necessary before a full interpretation can be made. In particular it is difficult to draw any firm conclusions from the results of experiments on withdrawal in which neurotransmitter levels are manipulated, since these may act at the level of the physical manifestations rather than having any direct interaction with the biochemical actions of ethanol.

4.2.2 Adaptive Changes

Chronic treatment with ethanol can result in the development of a metabolic tolerance due to increases of some of the enzyme systems involved in its breakdown. In addition, the spontaneous tolerance appears to vary between individuals (see, e.g. Schuckit and Rayses, 1979), and it has been speculated that this is due to the presence of one or more specific isoenzymes of liver alcohol dehydrogenase. One of these, the π-isoenzyme differs from the other common isoenzymes of human alcohol dehydrogenase in having a considerably higher K_m value for ethanol (about 20 mM at pH 7.5 compared with 0.4 mM for the others) (Li *et al.*, 1977). This suggests that it might be specifically involved in the metabolism of high concentrations of ethanol, and Li *et al.* (1977) have calculated that its activity would account for less than 15 per cent of total liver ethanol metabolism at an ethanol concentration of 0.5 mM rising to about 40 per cent at a concentration of 50 mM.

The activity of the above isoenzyme has been shown to vary considerably between individuals, suggesting that it might be the genetic cause of variations in individual tolerance. The significance of this isoenzyme is however hard to assess since, as mentioned earlier, it appears that the limiting factor in the oxidation of ethanol by the liver is generally not the activity of alcohol dehydrogenase but the ability to reoxidise the NADH produced (Videla and Israel, 1970; Lindross *et al.*, 1972). Thus an increased activity of alcohol dehydrogenase would not in itself be expected to result in an increase in the ability of the liver to metabolise it.

The atypical isoenzyme of liver alcohol dehydrogenase shows considerable variations between different population groups (varying from being present in some 5-10 per cent of the white British and American populations to about 85 per cent of the Japanese population) (von Wartburg *et al.*, 1974). It has an optimum pH for activity towards ethanol of about 8.5, whereas the optimum for the other isoenzymes is greater than pH 10.0. This results in the atypical isoenzyme being particularly active at physiological pH values, leading to a rapid formation of acetaldehyde following the ingestion of ethanol.

It has been suggested that the possession of this isoenzyme may be related to the phenomenon of alcohol sensitivity. This condition entails a strong reaction, including flushing, vasodilation and tachycardia, to the ingestion of ethanol. It is a common condition amongst Japanese and appears to have a percentage distribution similar to that of the atypical isoenzyme in different populations (von Wartburg *et al.*, 1974). A similar response to ingested ethanol can be induced in many cases by pretreatment of normal subjects with the aldehyde dehydrogenase inhibitor disulphiram, suggesting that the formation of abnormally high levels of acetaldehyde may be the biochemical basis of alcohol sensitivity.

Under normal conditions alcohol dehydrogenase activity accounts for more than 89 per cent of the metabolism of ethanol in liver (Havre *et al.*, 1977), the remainder being oxidised by catalase, which probably accounts for only about 2 per cent of the total ethanol metabolism (Lieber, 1977), and the microsomal ethanol oxidising system (MEOS) (see, e.g. Ohnishi and Lieber, 1977; Miwa *et al.*, 1978).

Chronic ethanol consumption has little effect on the activity of liver alcohol dehydrogenase or catalase, although it might result in an increased availability of H_2O_2 for the latter enzyme (see Lieber, 1977).

The activity of the MEOS is, however, significantly increased (Ohnishi and Lieber, 1977) in parallel with other enzyme activities associated with the smooth endoplasmic reticulum. This adaptive change in the capacity to oxidise ethanol, however, falls rather slowly on withdrawal, still persisting after the rate of ethanol oxidation has fallen to normal (Mezey, 1972). It has also been suggested that the effect of chronic ethanol consumption on mitochondrial structure may, by increasing ATPase activity, increase the capacity to reoxidise the NADH produced (see, e.g. Bernstein *et al.*, 1975).

An adaptive increase in the ability of the rat to metabolise tertiary butanol has also been reported, which may be due to increases in the activity of the microsomal glucuronidation system (McComb and Goldstein, 1979). The effects of ethanol itself on the activity of the glucuronidation system may, however, be more complicated, since it has been reported to be inhibited *in vitro*, although this inhibition is prevented by treatment with pyrazole (Moldéus *et al.*, 1978). These results were interpreted as indicating that the inhibition was due to alterations in the NAD^+ :NADH ratio.

The ethanol induced proliferation of the endoplasmic reticulum (see, e.g. Ishii *et al.*, 1973) increases the activity of a number of microsomal enzyme systems that are associated with 'detoxication' reactions which affect the behaviour of other drugs. Thus chronic ethanol ingestion increases the rate of metabolism of drugs such as pentobarbital (Misra *et al.*, 1971) and methadone (Borowsky and Lieber, 1978) giving rise to alcoholic drug resistance. On the other hand the toxicity of some compounds, such as carbon tetrachloride, which is rendered toxic by a mechanism involving hydroxylation, is increased (Traiger and Plaa, 1972).

The effects on enzymes of ethanol metabolism in brain are rather small. An increase in the activity of brain alcohol dehydrogenase has been reported to result from chronic ethanol consumption (Raskin and Sokoloff, 1972). A small increase in the activity of aldehyde dehydrogenase has also been reported, but this affects the cytoplasmic isoenzyme whereas the mitochondrial form is believed to play the dominant role in the oxidation of acetaldehyde.

4.2.3 Tissue Damage

Although the effects of ethanol on the liver may be more complicated than those in brain, more is known about the effects in the former organ, because much work has been devoted to attempts to understand the mechanisms of alcoholic hepatitis and cirrhosis. The mechanisms involved in liver damage are probably complex involving direct toxic effects of ethanol and its metabolite acetaldehyde as well as effects due to the increased $NADH:NAD^+$ ratio resulting from ethanol oxidation.

The processes involved in alcoholic liver damage have been reviewed in detail by Lieber and DeCarli (1977). Briefly, triglycerides are accumulated in the liver and the intracellular proteins tend to aggregate, resulting in destruction of the microtubular structures and swelling of the cells. This in turn leads to an impairment of secretory function in which proteins, such as albumin, transferrin and complement, are retained by the liver. This results in necrosis of the liver cells and inflammation which may, in turn, cause an autoimmune process that causes further liver cell damage (Leevy *et al.*, 1976).

The mechanisms involved in the various stages of these processes are still not completely clear. The decreased $NAD^+:NADH$ ratio that results from ethanol oxidation will inhibit the oxidation of fatty acids (Rawat, 1972; Ontoko, 1973) causing them to accumulate. It has also been suggested that the rate of fatty acid synthesis is increased (Nikkila and Ojala, 1963) and that peripheral lipid stores may be mobilised (Brodie *et al.*, 1961), but it appears that inhibition of degradation is the most important process (see, e.g. Guynn *et al.*, 1973; Rawat, 1978). The altered redox state will also lead to elevated levels of α-glycerophosphate which can be used for triglyceride synthesis; but the availability of this compound does not appear significantly to affect the rate of synthesis of triglycerides (Björkhem and Östling, 1978).

During the development of alcoholic liver damage, very low density lipoproteins become trapped inside the Golgi bodies and it has been suggested that this may be due to ethanol-induced membrane damage impairing their secretory function (Marinari *et al.*, 1978). Chronic ethanol ingestion also impairs liver mitochondrial protein synthesis (Hofmann and Hosein, 1978), but increases the rate of ribosomal protein synthesis (see, e.g. Kuriyama *et al.*, 1971).

A direct effect of ethanol on the cell membranes could also contribute to the damaged secretory properties of the liver, but it has been suggested that the hydrophobic condensation of intracellular proteins is the principal factor and that this is caused by acetaldehyde (Baraona *et al.*, 1977).

Since, as discussed earlier, ethanol ingestion does not result in the appearance of significant quantities of free acetaldehyde in the brain and does not cause any appreciable alteration of the $NAD^+: NADH$ ratio, the mechanisms involved in any damage to that organ should be simpler to understand, but at present little is known of the details of such processes.

Other processes which result from ethanol consumption include increases in the lactate:pyruvate and β-hydroxybutyrate:acetoacetate ratios which are themselves consequences of the altered redox state; these can lead to hyperuricaemia owing to the effects of lactate on the renal tubules, and ketoacidosis (see Weir, 1978 for review).

Although chronic ethanol consumption can result in the retention of very low density lipoproteins in the liver, this does not happen if consumption is more moderate, when they are released into the blood giving rise to hyperlipidaemia. The secretion of lipoproteins into the blood also includes a proportion of high density lipoproteins; and since these compounds are believed to exert a protective action against coronary heart disease it has been suggested that this may explain the relative resistance of chronic alcoholics to this condition (Yano *et al.*, 1977).

Chronic ethanol consumption in pregnancy can also affect the foetus, increasing the total lipids and triglycerides in the liver and the fatty acid levels in the plasma (Rawat, 1978), which may be one of the causative factors in the damage that can result in children born to severely alcoholic mothers (the 'foetal alcohol syndrome' – see Peiffer *et al.*, 1979, for a discussion of symptoms) (see, e.g. Jones and Smith, 1975; Quellette and Rosett, 1976; Rawat, 1978).

4.3 Conclusions

The effects of ethanol on peripheral tissues are complex owing to its diversity of action. Ethanol itself, acetaldehyde and the metabolic consequences of an altered cellular redox state probably all contribute to the aetiology of liver disease.

The effects in the CNS may be somewhat easier to interpret. No significant concentrations of free acetaldehyde can be detected in brain, the NAD^+:NADH ratio appears to be unaltered and behavioural tolerance to ethanol develops before any adaptive changes in enzyme levels are seen. Although the maintenance of tolerance may be influenced by these adaptive changes, the available evidence would suggest a primary action of ethanol on the CNS in the development of tolerance.

The primary effect of ethanol in the CNS appears to be a non-specific anaesthetic action on nerve membranes which affects electrical activity, sodium, potassium and calcium concentrations and neurotransmitter release. Although a mechanism for the development of tolerance can be postulated in terms of altered membrane fluidity, the maintenance of tolerance will be affected by secondary changes, giving rise to a myriad of biochemical adaptations, the full details of which are far from clear.

Acknowledgement

We are grateful to the Department of Education (Ireland) for the support of a grant.

References

Ahtee, L. and Eriksson, K. (1972), *Physiol. Behav.*, *8*, 123-6
Alivisatos, S.G.A. and Ungar, F. (1968), *Biochemistry*, *7*, 285-92
Allison, A.C. (1974) in Halsey, M.J., Millar, R.A. and Sutton, J.A. (eds.), *Molecular Mechanisms in General Anaesthesia*, Churchill, London
Badawy, A.A-B. and Evans, M. (1976) *Biochem. J.*, *160*, 315-24
Badawy, A.A-B., Punjani, N.F. and Evans, M. (1979), *Biochem. J.*, *178*, 575-80
Baraona, E. and Lindenbaum, J. (1977) in Lieber, C.S. (ed.), *Metabolic Aspects of Alcoholism*, MTP, Lancaster, 81-116
Baraona, E., Leon, M.A., Barowsky, S.A. and Lieber, C.S. (1977), *J. Clin. Invest.*, *60*, 546-54
Berger, D. and Weiner, H. (1977), *Biochem. Pharmac.*, *26*, 841-6
Bernstein, J.D. and Penniall, R. (1978), *Biochem. Pharmac.*, *27*, 2337-42
Bernstein, J.D., Videla, L. and Israel, Y. (1975), *J. Pharmac. Exp. Ther.*, *192*, 583-91
Björkhem, I. and Ostling, H. (1978), *Life Sci.*, *23*, 783-90
Blum, K. and Wallace, J. (1974), *Brit. J. Pharmac*, *51*, 109-11
Blum, K., Wallace, J.E. and Geller, I. (1972), *Science*, *176*, 292-4
Borowsky, S.A. and Lieber, C.S. (1978), *J. Pharmac. Exp. Ther.*, *207*, 123-9
Brodie, B.B., Butler, V.M., Horning, M.G., Maickel, R.D. and Maling, H.M. (1961), *Am. J. Clin. Nutr.*, *9*, 432-5
Cederbaum, A.I., Dicker, E. and Rubin, E. (1977), *Arch. Biochem. Biophys.*, *183*, 638-46
Chin, J.H. and Goldstein, D.B. (1977), *Mol. Pharmac.*, *13*, 435-41
Collier, H.O.J., Hammond, M.D. and Schneider, C. (1976), *Brit. J. Pharmac.*, *58*, 9-16
Cox, B.M. and Osman, O. (1970), *Brit. J. Pharmac.*, *38*, 157-70
Crabbe, J.C., Rigter, H., Uijlen, J. and Strijbos, C. (1979), *J. Pharmac. Exp. Ther.*, *208*, 128-33
Curran, M. and Seeman, P. (1977), *Science*, *197*, 910-11
Duncan, R.J.S. and Tipton, K.F. (1971), *Europ. J. Biochem.*, *22*, 538-43
Duncan, R.J.S., Kline, J.E. and Sokoloff, L. (1976), *Biochem. J.*, *153*, 561-6
Eriksson, C.J.P. (1973), *Biochem. Pharmac.*, *22*, 2283-92
Eriksson, C.J.P. and Graham, D.T. (1973), *J. Pharmac. Exp. Ther.*, *185*, 583-93
Eriksson, C.J.P. and Sippel, H.W. (1977), *Biochem. Pharmac.*, *26*, 241-7
Evans, M. and Badawy, A.A-B. (1977), *Biochem. Soc. Trans.*, *5*, 1037-8
Fenstermacher, J.D., Patlack, C.S. and Blasberg, R.G. (1974), *Fed. Proc.*, *33*, 2070-4
Frankel, D., Khanna, J.M., LeBlanc, A.E. and Kalant, H. (1975), *Psychopharmacologia*, *44*, 247-52
—— (1978), *Psychopharmac.*, *56*, 139-43
Geller, I. (1971), *Science*, *173*, 456-9
Goldstein, D.B. (1972), *J. Pharmac. Exp. Ther.*, *180*, 203-15
—— (1973), *J. Pharmac. Exp. Ther.*, *186*, 1-9
—— (1975), *Fed. Proc.*, *34*, 1953-61
Goldstein, D.B. and Judson, B.A. (1971), *Science*, *172*, 290-2

Gordon, E.R. and Lough, J. (1972), *Lab. Invest., 26,* 154-62
Griffiths, P.J., Littleton, J.M. and Ortiz, A. (1974), *Brit. J. Pharmac., 58,* 9-16
Guynn, R.W., Veloso, D., Harris, R.L., Lawson, J.W.R. and Veech, R.L. (1973).
    Biochem. J., 136, 639-47
Häkkinen, H-M. and Kulonen, E. (1976), *J. Neurochem., 27,* 631-3
Harris, R.A., Kraus, W., Goh, E. and Case, J. (1979), *Pharmac. Biochem.*
    Behav., 10, 343-7
Havre, P., Abrams, M.A., Corrall, R.J.M., Yu, L.C., Szczepanik, P.A., Feldman,
    H.B., Klein, P., Kong, M.S., Margolis, J.M. and Landau, B.R. (1977), *Arch.*
    Biochem. Biophys., 182, 14-23
Ho, A.K.S. and Kissin, B. (1975), *Adv. Exp. Med. Biol., 86,* 195-210
Hofmann, I. and Hosein, E.A. (1978), *Biochem. Pharmac., 27,* 457-63
Hosein, E.A., Hofmann, I. and Linder, E. (1977), *Arch. Biochem. Biophys., 183,*
    64-72
Hunt, W.A. and Majchrowicz, E. (1974), *J. Neurochem., 23,* 549-52
Ishii, H., Joly, J-G. and Lieber, C.S. (1973), *Biochim. Biophys. Acta., 291,*
    411-20
Israel, Y., Carmichael, F.J. and Macdonald, J.A. (1975), *Adv. Exp. Med. Biol.,*
    59, 55-68
Itokawa, Y. and Cooper, J.R. (1970), *Biochim. Biophys. Acta., 196,* 274-84
Jones, K.L. and Smith, D.W. (1975), *Teratol., 12,* 1-10
Kalant, H. (1978), *Proc. Europ. Soc. Neurochem., 1,* 317-31
Kalant, H. and Grose, W. (1967), *J. Pharmac. Exp. Ther., 158,* 386-93
Kalant, H., LeBlanc, A.E. and Gibbins, R.J. (1971), *Pharmac. Rev., 23,* 135-91
Kalant, H., Woo, N. and Endrenyi, L. (1978), *Biochem. Pharmac., 27,* 1353-8
Koivula, T., Koivusalo, M. and Lindros, K.O. (1975), *Biochem. Pharmac., 24,*
    1807-11
Kuriyama, K., Sze, P.Y. and Rauscher, G.E. (1971), *Life Sci., 10* (2), 181-9
LeBlanc, A.E. and Kalant, H. (1975), *Toxicol. Appl. Pharmac., 32,* 123-8
Leevy, C.M., Chen, T., Luisada-Opper, A., Kanagasundaram, N. and
    Zetterman, R. (1976) in Popper, H. and Schaffner, F. (eds.), *Progress in Liver*
    Disease, Grune and Stratton, New York, 516-30
Lehninger, A.L., Vercesi, A. and Bababunmi, E.A. (1978), *Proc. Nat. Acad. Sci.,*
    75, 1690-4
Li, T-K. (1977), *Adv. Enzymol., 45,* 427-83
Li, T-K., Bosron, W.F., Dafeldecker, W.P., Lange, L.G. and Valee, B.L. (1977),
    Proc. Nat. Acad. Sci., 74, 4378-81
Lieber, C.S. (1977) in Lieber, C.S. (ed.), *Metabolic Aspects of Alcoholism,* MTP,
    Lancaster, 1-29
Lieber, C.S. and DeCarli, L.M. (1977) in Lieber, C.S. (ed.), *Metabolic Aspects of*
    Alcoholism, MTP, Lancaster, 31-79
Lieber, C.S. and Rubin, E. (1968), *Amer. J. Med., 44,* 200-6
Lieber, C.S., Teschke, R., Hasumura, Y. and DeCarli, L.M. (1975), *Fed. Proc., 34,*
    2060-74
Lindross, K.O., Vihma, R. and Forsander, O.A. (1972), *Biochem. J., 126,* 945-52
McComb, J.A. and Goldstein, D.B. (1975), *Pharmacologist, 17,* 198
—— (1979), *J. Pharmac. Exp. Ther., 208,* 113-17
McIsaac, W.M., Taborsky, R.G. and Farrell, G. (1961), *Science 145,* 63-4
Magrinat, G., Dolan, J.P., Biddy, R.L., Miller, L.D. and Korol, B. (1973), *Nature,*
    244, 234-45
Marinari, U.M., Cottalasso, D., Gambella, G.R., Averame, M.M., Pronzato, M.A.
    and Nanni, G. (1978), *FEBS Lett., 86,* 53-6
Marshall, A. and Hirst, M. (1976), *Experientia, 32,* 201-3
Mezey, E. (1972), *Biochem. Pharmac., 21,* 137-42

Misra, P.S., Lefevre, A., Ishii, H., Rubin, E. and Lieber, C.S. (1971),
    Amer. J. Med., 51, 346-51
Miwa, G.T., Levin, W., Thomas, P.E. and Lu, A.Y.H. (1978), *Arch. Biochem.
    Biophys., 187*, 464-75
Moldéus, P., Andersson, B. and Norling, A. (1978), *Biochem. Pharmac., 27*,
    2583-8
Mukherji, B., Kashiki, Y., Ohyanagi, H. and Sloviter, H.A. (1975), *J. Neurochem.,
    24*, 841-3
Myers, R.D. (1978), *Ann. Rev. Pharmac. Toxicol., 18*, 125-44
Nikkila, E.A. and Ojala, K. (1963), *Proc. Soc. Exp. Biol. Med., 113*, 814-17
Noble, G.P. and Tewari, S. (1977) in Lieber, C.S. (ed.), *Metabolic Aspects of
    Alcoholism*, MTP, Lancaster, 149-85
Ohnishi, K. and Lieber, C.S. (1977), *J. Biol. Chem., 252*, 7124-31
Ontoko, J.A. (1973), *J. Lipid Res., 14*, 78-86
Peiffer, J., Majewski, F., Fischbach, H., Bierich, J.R. and Volk, B. (1979),
    J. Neurol. Sci., 41, 125-37
Pettersson, H. and Kiessling, K-H. (1977), *Biochem. Pharmac., 26*, 237-40
Quellette, E.M. and Rosett, H.L. (1976), *Ann. N.Y. Acad. Sci., 273*, 123-9
Rangaraj, N. and Kalant, H. (1978), *Biochem. Pharmac., 27*, 1139-44
Raskin, N.H. and Sokoloff, L. (1970), *J. Neurochem., 17*, 1677-87
—— (1972), *Nature, 236*, 138-40
Rawat, A.K. (1972), *Arch. Biochem. Biophys., 151*, 93-101
—— (1974), *J. Neurochem., 20*, 915-22
—— (1975) in Majchrowicz, E. (ed.), *Biochemical Pharmacology of
    Ethanol*, Plenum Press, New York, 165-77
—— (1978), *Biochem. J., 174*, 213-19
Rawat, A.K. and Kuriyama, K. (1972), *Science, 176*, 1133-5
Rtizmann, R.F. and Tabakoff, B. (1976), *Nature, 263*, 418-19
Roach, M.K., Khan, M.M., Coffman, R., Pennington, W. and Davis, D.L. (1973),
    Brain Res., 63, 323-9
Rogawski, M.A., Knapp, S. and Mandell, A.J. (1974), *Biochem. Pharmac., 23*,
    1955-62
Ross, D.H. (1976), *Ann. N.Y. Acad. Sci., 273*, 280-94
Ross, D.H., Medina, M.H. and Cardenas, H.L. (1974), *Science, 186*, 63-4
Sabelli, H.C. and Giardina, W.A. (1973) in Sabelli, H.C. (ed.), *Chemical
    Modulation of Brain Function*, Raven Press, New York, 2-33
Schuckit, M.A. and Rayses, V. (1979), *Science, 203*, 54-5
Seeman, P. (1972), *Pharmac. Rev., 24*, 583-665
—— (1974), *Experientia, 30*, 759-60
Smith, C.M. (1977), *Handbuch der Experimentellen Pharmakologie, 45*, 413-587
Tabakoff, B., Ritzmann, R.F. and Boggan, W.O. (1975), *J. Neurochem., 24*,
    1043-51
Taussig, P.E. (1979), *Int. J. Biochem., 10*, 183-91
Thadani, P.V. and Truitt, E.B. (1973), *Fed. Proc., 32*, 697
Thurman, R.G. and Pathman, D.E. (1975), *Finnish Found. Alc. Stud., 23*, 217-31
Tipton, K.F., Houslay, M.D. and Turner, A.J. (1977), *Essays in Neurochem.
    Neurobiol., 1*, 103-38
Tipton, K.F., Rivett, J.A. and Smith, I.L. (1978), *Proc. Europ. Soc. Neurochem.,
    1*, 332-45
Traiger, G.J. and Plaa, G.L. (1972), *J. Pharmac. Exp. Ther., 183*, 481-8
Truitt, E.B. and Walsh, M.J. (1971) in Kissin, B. and Begleiter, H. (eds.), *The
    Biology of Alcoholism*, Plenum Press, New York, *1*, 161-95
Turner, A.J., Illingworth, J.A. and Tipton, K.F. (1974), *Biochem. J., 144*, 353-60
Veloso, D., Passonneau, J.V. and Veech, R.L. (1972), *J. Neurochem., 19*, 2679-86

Videla, L. and Israel, Y. (1970), *Biochem. J., 118*, 275-81
von Wartburg, J.P., Berger, D., Buhlmann, Ch., Dubdied, A., and Ris, M.M. (1974)
   in Thurman, R.G., Yonetani, T., Williamson, J.R. and Chance, B. (eds.),
   Alcohol and Aldehyde Metabolising Systems, Academic Press, New York,
   33-44
Wallgren, H. (1960), *Acta Pharmac. Toxicol., 16*, 217-22
Wallgren, H., Kosunen, A.L. and Ahtee, L. (1973), *Isr. J. Med. Sci., 9*, Suppl.,
   63-71
Weir, D.G. (1978), *J. Clin. Invest., 8*, 263-5
Yano, K., Rhoads, G.G. and Kagan, A. (1977), *New Engl. J. Med., 297*, 405-10

5 THE TRANSPORT OF NUTRIENTS INTO THE BRAIN: THE EFFECT OF ALCOHOL ON THEIR SUPPLY AND UTILISATION

Oliver E. Pratt

The Evolution of Ideas on the Transport of Substances into the Brain

It has long been known that a lowering of the level of glucose in the blood leads to marked changes in the functioning of the brain. In patients who have been given an overdose of insulin, these changes are seen as clouding of consciousness and hallucinations, succeeded by coma, which may be accompanied by convulsions. These mental abnormalities are due to a lowering of the level of glucose in the blood and thus to a dimution in its supply to the brain. Although insulin overdosage is the usual cause of hypoglycaemia, the taking of alcohol also commonly reduces the blood sugar level. The nature of this disturbance of endocrine regulation caused by alcohol is considered in detail in Chapter 8. Hypoglycaemia is frequently seen in premature and small-for-date babies who as a result may suffer brain damage of greater or lesser severity (Johnson *et al.*, 1974).

Although the effects of hypoglycaemia on thought processes have been known for so long, the mechanisms by which glucose enters the brain have been worked out only more recently and ideas on the mechanisms involved owe much to the pioneer work of Widdas (1952) who studied the transport of glucose across the membrane of the erythrocyte. Widdas suggested that the cell membrane forms a barrier to many substances, with the exception of those which are small molecules or those which are soluble in lipids, but that there are specific carrier molecules located in the cell membrane which transport nutrient substances, such as glucose, into the cell.

These ideas have been widely exploited and have been greatly developed in the study of the passage, not only of glucose, but also of amino acids and ketone bodies into the brain; and this work on the way in which essential nutrients and metabolites move between the brain and the rest of the body has laid down the necessary basis for understanding how metabolic disturbances in the body can damage or alter the functioning of the brain.

Dementia and Alcoholism

There are five main groups of neuropsychiatric disorders associated with alcoholism (Victor, 1970). Of these, *acute intoxication* or drunkenness (in which alcohol acts mainly as a general anaesthetic) and the *withdrawal syndrome* — including nausea, irritability, hallucinations, seizures and delirium — may be severe at the time, but the effects are usually short-lived, subsiding in hours or days. A third group are the *nutritional disorders* which may develop when the normal diet is largely replaced by alcohol, including the Wernicke-Korsakoff syndrome and pellagra (Victor, Adams and Collins, 1971; Spillane, 1947).

A further cause of neuropsychiatric disorder is a group of diseases with organic changes in the brain which are associated with alcoholism but which have an *unknown pathogenesis.* These include alcoholic cerebellar degeneration with ataxia; primary degeneration of the corpus callosum (Marchiafava-Bigniami) and alcoholic cerebral atrophy with enlargement of the lateral ventricles. This latter condition is of interest because of evidence obtained from computerised axial tomography which suggests that early changes in brain shape have a higher incidence amongst alcoholics than was previously realised (Ron, Acker and Lishman, 1980; see also Chapters 10 and 11 of this volume).

The final group of neuropsychiatric disorders associated with alcoholism is that arising from *loss of liver function* as a result of cirrhosis and the consequent shunting of portal blood flow past the liver. This may lead either to coma or to chronic hepatocerebral degeneration with dementia. The key to an understanding of these conditions lies in the associated disorders of amino acid and protein metabolism, which must be considered in detail.

The Way in Which the Brain may be Damaged by Disturbances in the Metabolism of the Body

The effects of ethyl alcohol, or its first oxidation product acetaldehyde, upon the metabolism of various tissues of the body are many and varied. In addition, the effects of an excess of alcohol upon the liver and upon its metabolism, together with the other nutritional deficiencies associated with alcoholism, produce a spectrum of metabolic disturbance which is broad and diverse. Consideration has to be given, therefore, to which of the disturbances in the metabolism of the body that are caused by alcoholism and liver failure are most likely to damage the brain. The possibly damaging effects of such disturbances fall into two main groups:

(1)   *Deprivation.* When a substance which the brain needs fails to enter the cerebral cells in amounts which are sufficient to meet those needs it may be said that there is deprivation. For example, when too little of an essential amino acid is reaching the cerebral cells the brain is not able to re-form the cerebral protein that has been broken down, and is in a deprived state.

(2)   *Intoxication.* When too much of a substance which has a harmful effect enters the cerebral cells, the brain may be said to be suffering from intoxication.

Brain Damage due to Deprivation of a Nutrient or Metabolite

The first consideration is to determine what substances are needed by the brain, because some are essential to its functioning and trouble will be caused if the organ is deprived of them. What substances reach the brain?

Movement across the blood-brain barrier through the walls of the cerebral capillaries can take place in both directions. Normally influx, that is movement into the brain, exceeds efflux, which is movement out of the brain back into the circulation. There is thus a gain of the substance by the brain, i.e. a net uptake by the brain from the blood (see Table 5.1). Exceptions to this rule are some substances which are formed within the cerebral cells, e.g. lactate, pyruvate and glutamine, for which efflux normally exceeds influx (Daniel *et al.*, 1971 and 1972; Pratt, 1976).

For other substances it will be seen from Table 5.1 that the ratio of efflux to influx varies from zero to about 80 per cent, commonly being of the order of a half to two thirds. This ratio can be expected to fall sharply if the substance is one of which the brain is receiving inadequate amounts, for efflux only occurs when more of a substance is reaching the cerebral cells than they need for their metabolism.

The ketone bodies are an exception to this rule, however, as shown for example by 3-hydroxybutyrate of which the efflux is zero (Table 5.1). The cerebral cells do not need ketone bodies as long as adequate supplies of glucose are available. However, the brain cells use

Table 5.1: The movement of various substances into the brain across the blood-brain barrier (influx) together with the cerebral gain (net uptake) of each substance by the brain from the blood. The movement back into the blood (efflux) has been calculated as influx minus net uptake. Means ± SEM with no. of determinations in parentheses.

Substance	Concentration in blood plasma	Influx across the blood-brain barrier	Cerebral gain	Efflux	Ratio: efflux/influx
	$mmole\ l^{-1}$	$nmole\ min^{-1}$ g^{-1} of brain	$nmole\ min^{-1}$ g^{-1} of brain	$nmole$ $min^{-1}g^{-1}$ of brain	
glucose	7.63±0.66	970±130(10)	270±20(35)	700	0.72
glucose (hypoglycaemia)	1.35	250 (2)	210 (2)	40	0.16
lactate	0.99±0.34	40±3(4)	−107±43(4)	147	3.68
pyruvate	0.26±0.04	16±2(5)	6±1 (3)	22	1.38
leucine	0.10±0.01	11.7±0.9 (4)	2.5 (2)	9.2	0.79
lysine	0.34±0.01	8.4±1.6 (11)	3.0±0.1(3)	5.4	0.64
phenylalanine	0.050±0.002	5.5±0.4 (5)	1.8±0.5(9)	3.7	0.67
3-hydroxybutyrate	0.26±0.06	5±1 (14)	8±4 (7)	0	0
tyrosine	0.069±0.003	4.5±0.5(6)	2.1±0.2(3)	2.4	0.53
histidine	0.079±0.004	4.24±0.32(5)	1.34±0.03(5)	2.90	0.68

Based upon the data of Crockett *et al.*, (1977).

these substances readily when available (Daniel, Love and Pratt, 1977a, b) as an alternative to the oxidation of the pyruvate and lactate which are formed by glycolysis. Thus, a gain of ketone bodies by the brain is balanced by a corresponding loss of lactate (Daniel *et al.*, 1972; Oldendorf, 1973).

Brain Damage due to Intoxication

Experience shows that the blood-brain barrier is usually a highly effective screen which prevents toxic amounts of metabolites from reaching the brain from the blood, so that intoxication occurs only when such metabolites are formed within the brain at a rate which is faster than that at which they can be removed, as for example by transport out of the brain into the blood, efflux (see Figure 5.1).

On the whole, deprivation rather than intoxication by a metabolite, is a more likely cause of trouble in severe alcoholism. One clearly established example of the intoxication of the brain by a metabolite is seen when the brain swells during hypoxia. This occurs because of the accumulation of lactic acid in the cerebral cells, which takes place during hypoxia when there is an adequate supply of glucose (Myers, 1979). Hypoxia causes a sharp increase in the rate of glycolysis in the brain cells, which will be sustained if glucose is entering the brain fast enough. Pyruvate and lactate are thus formed at a high rate but cannot be oxidised because of the lack of oxygen. The carrier which transports these substances out of the brain back into the blood (Table 5.1) is overwhelmed so that lactic acid accumulates in the cerebral cells, leading to a fall in intracellular pH and swelling of the brain; this occurs as a result of the rise in osmotic pressure in the cells (Myers, 1979). Such a severe metabolic disturbance is not likely to occur just because of alcoholism, although the accumulation of lactic acid (Kreisberg, Owen and Siegel, 1971a, b) which results from alcohol intoxication may increase the liability to brain damage from lacticacidosis within the brain cells if an hypoxic episode occurs.

Figure 5.1: To show the sites of the two barriers between blood and brain and the fates of the nutrients that leave the capillaries and enter the brain. It is not known precisely where the breakdown of protein takes place, perhaps partly within the cerebral cells and partly along and at the ends of axons, or other cell processes.

Note that under normal conditions there is efflux of many nutrients back into the blood, so that the brain has an appreciable reserve against metabolic contingencies.

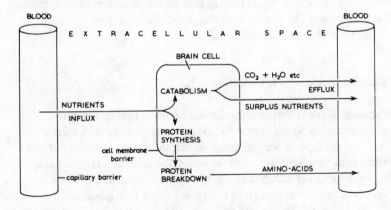

Consideration must also be given to the possibility that alcohol-induced liver damage interferes with the removal of waste nitrogen from the body. In these circumstances intoxication may result from an abnormal increase in the production of ammonia within the brain. Apart from this possibility, however, it seems more probable that deprivation of the brain of some essential metabolite or nutrient is the most likely mechanism of brain damage in severe alcoholism. Important for this consideration is the steady growth in knowledge of how substances move from the blood into the brain.

Is There a Barrier Between the Blood and the Brain?

The term 'blood-brain barrier' is sometimes rather misleading since substances, such as water, oxygen and, indeed ethyl alcohol, diffuse with the greatest facility from the blood into the brain, so that for these substances the barrier does not exist. However, many substances, such as certain dyes, are unable to enter the brain from the blood (Ehrlich, 1885) and this finding gave rise to the concept of a blood-brain barrier. (For a discussion of the history of ideas on the blood-brain barrier see Bradbury, 1979.)

All the early work on the entry of nutrients into the brain was done *in vitro*, generally with slices cut from the cerebral cortex, and it was found that both glucose and amino acids (substances which are essential for the nutrition of the brain) entered the tissue by some form of carrier-mediated transport system. Since such carrier-mediated processes in other tissues (Widdas, 1952) were known to be located in the membranes of the cells, it was clear that part of the blood-brain barrier was situated in the cerebral cell membranes (Lajtha, 1964).

However, brain slices and homogenates of brain tissue are devoid of a circulation and it was not until studies were made upon the entry of nutrients from the blood into the brain of living animals, that it became clear that a major part of the blood-brain barrier lies in the membranes of the endothelial cells of the cerebral capillaries and that the transport mechanisms which carry nutrients across these barriers (Figure 5.1) differ in important respects from those on the surfaces of brain cells (Baños *et al.*, 1970, 1971a, 1973a, 1975; Wade and Katzman 1975; Pratt, 1976; Pardridge and Oldendorf, 1975; Pardridge 1977; Sershen and Lajtha, 1979).

A third set of transport systems is found in the choroid plexus of the brain, which carries nutrients from the blood into the cerebro-spinal fluid (CSF). Since the CSF plays a relatively minor role in the nutrition of the brain it will not be considered further here and the reader is referred to Bradbury (1979) for a full discussion of such CSF transport systems.

Although, as will be shown later, glucose and amino acids pass into the brain mainly by means of carrier-mediated transport systems, the most important of which lie in the cell membranes of the endothelial cells of the cerebral capillaries, a small proportion of these nutrients may also enter the brain by passive diffusion. In the case of amino acids, the entry by diffusion may be of some importance, especially in certain diseases such as the aminoacidaemias (Pratt, 1976).

Whilst carrier-mediated transport systems play a major part in the entry of glucose and amino acids into the brain, that is in influx, it must not be forgotten that they also transfer these substances out of the cerebral cells and back into the blood, so that the net entry of substances into the brain is the result of influx minus efflux. It may therefore be concluded that a blood-brain barrier which is effective except for a few substances certainly does exist. Thus a large group of substances can only cross the barrier at an appreciable rate by making use of carrier-mediated transport processes, while large molecules, especially proteins, are completely excluded by the barrier, although a very few small molecules cross the barrier freely.

The Uptake and Utilisation of Glucose by the Brain

The substance which is the major source of energy for the brain is glucose, although under some circumstances the ketone bodies, acetoacetate and 3-hydroxybutyrate may supply a proportion of the energy requirements. These ketone bodies enter the brain by means of a carrier-mediated transport system (Daniel *et al.*, 1977b; Pratt, 1979a).

Methods Used for Studying Glucose Transport and Metabolism

Logically, transport must be studied before metabolism, since the cerebral cells must have glucose supplied to them from the blood before they are able to metabolise it. All the early studies of transport were made *in vitro* on brain slices or homogenates. One of the major difficulties with transport studies *in vivo* is that any change in the concentration of glucose in the blood is, under normal circumstances, accompanied by changes in the rate of secretion of insulin. However,

Figure 5.2: Shows the way in which a steady raised level of blood glucose was maintained over a two-hour period by means of a specially programmed intravenous injection, even though a high, steady level of insulin was also similarly maintained in the circulation. Means of 8 experiments with standard errors indicated by bars.

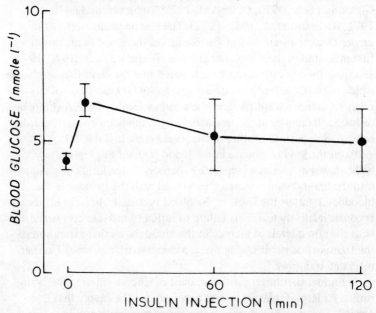

by means of a special technique (Daniel, Donaldson and Pratt, 1974, 1975a, 1976a; Donaldson and Pratt, 1975) in which steady raised levels of insulin can be maintained in the blood and at the same time a fall in the blood glucose can be prevented by an appropriate injection of glucose (see Figure 5.2), these difficulties can be largely overcome, and the transport of glucose into the brain, across the blood-brain barrier and into the cerebral cells can be studied.

In order to investigate the metabolism of glucose within the cerebral cells the essential first step is to determine how much glucose the cells are using *in vivo* by comparing the quantity of glucose entering the cells and that leaving them. This can best be done by measuring the difference in the concentration of glucose in the arterial blood and that in the venous blood leaving the brain, giving the cerebral arterio-venous differences.

Carrier-mediated Transport of Glucose into the Brain

The transport system which takes glucose across the blood-brain barrier shows the phenomenon of saturation and also shows stereo-specificity and competitive inhibition (Crone, 1965; Crone and Thompson, 1970; Gilboe and Betz, 1970; Oldendorf, 1971; Yudilevich and de Rose, 1971; Bachelard *et al.*, 1972, 1973). The kinetic parameters of the carrier-mediated transport of glucose across the blood-brain barrier were first measured in the living animal by us (Bachelard *et al.*, 1972, 1973) and from these results it can be calculated that the quantities of glucose which normally enter the brain are greater by far than those of any other substance except oxygen, the small molecule of which enters by diffusion. Examples of the quantities which the brain needs of glucose compared with various other nutrients are given in Table 5.1.

When the level of glucose in the blood is raised to progressively higher levels in a series of separate experiments, the influx of glucose into the brain does not increase in parallel with the increase in the blood level; but as the levels in the blood become higher, the influx becomes relatively less. This failure of influx to increase *pari passu* with the raised levels of glucose in the blood shows that saturation of the transport carrier is taking place, a characteristic feature of carrier-mediated transport.

In normal circumstances the amount of glucose entering the brain (influx) is large, far larger than is necessary for the energy that is needed. The excess of glucose leaves the cerebral cells and re-enters the blood, i.e. there is considerable efflux of glucose from the brain (Bachelard *et al.*, 1973). There is therefore a built-in safety factor in that there is an excess of glucose entering the brain, over and above the normal needs of the organ for energy. Thus, the brain is protected from damage if any moderate degree of hypoglycaemia develops.

The safety factor is greatest during adult life and is much lower both in the very young and the old, in whom the efflux of glucose from the brain is much reduced (Daniel, Love and Pratt, 1978; Pratt, 1979a; Love, 1980). Therefore at the two extremes of life mild degrees of hypoglycaemia may have deleterious effects on the cerebral cells, whose energy requirements in these circumstances cannot be met. The very young animal is able, to some extent, to use ketone bodies to supplement glucose for the energy requirements of its brain (Daniel *et al.*, 1971, 1972, 1977b) so that it is less vulnerable to hypoglycaemia than the old who cannot use ketone bodies as a supplement to glucose.

The Use of Glucose by the Cerebral Cells

The observation that the brain takes up glucose and oxygen and converts them to carbon dioxide and water gives an indication of the long-term overall result of cerebral metabolism which is rather misleading when one looks in more detail at what happens. Thus, if an animal is given an injection of radioactively labelled glucose, a considerable time elapses (of the order of 20-30 minutes) before any appreciable part of the tracer dose is excreted as carbon dioxide. Yet labelled glucose rapidly crosses the blood-brain barrier and enters into cerebral metabolism (Daniel, Love and Pratt, 1975c, 1977c).

Another puzzling observation is that giving insulin increases the rate at which the brain cells use glucose without any immediate increase in CO_2 production or in glycogen storage (Daniel, Love and Pratt, 1975c, 1977c). What happens is that a large part of the glucose taken up by the brain is not immediately used for energy production but is converted into other metabolites such as the non-essential amino acids, especially aspartate, N-acetylaspartate, glutamate and glutamine (Balázs, 1965; Cremer and Heath, 1974; Pratt, 1976).

Methods used to Study the Influx of Amino Acids

As with glucose, brain slices have been widely used to study the entry of amino acids into the brain, but here again the results of these *in vitro* methods have only limited value. The major disadvantage is that the activities of the carrier-mediated transport systems, which are located in the membranes of the endothelial cells of the capillaries and which are the main systems that carry amino acids into the brain, cannot be investigated *in vitro* and must be studied in the living animal with an intact cerebral circulation (Figure 5.1). Two main methods have been evolved for this *in vivo* work.

One is the 'bolus' method (Oldendorf, 1971; Pardridge and Oldendorf, 1975) in which a bolus consisting of saline containing a known amount of a trace amino acid is rapidly injected into the carotid artery. The head of the animal is immediately cut off and it is assumed that the bolus has made one circulation through the cerebral capillaries. The quantity of tracer amino acid taken up by the brain is calculated.

The second 'steady state' method consists in maintaining a steady raised level of an amino acid (radioactively labelled or unlabelled) in the circulation for 30 secs or 1 min (so that metabolic changes cannot occur), washing the blood out of the cerebral vessels for 20 sec (to avoid having a correction for the amino acid content of the blood in the vessels) and assaying the amino acid in the brain (Daniel *et al.*, 1974, 1975a, 1976a; Donaldson and Pratt, 1975; Pratt, 1974; Daniel *et al.*, 1974a). From a series of such experiments the rate at which the substance enters the brain is determined (Figure 5.3). The latter method is of particular value, since it can be used easily for the study of competitive inhibition, two amino acids being maintained steadily in the circulation simultaneously; the level of one is higher than normal and the effect of such a raised level on the transport into the brain of the other amino acid (of which only a tracer dose is injected) is measured.

Figure 5.3: The rate at which radioactivity accumulated within the brain in the time during which a steady specific activity of labelling of L-methionine was maintained in the circulating blood. Radioactivity in the brain, R_b, compared with radioactivity in the circulation, R_c. Each point represents a separate experiment.

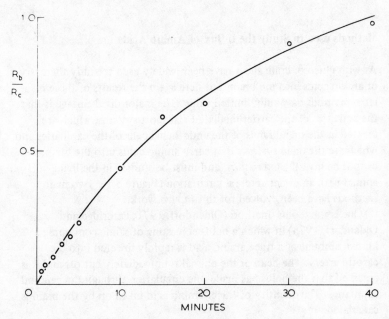

Source: Crockett, Daniel and Pratt, unpublished data.

The disadvantage of the 'bolus' method is that the amino acid is presented to the transport system at the blood-brain barrier in an abnormal fluid, saline, which does not contain all the amino acids, hormones, etc. which are present in normal blood, and which may interfere with or facilitate, the passage of amino acids into the brain (see Pratt, 1980b for a discussion of the ways in which the transport of one amino acid into the brain is influenced by the other amino acids which are present in the blood).

The Uptake and Utilisation of Amino Acids by the Brain

Although the needs of the brain for a steady and continuous supply of glucose have been realised for many years, the extent and diversity of the needs of the brain for amino acids were not appreciated until recently. One reason for the delay in appreciating these needs was the incorrect thinking with regard to the causes of the changes seen in the aminoacidurias, in which abnormally high levels of an amino acid were found in the blood and in which mental retardation was common (Stanbury *et al.,* 1978).

It was believed at first that the genetic abnormality in these children was not only a direct cause of the metabolic error (which, in the case of phenylketonuria, PKU, was a block in the hydroxylation of phenylalanine) but was also a direct cause of the abnormalities of the brain which led to mental retardation. Thus it was not necessary to consider any possible effects upon the brain of the raised level of phenylalanine in the blood, since the cerebral maldevelopment was explained as an independent genetic effect.

Another hypothesis which was subsequently suggested to explain the brain damage associated with the aminoacidurias was that the block in the metabolism of the amino acid caused abnormal metabolites to be produced which are toxic to nerve cells (Silberberg, 1969). However, no one seems to have been able to demonstrate conclusively that the abnormal metabolites are neurotoxic at the levels at which they are commonly found in patients with aminoacidurias.

More recently work done on such genetic disorders of metabolism has concentrated upon the nature of the metabolic defect and the high concentration of the amino acid (sometimes more than one amino acid) found in the blood in the aminoacidurias. This work has given encouragement to the view that high levels of an amino acid in the blood, e.g. of phenylalanine in phenylketonuria, cause excessive quantities of this amino acid to enter the cerebral cells, and that such an excess of one amino acid is toxic to these cells.

It was an important observation that abnormal patterns of amino acids in the blood lead to abnormal proportions of amino acids within the brain cells (O'Brien and Ibbot, 1966; McKean, Boggs and Peterson, 1968) and it was suggested that such imbalances within the brain could interfere with the synthesis of cerebral protein (Agrawal, Bone and Davison, 1970). A great deal of evidence has now accumulated that amino acid imbalance in the blood is likely to interfere with brain development (Davison, 1973; Pratt, 1979a; Pardridge, 1977, 1979); but what is not yet clear is whether, in an aminoaciduria such as phenylketonuria, protein synthesis in the brain is reduced by a toxic effect of too much phenylalanine within the brain cells, or alternatively by a lack of one or more of the other amino acids which are needed for the synthesis of cerebral protein (see Table 5.2). Later work, as will be discussed below, has shown that not only does a high level of an amino acid in the blood result in an excess of that amino acid entering the cells, but also, what may prove more important, such a raised blood level can affect severely the entry of other amino acids into the brain.

As in the case of glucose, most of the amino acids which are needed by the brain for its metabolism enter the cerebral cells from the blood by means of carrier-mediated transport processes. (A few rather unimportant amino acids enter by diffusion (Table 5.2) and, as will be shown later, there is a small element of diffusion in the influx of many amino acids; see Daniel, Pratt and Wilson, 1977d, e, f.) Again, the transport processes are stereospecific and only handle the L-isomers.

Transport Systems for Amino Acids from the Blood into the Brain

The carrier-mediated transport systems which transfer most amino acids across the blood-brain barrier can be saturated when the level of the amino acid in the blood is raised in successive experiments (see Figure 5.4). In this respect amino acid transport resembles glucose transport across the blood-brain barrier. However, a distinctive difference between the transport of amino acids and that of glucose is that a number of amino acids share each transport carrier. This means that competition for the carrier is part of the normal pattern of the transport of amino acids into the brain (Figure 5.5). Saturation and competition between substrates are commonly seen also in enzyme reactions: the ways in which the carrier molecules operate are remarkably similar to the ways in which enzymes operate (Dixon and Webb, 1979).

Table 5.2: Comparison of the contributions of carrier-mediated transport and passive diffusion to the movement of various substances across the blood-brain barrier. From the specific influx, that is the observed influx (v) divided by the level of the substance in the blood plasma (s), the apparent diffusion coefficient is subtracted to give the carrier-mediated component of the specific influx. Standard errors are given with the no. of determinations in parentheses. Figures in square brackets are likely values which are consistent with the other data. Units for each column: nmole min $^{-1}$ g $^{-1}$ of brain per mmole e $^{-1}$ of plasma.

Substance	Specific influx $\dfrac{v}{s}$	Apparent diffusion coefficient D	Carrier-mediated component of the specific influx
glucose	129±7(12)	<0.3	129
phenylalanine	110±7(11)	2.5±0.3 (8)	107
leucine	90±7 (5)	1.3±0.4 (6)	89
tyrosine	66±1 (6)	3.8±1.6 (6)	62
histidine	64±4 (5)	2.0±0.2 (9)	62
pyruvate	54±12(5)	[<0.3]	54
methionine	63±5 (6)	5.0±0.3 (6)	58
dihydroxyphenylalanine	48±3 (3)	[4]	44
lactate	43±6 (4)	[<0.3]	43
acetoacetate	37±7 (5)	[<0.3]	37
tryptophan	33±1(10)	4.9±1.5 (8)	28
isoleucine	26±3 (8)	1.6±0.3 (3)	24
lysine	26±5 (9)	<0.3	25
3-hydroxybutyrate	22±6 (8)	[<0.3]	22
threonine	18±3 (6)	0.8±0.2 (3)	17
cycloleucine	17±0.9 (5)	[1.3]	16
arginine	13±1(16)	<0.3	13
valine	12.8±1.4 (9)	1.2±0.2 (8)	12
serine	12.8±2.8 (8)	[0.8]	12
cysteine	11.1±2 (5)	[5]	6
citrulline	9±3 (3)	[<0.3]	9
alanine	8.7±2 (6)	[0.8]	8
glutamate	6.3±2.6 (4)	[0.8]	5
taurine	3.0±0.3 (5)	[<0.3]	3
proline	1.9±0.2 (7)	[1.9]	[0]
2-aminoisobutyrate	2.3±0.4 (7)	[2.3]	[0]
2-aminoadipate	1.9±0.4 (4)	[1.9]	[0]
thyroxine	0.6 (2)	[0.6]	[0]

Source: Based upon data from: Baños *et al.* (1974c, 1978); Crockett *et al.* (1977, 1978); Daniel *et al.* (1971, 1972, 1975b, 1977a, b, c, d, 1978); Pratt (1979a).

Figure 5.4: The effect of raising the concentration of L-leucine in the circulating blood of adult rats upon its influx into the brain. Each point represents a separate experiment and a curve has been fitted statistically to the data. Note that as a result of the saturation of the transport carrier the influx does not increase in proportion to the concentration of the amino acid in the blood. Influx in nmole min^{-1} g^{-1} of brain. Concentration in mmole l^{-1} of blood plasma.

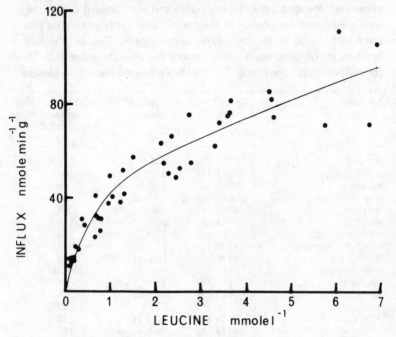

Source: Crockett, Daniel and Pratt, unpublished data.

The Way in Which a Raised Level of One Amino Acid in the Blood Excludes Other Amino Acids from the Brain

Competitive inhibition of chemically related substances for a shared carrier is a well established phenomenon in both the enzyme (Dixon and Webb, 1979) and in the transport fields (Neame, 1968). That such inhibition can operate in the transport of amino acids from the blood stream into the brain during life was first shown for the chemically related dibasic amino acids, arginine, lysine and ornithine (Baños *et al.*, 1971b, 1974a, c; Pratt, 1976), and later for various neutral amino acids (Oldendorf, 1973; Baños *et al.*, 1974b; Crockett, Daniel and Pratt, 1976).

Figure 5.5: Shows how an increase in the concentration of L-isoleucine in the blood can overcome the inhibitory effect of L-valine upon the transport of isoleucine across the blood-brain barrier. The curves were drawn by fitting equation (1) to the data of Daniel *et al.*, 1977f. The lower curve is one which has been fitted to the data from experiments in which the isoleucine level was not raised above the normal range (0.066-0.080 nmole l^{-1} of plasma). The middle curve was obtained by fitting this equation to the data from experiments in which the isoleucine level was raised to 1.1 to 1.3 nmole l^{-1} of plasma and the upper curve from those in which the isoleucine level was raised still further to 4.0 to 4.8 nmole l^{-1} of plasma. It will be seen that the inhibitory effect of a raised level of valine in the blood is progressively reduced as the isoleucine level is raised.

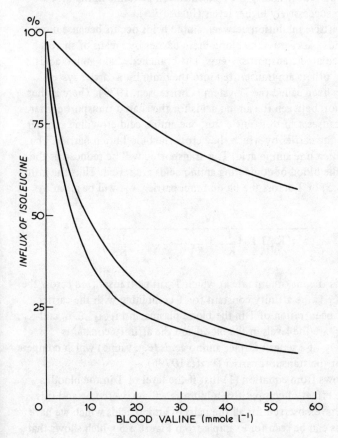

If one of the dibasic amino acids is present at a high concentration in the blood plasma, it largely prevents the others from entering the brain. This partial exclusion due to a high concentration of the *inhibiting amino acid* in the blood can be overcome if the concentration of the *excluded amino acid* in the blood is simultaneously increased (Baños *et al.*, 1974a, c). Another example of competition is provided by the interaction between the branched chain amino acids, isoleucine, leucine or valine. When any one of these is present in the circulating blood at a high concentration (of the order of 10 mmole 1^{-1} of plasma) not only does it saturate its own transport system, but it partially excludes the other branched chain amino acids from entering the brain. For example, a progressive diminution in the influx of leucine into the brain can be achieved by raising the concentration of valine in the blood plasma to successively higher levels (Figure 5.5).

Competitive inhibition between amino acids occurs because most amino acids pass across the blood-brain barrier by means of shared carrier-mediated transport systems. The branched chain amino acids and many others are transported into the brain by a carrier system which has been called the L-system (Christensen, 1979). There is thus competition between the amino acids for the shared transport carrier and this causes a sort of traffic jam, one amino acid crowding another out from the carrier by which they cross the blood-brain barrier. The rate at which one amino acid, T, is transported will be reduced as the levels in the blood of competing amino acids are raised. Thus the influx (Figure 5.5) of T across the blood-brain barrier, v_T, will be given by

$$v_T = \frac{sV}{s + K_T\left(1 + \frac{i_1}{K_1} + \frac{i_2}{K_2} + \ldots + \frac{i_n}{K_n}\right)} \tag{1}$$

where V is the maximum rate at which T can be transported across the barrier, K_T is the affinity constant for T combining with the carrier, s is the concentration of T in the blood plasma and $i_1, i_2, ..., i_n$ and K_1, $K_2, ..., K_n$ are the levels in the blood and the affinity constants respectively of a series of other amino acids (e.g. valine) which compete with T for the transport carrier (Pratt, 1979b).

It follows from equation (1) that if the level of T in the blood is raised the effect of competitive inhibitors will be overcome and this is what we have observed for all the pairs of amino acids which we have studied, as can be seen for example from Figure 5.5 which shows that raising the level of valine in the blood has little effect upon the influx of isoleucine into the brain if the level of the latter is first raised to about 4 mmole 1^{-1} of plasma.

The amino acids which are present in the highest concentration in the blood tend to monopolise the carrier molecules, which are thus unable to carry the other amino acids in the blood. There are a wide variety of carriers for amino acids on the surfaces of brain cells (Christensen, 1973, 1975, 1976, 1979; Sershen and Lajtha, 1979; Christensen and Handlogten, 1979). The carrier-system which transports most amino acids across the capillary endothelium into the brain is the L system which is not noticeably dependent upon a sodium gradient and is not affected by insulin (Christensen, 1979).

Some Effects of Alcoholism Upon the Metabolism of Amino Acids

The taking of alcohol in large quantities can affect the metabolism of amino acids in various ways. The liver is damaged and therefore its ability to metabolise amino acids is impaired. The chronic alcoholic usually fails to eat normally and tends especially to suffer from a lack of protein in the diet. (The chronic gastritis that is so often associated with alcoholism, also affects the absorption of the amino acids derived from the digestion of protein — Holdsworth, 1972; Schulz and Frizzell, 1975.) Finally, alcohol or its metabolites disturb the metabolism of amino acids in the body, and also perhaps in the brain (Sytinski *et al.,* 1975; Griffiths and Littleton, 1977).

Each of these effects of alcoholism may alter the levels of amino acids in the circulating blood, and as I shall show later, alterations in the pattern of amino acids in the blood may have profound effects on the supply of amino acids to the brain and therefore upon its function. Confirmation of the close relation between amino acids and alcoholism is provided by old evidence that amino acid administration is almost the only way of increasing the rate of metabolism of alcohol (Widmark, 1933; Le Breton, 1934). Most of these effects of alcohol upon the body are the result of disturbance of metabolism in liver and muscle. At the present time little is known about the effects of alcohol upon the metabolic activities of the brain cells themselves.

Amino Acids and Encephalopathy in Liver Failure

Neuropsychiatric disturbance in alcoholism is commonly the result of chronic liver failure due to a cirrhosis of mainly micronodular type (Laennec's cirrhosis), with associated shunting of blood from the portal to the systemic circulation, thus bypassing the liver. Cirrhosis is the scarred end stage of a chronic hepatitis. It develops in only 10 to 30 per cent of alcoholics and may also arise from causes unconnected with alcoholism (Popper, 1977). Nevertheless, alcoholic cirrhosis presents a growing problem, especially in the Western world. The incidence of cirrhosis among alcoholics is determined partly by genetic and partly by nutritional factors, although cirrhosis may develop even on an adequate diet.

The *chronic* liver failure of alcoholic cirrhosis is associated with encephalopathy. On the other hand *acute* liver failure, which develops more rarely from severe hepatic infection or poisoning (e.g. by paracetamol), causes coma, but the disorder is unrelated to alcoholism except in so far as pre-existing alcoholic cirrhosis may be a predisposing factor.

Imbalance of Blood Amino Acids in Liver Failure

How liver failure leads to encephalopathy is not yet clear but a common factor among many of the rival theories is that there is some disturbance of the metabolism of amino acids, of which the brain needs a continuous supply of some dozen or more from the circulation (see Table 5.2).

If the liver is completely removed from the body an imbalance develops progressively in the levels of the various amino acids in the bloodstream: the levels of most amino acids rise except for those of the branched chain amino acids, valine, leucine and isoleucine, which fall (McMenamy, Vang and Drapanas, 1965). The reason for this is that the branched chain compounds continue to be removed by the muscles (Baños *et al.*, 1973b) whereas the other amino acids would normally be removed mainly by the liver. We showed in 1972 (Knell *et al.*, 1972 and 1974) that this sort of imbalance also develops in human cases of acute hepatic failure. The levels of many amino acids are raised considerably above normal, especially methionine, some 20 to 30 times, and phenylalanine, tryptophan, tyrosine, glutamine, glutamate and aspartate, some 4 to 6 times above normal. On the other hand the levels of the branched chain amino acids are reduced considerably below normal. It has also become clear that although the changes are less striking in chronic liver failure, the same pattern of imbalance in amino acid levels develops, especially in comatose patients (Iber *et al.*, 1957; Fischer *et al.*, 1974; Zieve and Nicoloff, 1975; Rosen *et al.*, 1977).

Thus the levels of methionine and of the aromatic amino acids rise but only to some 1.5 to 3 times normal. In addition, the imbalance of amino acids in acute liver failure is probably aggravated by the effects of the high levels of insulin in the circulation (Daniel *et al.*, 1975b; Munro, Fernstrom and Wurtman, 1975).

The imbalance which develops in the proportions of the amino acids in the blood is likely to interfere with the transport of amino acids across the blood-brain barrier and there is a risk that the brain will be deprived of one or more of the branched chain amino acids, all of which it needs as nutrients (see Tables 5.3 and 5.4). Most important are four of the amino acids whose levels rise in the blood in liver failure. These are methionine, phenylalanine and tyrosine, as well as tryptophan, of which the rise is in the free fraction of the tryptophan, i.e. that not bound to blood albumin (as most of it normally is). These four amino acids all have a high affinity for the main transport carrier, i.e. the one which takes most of the neutral amino acids across the barrier constituted by the cells of the brain capillary blood vessels. Their affinities for the carrier are generally greater than those of the branched chain amino acids and a rise in their blood levels combined with a fall in those of the branched chain amino acids brings together the factors (see Table 5.3) which are most likely to lead to a block in transport across the capillary barrier.

Table 5.3: Conditions Which Increase the Danger of the Brain Being Deprived of a Nutrient Through Competitive Inhibition of the Carrier-mediated Transport of the Nutrient Across the Blood-brain Barrier

	Concentration in the blood	Affinity for the carrier*	Rate of use by the brain	Diffusion rate across blood-brain barrier
Nutrient	low	low	high	low
Inhibitor	high	high	–	–

*A low affinity for the carrier means a high value of the affinity constant, K, and vice versa, see equation (1).

The kinetic parameters of transport across the blood-brain barrier *in vivo* have now been evaluated for all the amino acids which are present in the blood in reasonable amounts (Tables 5.2 and 5.4), and by substituting these values into equation (1) the rate at which each amino acid is taken into the brain by the carrier for neutral amino acids can be estimated, provided that the levels of the various amino acids in the bloodstream are known (Pratt, 1979b). Whilst such an estimate is only an approximate one, since the parameters of the transport processes cannot be measured in man, valuable indications are given of the effects upon transport of changes in the pattern of amino acids levels like those which are seen in hepatic failure.

Table 5.4: Estimates of the values of the kinetic parameters for the carrier-mediated transport of various nutrient substances across the blood-brain barrier. V is the maximum rate of carrier-mediated transport when there is an excess of the substance in the circulation. K is the equlibrium constant for the combination of the substance with the carrier. (This measures its affinity for the carrier – the higher K is, the lower the affinity.) Standard errors are given with the number of estimates of K in parentheses. Estimates of V are based upon the results of from 10 to 60 experiments. Where standard errors are not given the value shown is a likely one consistent with other data.

Substance	Maximum carrier-mediated transport rate V nmole min^{-1} g^{-1} of brain		Equilibrium constant K mmole l^{-1}		
glucose	2,200	± 100	10.5	± 1.2	(3)
pyruvate	310		5.8	± 1.3	(5)
lactate	250		5.7	± 0.8	(4)
acetoacetate	> 300		> 30		
3-hydroxybutyrate	> 300		> 30		
alanine	39.1		0.72	± 0.20	(3)
arginine	28	± 1	0.58	± 0.20	(4)
glutamine	290		9.3		(2)
glycine	119		8.9	± 3.4	(4)
histidine	49	± 11	0.13	± 0.03	(5)
isoleucine	73	± 21	0.38	± 0.09	(7)
leucine	86	± 7	0.13	± 0.03	(3)
lysine	189	± 13	2.1	± 0.6	(4)
methionine	42	± 2	0.144	± 0.05	(4)
phenylalanine	50	± 3	0.092	± 0.016	(7)
serine	52	± 5	4.6	± 1.1	(3)
threonine	64	± 17	1.33	± 0.23	(4)
tryptophan	47	± 2	0.15	± 0.03	(6)
tyrosine	58	± 11	0.15	± 0.03	(3)
valine	90	± 10	0.73	± 0.15	(7)

Sources: Baños *et al.*, 1978; Crockett *et al.*, 1976; Daniel *et al.*, 1971, 1972, 1975c, 1977b, f, 1978; Pratt 1976, 1979b.

Both in acute and in chronic liver failure, the raised levels of the various amino acids acting together will inhibit severely the transport of the branched chain amino acids into the brain, reducing it to a small fraction of the normal (see Figure 5.6). This is one way in which the metabolism of the brain may be disturbed severely enough to cause encephalopathy. If the metabolism of the brain is being disturbed in this way it would be expected that the deprivation of branched chain amino acids suffered by the brain as a consequence of competition for the transport carrier could be prevented by raising the levels of these branched chain amino acids above normal in the bloodstream (see Figure 5.5, Table 5.3). Imbalance in the amino acid levels in the blood is most severe in acute hepatic failure and even though coma is common in this condition, the part played by the amino acid imbalance is far from clear.

Dogs with acute hepatic failure following a portacaval shunt show an improvement in their mental state when given an amino acid mixture containing large amounts of the branched amino acids (Fischer *et al.*, 1975), but it has been pointed out that this result has an alternative explanation: at the same time as the levels of the branched chain amino acids were increased in the mixture given to the dogs the levels of other amino acids were reduced. These other amino acids included those from which ammonia is formed most readily (e.g. glycine) so that the improvement reported might have been due to a reduction in the toxic effect of ammonia upon the brain (Zieve, 1979). In addition, no clear correlation has been found in acute hepatic failure between the imbalance of the amino acids in the blood and the degree of coma (Chase *et al.*, 1978). Also high levels even of the branched chain amino acids have been found in the brains of patients dying of acute hepatic failure (Record *et al.*, 1976), which is not what would be expected if the brain were being deprived of these nutrients.

What happens in acute liver failure produced experimentally is that the blood-brain barrier breaks down owing to cerebral oedema. The result of this breakdown is that not only all the amino acids but also substances like insulin, which are normally excluded from the brain, enter the organ freely (Livingstone *et al.*, 1977; James *et al.*, 1978). This suggests that the imbalance in amino acids in the circulation does indeed play a key role in the pathogenesis of coma in acute liver failure, but probably not by excluding branched chain amino acids from the brain. The mechanism is more likely to be the toxic effect of an excessively high level of ammonia in the brain following abnormal deamination of the amino acids released by the autolysis of hepatic

Figure 5.6: Estimated Influx into the Brain of the Three Branched-chain Amino Acids, L-Leucine (LEU), L-Valine (VAL) and L-Isoleucine (ILE) in Normal Controls (Blank Columns) in Patients with Chronic Liver Failure (Shaded), and in Patients with Acute Liver Failure (Black)

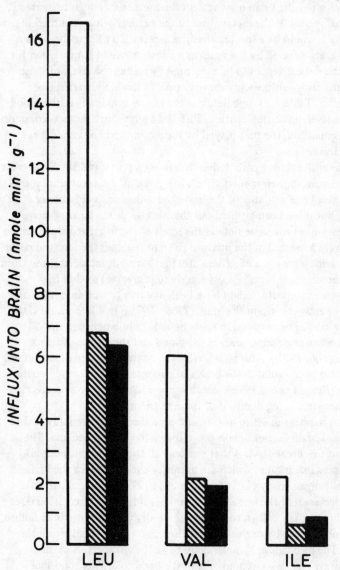

Source: Based on data of Rosen *et al.*, 1977.

cells. Coma can be produced experimentally by giving infusions of amino acids and can be prevented if arginine is also given (Fahy *et al.*, 1958). In acute hepatic failure arginine levels are not raised appreciably, so that it is useful to give this amino acid as a supplement (Zieve, 1979). A similar need to give arginine supplements to cope with amino acid imbalance has been found in the intravenous feeding of neonates (Shaw, 1973; Pratt, 1979a).

Ammonia Intoxication

Evidence for a possible damaging effect of ammonia upon the brain is also provided by the raised levels of glutamine in the cerebrospinal fluid in patients with hepatic failure. These levels are especially high when there is coma (Knell *et al.*, 1972; Zieve and Nicoloff, 1975; Record *et al.*, 1976; Jeppsson *et al.*, 1979). It must be remembered, however, that the glutamine which the brain forms in order to remove potentially toxic ammonia leaves the organ mainly by transport out across the endothelium of the cerebral capillaries, rather than via the cerebrospinal fluid (Pratt, 1979a, 1980a, b). Rapid transport of glutamine across the blood-brain barrier outwards will play a part in preventing toxic damage to the brain from ammonia. Conversely a breakdown in the transport of glutamine out of the brain in liver failure may precipitate encephalopathy.

There is evidence that the amino acid imbalance in acute hepatic failure also leads to altered metabolism of the central neurotransmitters which are formed from the aromatic amino acids phenylalanine, tyrosine and tryptophan (Curzon *et al.*, 1973; Knell *et al.*, 1974; Daniel *et al.*, 1975b, 1976b; Cumings *et al.*, 1976a; Bloxham and Curzon, 1978). Thus, high levels of the metabolites of the neurotransmitter serotonin were found in the cerebrospinal fluid in patients with acute hepatic failure (Knell *et al.*, 1972) and a marked increase has been reported in the level of octopamine (a false neurotransmitter which interferes with the action of noradrenaline) in the blood of parients with fulminant hepatic failure (Chase *et al.*, 1978); although the levels did not correlate closely with the degree of coma.

Disturbance of Neurotransmitter Metabolism

Neurotransmitter metabolism in the brain is likely also to be disturbed in chronic hepatic failure. Thus, the tryptophan level was found to be raised above normal in the cerebrospinal fluid of patients with cirrhosis of the liver, indicating that an excess of tryptophan is reaching the brain (Young *et al.*, 1975; Cumings *et al.*, 1976b), but this was so whether the patients were in coma or not. In chronic hepatic failure, in contrast to the acute condition, competition between amino acids for transport across the blood-brain barrier may well cause the brain to be deprived of some of the branched chain amino acids which it needs. Thus, the condition of patients with chronic liver failure from cirrhosis can be improved by giving them supplements of the branched chain amino acids (Fischer *et al.*, 1976).

More recently it has been shown that a combined injection of phenylalanine and of tryptophan given over a period of hours to otherwise normal dogs, so as to deprive the brain of branched chain amino acids, causes a state resembling hepatic coma, and that this can be prevented if branched chain amino acids are also given (Freund *et al.*, 1978). It seems clear therefore that deprivation of the brain of some of the amino acids which it needs (see Figure 5.6, and Table 5.3) constitutes one important pathogenic mechanism which can be responsible for the encephalopathy seen in chronic liver failure caused by a cirrhosis associated with alcoholism.

How Amino Acid Metabolism is Disturbed in Alcoholism

The imbalance of amino acids in the circulation in cirrhosis develops primarily as a result of chronic liver failure associated with shunting of blood from the portal to the systemic circulation. The imbalance of amino acids in the blood may be made worse by other factors. There may be various nutritional deficiencies, especially of amino acids or of vitamins, which develop because alcohol forms a large part of the diet or because alcohol interferes with the transport of nutrients across the intestinal wall. In addition alcohol has the direct effect of altering the balance of oxidation-reduction between pairs of metabolites of glucose.

Thus both in the cerebral cells and in the cells of the body there is an accumulation for example of lactate rather than pyruvate and of 3-hydroxybutyrate rather than acetoacetate. There are a number of such pairs of metabolites of which the oxidised form undergoes transamination and thus produces a non-essential amino acid (see Table 5.5). The shift in the equilibrium between the reduced and the oxidised pairs which is caused by the metabolism of alcohol will lower the concentration of the oxidised form within the cells and thus will interfere indirectly with the synthesis of the amino acid. This disturbance in the metabolism of amino acids will interfere in turn with protein synthesis and also with the synthesis of glucose from amino acids by the liver.

Table 5.5: Ways in which the prolonged metabolism of alcohol can affect carbohydrate metabolism and, indirectly, amino acid metabolism, in the cells of the brain and the body. Each of the pairs of metabolites of glucose shown below are in equilibrium in the cells, the second being the oxidised form of the first. The oxidised form is, in turn, converted to an amino acid by transamination. Prolonged metabolism of alcohol shifts the equilibrium between the oxidised and reduced forms of each pair, decreasing the proportion of the oxidised form, which indirectly reduces the rate at which the amino acid can be synthesised.

Reduced forms of the metabolites of glucose which accumulate in alcoholism	Oxidised forms of metabolites of glucose which are depleted in alcoholism	Amino acid which can be made from the oxidised form of the metabolite by transamination
Lactate	Pyruvate	Alanine
Malate	Oxaloacetate	Aspartate
2-Hydroxyglutarate	2-Ketoglutarate	Glutamate, Glutamine

An unresolved problem is the extent to which neuropsychiatric disturbance (short of dementia) develops before there is a serious loss of liver function. That there are organic changes in the brain in chronic alcoholism is suggested by recent work which shows that some degree of cerebral atrophy is not uncommon (see Chapter 11 of this volume; Ron *et al.*, 1980). These findings pose the question of how the shrinkage of the brain is brought about in alcoholism. For instance, do disturbances in the metabolism of certain amino acids cause alterations in osmotic pressure within the cells of the brain? This seems possible, since the amino acids aspartate, *N*-acetylaspartate and glutamate are known to be concerned with the regulation of the osmotic pressure within the cerebral cells (Pratt, 1976; Bradbury, 1979).

The Role of the Muscles in Alcoholism (Addendum by E. Spargo)

Spargo *et al.* (1979a, b) have recently drawn attention to another way in which alcohol may affect the metabolic regulation of the body. This is by its effect on the metabolism of the skeletal muscles, which although not usually considered as a single 'organ' do in fact have a mass which is some 21 times as great as that of the liver. Alcohol-induced changes in muscle metabolism may have a considerable effect on the overall metabolic balance of the body, since the important role of the muscles in the regulation of glucose and amino acid metabolism has become clear from recent work (Daniel, Pratt and Spargo, 1977a, b; Chang and Goldberg, 1978a, b; Goldberg *et al.*, 1978; Spargo *et al.*, 1979a).

When there is an increased demand for hepatic glucose production, e.g. in fasting, muscle proteins can be broken down into their constituent amino acids, many of which are converted within the muscles into one of the three gluconeogenic amino acids glycine, glutamine or alanine, which together account for some 85 per cent of the amino acid release from muscle under such circumstances. The level of alanine in the circulation appears to control the amino acid release from the muscles (Daniel, Pratt and Spargo, 1979), since a fall in its level produces increased output from the muscles, whereas a rise leads to increased uptake.

Alcohol can interfere with various steps in this process within the muscles, but the main effects are likely to be due to alcohol-induced shift in the balance between pyruvate and lactate, very much in favour of lactate (Kreisberg *et al.*, 1971a, b; Axelrod, 1974). This altered balance will also affect the metabolism of other substances which are involved in both amino acid and glucose metabolism, e.g. oxaloacetate and α-ketoglutarate; and such changes are likely to interfere with the conversion within the muscles of one amino acid into another or of pyruvate to alanine. Therefore, since we have shown that a reduction in the 'functional' muscle mass impairs the ability to regulate blood alanine levels in both experimental conditions (Daniel, Pratt, Spargo and Taylor, 1977b) and in pathological conditions (Spargo *et al.,* 1979b), it seems likely that the myopathy associated with chronic alcoholism may be an important factor contributing to the defective regulation of blood glucose and amino acid levels. This defective regulation will affect the availability of these substances to the brain.

Conclusion

It can be concluded that a factor which must play an important part in the pathogenesis of the neuropsychiatric disturbances associated with chronic alcoholism is the imbalance of amino acids in the circulation which is commonly seen. This imbalance takes the form of low levels of the branched chain amino acids leucine, valine and isoleucine, and raised levels especially of methionine, phenylalanine, tryptophan and tyrosine. It develops primarily as a result of alcohol-induced chronic liver failure, although it is likely to be aggravated by the direct effects of alcohol upon intermediary metabolism. In addition, chronic alcoholism results in various nutritional deficiencies, especially of amino acids and vitamins.

There are several possible reasons for the encephalopathy and brain damage caused by this imbalance of amino acids. One important reason is that the brain is deprived of branched chain amino acids, as a result of competitive inhibition of their transport across the blood-brain barrier by other amino acids. These branched chain amino acids are essential to the brain for its metabolism, and such deprivation will interfere with the resynthesis of cerebral protein which is continually being broken down and reformed. Another possible reason is the intoxication of the brain by the ammonia which is formed from the excessive quantities of some amino acids which are reaching the cerebral cells. Such intoxication will be aggravated if a breakdown of transport mechanisms across the blood-brain barrier interferes with the detoxication of ammonia. Other possible pathogenic mechanisms by which the imbalance of amino acids in the blood leads to encephalopathy include disturbances in the metabolism of central neurotransmitters. Such disturbances may arise because the amounts of the amino acid precursors of these neurotransmitters which are supplied to the brain are abnormal.

Further study of the transport of nutrient substances and metabolites, especially amino acids, across the blood-brain barrier will be necessary in order to assess the relative importance of these different pathogenic mechanisms which may cause encephalopathy in chronic alcoholism.

Acknowledgements

Much of the work on which this review is based was supported by grants from the Nuffield Foundation, the National Fund for Research into Crippling Diseases, the Wellcome Trust and the Kennedy Trust.

References

Agrawal, H.C., Bone, A.H. and Davison, A.N. (1970), 'Effect of phenylalanine on protein synthesis in the developing rat brain', *Biochem. J., 117*, 325-31

Axelrod, D.R. (1974), 'Metabolic and endocrine aberrations in alcoholism' in *The Biology of Alcoholism, 3* (Kissin, B. and Begleiter, H., eds.), Plenum Press, New York, 291-302

Bachelard, H.S., Daniel, P.M., Love, E.R. and Pratt, O.E. (1972), 'The *in vivo* influx of glucose into the brain of the rat compared with the net cerebral uptake', *J. Physiol. Lond., 222*, 149-50*P*

—— (1973), 'The transport of glucose into the brain of the rat *in vivo*', *Proc. Roy. Soc. Lond.*, B., *183*, 71-82

Balázs, R. (1965), 'Control of glutamate metabolism. The effect of pyruvate', *J. Neurochem., 12*, 63-76

Baños, G., Daniel, P.M., Moorhouse, S.R. and Pratt, O.E. (1970), 'The passage of amino acids into the rat's brain', *J. Physiol., 210*, 149*P*

—— (1971a), 'The entry of amino acids into the brain of the rat during the post-natal period', *J. Physiol., 213*, 45-6*P*

—— (1973a), 'The influx of amino acids into the brain of the rat *in vivo:* the essential compared with some non-essential amino acids', *Proc. Roy. Soc. Lond.*, B., *183*, 59-70

—— (1973b), 'The movement of amino acids between blood and skeletal muscle in the rat', *J. Physiol., 235*, 459-75

—— (1974a), 'Inhibition of entry of some amino acids into the brain, with observations on mental retardation in the aminoacidurias', *Psychol. Med., 4*, 262-9

—— (1975), 'The requirements of the brain for some amino acids', *J. Physiol., 246*, 539-48

Baños, G., Daniel, P.M., Moorhouse, S.R., Pratt, O.E. and Wilson, P. (1974b), 'Inhibition of neutral amino acid entry into the brain of the rat *in vivo*', *J. Physiol., 237*, 22-3*P*

Baños, G., Daniel, P.M. and Pratt, O.E. (1971b), 'Inhibition of entry of L-arginine into the brain of the rat, *in vivo*, by L-lysine or L-ornithine', *J. Physiol., 214*, 24-5*P*

—— (1974c), 'Saturation of a shared mechanism which transports L-arginine and L-lysine into the brain of the living rat', *J. Physiol., 236*, 29-41

—— (1978), 'The effect of age upon the entry of some amino acids into the brain, and their incorporation into cerebral protein', *Develop. Med. Child Neurol., 20*, 335-46

Bloxham, D.L. and Curzon, G. (1978), 'A study of proposed determinants of brain tryptophan concentration in rats after portocaval anastomosis or sham operation', *J. Neurochem., 31*, 1255-63

Bradbury, M. (1979), *The Concept of a Blood-brain Barrier*, Wiley, Chichester, New York, Brisbane, Toronto

Cascino, A., Cangiano, C., Calcaterra, V., Rossi-Fanelli, F. and Capocaccia, L. (1978), 'Plasma amino acids imbalance in patients with liver disease, *Am. J. Dig. Dis., 23*, 591-8

Chang, T.W. and Goldberg, A.L. (1978a), 'The origin of alanine produced in skeletal muscle', *J. Biol. Chem., 253*, 3677-84

—— (1978b) 'The metabolic fates of amino acids and the formation of glutamine in skeletal muscle', *J. Biol. Chem., 253*, 3685-95

Chase, R.A., Davies, M., Trewby, P.N., Silk, D.B.A. and Williams, R. (1978), 'Plasma amino acid profiles in patients with fulminant hepatic failure treated by repeated polyacrylonitrile membrane hemodialysis', *Gastroenterology, 75*, 1033-40

Christensen, H.N. (1973), 'On the development of amino acid transport systems', *Fed. Proc., 32*, 19-28

—— (1975), *Biological Transport*, Benjamin, New York

—— (1976), 'Metabolite transport at cell membranes' in Levi, G., Battistin, L. and Lajtha, A. (eds.), *Transport Phenomena in the Nervous System*, Plenum Press, New York, 3-12

—— (1979), 'Developments in amino acid transport, illustrated for the blood-brain barrier', *Biochem. Pharmacol., 28*, 1989-92

Christensen, H.N. and Handlogten, M.E. (1979), 'Interaction between parallel transport systems examined with tryptophan and related amino acids', *J. Neural. Trans. Suppl., 15*, 1-13

Cremer, J.E. and Heath, D.F. (1974), 'The estimation of rates of utilization of glucose and ketone bodies in the brain of the suckling rat using compartmental analysis of isotopic data', *Biochem. J., 142*, 527-44

Crockett, M.E., Daniel, P.M., Love, E.R., Moorhouse, S.R. and Pratt, O.E. (1977), 'Exchange of nutritional substances between blood and brain', *J. Physiol., 271*, 24-6P

Crockett, M.E., Daniel, P.M. and Pratt, O.E. (1976), 'Competition between some neutral amino acids for carrier-mediated transport into the brain *in vivo*', *J. Physiol., 263*, 206-7P

—— (1978), 'A comparison of the transport systems which carry L-methionine across the blood-retinal barrier', *J. Physiol., 280*, 39P

Crone, C. (1965), 'Facilitated transfer of glucose from blood into brain tissue', *J. Physiol. Lond., 181*, 103-13

Crone, C. and Thompson, A.M. (1970), 'Permeability of brain capillaries' in *Capillary Permeability*, Crone, C. and Lassen, N.A. (eds.), Munksgaard, Copenhagen, 447-53

Cumings, M.G., James, J.H., Soeters, P.B., Keane, J.M., Foster, J. and Fischer, J.E. (1976a), 'Regional brain study of indoleamine metabolism in the rat in acute hepatic failure', *J. Neurochem., 27*, 741-6

Cumings, M.G., Soeters, P.B., James, J.H., Keane, J.M. and Fischer, J.E. (1976b), 'Regional brain indoleamine metabolism following chronic portacaval anastomosis in the rat', *J. Neurochem., 27*, 501-9

Curzon, G. (1979), 'Relationships between plasma, CSF and brain tryptophan', *J. Neural. Trans. Suppl., 15*, 81-92

Curzon, G., Kantamanini, B.D., Fernando, J.C., Woods, M.S. and Cavanagh, J.B. (1975), 'Effects of chronic portecaval anastomosis on brain tryptophan, tyrosine and 5-hydroxytryptamine', *J. Neurochem., 24*, 1065-70

Curzon, G., Kantamanini, B.D., Winch, J., Rojas-Bueno, A., Murray-Lyon, I.M. and Williams, R. (1973), 'Plasma and brain tryptophan changes in experimental acute hepatic failure', *J. Neurochem., 21*, 137-45

Curzon, G., Knott, P.J., Murray-Lyon, I.M., Record, C.O. and Williams, R. (1975), 'Disturbed brain tryptophan metabolism in hepatic coma', *Lancet, I*, 1092-3

Daniel, P.M., Donaldson, J. and Pratt, O.E. (1974), 'The rapid achievement and maintenance of a steady level of an injected substance in the blood plasma', *J. Physiol., 237*, 8-9P

—— (1975a), 'A method for injecting substances into the circulation to reach rapidly and to maintain a steady level', *Med. Biol. Engineer., 13*, 214-27

—— (1976a), 'Infusion schedules for prescribed blood concentration time courses', *J. Appl. Physiol., 41*, 608

Daniel, P.M., Love, E.R., Moorhouse, S.R. and Pratt, O.E. (1975b), 'Amino acids, insulin, and hepatic coma', *Lancet, 2*, 179-80

Daniel, P.M., Love, E.R., Moorhouse, S.R., Pratt, O.E. and Wilson, P. (1971), 'Factors influencing utilisation of ketone-bodies by brain in normal rats and rats with ketoacidosis', *Lancet, 2*, 637-8

—— (1972), 'The movement of ketone bodies, glucose, pyruvate and lactate between the blood and the brain of rats', *J. Physiol., 221*, 22-3P

—— (1974a), 'A method for rapidly washing the blood out of an organ or tissue of the anaesthetized living animal', *J. Physiol., 237*, 11-*12P*

Daniel, P.M., Love, E.R. and Pratt, O.E. (1977a), 'The influence of age on the influx of ketone bodies into the brain of the rat', *J. Physiol., 268*, 15-16*P*

—— (1977b), 'The transport of ketone bodies into the brain of the rat *(in vivo)*', *J. Nuerol. Sci., 34*, 1-13

—— (1975c), 'Insulin and the way the brain handles glucose', *J. Neurochem., 25*, 471-6

—— (1977c), 'The influence of insulin upon the metabolism of glucose by the brain', *Proc. Roy. Soc. Lond.*, B., *196*, 85-104

—— (1978), 'The effect of age upon the influx of glucose into the brain', *J. Physiol., 274*, 141-8

Daniel, P.M., Moorhouse, S.R. and Pratt, O.E. (1976b), 'Amino acid precursors of monoamine neurotransmitters and some factors influencing their supply to the brain', *Psychol. Med., 6*, 277-86

—— (1978), 'Partial exclusion of tryptophan from the brain due to saturation of the transport carrier', *J. Physiol., 282*, 9-10*P*

Daniel, P.M., Pratt, O.E. and Spargo, E. (1977a), 'The metabolic homoeostatic role of muscle and its function as a store of protein', *Lancet, 2*, 446-8

—— (1979), 'Blood alanine as a regulator of amino acid release from muscle in rats', *J. Physiol. (London), 295*, 12-13*P*

Daniel, P.M., Pratt, O.E., Spargo, E. and Taylor, D.E.M. (1977b), 'The 'Effect of bilateral hind-limb ischaemia on the patterns of free amino acids in the circulation in the rat', *J. Physiol. (London), 272*, 103-*4P*

Daniel, P.M., Pratt, O.E. and Wilson, P.A. (1977d), 'The influx of isoleucine into the cerebral hemispheres and cerebellum: carrier-mediated transport and diffusion', *Quart. J. Exp. Physiol., 62*, 163-73

—— (1977e), 'The transport of L-leucine into the brain of the rat *in vivo:* saturable and non-saturable components of influx', *Proc. Roy. Soc. Lond.*, B., *196*, 333-46

—— (1977f), 'The exclusion of L-isoleucine or of L-leucine from the brain of the rat, caused by raised levels of L-valine in the circulation, and the manner in which this exclusion can be partially overcome', *J. Neurol. Sci., 31*, 421-31

Davison, A.N. (1973), 'Inborn errors of amino acid metabolism affecting myelination of the central nervous system' in *Inborn Errors of Metabolism*, (Holmes, F.A. and van den Berg, C.J., eds.), Academic Press, London and New York

Dixon, M. and Webb, E.C. (1979), *Enzymes,* 3rd edn, Longmans, London, 318-20

Donaldson, J. and Pratt, O.E. (1975), 'A method for displaying the effect of altering the constants of a function and an application to the problem of maintaining steady blood concentrations', *J. Physiol., 252*, 5-6*P*

Ehrlich, P. (1885), *Das Sauerstoff-Bedürfniss des Organismus. Eine Farbendanalytische Studie*, A. Hirshwald, Berlin, 69ᵈ

Fahey, J.L., Perry, R.S. and McCoy, P.F. (1958), 'Blood ammonia elevation and toxicity from intravenous L-amino acid administration to dogs: the protective role of L-arginine', *Am. J. Physiol., 192*, 311-17

Fischer, J.E., Funovics, J.M., Aguirre, A., James, J.H., Keane, J.M., Wesdorp, R.I.C., Yoshimura, N. and Westman, T. (1975), 'The role of plasma amino acids in hepatic encephalopathy', *Surgery, 78*, 276-88

Fischer, J.E., Rosen, H.M., Ebeid, A.M., James, J.H., Keane, J.M. and Soeters, P.B. (1976), 'The effect of normalization of plasma amino acids on hepatic encephalopathy in man', *Surgery, 80*, 77-91

Fischer, J.E., Yoshimura, N., Aguirre, A., James, J.H., Cummings, M.G., Abel, R.M. and Deindoerfer, F. (1974), 'Plasma amino acids in patients with hepatic encephalopathy – effects of amino acid infusions', *Am. J. Surg., 127*, 40-7

Freund, H., Krause, R., Rossi-Fanelli, F., Smith, A.R. and Fischer, J.E. (1978), 'Amino acid induced coma in normal animals: prevention by branched chain amino acids', *Gastroenterology, 74*, 1167

Gilboe, D.D. and Betz, A.L. (1970), 'Kinetics of glucose transport in the isolated dog brain', *Am. J. Physiol., 219*, 774-8

Goldberg, A.L. and Chang, T.W. (1978), 'Regulation and significance of amino acid metabolism in skeletal muscle', *Federation Proc., 37*, 2301-7

Green, A.R. (1978), 'The effect of dietary tryptophan and its peripheral metabolism on brain 5-hydroxytryptamine synthesis and function', *Essays on Neurochem. Neuropharm., 3*, 104-27

Griffiths, P.J. and Littleton, J.M. (1977), 'Concentrations of free amino acids in brains of mice during the induction of physical dependence on ethanol and during the ethanol withdrawal syndrome', *Br. J. Exp. Path., 58*, 19-27

Holdsworth, C.D. (1972), 'Absorption of protein, amino acids and peptides – a review', in *Transport Across the Intestine* (Burland, W.L. and Samuel, P.D., eds.), Churchill Livingstone, Edinburgh and London, 136-52

Iber, F.L., Rosen, H., Levenson, S.M. and Chalmers, T.C. (1957), 'The plasma amino acids in patients with liver failure', *J. Lab. Clin. Med., 50*, 417-25

James, J.H., Escourrou, J. and Fischer, J.E. (1978), 'Blood-brain neutral amino acid transport activity is increased after portacaval anastomosis', *Science, 200*, 1395-7

James, J.H., Hodgman, J.M. and Fischer, J.E. (1976), 'Alterations of brain octapamine and brain tyrosine following portacaval anastomosis in rats', *J. Neurochem., 27*, 223-7

Jeppsson, B., James, J.H., Ziparo, V. and Fischer, J.E. (1979), 'The role of central nervous system glutamine in increasing uptake of aromatic amino acids by brain following portacaval shunt', *Gastroenterology, 76*, 1286

Johnson, J.D., Malachowski, N.C., Grobenstein, R., Welsh, D., Daily, W.J.R. and Sunshine, P. (1974), 'Prognosis of children surviving with the aid of mechanical ventilation in the newborn period', *J. Pediat., 84*, 272-6

Knell, A.J., Pratt, O.E., Curzon, G. and Williams, R. (1972), 'Changing ideas in hepatic encephalopathy' in Neale, G. (ed.), *Eighth Symposium on Advanced Medicine*, Pitman, London, 156-70

Knell, A.J., Davidson, A.R., Williams, R., Kantamaneni, B.D. and Curzon, G. (1974), 'Dopamine and sertonin metabolism in hepatic encephalopathy', *Br. Med. J., 1*, 549-51

Kreisberg, R.A., Owen, W.C. and Siegal, A.M. (1971a), 'Ethanol-induced hyperlacticacidemia: inhibition of lactate utilization', *J. Clin. Invest., 50*, 166-74

Kreisburg, R.A., Siegal, A.M. and Owen, W.C. (1971b), 'Dopamine and sertonin metabolism in hepatic encephalopathy', *J. Clin. Invest., 50*, 175-85

Lajtha, A. (1964), 'Protein metabolism of the nervous system', *Int. Rev. Neurobiol., 6*, 1-98

Le Breton, E. (1934), 'Influence de la nature de l'aliment brûlé sur la vitesse d'oxydation de l'alcool dans l'organisme; cas de protides', *C.R. Soc. Biol. Paris, 17,* 709-12

Livingstone, A.S., Potvin, M., Goresky, C.A., Finlayson, M.H. and Hinchey, E.J. (1977), 'Changes in the blood-brain barrier in hepatic coma after hepatectomy in the rat', *Gastroenterology, 73,* 697-704

Love, E.R. (1980), 'Some aspects of the transport of glucose and ketone bodies into the brain and retina', in *Transport and Inherited Metabolic Disease,* Toothill, C. and Belton, N.R. (eds.), MTP, Lancaster

McKean, C.M., Boggs, D.E. and Peterson, N.A. (1968), 'The influence of high phenylalanine and tyrosine on the concentrations of essential amino acids in brain', *J. Neurochem., 15,* 235-41

McMenamy, R.H., Vang, J. and Drapanas, T. (1965), 'Amino acid and α-keto acid concentrations in plasma and blood of the liverless dog', *Am. J. Physiol., 209,* 1046-52

Marks, V. and Rose, C.F. (1965), *Hypoglycaemia,* Blackwell, Oxford

Munro, H.N., Fernstrom, J.D. and Wurtman, R.J. (1975), 'Insulin plasma amino acid imbalance and hepatic coma', *Lancet, 1,* 722-4

Myers, R.E. (1979), 'Lactic acid accumulation as cause of brain edema and cerebral necrosis resulting from oxygen deprivation' in *Advances in Perinatal Neurology, 1,* Korobkin, R. and Guilleminault, C. (eds.), Spectrum Publications, New York and London, 85-114

Neame, K.D. (1968), 'Transport, metabolism and pharmacology of amino acids in brain', in *Applied Neurochemistry,* Davison, A.N. and Dobbing, J. (eds.), Blackwell Scientific Publications, Oxford, 119-77

O'Brien, D. and Ibbot, F.A. (1966), 'Effect of prolonged phenylalanine loading on the free amino-acid and lipid content of the infant monkey brain', *Develop. Med. Child Neurol., 8,* 724-8

Oldendorf, W.H. (1971), 'Brain uptake of radiolabeled amino acids, amines, and hexoses after arterial injection', *Am. J. Physiol., 221,* 1629-39

——— (1973), 'Carrier-mediated blood-brain barrier transport of short-chain monocarboxylic organic acids', *Am. J. Physiol., 224,* 1450-3

Pardridge, W.M. (1977), 'Regulation of amino acid availability to the brain' in Wurtman, R.J. and Wurtman, J.J. (eds.), *Nutrition and the Brain,* Raven Press, New York, 141-204

——— (1979), 'The role of blood-brain barrier transport of tryptophan and other neutral amino acids in the regulation of substrate-limited pathways of brain amino acid metabolism', *J. Neural Trans., Suppl. 15,* 43-54

Pardridge, W.M. and Oldendorf, W.H. (1975), 'Kinetic analysis of blood-brain barrier transport of amino acids', *Biochim. Biophys. Acta., 401,* 128-36

Popper, H. (1977), 'Pathologic aspects of cirrhosis: a review, *Am. J. Pathol., 87,* 228-64

Pratt, O.E. (1974), 'An electronically controlled syringe drive for giving an injection at a variable rate according to a preset programme', *J. Physiol. Lond., 237,* 5-6P

——— (1976), 'The transport of metabolizable substances into the living brain' in *Transport Phenomena in the Nervous System: Physiological and Pathological Aspects,* Levi, G., Battistin, L. and Lajtha, A. (eds.), Plenum Press, New York, 55-75

——— (1979a), 'Adequate nutrition of the developing brain' in *Advances in Perinatal Neurology, 1,* Korobkin, R. and Guilleminault, C. (eds.), Spectrum Publications, New York and London, 21-55

——— (1979b), 'Kinetics of tryptophan transport across the blood-brain barrier', *J. Neural Trans., Supp. 15,* 29-42

—— (1980a), 'A new approach to the treatment of phenylketonuria' *J. Ment. Def. Res.,* in press

—— (1980b), 'The needs of the brain for amino acids and their transport across the blood-brain barrier' in *Transport and Inherited Metabolic Disease,* Toothill, C. and Beeton, N.R. (eds.), MTP, Lancaster

Record, C.O., Buxton, B., Chase, R.A., Curzon, G., Murray-Lyon, I.M. and Williams, R. (1976), 'Plasma and brain amino acids in fulminant hepatic failure and their relationship to hepatic encephalopathy', *Eur. J. Clin. Invest., 6,* 387-94

Ron, M.A., Acker, W. and Lishman, W.A. (1980), 'Morphological abnormalities in the brain of chronic alcoholics; a clinical psychological and computerised axial tomographic study', *Fed. Proc. Symposium Magnus Huss,* Stockholm, in press

Rosen, H.M., Yoshimura, N., Hodgman, J.M. and Fischer, J.E. (1977), 'Plasma amino acid patterns in hepatic encephalopathy of differing etiology', *Gastroenterology, 72,* 483-7

Schultz, S.G. and Frizzell, R.A. (1975), 'Amino acid transport by the small intestine', in *Intestinal Absorption and Malabsorption,* Csáky, T.Z. (ed.), Raven Press, New York

Sershen, H. and Lajtha, A. (1979), 'Inhibition pattern by analogs indicates the presence of ten or more transport systems for amino acids in brain cells', *J. Neurochem., 32,* 719-26

Shaw, J.C.L. (1973), 'Parenteral nutrition in the management of sick low birthweight infants', *Pediatr. Clin. North Am., 20,* 333-58

Silberberg, D.H. (1969), 'Maple syrup urine disease metabolites studies in cerebellum cultures', *J. Neurochem., 16,* 1141-6

Spargo, E., Pratt, O.E. and Daniel, P.M. (1979a), 'Metabolic functions of skeletal muscles of man, mammals, birds and fishes', *J. Roy. Soc. Med., 72,* 921-5

—— (1979b), 'The effects of murine muscular dystrophy on the metabolic and homeostatic functions of the skeletal muscles', *J. Neurol. Sci., 43,* 277-90

Spillane, J.D. (1947), *Nutritional Disorders of the Nervous System,* E. and S. Livingstone, Edinburgh

Stanbury, J.B., Wyngaarden, J.B. and Fredrickson, D.S. (1978), *The Metabolic Basis of Inherited Disease,* 4th edn, McGraw-Hill, New York and London

Sytinsky,I.A., Guzikov, B.M., Gommanko, V.P., Eremin, V.P. and Konovalova, N.N. (1975), 'The gamma-amino-butyric acid system in brain during acute and chronic ethanol intoxication', *J. Neurochem., 25,* 43-8

Victor, M. (1970), 'The treatment of alcoholism' in *Alcohol and Derivatives, 2,* Trémolières, J. (ed.), Pergamon Press, Oxford, London, New York, 413-44

Victor, M., Adams, R.D. and Collins, G.H. (1971), *The Wernicke-Korsakoff Syndrome,* Blackwell, Oxford

Wade, L.A. and Katzman, R. (1975), 'Synthetic amino acids and the nature of L-DOPA transport at the blood-brain barrier', *J. Neurochem., 25,* 837-42

Widdas, W.F. (1952), 'Inability of diffusion to account for placental glucose transfer in the sheep and consideration of the kinetics of a possible carrier transfer', *J. Physiol. Lond., 118,* 23-39

Widmark, E.M.P. (1933), 'Über die Einwirkung von Aminosäuren auf den Alkoholgehalt des Blutes', *Biochem. Zeitschr., 265,* 237-40

Wurtman, R.J. and Pardridge, W.M. (1979), 'Circulating tryptophan, brain tryptophan, and psychiatric disease', *J. Neural Trans., Supp. 15,* 227-36

Young, S.N., Lal, S., Sourkes, T.L., Feldmuller, F., Aronoff, A. and Martin, J.B. (1975), 'Relationships between tryptophan in serum and CSF, and 5-hydroxyindole acetic acid in CSF of man: effect of cirrhosis of liver and probenecid administration', *J. Neurol. Neurosurg. Psychiat., 38,* 322-30

Yudilevich, D.L. and de Rose, N. (1971), 'Blood-brain transfer of glucose and other molecules measured by rapid indicator dilution', *Am. J. Physiol., 220*, 841-6

Zieve, L. (1979), 'Amino acids in liver failure', *Gastroenterology, 76*, 219-21

Zieve, L. and Nicoloff, D.M. (1975), 'Pathogenesis of hepatic coma', *Am. Rev. Med., 26*, 143-57

6 ANOMALIES IN THE FUNCTION OF DOPAMINE SYSTEMS IN ETHANOL-WITHDRAWN ANIMALS

B. Tabakoff, S. Urwyler and P.L. Hoffman

The dopamine systems of brain have been postulated to be involved in the control of various behavioural and physiological processes (Jenner *et al.*, 1978). Since withdrawal of animals or man from chronic treatment with ethanol results in the appearance of withdrawal symptoms (Gross *et al.*, 1974; Goldstein, 1975; Ritzmann and Tabakoff, 1976) (e.g. temperature aberrations and tremor), which may reflect a malfunction of the dopamine systems of brain, and since tolerance develops to several effects of ethanol which are thought to be mediated through activity of dopamine neurons (Hunt and Overstreet, 1977; Tabakoff *et al.*, 1978), we examined various parameters of dopaminergic function in animals chronically treated with and withdrawn from ethanol. We reasoned that by monitoring the time course of the neurochemical changes, we could discern whether the change was related to the overt manifestations of tolerance or of physical dependence (i.e., withdrawal symptoms), since these phenomena follow different time courses of disappearance after ethanol withdrawal (Ritzmann and Tabakoff, 1976).

Previous studies on dopamine turnover in brains of ethanol-withdrawn animals have produced conflicting results (Hunt and Majchrowicz, 1974; Ahtee and Svarstrom-Fraser, 1975) and hence we approached the study of the effects of ethanol on dopaminergic systems from a different viewpoint. The presence of ethanol in the neuronal milieu has been postulated to alter the physical characteristics of the neuronal plasma membranes (Seeman, 1972; Chin and Goldstein, 1976) and one could expect that the function of membrane-bound receptors and enzymes would be affected by both acute and chronic administration of ethanol. Our studies were, therefore, concentrated on distinguishing the effects of ethanol on dopamine *receptor-mediated* processes, such as adenylate cyclase activity and the modulation of tyrosine hydroxylase activity within the dopamine neurons. Agents used to alter tyrosine hydroxylase activity were ones known to act on neuronal receptors which, in turn, modulate the electrophysiological activity of the dopamine neurons. Behavioural concomitants of dopamine receptor function in ethanol-withdrawn and control animals were also monitored. Our results not only indicated that ethanol has a significant effect on brain dopamine systems and that these effects may be related to the development of ethanol tolerance, but they gave further insight into some of the normal characteristics of the dopamine systems of the brain.

Male C57B1 mice were used for our studies, and during experiments which involved the chronic administration of ethanol, the animals were fed a liquid diet containing 59.6 g/l ethanol (Ritzmann and Tabakoff, 1976). Control animals were fed a diet which contained sucrose in place of the ethanol, and the daily intake of the sucrose-containing diet by control animals was restricted to equal the mean caloric intake of the animals imbibing the ethanol-containing diet.

After consuming the ethanol-containing diet for seven days, all mice were offered a liquid diet containing sucrose. This constituted withdrawal. The presence of physical dependence in animals fed the ethanol-containing diet was determined by monitoring physiological and behavioural signs occurring during the 24-hour period following the withdrawal of ethanol from the diet. At various times after withdrawal, tyrosine hydroxylase activity within the striatum was measured *in vivo*, by monitoring the accumulation of dihydroxyphenylalanine (DOPA) after injection of NSD-1024 (an inhibitor of brain aromatic amino acid decarboxylase). The response of the dopamine systems to administration of dopamine receptor blockers or dopamine receptor agonists was investigated by measuring DOPA accumulation after animals were injected i.p. with pimozide, haloperidol or apomorphine. The neuroleptics were administered 120 minutes, and apomorphine was administered 30 minutes, prior to sacrifice. The accumulation of DOPA, after inhibition of aromatic amino acid decarboxylase, also served as a measure of dopaminergic response to morphine, which was administered 45 minutes prior to sacrifice. Previous studies (Pollard *et al.*, 1978) have shown that morphine acts on opiate receptors residing on terminals of dopamine neurons.

Soluble tyrosine hydroxylase activity was prepared and measured *in vitro* by a modification of the procedure described by Morgenroth *et al.* (1975). Kinetic constants were derived from double reciprocal plots using at least five different concentrations of the cofactor, $DMPH_4$. Further procedural details are contained in other published reports from our laboratories (Tabakoff and Hoffman, 1978).

Adenylate cyclase activity was assayed as described by Kebabian *et al.* (1972) with minor modifications. The production of cyclic AMP was determined both in the presence and absence of various concentrations of dopamine. In certain of these experiments, subcortical areas were subdivided into striatal and mesolimbic regions, and homogenates prepared with tissue from those regions were assayed separately. Specific binding of ^{3}H-haloperidol and ^{3}H-spiroperidol to homogenates of striatal and mesolimbic regions of mouse brain was determined according to a modification of the method of Seeman *et al.* (1978).

All assays were done in sextuplicate with six tubes containing (+)-butaclamol and six tubes containing (−)-butaclamol (10^{-7} M). The response of dopamine-sensitive adenylate cyclase to dopamine receptor agonists was also tested *in vivo* by monitoring the accumulation of c-AMP in the striatum of ethanol-withdrawn and control mice after injections of apomorphine (1 mg/kg). Mice were sacrificed by microwave irradiation and c-AMP was quantitated by radioimmunoassay.

The behavioural and physiological correlates of dopamine receptor function in the ethanol-withdrawn and control animals were assessed by monitoring the decrease in body temperature produced by administration of piribedil or apomorphine and by monitoring apomorphine-induced changes in locomotor activity within an open field. During open field testing, the number of line crossings, in three consecutive three-minute sessions within the field, the area of which was divided into two-inch squares, were summed to obtain a pre-injection activity score. Locomotor activity was again determined ten minutes after an i.p. injection of apomorphine. At least 30 minutes elapsed between the pre-injection testing session and the injection of apomorphine.

The data in Table 6.1 demonstrate that animals withdrawn from the ethanol-containing diet are less sensitive to the hypothermic and locomotion-altering effects of dopamine receptor agonists. The changes in the animals' responsiveness to the dopamine receptor agonist remained evident for approximately three days after the withdrawal of animals from the ethanol-containing diet. Results reported for ethanol-withdrawn animals were obtained with mice which showed definite signs of physical dependence and tolerance as determined by criteria previously established in our laboratories (Ritzmann and Tabakoff, 1976).

Differences in locomotor activity between ethanol-withdrawn and control animals were evident only after injections of the high dose of apomorphine (4 mg/kg). Ethanol-withdrawn and control animals responded in a similar manner to the injection of a low dose of

Table 6.1: Effect of Apomorphine on Field Activity and Body Temperature of Mice
(Results expressed as the mean ± S.D.)

Group	Apomorphine (mg/kg)	Time after Withdrawal (days)	Activity Pre-injection	Activity Post-injection	Δ
Control	4	1	315±95	615±71	300±76
		3	338±25	695±55	321±73
		7	285±32	618±13	332±32
Ethanol	4	1	275±61	398±140	123±109*
		3	322±34	424±33	101±38 *
		7	296±39	612±78	316±54
Control	0.05	1	328±28	170±36	−150±23
Ethanol	0.05	1	312±42	154±38	−158±29
			Change In Body Temperature (¼C)		
Control	4	1	−6.1±0.7		
Ethanol	4	1	−3.0±0.3*		

*$<$0.01 compared to control animals.

apomorphine (i.e. 0.05 mg/kg). The high dose of apomorphine (4 mg/kg) also produced significantly less hypothermia in the ethanol-withdrawn animals compared with sucrose-fed controls. Similar results were obtained if piribedil was used in place of apomorphine as a dopamine receptor agonist (Hoffman and Tabakoff, 1977).

In attempts to ascertain the biochemical determinants of the observed 'subsensitivity' of the ethanol-withdrawn animals to dopamine receptor agonists, we measured dopamine-stimulated adenylate cyclase activity in striatal and mesolimbic regions of the brain of these animals. The adenylate cyclase activity in subcortical tissue from brains of ethanol-treated animals was less responsive to stimulation by dopamine compared with tissue obtained from control animals (Hoffman and Tabakoff, 1977). The differences were most evident 24 hours after withdrawal, but returned to normal after approximately three days.

The differences in dopamine-stimulated adenylate cyclase between ethanol-withdrawn and control animals were localised to the striatal regions. No differences in basal or dopamine-stimulated adenylate cyclase activity were noted when tissue from mesolimbic regions of brains of ethanol-withdrawn and control animals was used for assay of adenylate cyclase activity (Tabakoff and Hoffman, 1979).

Since several coupling factors are important in the proper expression of dopamine DA-sensitive adenylate cyclase activity, and since these factors may not be functional within the *in vitro* assays (Tabakoff and Hoffman, 1979) utilised in our studies, we monitored the c-AMP levels in striatum of ethanol-withdrawn and control mice after *in vivo* administration of apomorphine. The data in Table 6.2 illustrate that, as would be predicted from *in vitro* results, the production of cAMP is not elevated by administration of apomorphine in ethanol-withdrawn mice.

Table 6.2: Striatal cyclic AMP levels after treatment of C57B1 mice with apomorphine.

	cAMP (pmole/mg protein)	
	Saline	apomorphine (1 mg/kg)
Control	24.6±5.9 (6)	43.2±13.6 (6) *
Ethanol-treated	24.0±8.0 (5)	27.2± 9.3 (5)

a. Male C57B1 mice were exposed to an ethanol-containing liquid diet or a diet containing equicaloric amounts of sucrose (controls) for seven days. Twenty-four hours after ethanol withdrawal, animals received i.p. injections of saline or apomorphine (1 mg/kg). After 10 minutes they were sacrificed by focused microwave irradiation, brains were removed and the caudate nucleus was dissected. Pooled tissue from two animals was homogenised, chromatographed and assayed for cAMP, using a radioimmunoassay. Values represent mean ± standard deviation; numbers in parentheses represent the number of determinations in each group.

Results expressed as mean ± SD.

* $P < 0.02$, apomorphine-treated compared to saline-treated control animals.

To further assess the biochemical correlates of dopamine receptor function and the function of receptors which reside on dopamine neurons, we monitored the increase in tyrosine hydroxylase activity after administration of neuroleptics or morphine to ethanol-withdrawn and control animals. It can be seen from Table 6.3 that DOPA accumulation, after inhibition of aromatic amino acid decarboxylase, was slightly lower in ethanol-withdrawn than in control animals in the absence of neuroleptics or morphine. Furthermore, DOPA accumulation measured after injection of pimozide or haloperidol was significantly less in the ethanol-withdrawn animals compared with the sucrose-fed controls.

Similarly (see Table 6.3) ethanol-withdrawn animals did not demonstrate an increased tyrosine hydroxylase activity after morphine administration as did the control mice. The lack of responsiveness of tyrosine hydroxylase activity, as measured by DOPA accumulation after administration of neuroleptics, was evident for approximately three days after animals were removed from the ethanol-containing diet. Apomorphine, which diminishes DOPA synthesis in control animals, was also found to be less effective in ethanol-withdrawn mice.

Table 6.3: DOPA Accumulation in Striatum of Control and Ethanol-Withdrawn Mice[a]

Group	DOPA(nmol/g)	Percent Change	DA (nmol/g)	Percent Change
Control (13)	2.48 ± 0.23	–	29.7 ± 1.2	–
Control and Morphine (10)	3.67 ± 0.60	+50	30.2 ± 0.9	+ 1
Control and Haloperidol (8)	4.21 ± 0.47	+70	23.8 ± 1.1	−20
Control and Apomorphine (9)	1.99 ± 0.26	−20	33.5 ± 1.2	+13
Ethanol-withdrawn (16)	2.21 ± 0.20	–	31.1 ± 1.5	–
Ethanol-withdrawn and Morphine (6)	2.11 ± 0.52*	− 5	33.4 ± 3.5	+ 7
Ethanol-withdrawn and Haloperidol (6)	3.20 ± 0.52*	+44	30.0 ± 1.3*	− 3
Ethanol-withdrawn and Apomorphine (10)	1.96 ± 0.24	−11	31.4 ± 0.8	+ 1

a. Animals were treated chronically with ethanol and striatal DOPA accumulation was measured at 24 hours after withdrawal. DOPA and DA in striata of individual mice were detected and quantitated simulatenously by HPLC, using fluorimetric detection. The dose of morphine was 10 mg/kg, haloperidol was 0.1 mg/kg, and the apomorphine dose was 1.0 mg/kg. All animals were treated with NSD-1024, 30 minutes prior to sacrifice. Apomorphine was injected 30 minutes, morphine 45 minutes, and haloperidol 120 minutes, prior to sacrifice.

* $P < 0.05$, control compared to ethanol-withdrawn. Results are mean ± SD.

The *in vitro* measurements of tyrosine hydroxylase activity supported the *in vivo* findings that little difference existed in the activity of tyrosine hydroxylase in ethanol-withdrawn and control animals when animals *were not injected* with a neuroleptic or other drug. The K_m determined for $DMPH_4$ with tissue obtained from control mice was 1.8×10^{-4} M. The V_m was 19.6 pmoles DOPA formed/minute/mg soluble protein. The K_m and V_m values for ethanol-withdrawn mice were 1.9×10^{-4} M and 22.2 pmoles DOPA formed/minute/mg protein, respectively.

One possible explanation for the diminished responsiveness to neuroleptics, and the 'subsensitivity' of dopamine-sensitive adenylate cyclase in the ethanol-withdrawn animals, is that chronic ethanol ingestion reduces the number of dopamine or neuroleptic receptors in the brain of mice. Data in Table 6.4, however, demonstrate that no significant differences were noted in specific binding of haloperidol or spiroperidol to homogenates of striatal or mesolimbic tissues from ethanol-withdrawn and control animals. The lower concentration of neuroleptic used for the binding studies was approximately the K_D value for the neuroleptic as determined by Scatchard analysis and the higher concentration was assumed to be a saturating level of the compound.

Table 6.4: Effect of Chronic Ethanol Treatment on Specific Binding of ^{3}H-Haloperidol and ^{3}H-Spiroperidol in Mouse Brain [a]

| | Neuroleptic Added (nM) | ^{3}H-Neuroleptic Bound (fmol/mg protein) | |
		Control	Ethanol-withdrawn
Striatal Tissue	Spiroperidol (0.2)	29.5± 2.9	26.5± 0.8
	(2.0)	95.0±17.5	102.1±11.1
	Haloperidol (2.0)	66.7±19.2	78.4±11.6
	(8.0)	243.5±73.5	269.3±76.1
Mesolimbic Tissue	Spiroperidol (0.2)	18.1± 1.3	17.2± 1.6
	(2.0)	60.1± 8.6	58.0± 8.5
	Haloperidol (2.0)	18.9	18.2
	(8.0)	270.9	253.4

a. Ethanol-fed animals had been withdrawn from ethanol for 24 hours at the time of sacrifice. Each experiment was performed in sextuplicate and the values represent the mean ± S.D. of three to six experiments. (Haloperidol was used with mesolimbic tissue in only one experiment.) Values for specific binding represent the difference between mean concentrations of spiroperidol bound in the presence of 10^{-7} M (−) and (+)-butaclamol.

Discussion

The behavioural, physiological and biochemical measures used to assess
the function of dopamine systems in ethanol-withdrawn animals
indicated that the chronic consumption of ethanol resulted in a
diminished responsiveness of the dopamine systems to perturbation by
either dopamine agonists or antagonists and other drugs
(e.g. morphine). A diminished responsiveness to both dopamine
agonists and antagonists is difficult to reconcile within the framework
of theories currently being used to explain the development of super-
or subsensitivity in dopaminergic or adrenergic systems of brain
(Creese, Burt and Snyder, 1977; Lekfkowitz, 1978; Seeman, Tedesco,
Lee *et al.*, 1978). The results in Table 6.4 certainly indicate that an
increase or decrease in receptor number is *not* a viable explanation of
the effects produced in the dopamine systems by chronic ethanol
feeding to mice. Although some controversy surrounds any conclusions
based on data which may equate dopamine binding sites associated with
adenylate cyclase activity and neuroleptic binding sites in brain, one
could argue that the lack of difference in neuroleptic binding between
tissue of ethanol-withdrawn and control animals, as noted in the
present studies, would also indicate that changes in receptor number or
affinities are not primarily responsible for the diminished sensitivity of
adenylate cyclase to stimulation by dopamine in the ethanol-
withdrawn animals.

Since the addition of ethanol to biological or artificial membranes
alters the 'fluidity' of such membranes (Seeman, 1972; Chin and
Goldstein, 1976), one should consider that changes in membrane
microenvironments could alter the coupling between the dopamine
receptor and adenylate cyclase, or other intracellular effectors. The
chronic administration of ethanol has, on the other hand, been found
to result in an adaptive change in the composition of neuronal
membranes (Littleton and John, 1977), and such changes would also be
expected to alter protein function within neuronal membranes of the
ethanol-fed animals.

Our recent studies (Tabakoff and Levental, 1979) have clearly
demonstrated membrane dependent changes in the activity of
$(Na\pm K\pm)$ ATPase and the response of this enzyme to ethanol in ethanol-
withdrawn animals as compared with control mice. The changes in
membrane characteristics after chronic administration of ethanol may,
as well, be responsible for changes in the function of the membrane-
bound, dopamine-sensitive adenylate cyclase. In addition, if the
changes in membrane characteristics after chronic ethanol treatment

truly represent an adaptive response in neuronal systems, then such changes should be considered within the context of normal regulatory mechanisms for controlling receptor sensitivities.

When one discusses the coupling between the dopamine receptors and the systems that control the activity of tyrosine hydroxylase, one must not ignore the possibility that such coupling involves, not only the immediate environment of the dopamine receptor, but the function and responsiveness of several interneurons. Both cholinergic and GABA neurons have been postulated to be components of a feedback loop which acts to control striatal tyrosine hydroxylase activity (Perez de la Mora and Fuxe, 1977). Substance P has also been postulated to play an important role in control of dopamine synthesis within the nigrostriatal dopamine system (Hökfelt *et al.*, 1975).

At present, little is known of the effects of chronic ethanol consumption on neuronal systems which use substance P as a neurotransmitter. The chronic administration of ethanol to rodents has, however, been shown to produce an increase in acetylcholine synthesis in various areas of brain after ethanol withdrawal (Hunt and Dalton, 1976) and to produce a decrease in brain GABA levels at certain times after ethanol withdrawal (Sutton and Simmonds, 1973).

If one examines the time course of changes in GABA or acetylcholine levels noted in ethanol-withdrawn animals by other workers (Hunt and Dalton, 1976; Sutton and Simmonds, 1973), one finds that such changes do not well correlate with the time course of changes in the responsiveness of tyrosine hydroxylase to neuroleptics noted in our work. We have, in preliminary studies, however, noted that the response of dopamine neurons of ethanol-withdrawn mice to GABA receptor agonists is significantly less than the response noted in control mice. Such results do indicate that chronic ingestion of ethanol produces changes in the function of neuronal systems that constitute the components of the striato-nigral feedback loop and may explain the ineffectiveness of neuroleptics in altering dopamine synthesis in the ethanol-withdrawn animal.

It has been proposed that the response to high doses of apomorphine represents the effects of this drug at post-synaptic receptors (Strombom, 1975). If one is to accept such a postulate, one would conclude that chronic ethanol treatment and withdrawal results in changes primarily at the post-synaptic dopamine receptors. Such a conclusion would be supported by findings of changes in the responsiveness of dopamine-sensitive adenylate cyclase in the ethanol-withdrawn animals, since the dopamine-sensitive adenylate cyclase activity has been postulated to be primarily located post-synaptically to the dopamine neurons which enter the striatum from the substatia nigra (Kebabian, 1977).

The conclusion that ethanol feeding affects the function of post-synaptic dopamine receptors, and our results with tyrosine hydroxylase, would be in accord with the contention of Zivkovic *et al.* (1975) and Gale *et al.* (1978), that tyrosine hydroxylase activity of the through presynaptic dopamine receptors. However, it is clear from our through pre-synaptic dopamine receptors. However, it is clear from our studies with morphine (see Table 6.3) and GABA agonists, that the function of receptors located directly on the dopamine neuron of the nigro-striatal pathway is also altered. We, at present, hypothesise that changes in the membrane environment of receptors in the ethanol-treated animal represent the mechanism by which receptor function is altered. Since the time course of the changes in receptor function follows the time course for the presence of ethanol tolerance, we postulate a relationship between the two phenomena.

Acknowledgements

This work was supported in part by grants from the National Institute of Alcohol Abuse and Alcoholism (AA 2696), the National Institute of Drug Abuse (DA-2024), the State of Illinois Department of Mental Health and Developmental Disabilities (720), and the National Science Foundation (BNS 76-11779).

S. Urwyler is a Swiss National Science Foundation Fellow.

References

Ahtee, L. and Svarstrom-Fraser, M. (1975), 'Effect of ethanol dependence and withdrawal on the catecholamines in rat brain and heart', *Acta. Pharm. and Toxicol., 36*, 289-98

Chin, J.H. and Goldstein, D.B. (1976), 'Drug tolerance in biomembranes: A spin label study of the effects of ethanol', *Science, 196*, 684-5

Creese, I., Burt, D.R. and Snyder, S.H. (1977), 'Dopamine receptor binding enhancement accompanies lesion-induced behavioural supersensitivity', *Science, 197*, 596-8

Gale, K., Costa, E., Toffano, G., Hong, J.-S. and Guidotti, A. (1978), 'Evidence for a role of nigral gamma-aminobutyric acid and substance P in the haloperidol-induced activation of striatal tyrosine hydroxylase', *J. Pharmacol. Exp. Ther., 206*, 29-37

Goldstein, D.B. (1975), 'Physical dependence on alcohol in mice', *Fed. Proc.,*

34, 1953-61

Gross, M.M., Lewis, E. and Hastey, J. (1974), 'Acute alcohol withdrawal syndrome', in *The Biology of Alcoholism, 3*, Kissin, B. and Begleiter, H. (eds.), Plenum Press, New York, 191-264

Gruber, B., Dinovo, E.C., Noble, E.P. and Tewari, S. (1977), 'Ethanol-induced conformational changes in rat brain microsomal membranes', *Biochem. Pharmacol., 26*, 2181-5

Hoffman, P.L. and Tabakoff, B. (1977), 'Alterations in dopamine receptor sensitivity by chronic ethanol treatment', *Nature, 268*, 551-3

Hökfelt, T., Kellerth, J.O., Nilsson, G. and Pernow, B. (1975), 'Substance P: Localization in the central nervous system and in some primary sensory neurons', *Science, 190*, 889-90

Hunt, G.P. and Overstreet, D.H. (1977), 'Evidence for parallel development of tolerance to the hyperactivating and discoordinating effects of ethanol', *Psychopharmacol., 55*, 75-81

Hunt, W.A. and Dalton, T.K. (1976), 'Regional brain acetylcholine levels in rats acutely treated with ethanol or rendered ethanol dependent', *Brain Res., 109*, 628-31

Hunt, W.A. and Majchrowicz, E. (1974), 'Alterations in the turnover of brain norepinephrine and dopamine in alcohol-dependent rats', *J. Neurochem., 23*, 549-52

Jenner, P., Clow, A., Reavill, C., Theodoron, A. and Marsden, C.D. (1978), 'A behavioral and biochemical comparison of dopamine receptor blockade produced by haloperidol with that produced by substituted benzamide drugs', *Life Sci., 23*, 545-50

Kebabian, J.W. (1977), 'Biochemical regulation and physiological significance of cyclic nucleotides in the nervous system' in *Advances in Cyclic Nucleotide Research, 8*, Greengard, P. and Robinson, G.A. (eds.), Raven Press, New York, 421-508

Kebabian, J.W., Petzold, G.L. and Greengard, P. (1972), 'Dopamine-sensitive adenylate cyclase in caudate nucleus of rat brain and its similarity to the "dopamine receptor"', *Proc. Natl. Acad. Sci., 69*, 2145-9

Lefkowitz, R.J. (1978), 'Identification and regulation of alpha- and beta-adrenergic receptors', *Fed. Proc., 37*, 123-9

Littleton, J.M. and John, G. (1977), 'Synaptosomal membrane lipids of mice during continuous exposure to ethanol', *J. Pharm. Pharmacol., 29*, 579-80

Morgenroth III, V.H., Boadee-Biber, M. and Roth, R.H. (1975), 'Activation of tyrosine hydroxylase from central noradrenergic neurons by calcium', *Molec. Pharmacol., 11*, 427-35

Perez de la Mora, M. and Fuxe, K. (1977), 'Brain GABA, dopamine and acetylcholine interactions. I. Studies with oxotremorine', *Brain Res., 135*, 107-22

Pollard, H., Llorens, C., Schwartz, J.C., Gros, C. and Dray, F. (1978), 'Localization of opiate receptors and enkephalins in the rat striatum in relationship with the nigro-striatal dopaminergic system: Lesion studies', *Brain Res, 151*, 392-8

Ritzmann, R.F. and Tabakoff, B. (1976), 'Body temperature in mice: A quantitative measure of alcohol tolerance and physical dependence', *J. Pharmacol. Exp. Ther., 199*, 158-70

Seeman, P. (1972), 'The membrane actions of anesthetics and tranquillizers', *Pharmacol. Rev., 24*, 583-655

Seeman, P., Tedesco, J.L., Lee, T., Chau-Wong, M., Muller, P., Bowles, J., Whitaker, P.M., McManus, C., Tittler, M., Weinreich, P., Friend, W.C. and Brown, G.M. (1978), 'Dopamine receptors in the central nervous system',

Fed. Proc., 37, 130-6

Strombom, U. (1975), 'On the functional role of pre- and postsynaptic catecholamine receptors in brain', *Acta. Physiol. Scand. Suppl., 431,* 1-43

Sutton, I. and Simmonds, M.A. (1973), 'Effects of acute and chronic ethanol on the gamma-aminobutyric acid system in rat brain', *Biochem. Pharm., 22,* 1685-92

Tabakoff, B. and Hoffman, P.L. (1978), 'Alterations in receptors controlling dopamine synthesis after chronic ethanol administration', *J. Neurochem., 31,* 1223-9

——— (1979), 'Development of functional dependence on ethanol in dopaminergic systems', *J. Pharmacol. Exper. Ther., 208,* 216-22

Tabakoff, B., Hoffman, P.L. and Ritzmann, R.F. (1978), 'Integrated neuronal models for development of alcohol tolerance and dependence,' in *Currents in Alcoholism, 3,* Frank Sexias (ed.), Grune and Stratton, New York, 97-117

Tabakoff, B. and Levental, M. (1979), 'Chronic ethanol feeding alters membrane environment and function of membrane bound enzymes', *Fed. Proc., 30,* 1030

Zivkovic, B., Guidotti, A., Revuelta, A. and Costa, E. (1975), 'Effects of thioridazine, clozapine and other antipsychotics on the kinetic state of tyrosine hydroxylase and on the turnover rate of dopamine in striatum and nucleus accumbens', *J. Pharmacol. Exp. Ther., 194,* 37-46

7 OPIOID PEPTIDES: THEIR ROLE IN DRUG DEPENDENCE

Albert Herz

Introduction

The basic mechanisms underlying addictive processes are, unfortunately, not as yet well understood. This remains true for the opiates, although spectacular progress has been made over the last half decade in this field, in which two central discoveries have immensely improved our understanding of their acute actions. These are the identification of their specific binding sites (receptors) in the central nervous system, followed, a few years later, by the detection of the endogenous (peptide) ligands of the opiate receptors (see Herz, 1978).

These new developments substantially accelerated the rate of research into opiate addiction, since they greatly facilitated our understanding of the biochemical and molecular mechanisms underlying the phenomena of opiate tolerance and dependence.

In the following sections various aspects of these investigations into the relationship between opioid peptides (endorphins) and addiction problems will be discussed. These include: first, the changes in endogenous endorphin levels brought about by continuous occupation of opiate receptors by exogenous ligands; secondly, the dependence liabilities of endorphins (and endorphin derivatives), and the implications of these in view of the possible biological functions of endorphins; and thirdly, the postulated role of endorphins in reward mechanisms, these being of particular interest in view of the psychic dependence phenomena.

Changes in Endorphin Systems After Chronic Opiate Treatment

It is well known from neurotransmitter and hormone studies that the activity of particular mediator systems can be regulated by specific feedback mechanisms. Thus, it has been postulated that the prolonged stimulation of opioid receptors during chronic exposure to opiates might cause a suppression of endorphin synthesis and/or release. One feature of the withdrawal syndrome would then reflect a deficit of endorphins at their receptors after discontinuation of the exogenous

141

opiate supply (Kosterlitz and Hughes, 1975; Goldstein, 1978). It has further been speculated that a considerable length of time may be required before normal function of the endorphin system(s) is (are) re-established, and that this might explain the continuing disturbances of protracted withdrawal.

A number of investigations were undertaken to provide experimental support for this concept. Concerning the enkephalins, several groups were unable to discover significant changes in the enkephalin content of various regions of rat brain after chronic morphine treatment. Further, no differences with respect to controls were seen after naloxone-precipitated withdrawal in these animals (Childers *et al.*, 1977; Fratta *et al.*, 1977; Wesche *et al.*, 1977).

Changes in β-endorphin levels, however, have been recently reported from this laboratory (Höllt *et al.*, 1978a; Przewłocki *et al.*, 1979). Whilst β-endorphin-like immunoreactivity (β-ELI) in brain and pituitary was unchanged in rats after 10 days of opiate treatment, a decrease in β-ELI in the anterior pituitary lobe and in the hypothalamus, accompanied by a considerable increase in β-ELI in the plasma, was observed after naloxone-precipitated withdrawal in these animals. Probably these changes should be regarded as stress phenomena, which do not represent opiate-specific effects.

A quite different pattern of changes was observed when the time of exposure to morphine (implanted as pellets) was prolonged from 10 days to one month or more. There was then a 60 per cent decrease in β-endorphin in the intermediate/posterior lobe of the pituitary, but no significant change in the anterior lobe. A decrease in β-endorphin in some brain areas, e.g. midbrain, and in met-enkephalin in the striatum, was also present after this long-term morphine treatment prior to withdrawal. In this context, it is interesting that an increase in the activity of a high-affinity enkephalin-degrading peptidase in brain has recently been observed after chronic morphine treatment (Malfroy *et al.*, 1978). This finding might at least partially explain the decreased enkephalin levels detected.

It is unlikely that these changes in endorphin levels after prolonged morphine treatment are the results of opiate receptor-coupled feedback inhibition of endorphin synthesis. This conclusion is based on recent experiments in which opiate agonists with high receptor affinity, such as etorphine or levorphanol, were implanted (as pellets) in rats over a period of one month. Although these animals displayed a very high degree of tolerance to morphine, no significant changes in β-endorphin or enkephalin content in brain or pituitary could be found (Wüster *et al.*, 1980). Also, the fact that it was not possible to modulate the potassium-evoked release of met-enkephalin from striatal slices *in vitro* by morphine, and that this release was unchanged in slices from tolerant/dependent rats, does not support the notion that the reduced endorphin levels in chronically morphine-treated rats are a result of feedback inhibition of endorphin synthesis mediated by 'autoreceptors' (Osborne and Herz, 1980).

Changes in endorphin levels in brain and pituitary similar to those observed after chronic morphine treatment were recently observed after chronic exposure of rats and guinea pigs to ethanol: 2-3 weeks after continuous intake of ethanol in the drinking water (ethanol concentration 5-20 per cent), the β-endorphin content of the intermediate/posterior lobe greatly decreased, whereas in the anterior lobe only smaller changes were observed. A decrease in the β-endorphin and met-enkephalin content of particular brain areas was also seen (Schulz *et al.*, in preparation).

The similarities between the changes in endorphin content in pituitary and brain after chronic treatment with morphine and ethanol are striking, although it is not proven that a common mechanism is responsible for the changes effected. It seems improbable that these effects are caused by toxic actions of the drugs. The pronounced changes observed, particularly in the intermediate/posterior pituitary lobe − the release of β-endorphin from this lobe is probably dopamine-modulated (Przewłocki *et al.*, 1979) − and in the striatum, points to an interference with dopaminergic mechanisms. In contrast to morphine and ethanol, a chronic blockade of dopamine receptors by haloperidol increases β-endorphin in the intermediate/posterior pituitary and met-enkephalin in the striatum (Höllt *et al.*, 1980; Hong *et al.*, 1979). For both morphine and ethanol an interference with dopaminergic systems is well established. Whether these effects are directly related to addictive processes has to be shown. The development of methods appropriate to the study of the turnover of various endorphins is also a prerequisite for further inquiries into this question.

Even prior to the discovery of endorphins, Dole and Nyswander (1967) suggested that some type of metabolic disorder may underlie the phenomenon of narcotic addiction. Although the present data could be interpreted in support of such a notion, the specificity of these changes in endorphin levels remains a matter for discussion. Still more difficult to prove is the theory of Goldstein (1978), according to which a genetic deficiency in endorphins might predispose to opiate addiction; this theory postulates that for a given availability of heroin and given conditions of social stress, some individuals will be more vulnerable to addiction than others. The endorphin levels in plasma and CSF of normal human individuals are very low and, in addition, in view of the high cross-reactivity between β-endorphin and β-lipotropin of the β-endorphin antisera available, it is necessary to separate opioid-active and -inactive peptides by chromatographic methods (Höllt *et al.*, 1978b, 1979). Nevertheless, it might eventually be feasible to test whether addicts, post-recovery, have lower endorphin levels in plasma (and cerebrospinal fluid?) than control individuals. No such data are, as yet, available.

Dependence Liability of Endorphins

The detection of the endogenous ligands of the opiate receptors raised the hope that it might be possible to develop analgesic drugs structurally related to endogenous peptides with low (or even lacking) dependence liability. This expectation was based on the notion that compounds normally present in the organism might not induce the adaptive changes underlying tolerance and dependence. Unfortunately, however, this expectation has not been fulfilled. There is now overwhelming evidence that the dependence liability of naturally occurring opiate-like peptides does not differ from those of typical exogenous opiates (Wei and Loh, 1976; Herz *et al.*, 1978; Miglécz *et al.*, 1979).

Clearly, tolerance also develops to endogenously released endorphins. This may be concluded from the observation that the pain relief obtained by electrical stimulation of periventricular brain areas via chronically implanted electrodes in chronic pain patients rapidly diminishes upon repeated stimulation (Hosobuchi *et al.*, 1977). It seems justified to interpret this observation in terms of stimulation-induced release of endorphins and the development of acute tolerance to these endorphins. A rapid development of tolerance (and dependence) is also observed for the inhibitory effect of met-enkephalin when administered microelectrophoretically to single neurones of the rat brain (Fry *et al.*, 1978). Tolerance/dependence seems to develop when synthetic enkephalin analogues are repeatedly applied and tolerance/dependence is tested in the usual way. (A few reports claiming lower dependence liability of particular enkephalin derivatives (Frederickson *et al.*, 1978) should be interpreted with caution until confirmed by further investigations.)

In spite of this scepticism, in view of the concept of the multiplicity of opiate receptors (Martin *et al.*, 1976; Lord *et al.*, 1977), it might be possible to develop opioids with lower dependence liability. It may be that opioid effects mediated by various types of opiate receptors adapt in different ways and/or at a different rate. Thus, it has been shown that the development of tolerance/dependence in the mouse vas deferens – an organ containing mainly presynaptically located 'δ-receptors' – is very low in comparison to that developed by the guinea-pig ileum, a preparation which contains mainly 'μ-receptors' (Schulz *et al.*, 1980).

It has also been shown that some benzomorphanes, which do not substitute for morphine in the dependent monkey, need a higher amount of naloxone for their antagonism than morphine (Hutchinson *et al.*, 1975; Kosterlitz and Hughes, 1975). Since higher amounts of naloxone are necessary to antagonise enkephalins than morphine (Lord *et al.*, 1977), it may be suggested that these benzomorphanes induce their actions via the δ-receptors. It might therefore be productive to search for less addictive opioids – peptides or non-peptides – on the basis of such a concept.

The generally observed dependence liability of naturally occurring endorphins is of interest in view of their putative physiological functions as neurotransmitters/neuromodulators in the central nervous system. The lack of, or at most very discrete effects of, the opiate antagonist, naloxone, when applied to non-opiate-pretreated animals or humans suggests that the endorphinergic systems are not tonically active to a high degree. It seems that such systems become activated under particular circumstances, for instance, under stress or pain. (A significant endorphinergic basal activity, however, seems to regulate the release of prolactin and growth hormone from the pituitary (Grandison and Guidott, 1977; Shaar *et al.*, 1977).)
however, seems to regulate the release of prolactin and growth hormone from the pituitary (Grandison and Guidotti, 1977; Shaar *et al.*, 1977).)

The minimal amounts of endorphins occupying the receptors under 'normal' conditions are evidently unable to induce considerable adaptive changes in these systems. The rapid breakdown, at least of the enkephalins, is in line with this notion. On the other hand, it must be accepted that some changes in the sensitivity of the effector system should be regarded as quite 'physiological', as has been postulated for (other) neurotransmitter systems (Klee, 1978). Such small adaptive changes occurring in particular neuronal systems may be completely different from the situation occurring during massive flooding of the brain by the application of large amounts of opiates over a long period.

Endorphins and Reward

Closely related to the above-mentioned dependence liability of the
endorphins is the fact that these peptides are self-administered in rats
implanted with permanently indwelling intraventricular cannulae (van
Ree *et al.*, 1978; Stein and Belluzzi, 1979). Self-administration is
characteristic for drugs giving rise to the development of psychological
dependence. Thus, the question of the role of endorphins in reward is
closely connected to the addiction problem. In view of this it might be
expected that not only exogenously applied endorphins, but also those
released by an activation of endorphinergic pathways, may be
rewarding. Indeed, a natural physiological role for these substances in
reward is suggested by the experiments performed in our laboratories
(Dum and Herz, 1980).

It was found that the consumption of a preferred food by satiated
rats, an activity primarily motivated by pleasure, can be suppressed by
a moderate dose of the opiate antagonist, naloxone. Furthermore,
certain behavioural changes induced by a rewarding situation, that is, a
decrease in sensitivity to pain and an increase in exploratory behaviour,
can also be reversed or reduced by the same dose of antagonist. In line
with this evidence is the fact that there is a high concentration of
endorphins, particularly enkephalins, in some limbic areas, which also
have a high opiate receptor density, and which are known to be
effective sites for self-stimulation.

Experiments of Stein and Belluzzi (1979) in rats with electrodes
implanted in the central gray, substantia nigra or stria terminals
revealed effective self-stimulation which was antagonised by naloxone.
This gives support to the hypothesis that endorphins are released by
this stimulation. However, block of catecholamine synthesis also
reduced the self-stimulation rate, indicating that catecholaminergic,
probably dopaminergic mechanisms, may also be involved. This is not
surprising in view of various other indications that a close
interrelationship between endorphinergic and dopaminergic
mechanisms exists (see also above). In any case, these results suggest
that the phenomenon of psychological dependence, as observed for
opiates, may be related to a direct, pharmacological effect exerted upon
the natural rewarding processes of the brain.

Acknowledgement

Part of the work was supported by Bundesministerium für Jugend, Familie und Gesundheit.

References

Childers, S.R., Simantov, R. and Snyder, S.H. (1977), 'Enkephalin: Radioimmunoassay and radioreceptorassay in morphine dependent rats', *Europ. J. Pharmacol., 46*, 289-93

Dole, V.P. and Nyswander, M. (1967), 'Heroin-addiction – a metabolic disease', *Arch. int. Med., 120*, 19-24

Dum, J. and Herz, A. (1980) , 'The activation of endorphin(s) by reward' in *Endogenous and Exogenous Opiate Agonists and Antagonists*, Way, E.L. (ed.), Pergamon Press, New York, 431-4

Fratta, W., Yang, H.Y., Hong, J. and Costa, E. (1977), 'Stability of met-enkephalin content in brain structures of morphine dependent or foot shock stressed rats', *Nature, 268*, 452-3

Frederickson, R.C.A., Smithwick, E.L. and Shuman, R. (1978), 'Opioid peptides: Structure activity studies and development of analogues with clinical potential' in *Characteristics and Function of Opioids*, van Ree, J.M. and Terenius, L. (eds.), Elsevier/North-Holland Biomedical Press, Amsterdam, 215-16

Fry, J., Zieglgänsberger, W. and Herz, A. (1978), 'Tachyphylaxis to enkephalin tolerance and dependence at the single neurone level?' in *Iontophoresis and Transmitter Mechanisms in the Mammalian Central Nervous System*, Ryall, R.W. and Kelly, J.S. (eds.), Elsevier/North-Holland Biomedical Press, Amsterdam, 323-5

Goldstein, A. (1978), 'Endorphins: Physiology and clinical implications' in *Recent Developments in Chemotherapy of Narcotic Addiction*, Kissin, B., Lowinson, J.H. and Millman, R.B. (eds.), The New York Academy of Sciences, New York, 49-55

Grandison, L. and Guidotti, A. (1977), 'Regultion of prolactin release by endogenous opiates', *Nature, 270*, 357-9

Herz, A. (1978), in *Developments in Opiate Research*, Herz, A. (ed.), Dekker, New York

Herz, A., Bläsig, J., Fry, J., Schulz, R. and Zieglgänsberger, W. (1978), 'Dependence liability of opiate-like peptides' in *Neuro-Psychopharmacology, 2*, Deniker, P., Radouco-Thomas, C. and Villeneuve, A. (eds.), Pergamon Press, Oxford-New York, 1307-12

Höllt, V., Przewłocki, R. and Herz, A. (1978a), 'β-Endorphin-like immunoreactivity in plasma, pituitaries and hypothalamus of rats following treatment with opiates', *Life Sci., 23*, 1057-66

Höllt, V., Emrich, H.M., Müller, O.A. and Fahlbusch, R. (1978b), 'β-Endorphin-like immunoreactivity (β-ELI) in human plasma and cerebrospinal fluid (CSF)' in *Characteristics and Function of Opioids*, van Ree, J.M. and Terenius, L. (eds.), Elsevier/North-Holland Biomedical Press, Amsterdam, 279-80

Höllt, V., Müller, O.A. and Fahlbusch, R. (1979a), 'β-Endorphin in human plasma: Basal and pathologically elevated levels', *Life Sci., 25*, 37-44

Höllt, V., Przewłocki, R., Bergmann, M., Haarmann, I. and Duka, Th. (1980) 'Increased biosynthesis of β-endorphin in the pars intermedia of rat pituitaries after long-term treatment with haloperidol' in *Endogenous and Exogenous Opiate Agonists and Antagonists*, Way, E.L. (ed.), Pergamon Press, New York, 325-8

Hong, J.S., Yang, H.-Y.T., Gillin, J.C., Fratta, W. and Costa, E. (1979), 'Participation of [met⁵]-enkephalin in the action of antipsychotic drugs' in *Endorphins in Mental Health Research*, Usdin, E., Bunney Jr., W.E. and Kline, N.S. (eds.), Macmillan Press, London, 105-14

Hosobuchi, Y., Adams, J.E. and Linchitz, R. (1977), 'Pain relief by electrical stimulation of the central grey matter in humans and its reversal by naloxone', *Science, 197*, 183-6

Hutchinson, M., Kosterlitz, H.W., Leslie, F.M., Waterfield, A.A. and Terenius, L. (1975), 'Assessment in the guinea-pig ileum and mouse van deferens of benzomorphans which have strong anti-nociceptive activity', *Brit. J. Pharmacol., 55*, 544-7

Klee, W.A. (1978), 'Dual regulation of adenylate cyclase: A biochemical model for opiate tolerance and dependence' in *The Bases of Addiction*, Fishman, J. (ed.), Dahlem Konferenzen, Berlin, 431-40

Kosterlitz, H.W. and Hughes, J. (1975), 'Some thoughts on the significance of enkephalin, the endogenous ligand', *Life Sci., 17*, 91-6

Lord, J.A.H., Waterfield, A.A., Hughes, J. and Kosterlitz, H.W. (1977), 'Endogenous opioid peptides: Multiple agonists and receptors', *Nature, 267*, 495-9

Malfroy, B., Swerts, J.P., Guyon, A., Roques, B.P. and Schwartz, J.C. (1978), 'High-affinity enkephalin-degrading petidase in brain is increased after morphine', *Nature, 276*, 523-6

Martin, W.R., Eades, C.G., Thompson, J.A., Huppler, R.E. and Gilbert, P.E. (1976), 'The effects of morphine- and nalorphine-like drugs in the nondependent and morphine-dependent chronic spinal dog', *J. Pharmacol. exp. Ther., 197*, 517-32

Miglécz, E., Székely, J.I. and Dunai-Kovács, Z. (1979), 'Comparison of tolerance: development and dependence capacities of morphine, β-endorphin, and [D-met², pro⁵]-enkephalinamide', *Psychopharmacology, 62*, 29-34

Osborne, H. and Herz, A. (1980), 'K⁺-evoked release of met-enkephalin from rat striatum in vitro: effect of putative neurotransmitters and morphine', *Naunyn-Schmiedeberg's Arch. Pharmacol., 310*, 203-9

Przewłocki, R., Höllt, V. and Herz, A. (1978), 'Substances modulating the release of β-endorphin-like immunoreactivity (β-ELI) from rat pituitary in vitro' in *Characteristics and Function of Opioids*, van Ree, J.M. and Terenius, L. (eds.), Elsevier/North-Holland Biomedical Press, Amsterdam, 285-6

Przewłocki, R., Höllt, V., Duka, Th., Kleber, G., Gramsch, Ch., Haarmann, I. and Herz, A. (1979), 'Long-term morphine treatment decreases endorphin levels in rat's brain and pituitary', *Brain Res., 174*, 357-61

Schulz, R., Faase, E., Illes, P. and Wüster, M. (1980), 'Development of opiate tolerance/dependence in the guinea-pig myenteric plexus and the mouse van deferens' in *Endogenous and Exogenous Opiate Agonists and Antagonists*, Way, E.L. (ed.), Pergamon Press, New York, 135,138

Shaar, C.J., Frederickson, R.C.A., Dinninger, N.B., Clemens, J.A. and Hull, R.H. (1977), 'Enkephalin analogues and naloxone modulate release of growth hormone and prolactin. Evidence for regulation by an endogenous opioid peptide in brain', *Life Sci., 21*, 853-60

Stein, L. and Belluzzi, J.D. (1979), 'Brain endorphins: Possible mediators of pleasurable states' in *Endorphins in Mental Health Research*, Usdin, E., Bunney Jr., W.E. and Kline, N.S. (eds.), Macmillan Press, London, 375-89

Van Ree, J.M., Dorsa, D.M. and Colpaert, F.C. (1978), 'Neuropeptides and drug

dependence' in *Characteristics and Function of Opioids*, van Ree, J.M. and
Terenius, L. (eds.), Elsevier/North-Holland Biomedical Press, Amsterdam, 1-12
Wei, E. and Loh, H.H. (1976), 'Physical dependence on opiate-like peptides',
Science, 193, 1262-3
Wesche, D., Höllt, V. and Herz, A. (1977), 'Radioimmunoassay of enkephalins.
Regional distribution in rat brain after morphine treatment and
hypophysectomy', *Naunyn-Schmiedeberg's Arch. Pharmacol., 301*, 79-82
Wüster, M., Schulz, R. and Herz, A. (1980). 'Inquiry into endorphinergic
feedback mechanisms during the development of opiate tolerance/dependence',
Brain Res., 189, 403-11

PART TWO

CLINICAL INVESTIGATIONS

8 THE EFFECTS OF ETHANOL ON THE ENDOCRINE SYSTEM

Vincent Marks

Introduction

Few of the endocrine glands escape completely from the pharmacological effects of alcohol. The fact that quite small doses of alcohol can stimulate release of 5-hydroxytryptamine from certain carcinoid tumours has, for example, been recognised for many years, and its ability to stimulate release of calcitonin from medullary carcinomas of the thyroid is sufficiently predictable (Dymling *et al.*, 1976) to make it useful diagnostically.

It is important in any discussion of alcohol to distinguish between those effects produced by small to moderate subinebriating amounts and those produced by large intoxicating doses. Similarly, it is important to differentiate between the acute effects of alcohol in previously healthy subjects and those resulting from long-term alcohol abuse. The latter may produce different effects, depending on whether the abuse is still continuing, as in the drinking alcoholic, or whether it has been discontinued either recently, i.e. in the acutely withdrawn alcoholic, or in the remote past, i.e. in the recovered alcoholic.

Comparatively little of the experimental work carried out on animals, which has recently been reviewed (Marks and Chakraborty, 1973), is immediately relevant to man. The doses used in order to produce changes in endocrine function have generally been excessive and the methods used to assess their effects too crude to be scientifically useful. I will, therefore, draw upon the older literature only when it helps to explain current attitudes and concepts and will utilise, as far as possible, knowledge derived from the study of human subjects under experimental and clinical conditions by modern analytical techniques.

Enteroinsular Axis

In moderate doses, e.g. 50 g, alcohol exaggerates the hypoglycaemic rebound observed in normal healthy subjects following the ingestion of sugary drinks sufficiently, occasionally, to produce neuroglycopenic

153

symptoms (O'Keefe and Marks, 1977; Marks and Wright, 1977). The effect is mediated by a greater rise in plasma insulin produced by the combination of sugar and alcohol than by sugar alone. Alcohol drunk by itself in the amounts used in these experiments, which simulated those of normal alcohol usage, has no effect upon either plasma insulin or blood glucose levels. In large doses, or when taken after a 24-hours or longer fast, it produces a fall in both plasma insulin and blood glucose levels due to inhibition of gluconeogenesis.

When fructose — a non-insulinotropic sugar — is substituted for sucrose in the mixture, there is no significant rise in plasma insulin and consequently no hypoglycaemic rebound (Marks and Wright, 1979). Conversely, increasing the insulinogenic stimulus by raising the concentration and/or amount of sucrose in the mixture, increases the incidence and severity of the hypoglycaemic rebound. Consequently, eating solid food with an alcoholic drink does not necessarily delay or prevent hypoglycaemic rebound unless the meal is either rich in fat and protein and poor in starch content, or contains a large amount of dietary fibre such as celery and little rapidly absorbable carbohydrate (unpublished observations).

Although the initial work on alcohol potentiated reactive hypoglycaemia was performed using virtually pure alcohol and pure sucrose solutions, taken in the form of gin and tonic, there is every reason to believe that all other drinks containing a combination of alcohol and an insulinogenic sugar, such as whisky and ginger ale, rum and Coca Cola, vodka and lime, sweet sherry and port, and some types of beer — especially when drunk mixed with sucrose-rich solutions such as lager and lime — would be equally effective in producing symptomatic reactive hypoglycaemia.

The social, medical and forensic consequences of this newly described syndrome of alcohol-induced reactive hypoglycaemia are far from fully understood. Undoubtedly it contributes to the afternoon malaise occasionally observed following the drinking of even modest amounts of alcohol at lunchtime, especially when taken with only a light snack consisting mainly of starchy foods. Unknown, however, is the importance of alcohol-induced reactive hypoglycaemia in the causation of accidents, either on the road or in the home, through its ability to summate with the intoxicating effects of alcohol. Alcohol-induced reactive hypoglycaemia is probably also important in the genesis of the epidemic of 'non-hypoglycaemia' that has been described in the USA (Yager and Young, 1974) and which is characterised by a feeling of general malaise punctuated by episodes of more acute symptoms resembling those observed during hypoglycaemic attacks in insulin-treated diabetics.

Contrary to expectations, in view of its well-known ability to provoke gastric acid production, alcohol does not stimulate gastrin secretion to any significant extent. It does, however, through its effect on gastric acidity, stimulate secretin secretion (Strauss *et al.*, 1975), but only under circumstances in which intraduodenal or intrajejunal pH falls below 4.0 (Hacki *et al.*, 1978). There is no evidence that alcohol itself has a direct effect upon the secretin-producing cells of the intestinal mucosa, nor does it appear to stimulate secretion of GIP (unpublished observations) currently believed to be the most important mediator of intestinal augmentation of glucose stimulated insulin release. The effect of alcohol on vasoactive intestinal peptide (VIP), motilin, pancreozymin, caerulin, neurotensin, somatostatin, pancreatic polypeptide and glicentin has not been investigated thoroughly, but might be expected to throw some light on the way that alcohol contributes to, or causes, acute and chronic pancreatitis, as well as the mechanism of alcohol-induced reactive hypoglycaemia.

Alcohol does not affect glucagon secretion directly but may do so indirectly by depressing blood glucose levels in fasting, malnourished or dieting subjects, thereby suppressing insulin secretion and removing its inhibitory effect upon glucagon release.

Despite convincing evidence — only briefly alluded to here and dealt with in greater detail elsewhere (Marks, 1978) — that alcohol can, under certain circumstances, produce moderate to severe hypoglycaemia in man through a variety of mechanisms, there is absolutely no evidence that hypoglycaemia predisposes to the drinking of alcohol. The belief that it does has been used as the basis of a chemical theory of alcoholism. According to this theory, a tendency towards the development of hypoglycaemia due to defective adrenocortical function leads to the seeking out and drinking of alcohol in an attempt to restore the blood glucose level to normal (Tintera and Lovell, 1949; Tintera, 1966).

This theory of the causation of alcoholism and other types of debility, is based upon a number of misconceptions. Nevertheless, it has many adherents in the USA and even in this country, and was recently the subject of a joint warning by the American Medical Association, American Diabetes Association and Endocrine Societies (Diabetes, 1973). It is true that alcohol can raise the blood glucose level in normal subjects and experimental animals, but only when consumed in intoxicating amounts in recently well fed individuals. When taken in subinebriating quantities alcohol has no effect on blood sugar levels, and when drunk by fasting, malnourished or carbohydrate-depleted (e.g. dieting) subjects it may cause severe and even fatal hypoglycaemia (Marks, 1978). Adrenal function is not impaired in heavy alcohol users (Wright, 1978) though, due to alterations brought about by heavy alcohol use in metabolic pathways concerned with degradation of biologically active endogenous steroids to inactive ones, there may be quantitative and qualitative changes in urinary steroids which superficially resembled those observed in patients with proven adrenocortical insufficiency. Finally, the adrenocortical preparation, namely adrenocortical extract (ACE), claimed to be specific for replacement of the missing or reduced endogenous steroids is almost biologically inert and, though expensive, serves only as a placebo.

Hypothalamic-pituitary-adrenal AXIS

Whilst there is no evidence that impaired adrenocortical function predisposes to increased alcohol consumption, there is ample evidence that alcohol can affect adrenocortical function. Small to moderate doses of alcohol have no consistent effect upon adrenocortical activity in healthy human subjects, but in large doses it activates cortisol release, probably through stimulation of regulatory centres in the hypothalamus and above. The stimulation is, however, almost certainly an indirect effect of intoxication rather than caused by alcohol itself, as it is not observed in alcohol-tolerant subjects given similar amounts of alcohol to those that are stimulatory in naive subjects.

In a small proportion of cases chronic alcohol consumption is associated with the appearance of Cushing's syndrome due to adrenocortical hyperfunction (Rees *et al.*, 1977; Smals *et al.*, 1977). Morning plasma cortisol levels are raised and are not suppressed normally after overnight dexamethasone administration. Diurnal plasma cortisol rhythms are disturbed and urinary free cortisol excretion is increased, though not to as great an extent as the plasma cortisol levels and clinical severity of the disease would lead one to expect. Urinary 17-oxogenic steroids are usually normal or only moderately increased and 17-oxosteroids (previously known as 17-ketosteroids) are generally normal or low. Plasma ACTH levels are inappropriately high in the presence of hypercortisolaemia, but are rarely raised to levels as high as would be expected if excessive pituitary ACTH secretion was the sole cause of the adrenal hyperfunction.

Differentiation from other types of Cushing's syndrome, especially the so-called idiopathic, hypophyseal or hypothalamic variety, may be difficult, but once suspicion has been aroused other evidence of excessive alcohol use, such as an increase in red cell size, raised plasma levels of urate, triglyceride, alphalipoprotein, aspartate transferase and gamma-glutamyl transferase, can generally be found. The most telling point, however, is that alcohol-induced Cushing's syndrome remits completely on withdrawal of the patient from alcohol, though many of the physical stigmata persist for weeks or even months after the event.

It is unknown why Cushing's syndrome is seemingly so rare amongst heavy alcohol users, since morning plasma cortisol levels are generally high or very high in heavy drinkers even though, in complete contrast to those of normal subjects, they tend to fall, instead of rising, following the ingestion of 100 g of alcohol on an empty stomach (Merry and Marks, 1972). This difference in behaviour could constitute the basis of a laboratory test for detection of potentially harmful chronic alcohol abuse, although the unpleasant side effects experienced by non-alcoholic subjects given this amount of alcohol tends to limit its usefulness.

There is no evidence that primary adrenocortical insufficiency is commoner amongst heavy alcohol users than in the general population, although in upwards of 25 per cent of chronic alcoholics admitted to hospital for rehabilitation there is evidence of defective hypothalamic-pituitary-adrenocortical activation in response to insulin-induced hypoglycaemia (Wright, 1978; Chalmers *et al.*, 1978). In a small proportion of cases the abnormality is sufficiently profound to produce symptoms attributable to secondary adrenocortical insufficiency — the alcoholic aetiology of which may go completely unnoticed unless specifically sought (Steer *et al.*, 1969). The impairment of stress-stimulated hypothalamic-pituitary-adrenocortical activity undoubtedly contributes to the pathogenesis of alcohol-induced fasting hypoglycaemia and possibly also accounts for some of the sudden unexplained deaths in chronic alcoholics.

Older work purporting to delineate adrenocortical function in heavy alcohol users was based mainly on urinary steroid measurements which modern analytical techniques have shown to be virtually worthless. There is more or less general agreement that in the main, chronic alcoholics excrete smaller amounts of total 17-oxosteroids than age-matched controls. It is now almost certain that this is due to changes in the metabolism of their precursors in the liver rather than to a reduction in the total amount of steroids produced by the adrenal glands. Drinking male alcoholics, for example, were found to excrete significantly smaller amounts of 3α-hydroxy-5α-androstane-17-one (androsterone) than normal subjects, but normal amounts of 3α-hydroxy-5β-androstane-17-one (aetiocholanolone). The ratio of urinary 5α to 5β C_{19}-steroids was reduced by 50 per cent in drinking alcoholics compared with normal subjects. This was not observed in abstinent alcoholics but was matched by a similar reduction in adult epileptic patients on anticonvulsant drugs, suggesting that hepatic enzyme induction, whatever its cause, might be responsible for the changes in urinary steroid pattern observed (Seddon, 1974).

Though similar findings were reported by Farmer and Fabre (1975), they are difficult to reconcile with observations made on rat livers and on hepatic biopsies from men, that steroid A-ring 5α-reductase activity is *increased* by alcohol pre-treatment (Gordon and Southren, 1977). Such a reduction would be expected to produce an increase in 5α:5β-C_{19} steroid ratio rather than the decrease observed. One explanation for the apparent discrepancy is that the changes observed in chronic alcoholics are due to incipient cirrhosis in which the urinary 5α:5β ratio is decreased, rather than to changes brought about by alcohol *per se*. This explanation is unlikely, however, at least in the cases studied by Seddon (1974) in which evidence of hepatic damage was scanty or absent.

Whether the alterations in the catabolism of adrenal (and, incidentally, of testicular and ovarian) steroids produced by alcohol are important in the pathogenesis of Cushing's syndrome, feminisation and virilism, previously attributed almost exclusively to liver damage, is still unknown but clearly warrants further investigation as does the mechanism of their production.

Pituitary-thyroidal Axis

Animals rendered hypothyroid by drugs or by thyroidectomy increase their intake of alcohol voluntarily, whilst those rendered hyperthyroid consume less alcohol than their respective untreated controls. These observations, which have not gone unchallenged, prompted studies of thyroid function in chronic alcoholics and led to the description by a single author of a remarkably high incidence of hypothyroidism amongst two different groups of patients. Subsequent investigations using more reliable diagnostic methods have, however, consistently failed to find evidence of thyroid dysfunction in chronic alcoholics, whether they are still actively drinking or dried out (Loosen and

Prange, 1977; Wright, 1978).

Serum triiodothyronine levels are not infrequently low (less than 1.2 nmol/l) in actively drinking alcoholics but return rapidly to normal within a week of alcohol withdrawal (Wright, 1978). These low levels probably represent no more than the general, non-specific reduction in plasma triiodothyronine levels often observed in chronically ill people, possibly due to impaired peripheral conversion from thyroxine, the plasma concentration of which is almost invariably normal. The conclusion seems inescapable that thyroid function, almost uniquely amongst endocrine functions, is neither disturbed by chronic alcohol abuse nor a contribution to its pathogenesis.

Prolactin

The secretion of prolactin and TSH by the pituitary gland are interrelated, though the precise nature of the connection is still obscure. Plasma prolactin levels are often raised in hypothyroid patients and returned to normal on restoration of euthyroidism by thyroxine replacement therapy. Thyrotrophin-releasing hormone (TRH) stimulates the secretion of both TSH and prolactin, though not necessarily to the same extent in all situations, and other, still unknown, factors must modulate the responses observed in the two pituitary hormones. Moderate (50 g) doses of alcohol taken orally, for example, produce a rise in plasma prolactin, but not of TSH levels, in a small proportion of normal subjects (unpublished observations). Similar doses of alcohol produce no prolactin response in regular drinkers. The reason for these differences is not known.

In our own case material of recently admitted chronic alcoholic patients without overt evidence of liver disease or gynaecomastia, 5 out of 41 had raised plasma prolactin levels, i.e. above 500 mU/l, an incidence resembling that reported by Majumdar (1979) in a series of 10 similar patients.

The relevance or clinical significance of the hyperprolactinaemia is unknown, but it is tempting to link it with the well-known occurrence of impotence in alcoholic men and irregularity of menstruation in women. At present there is little evidence to support the suggestion (Williams, 1976) that the association between long-continued alcohol ingestion and an increased occurrence of breast cancer in women might be due to stimulation of prolactin secretion through the reserpine-like action of alcohol on dopaminergic centres in the hypothalamus.

Hypothalamic-pituitary-growth-hormone Activity

Small doses of alcohol have no effect on plasma growth hormone in normal healthy subjects, but larger inebriating (e.g. 100 g) doses do cause a rise in plasma growth hormone, though not to as high levels as might be expected in view of the 'stress' experienced. Of greater interest than the dissociation between 'stress' and growth hormone is the ability of quite modest amounts of alcohol acutely to attenuate plasma growth hormone responses to hypoglycaemic or arginine stimulation in healthy volunteer subjects. The mechanism is still unknown (Wright, 1978), but probably involves inhibition of the hypothalamic centres responsible for regulating growth hormone release.

Plasma growth hormone levels are generally normal in recently withdrawn alcoholic subjects despite their frequently obvious clinical distress. The possibility that this might be due to an inhibitory effect of long-term alcohol ingestion on growth hormone regulatory centres in the hypothalamus is supported by observations that in a series of 24 recently abstinent men, 9 had absent or impaired growth hormone responses to insulin-induced hypoglycaemia (Chalmers *et al.*, 1978). Many of these latter subjects also failed to produce the expected rises in plasma cortisol and prolactin that occur in response to insulin-induced hypoglycaemia, suggesting the existence of a more general impairment of hypothalamic-pituitary function in chronic alcoholic subjects than is often recognised. Evidence that recovery of hypothalamic-pituitary function can occur after prolonged abstinence from alcohol is currently confined to a few observations (Merry and Marks, 1972; Andreani *et al.*, 1976) mainly because it has not been more widely sought.

Hypothalmic-pituitary-gonadal Function

This is at the same time one of the most important and most confused areas of interest in the endocrinology of alcoholism, and it has already attracted a large and often conflicting literature (Editorial, 1974; Editorial, 1976). Impotence in men and sexual dysfunction in women are amongst the commonest of the psychosomatic symptoms experienced by alcoholics; yet the biological causes are still poorly understood. One of the main reasons for this has been the difficulty of separating abnormalities of sexual endocrine function caused by liver disease from those due to alcohol *per se*.

It has long been recognised that the hormonal and spermatogenic functions of the testis are both impaired in chronic alcoholic subjects suffering from alcohol-induced liver disease. In the absence of chronic liver disease, however, long continued heavy alcohol usage has seemingly little adverse effect on either modality of testicular function. Plasma testosterone levels, whether measured by radioimmunoassay or by competitive protein binding as 17-hydroxyandrogens, are generally normal or high in non-cirrhotic alcoholic subjects compared with non-alcoholic controls (Wright, 1978). One explanation for the occasional high plasma testosterone level observed in such individuals is that it is due to an increase in plasma sex hormone-binding globulin secondary to chronic alcohol ingestion thereby producing a change in the bound to free ratio of testosterone rather than a genuine hyperandrogenism. Another possible explanation is that high plasma testosterone levels represent a rebound from previously depressed or 'compensated' normal levels present during the period of active heavy drinking (Kricka and Clark, 1979). Support for this latter suggestion comes from the observation that plasma LH levels are often raised in drinking alcoholics (Wright *et al.*, 1976) and rise excessively in response to exogenous gonadotrophin-releasing hormones (LH-RH).

The acute ingestion of large doses of alcohol by normal volunteers has been reported to depress plasma testosterone levels (Gordon *et al.*, 1976; Dotson *et al.*, 1975; Ylikahri *et al.*, 1974), but this has not been universally observed even by the same investigators on different occasions (Ylikahri *et al.*, 1978). In one series of experiments, for example, the ingestion of large doses of alcohol by normal volunteers was followed by a small fall in plasma testosterone concentration accompanied by a slight, presumably compensatory, rise in plasma LH levels (Mendelson *et al.*, 1977). On the other hand, in rats, which have relatively high and easily measurable basal LH levels, large doses of alcohol produce a temporary but quite dramatic fall in plasma LH, which is accompanied by an almost equally profound, and presumably secondary, fall in plasma testosterone (Symons and Marks, 1975; Cicero, 1977). Whether the differences in the response to alcohol in rats and in man represent genuine species differences or merely differences in experimental design awaits elucidation.

Currently our own view on the likely sequence of events in man is that long continued heavy alcohol use produces a primary depression in testicular testosterone production and secretion — and possibly a reduction in the ratio of free to protein bound testosterone in the plasma — leading, in the initial stages, to a compensatory increase in hypothalamic-pituitary LH secretion and increased sensitivity to exogenous LH-RH. Later, possibly as a result of a direct effect of alcohol on hypothalamic centres, the adenohypophysis no longer secretes sufficient LH to maintain plasma testosterone levels within the normal range, and evidence of hypogonadism begins to appear. The clinical picture can alter markedly at any time through superimposition of changes brought about by liver damage and which have, in many earlier studies, done so much to obscure the primary effects of alcohol on hypothalamic-pituitary-gonadal function in man.

Acute alcohol administration has no significant effect upon basal FSH levels in healthy men (Leppalusto *et al.*, 1975). In chronic alcoholic male subjects plasma FSH levels are generally normal, but may be raised in the presence (Van Thiel *et al.*, 1974) or even absence (Wright *et al.*, 1976) of liver damage. These observations are consistent with the known fecundity of chronic alcoholics, which may, however, turn to sterility when liver damage supervenes, or even earlier if impotence becomes a factor.

Information relating to hypothalamic-pituitary-gonadal function in alcoholic women is sparse and almost impossible to disentangle from the changes wrought by superimposed liver disease, social and psychological disturbances and the menopause. What scanty information is available suggests that a condition not unlike that observed in men can occur. It has, however, recently been reported that in healthy, non-alcoholic women moderately large doses of alcohol (1 g/kg body wt) had no effect on the plasma concentration of any of the ovarian or pituitary sexual hormones (McNamee *et al.*, 1979).

Sympathetico-adrenomedullary Function

There is ample evidence from experiments on animals and both experimental and clinical observations in man that intoxicating doses of alcohol activate sympathetico-adrenomedullary activity (Marks and Chakraborty, 1973). What is much less certain, however, is whether smaller subinebriating doses, or chronic alcohol abuse, have similar effects. Very few studies have been made using modern analytical techniques with the requisite sensitivity and specificity to detect small but significant changes in plasma adrenaline and noradrenaline levels. One such study, using an isotope derivatisation technique with chromatographic separation of adrenaline and noradrenaline, which was carried out in our own laboratory, revealed that alcohol given on an empty stomach to healthy volunteers in doses sufficient to raise blood alcohol levels to 0.5-1.0 g/l had no effect upon plasma adrenaline and only a small, clinically unimportant stimulatory effect on plasma noradrenaline levels unless the subjects experienced symptoms of alcoholic intoxication. Under these circumstances the plasma levels of both catecholamines rose dramatically.

Indirect evidence of the failure of subinebriating doses of alcohol to activate the sympathetico-adrenomedullary system comes from the well-known ability of alcohol to depress rather than to elevate plasma non-esterified fatty acid (NEFA) levels (an extremely sensitive indicator of sympathetic nervous activity) and its failure to produce a rise in blood glucose concentration or pulse rate when drunk in socially acceptable but still euphoric amounts. Indeed, it has been suggested that small doses of alcohol can, by allaying the concern occasioned by the undertaking of anxiety-provoking tests, actually reduce sympathetico-adrenomedullary activity.

Catecholamine production is markedly increased by alcoholic inebriation as well as by alcohol withdrawal. There do, however, appear to be a certain number of chronic alcoholics — 2 out of 12 in our own series (Wright, 1978) — who show no sympathetico-adrenomedullary response to insulin-induced hypoglycaemia, suggesting that hypothalamic depression noted in respect of growth hormone and ACTH secretion might also extend to the autonomic nervous system. Such individuals might be especially at risk when subjected to unusually stressful situations. Suppression of sympathetico-adrenomedullary activation by alcohol is not confined to chronic alcohol users, however. Quite modest amounts of alcohol prevent the normal homeostatic restoration of blood glucose to normal following its experimental depression by exogenous insulin, and a combination of alcohol and exercise in the cold can lead to severe and potentially dangerous hypoglycaemia in perfectly healthy normal volunteers (Marks, 1978).

Conclusions relating to sympathetico-adrenomedullary function in alcoholics based on urinary analysis are complicated by the fact that alcohol alters the metabolism of the catecholamines through changes in redox potential in the liver, with the result that urinary excretion of 3-methoxy-4-hydroxy mandelic acid (HMMA; VMA), the normal major product of adrenaline and noradrenaline catabolism, decreases and is accompanied by a corresponding increase in 3-methoxy-4-

hydroxy-phenylglycol (MOPG) excretion (Ogata *et al.*, 1971; Akhter
et al., 1978).

Other Endocrine Systems

There is clear evidence that alcohol can alter the metabolism of
calcium, water, magnesium and other electrolytes, possibly through an
effect on the endocrine glands concerned with their regulation. It also
has a profound effect upon the secretion, synthesis and catabolism of
a number of neurotransmitters (Littleton, 1978), and of intracellular
'second-messengers'. Indeed, this may be the agency through which
the manifold actions of alcohol on endocrine systems are exerted. In
this contribution consideration is given only to the possible role of
cyclic adenosine monophosphosphate (cAMP) in mediating alcohol-
induced changes in endocrine function, since it is well known to be
important in regulating hormone release from a number of the
ductless glands.

Cyclic AMP

Ethanol has been reported to elevate cytoplasmic cAMP levels in
several tissues including thyroid, intestine, liver, pancreas and brain.
In the islets of Langerhans, studied *in vitro*, ethanol (Kuo *et al.*, 1973)
had a relatively greater effect on the rate of cyclic AMP synthesis at
low than at high concentrations. This fits well with observations made,
in vivo, that ethanol augments the insulinotropic effects of glucose
only between relatively narrow concentration limits that coincide
with those achieved during moderate but not heavy drinking (Kuhl
et al., 1976). The mechanisms generally proposed for the increase in
tissue cAMP produced by alcohol is activation of adenylate cyclase.
Nevertheless, though not yet demonstrated *in vitro*, inhibition of
phosphodiesterase — the enzyme system responsible for inactivation
of cAMP — remains a possibility, especially since changes in cyclic
nucleotide metabolism are not confined to the effects of alcohol upon
cAMP. In rats, for example (Mailman *et al.*, 1978), alcohol caused a
dose-dependent decline in cerebellar guanosine-3'5'-monophosphate
(cGMP) that could be prevented by administration of thyrotrophin-
releasing hormone (THR). Cyclic AMP, on the other hand, was
unaffected. In man 50 g alcohol produced a significant fall in the

plasma cAMP level but caused a small but significant rise in plasma cGMP (Wright *et al.*, 1979). Moreover, it enhanced the rise in plasma cAMP produced by glucagon but reduced the effect produced by bovine parathyroid hormone (PTH).

Clearly, therefore, much more experimental work must be done before the demonstrable effects of alcohol on cyclic nucleotide metabolism can be synthesised into a unifying theory to explain the diverse effects of alcohol on endocrine functions, if indeed this is the mechanism through which it works. Nevertheless, it remains an intriguing possibility and one we are actively pursuing.

References

Akhter, M.I., Clark, P.M.S., Kricka, L.J. and Nicholson, G. (1978), 'Urinary metabolites of tryptophan, serotonin and norepinephrine', *Journal of the Study of Alcoholism, 39*, 833-41

Andreani, D., Tamburrano, G., Javicoli, M. (1976), 'Alcohol hypoglycemia: hormonal changes', in *Hypoglycemia: Proceedings of the European Symposium, Rome*, Andreani, D., Lefebvre, D. and Marks, V. (eds.), Thieme, Stuttgart, 99-105

Chalmers, R.J., Bennie, E.H., Joynson, R.H. and Masterton, G. (1978), 'Growth hormone, prolactin and corticosteroid responses to insulin hypoglycaemia in alcoholics', *British Medical Journal, 1*, 745-8

Cicero, T.J. (1977), 'A comparative analysis of the acute and chronic effects of alcohol, the barbiturates and narcotics on several endocrine systems in *Alcohol Intoxication and Withdrawal*', Gross, M.M. (ed.), *Experimental Studies, IIIb*, Plenum Press, New York, 95

Diabetes (1973), 'Statement on hypoglycemia', *Diabetes, 22*, 137

Dotson, L.E., Robertson, L.S. and Tuckfeld, B. (1975), 'Plasma alcohol, smoking, hormone concentrations and self-reported aggression', *Journal of the Study of Alcoholism, 36*, 578-86

Dymling, J.F., Ljungberg, O., Hillyard, C.J., Greenberg, P.B., Evans, I.M.A. and MacIntyre, I. (1976), 'Whisky: A new provocative test for calcium secretion', *Acta Endocrinologica, 82*, 500-9

Editorial (1974), 'Sex and alcohol', *The New England Journal of Medicine, 291*, 251-3

———— (1976), 'Sex and alcohol: a second peek', *The New England Journal of Medicine, 295*, 835-6

Farmer, R.W. and Fabre, L.F. (1975), 'Some endocrine aspects of alcoholism', in *Advances in Experimental Medicine and Biology (Biochemical Pharmacology of Ethanol), 56*, Majchrowcia, E. (ed.), Plenum Press, London, 277

Gordon, G.G., Altman, K., Southren, A.L., Rubin, E. and Lieber, C.S. (1976), 'Effect of alcohol (ethanol) administration on sex hormone metabolism in normal man', *The New England Journal of Medicine, 295*, 793-7

Gordon, G.G. and Southren, A.L. (1977), 'Metabolic effects of alcohol on the endocrine system', in *Metabolic Aspects of Alcoholism*, Lieber, C.S. (ed.), MTP, Lancaster, 249-302

Hacki, W.H., Greenberg, G.R. and Bloom, S.R. (1978), 'Role of secretin in man' in *Gut Hormones*, Bloom, S.R. (ed.), Churchill-Livingstone, Edinburgh, 182-92

Kricka, L.J. and Clark, P.M.S. (1979), *Biochemistry of Alcohol and Alcoholism*, Ellis Horwell, Chichester

Kuhl, C., Andersen, O., Jensen, S.L. and Nielsen, O.V. (1976), 'Effect of ethanol on glucose-mediated insulin release in triply catheretized anaesthetized pigs', *Diabetes, 25*, 752-7

Kuo, W.-N., Hodsgins, D.S. and Kuo, J.F. (1973), 'Adenylate cyclase in islets of Langerhans', *The Journal of Biological Chemistry, 248*, 2705-11

Leppaluoto, J., Rapeli, M., Varis, R. and Ranta, T. (1975), 'Secretion of anterior pituitary hormones in man: effects of ethyl alcohol', *Acta. Psysiologica Scandinavika, 95*, 400-6

Littleton, J.L. (1978), 'Alcohol and neurotransmitters', in *Clinics in Endocrinology and Metabolism: Metabolic Effects of Alcohol*, Marks, V. and Wright, J. (eds.), Saunders, Eastbourne, 369-84

Loosen, P.T. and Prange, A.J. (1977), 'Alcohol and anterior pituitary secretion', *Lancet, 2*, 985

McNamee, B., Grant, J., Ratcliffe, J., Ratcliffe, W. and Oliver, J. (1979), 'Lack of effect of alcohol on pituitary-gonadal hormones in women', *British Journal of Addiction, 74*, 316-17

Mailman, R.B., Frye, G.D., Mueller, R.A. and Breese, G.R. (1978), 'Thyrotropin-releasing hormone reversal of ethanol-induced decreases in cerebellar cGMP', *Nature, 272*, 832-3

Majumdar, S.K. (1979), 'Serum prolactin in chronic alcoholics', *The Practitioner, 222*, 693-5

Marks, V. and Chakraborty, J. (1973), 'The clinical endocrinology of alcoholism', *Journal of Alcoholism, 8*, 94-103

Marks, V. (1978), 'Alcohol and carbohydrate metabolism', *Clinics in Endocrinology and Metabolism, 7*, 333-49

Marks, V. and Wright, J.W. (1977), 'Endocrinological and metabolic effects of alcohol', *Proceedings of the Royal Society of Medicine, 70*, 337-48

——— (1980), 'Alcohol provoked reactive hypoglycaemia', in *Current Views on Hypoglycemia and Glucagon; Second European Symposium*, Andreani, D., Lefebevre, P.J. and Marks, V. (eds.), Academic Press, London, 283-95

Mendelson, J.H., Mello, N.K. and Ellingboe, J. (1977), 'Effects of acute alcohol intake on pituitary-gonadal hormones in normal human males', *Journal of Pharmacology and Experimental Therapeutics, 206*, 676-82

Merry, J. and Marks, V. (1972), 'The effect of alcohol, barbiturate, and diazepam on hypothalamic-pituitary-adrenal function in chronic alcoholics', *Lancet, 2*, 990-1011

Ogata, M., Mendelson, J.H., Mello, N.K. and Majchrowicz, E. (1971), 'Adrenal function and alcoholism. II. Catecholamines', *Psychosomatic Medicine, 33*, 159-80

O'Keefe, S.J. and Marks, V. (1977), 'Lunchtime gin and tonic; a cause of reactive hypoglycaemia', *Lancet, 1*, 1286

Rees, L.H., Besser, G.M., Jeffocate, W.J., Goldie, D.J. and Marks, V. (1977), 'Alcohol-induced pseudo Cushing's syndrome', *Lancet 1*, 726-8

Seddon (1974), 'Urinary steroid profiles with special reference to chronic alcoholism', MSc Thesis, University of Surrey

Smals, A.G.H., Njo, K.T., Knoben, J.M., Ruland, C.M., Kloppenborg, P.W.C. (1977), 'Alcohol-induced Cushingoid syndrome', *Journal of the Royal College of Physicians, 12*, 36-41

Steer, P., Marnell, R. and Werk, E.E. (1969), 'Clinical alcohol hypoglycemia and isolated adrenocorticotrophic hormone deficiency', *Annals of Internal*

Medicine, 71, 343-8

Strauss, E., Urbach, H.J. and Yalow, R.S. (1975), 'Alcohol stimulated secretion of immunoreactive secretin', *The New England Journal of Medicine, 293*, 1031-2

Symons, A.M. and Marks, V. (1975), 'The effects of alcohol on weight gain and the hypothalamic-pituitary-gonadotrophin axis in the maturing male rat', *Biochemical Pharmacology, 24*, 955-8

Tintera, J.W. and Lovell, H.W. (1949), 'Endocrine treatment of alcoholism', *Geriatrics, 4*, 274-80

Tintera, J.W. (1966), 'Stabilizing homeostasis in the recovered alcoholic through endocrine therapy: evaluation of the hypoglycemia factor', *Journal of the American Geriatrics Society, 14*, 126-50

Van Thiel, D.H., Lester, R. and Sherins, R.J. (1974), 'Hypogonadism in alcoholic disease: evidence for a double defect', *Gastroenterology, 67*, 1188-99

Williams, R.R. (1976), 'Breast and thyroid cancer and malignant melanoma promoted by alcohol-induced pituitary secretion of prolactin', T.S.H. and M.S.H., *Lancet, 1*, 996-9

Wright, J. (1978), 'Endocrine effect of alcohol', *Clinics in Endocrinology and Metabolism, 7*, 351-67

Wright, J.W., Fry, D.E., Merry, J.W. and Marks, V. (1976), 'Abnormal hypothalamic-pituitary-gonadal function in chronic alcoholics', *British Journal of Addiction, 71*, 211-15

Wright, J., Wood, P.J. and Marks, V. (1979), 'The effect of alcohol on plasma and urinary cyclic AMP and on the cyclic AMP response to glucagon in man' (Abstract), *Annals of Clinical Biochemistry, Supplement 1*, 27

Yager, J. and Young, R.T. (1974), 'Non-hypoglycemia is an epidemic condition', *The New England Journal of Medicine, 291*, 907-8

Ylikhari, R., Huttunen, M., Harkonen, M., Seuderling, V., Onikki, S., Karonen, S.L. and Adlercreutz, H. (1974), 'Low plasma testosterone values in men during hangover', *Journal of Steroid Biochemistry, 5*, 655-60

Ylikahri, R.H., Huttunen, M.O., Harkonen, M., Leino, T., Helenius, T., Liewendahl, K. and Karonen, S.-L. (1978), 'Acute effects of alcohol on anterior pituitary secretion of the tropic hormones', *Journal of Clinical Endocrinology and Metabolism, 46*, 715-20

9 IMPAIRMENTS OF THE NERVOUS SYSTEM IN ALCOHOLICS

Vladimir Hudolin

Introduction

Diagnosing alcoholism may be difficult, but diagnosing different organic neurological syndromes complicating alcoholism is much easier — only first one must define them. For many years we have tried to measure objectively, describe and diagnose clinically certain neurological impairments in alcoholics, particularly brain damage. In this chapter some of our investigations will be reported. The following investigations will be described:

(1) As far back as 1962 we published the results of a study of 161 alcoholics using pneumoencephalography (Hudolin, Vi., 1962). Since that time we have continued our studies, using pneumoencephalography, electroencephalography, gammaencephalography, echoencephalography and computerised axial tomography (Hudolin, Vi., 1967; Hudolin Vi., and Kryzanovski, 1977).

(2) Since 1 January 1965, we have been studying cases of alcoholism admitted for treatment to our department, or to other psychiatric hospitals and psychiatric services in general hospitals in the Socialist Republic of Croatia, in an attempt to identify the main characteristics of the alcoholic disease and to evaluate our therapeutic and rehabilitation programmes. We have examined computerised registers of all alcoholics hospitalised in Croatia between 1 January 1965 and 1 January 1977.

(3) Also, we have made a detailed examination of the computerised data of all patients treated in our Department for Neurology, Psychiatry, Alcoholism and Other Dependencies in Zagreb in the course of 1978, who had alcoholism recorded as a diagnosis on discharge from the department, regardless of the nature of the primary disease for which they were admitted.

The starting assumption in our work was that alcoholism, when clinically diagnosed, is a form of encephalopathy caused by metabolic disorders and partly also due to the direct effects of alcohol on the

168

tissues. The hypersensitivity to alcohol of persons suffering from the post-traumatic cerebral syndrome is very much like the hypersensitivity to alcohol shown by patients in the advanced stages of the alcoholic disease. The hypersensitivity is seen first of all in the symptoms of heavy intoxication after the intake of even small amounts of alcohol (with a rapid depressive effect on the brain) and in the almost universal inability of alcoholic patients to control the amounts of alcohol drunk. This inability persists for a long time or permanently.

Our most recent studies have not, admittedly, been directed primarily to the study of the clinical picture of alcoholic brain damage. We have tried rather to evaluate our therapeutic procedures and test our medical model of approach to the control of alcoholism and to the difficulties in general related to alcohol consumption. We have looked for answers to the following questions:

(1)   What is the incidence and what are the types of clinical pictures pointing to major cerebral impairment in alcoholics?
(2)   What is the effectiveness (established on the basis of evaluation) of the medical model of approach to the control of alcoholism and other disturbances related to alcohol consumption?
(3)   What is the most effective programme of prevention of alcohol-related problems?

Pneumoencephalographic Studies of Alcoholics

Both pneumoencephalographic and post-mortem examinations of alcoholics show that the damage to the brain is most frequently linked with cerebral atrophy. The question arises, as to what extent the rehabilitation of individual serious cases can be achieved, when it is known that in the course of time alcoholism produces in many cases irreversible lesions in different organs and especially in the central nervous system.

We approached the investigation of pneumoencephalographic aspects of brain lesions in alcoholics with the aim of ascertaining its significance in practical clinical work. The brain lesions caused by alcoholism are closely allied to the concept of alcoholic encephalopathy. Wernicke (1881) in his *Textbook of Neurology* gave the classical pathological-anatomical description of the syndrome which has been named after him. Korsakow from 1887 to 1890 published his papers about the disease which bears his name (Benedek and Juba, 1944). Many authors describe in detail the pathological anatomy of alcoholic brain lesions (Benedek and Juba, 1944; Boudin *et al.*, 1959; Courville, 1955; Delay *et al.*, 1956; Delay *et al.*, 1959; Enkin, 1957; Gamper, 1928; Gudden, 1896; Guillain *et al.*, 1939; Gullotta and Mazzoleni, 1959; Huber, 1954; Környey and Saethre, 1937; Lapresle and Claz, 1959; Marchiafava and Bignami, 1903; Menzi, 1955).

Marchiafava and Bignami (1903) described necrosis of the corpus callosum in chronic alcoholics, Morel (1939) and Morel and Dunman (1940) described the 'laminar cortical sclerosis of alcoholics', and later niacin encephalopathy was described by Jolliffe (1940) and Jolliffe *et al.* (1940). After that, cerebellar atrophies of alcoholics were described more frequently (Alajouanine *et al.*, 1959a). Individual authors have described pneumoencephalographic aspects of alcoholic encephalopathy as a casual finding or as a result of systematic investigations (Meyer, 1930; Flügel, 1932 in the earlier literature and Pluvinage, 1954; Lereboullet, 1957; Lereboullet and Pluvinage, 1956; Lereboullet *et al.*, 1954, 1956a, b, 1959; Postel and Cossa, 1956; Tumarkin *et al.*, 1955, more recently). In addition, alcoholism has national characteristics and for this reason national groups of alcoholics should be investigated, as some others have done (Greenblatt *et al.*, 1944; Bleuler, 1955). Also no pneumoencephalographically investigated group has until now been compared with a control group of nonalcoholics.

Methods Used at Zagreb

In the period 1 January 1958 to 1 December 1960 there were 3327 hospitalised patients in the Department, of whom 400 (or 12 per cent) were alcoholics. Pneumoencephalographic investigations were done routinely on 161 (or 40.3 per cent) of the patients. The investigation was carried out in the case of every patient who consented, where pneumoencephalography could give data of value for therapeutic purposes, where we expected that the pneumoencephalogram would give findings of diagnostic or prognostic interest, where there was no contra-indication, and in all cases where it was indicated from the point of view of differential diagnosis.

No complications developed in our patients from the use of the pneumoencephalographic procedure. The procedure was not undertaken in any case where there was an absolute contra-indication or an acute clinical picture.

Pneumoencephalography was always done by the lumbar route, injecting 20-40 cc of air. In every case pictures in 6 standard views were done:

(1)　antero-posterior sagittal view;
(2)　postero-anterior sagittal view;
(3)　left lateral view of the head lying sideways;
(4)　right lateral view of the head lying sideways;
(5)　lateral view with brow up;
(6)　lateral view with brow down.

These views were supplemented in individual cases by pictures taken in special positions or by tomography. In a certain number of cases pneumoencephalographic pictures were also taken 24 hours after the injection of air (especially in cases where cranial cerebral trauma was suspected).

The assessment of a pneumoencephalogram is always very difficult, and especially so when judging atrophic changes. We assessed the pneumoencephalogram on the basis of the general criteria which have been described in the medical literature, and measurements were made only in rare instances.

Normal pneumoencephalographic findings were established in 17 (or 10.5 per cent) of all cases examined. Usually the following pathological pneumoencephalographic changes, isolated or interrelated, were found:

(1)　enlargement of ventricles;
(2)　enlargement of subarachnoid spaces on the surface of the brain (uniformly diffused or mainly localised in different regions);
(3)　isolated enlargement of the third ventricle or a greater enlargement of the third ventricle in comparison with the general enlargement of the other ventricles;
(4)　enlargement of the subarachnoid spaces in the posterior cranial fossa;
(5)　atrophy of the corpus callosum;
(6)　enlargement of the basal cisternae; and
(7)　difficulties in the distribution of air.

We divided the pneumoencephalographic findings, on the basis of the degree of changes that were revealed, into slight atrophy, medium atrophy, severe atrophy and very severe atrophy.

Subcortical Atrophy (Hydrocephalus internus)

In the group of 161 patients that were investigated by pneumoencephalography, 17 had normal findings: in one case the subarachnoid spaces and ventricles did not fill with air. In the remaining 143 cases were found:

normal ventricles	6 cases (N)
slight enlargement of ventricles	28 cases (+)
medium enlargement of ventricles	38 cases (++)
severe enlargement of ventricles	63 cases (+++)
very severe enlargement of ventricles	6 cases (++++)
air did not enter ventricles	2 cases

When divided into different age groups the results were as follows:

0 to 30 years		15 patients
normal ventricles	(N)	4 cases
slight enlargement of ventricles	(+)	4 cases
medium enlargement of ventricles	(++)	4 cases
severe enlargement of ventricles	(+++)	3 cases

31 to 40 years		46 patients
normal ventricles	(N)	2 cases
slight enlargement of ventricles	(+)	11 cases
medium enlargement of ventricles	(++)	12 cases
severe enlargement of ventricles	(+++)	10 cases
very severe enlargement	(++++)	11 cases

41 to 50 years		46 patients
air did not enter ventricles		1 case
normal ventricles	(N)	6 cases
slight enlargement of ventricles	(+)	11 cases
medium enlargement of ventricles	(++)	12 cases
severe enlargement of ventricles	(+++)	13 cases
very severe enlargement of ventricles	(++++)	3 cases

51 to 60 years   31 patients

normal ventricles	(N)	1 case
slight enlargement of ventricles	(+)	1 case
medium enlargement of ventricles	(++)	8 cases
severe enlargement of ventricles	(+++)	18 cases
very severe enlargement of ventricles	(++++)	3 cases

Over 60 years   23 patients

normal ventricles	(N)	1 case
medium enlargement of ventricles	(++)	4 cases
severe enlargement of ventricles	(+++)	18 cases

Cortical Atrophy (External Hydrocephalus)

In 17 cases there were normal pneumoencephalograms and in one case the air did not enter subarachnoid spaces and ventricles. The remaining 143 cases showed the following cortical changes:

normal surface of the brain	(N)	7 cases
slight enlargement of subarachnoid spaces	(+)	18 cases
medium enlargement	(++)	47 cases
severe enlargement	(+++)	64 cases
very severe enlargement	(++++)	7 cases

The findings according to the age group of the patients are especially interesting:

0 to 30 years   15 patients

normal surface of the brain	(N)	3 cases
slight enlargement of subarachnoid spaces	(+)	4 cases
medium enlargement	(++)	5 cases
severe enlargement	(+++)	3 cases

31 to 40 years   46 patients

air did not enter subarachnoid spaces
on the surface of the brain   1 case
normal surface of the brain   (N)   11 cases
slight enlargement of subarachnoid spaces(+)   5 cases
medium enlargement   (++)   18 cases
severe enlargement   (+++)   10 cases
very severe enlargement   (++++)   1 case

41 to 50 years   46 patients

normal surface of the brain   (N)   6 cases
slight enlargement of subarachnoid spaces(+)   9 cases
medium enlargement   (++)   12 cases
severe enlargement   (+++)   16 cases
very severe enlargement   (++++)   3 cases

51 to 60 years   31 patients

normal surface of the brain   (N)   2 cases
medium enlargement of subarachnoid
spaces   (++)   8 cases
severe enlargement   (+++)   18 cases
very severe enlargement   (++++)   3 cases

Over 60 years   23 patients

normal surface of the brain   (N)   2 cases
medium enlargement of subarachnoid
spaces   (++)   4 cases
severe enlargement   (+++)   17 cases

From the findings shown above according to the age group it is clear
that in the older group the changes were more severe. In some cases
severe local enlargements in some regions were found, giving the
impression of porencephaly. There were seven of these cases.

Although most of the patients showed general diffused cortical
atrophy, more careful investigation of our X-ray pictures revealed
in almost all cases that the frontal region, the Sylvian regions and basal
temporal regions were more severely affected.

The State of the Third Ventricle. Special attention was given to the
state of the third ventricle because it was noticed that this was

sometimes much more enlarged than the other ventricles. In some cases the enlargement of the third ventricle was an isolated finding. In these two categories there were 38 cases. The most important aspects of the clinical picture in these cases were vegetative symptoms and pronounced personality changes. It seemed to us that the cases with pronounced enlargement of the third ventricle were the most resistant to treatment.

Alcoholic encephalopathies show, from the pathological anatomical point of view also, the greatest changes in the neighbourhood of the third ventricle and of the truncus.

Corpus Callosum. In some cases the impression was given of an atrophied corpus callosum, since the portion between the sulcus corporis callosi and the third ventricle was narrowed when seen on the pneumoencephalograms. Similar findings have been described by other authors: Frau and Chateau (1956); Levin and Greenblatt (1948); Postel and Cossa (1956); Perrin (1951); Lereboullet *et al.* (1959), and others. In all there were 28 cases with signs of atrophied corpus callosum in our material.

Cisternal Changes. Deep and wide cisternae were, in our investigations, among the signs forming the criteria for the pneumoencephalographic diagnosis of cerebral atrophy. In some cases the cisternae were exceptionally large.

Disturbances of Air Filling. In any group of patients subjected to pneumoencephalographic procedures there are always a certain number of cases which show disturbances of the air filling. Sometimes it is difficult to judge whether these are due to poor technical manipulations during the course of the procedure or to some pathological intracranial changes.

In our group of patients, in only one case did the cerebrospinal fluid space not fill with air.

Control Group

A special problem which arises in all scientific investigations in the pneumoencephalographic field is the question of a control series. One might ask, whether it is possible to find similar cerebral changes in a group of nonalcoholics of the same age distribution. Indeed the question of the characteristics of the so-called normal pneumoencephalogram is still under discussion.

In our control series we included 135 pneumoencephalograms of

patients with neurotic disturbances with headache, and where
pneumoencephalography was carried out for differential diagnostic
reasons. These cases were divided into age groups similar to those of
the alcoholics:

(1)   In the age group 0 to 30 years there were 58 cases. In this group
        we found changes in only 3 cases (in 2 cases slight enlargement
        of the ventricles and in one, in addition to the slight enlargement
        of the ventricles, an even more pronounced enlargement of the
        third ventricle). In one case the cerebrospinal fluid spaces did not
        fill with air and in two cases the air did not enter one of the
        lateral ventricles.

(2)   The age group 31 to 40 years had 43 patients. Slight cortical and
        subcortical atrophy were found in only 3 cases; in 4 cases there
        was a slight enlargement of ventricles; in one case isolated
        enlargement of the third ventricle; and in one case slight
        enlargement of ventricles with a more pronounced enlargement
        of the third ventricle.

(3)   The age group 41 to 50 years had 22 patients. In one case the
        ventricles did not fill with air; one case showed medium cortical
        and subcortical atrophy; one case showed slight cortical atrophy;
        one slight enlargement of ventricles; one medium enlargement of
        the cortical subarachnoid spaces; and one medium enlargement
        of the ventricles.

(4)   The age group 51 to 60 years had only 11 patients. One of these
        showed slight cortical atrophy and one slight cortical and
        subcortical atrophy.

(5)   In the over 60-year category there was only one case. Given the
        subject's age, the pneumoencephalogram was normal.

The high percentage of abnormal pneumoencephalograms in the group
of alcoholics is evidence that the changes we have found in this group
are significant. When assessing the results of pneumoencephalography
due consideration was given to the age of the patient.

In the control series, cases above the age of 50 years occur rarely,
as people in this age group rarely present themselves for hospital
treatment and pneumoencephalography on account of neurotic
headache. But 135 pneumoencephalograms from our control series
with a minimal percentage of pathological changes give clear evidence
that the findings in our group of alcoholics were significant.

Doubtful Cases

Of 161 cases of alcoholics who had undergone pneumoencephalography, there were parallel diseases in 19 cases (sclerosis cerebri, general arteriosclerosis, syphilis, and others) and in this group judgement should be reserved.

General Characteristics of our Alcoholic Group

The majority of our patients were admitted in a very grave condition as emergency cases. Analysis of our material shows the following number of cases:

delirium tremens	22
alcoholic epilepsies	19
alcoholic psychoses	13
alcoholic dementias	9
Korsakow psychoses	6
suicidal attempts	6
Total	75

Sex and Age

In the alcoholic group there were 143 males (88.8 per cent) and 18 females (11.2 per cent), a ratio of 8 to 1. In the age group 31 to 50 there were 57.8 per cent of cases, and above 60 only 14.3 per cent of cases.

In general, on the basis of our experience, it is possible to say:

(1)   Strongly emphasised pneumoencephalographic changes are found frequently in cases with grave clinical symptoms.

(2)   In the cases with marked cortical atrophy, personality changes and general deterioration in the clinical picture are more pronounced than in the cases with ventricular enlargements of the same degree.

(3)   A more pronounced enlargement of the third ventricle, than can be expected from the rest of the pneumoencephalographic findings, is normally found in cases of graver clinical symptomatology and prognosis, with outstanding vegetative symptoms.

(4)   In cases showing corpus callosum atrophy, the clinical picture revealed severe personality changes and gross intellectual deterioration.

Conclusions

On the basis of 161 pneumoencephalograms or 40.3 per cent of 400 cases of alcoholism, the following conclusions can be drawn:

(1)   It is clear that alcoholism causes cerebral atrophy. In 90 per cent of our cases we have found cerebral atrophies which could not be attributed to age or to any parallel pathological state.

(2)   In our control group of 135 cases with neurotic headache, cerebral atrophies were negligible.

(3)   Different combinations of these characteristics were found in the great majority of our cases. Isolated cortical or subcortical atrophy was only exceptionally present.

(4)   The pneumoencephalographic picture revealed by our cases is not a specific one for alcoholism, although cerebellar atrophy and atrophy of corpus callosum were more often present in our cases than has been described in other pathological conditions.

(5)   In view of the fact that alcoholism is chiefly caused by secondary alimentary deficiencies in alcoholics and not by the direct action of alcohol, the pneumoencephalographic picture of chronic alcoholism is very similar to that of the pneumoencephalograms of other deficiency diseases and cannot be differentiated from them.

(6)   The atrophic process appears relatively early, and in the period between the ages of 40-60 years it is clearly defined.

Practical Applications

In 1962 when our investigations were done we drew the following conclusions:

The clinical picture of alcoholic lesions of the periopheral nervous system was found in our cases much less frequently than had been described in the earlier medical literature.

Terminologically, every case of alcoholism which shows even minor lesions of the central nervous system, should be encompassed by the term 'alcoholic encephalopathy', and within this framework specific clinical syndromes could be defined.

Clinical differences between individual alcoholic syndromes do not necessarily imply different pathological and anatomical pictures. In our patients, even the pneumoencephalograms do not show important basic differences, but mostly variations in the degree of atrophy.

The gravity of the acute clinical picture does not necessarily run parallel with the gravity of the cerebral atrophy. There were cases with severe cerebral atrophy and a minor clinical picture, and vice versa, but in chronic and subchronic alcoholic states with no acute clinical picture there is usually a correlation between the severity of cerebral atrophy and the severity of the clinical condition.

Individual cases of alcoholism may compensate for a long time, but they can frequently lose this compensation as a result of even minor external events. Sometimes even therapy itself (antabuse) can produce this loss of compensation.

Treatment of alcoholism should be started as early as possible. Once severe cerebral atrophy of an irreversible kind has developed, the prognosis becomes very difficult and uncertain. In more severe cases it is necessary to undertake long-term rehabilitation, as it is not possible to expect improvement by the use of short-term methods.

Finally, it must be emphasised that it is not possible in individual cases to base the prognosis on the pneumoencephalogram alone, as sometimes a patient with severe atrophy will make good improvement and vice versa. It seems to us that it is not possible to speak about particular clinical pictures in correlation with particular pneumoencephalographic findings. In an individual case prolonged clinical study will give more detailed insight into the condition.

Electroencephalographic Studies of Alcoholics

During the war (Greenblatt *et al.*, 1944) and in the postwar period (Levin and Greenblatt, 1948; Perrin, 1951; Courjon and Perrin, 1952a, b; Little and McAvoy, 1952; Vercelletto, 1952; Funkhouser, 1953; Horsey and Akert, 1953; Lereboullet *et al.*, 1956a, b; Lafon *et al.*, 1956a; Newman, 1956; Prudent, 1956; Sisson and Elligson, 1956; Delay *et al.*, 1957; Marinacci, 1957; Limeno, 1958; Subbotnik and Špilberg, 1959; Lynch, 1960; Müller and Rutenfranz, 1960; Bonetti, 1961; Dyken *et al.*, 1961; Lundervold *et al.*, 1962; Mukasa, 1962; Streljčuk and Melehova, 1962; Hudolin, Vi. and Gubarev, 1965; Hudolin, Vi. *et al.*, 1966) considerable attention was paid to studies of brain damage in alcoholics and to electroencephalographic examination. EEG examinations were made in cases of acute alcohol intoxication, individual neurological and psychiatric clinical states in the course of the alcoholic disease, and in so-called simple, uncomplicated alcoholic conditions (Dréano, 1953; Hudolin, Vi., 1965, 1966, 1967; Hudolin, Vi. and Gubarev, 1967; Grioire *et al.*, 1956; Lafon *et al.*, 1956b; Thompson, 1957; Marinacci and Courville, 1958; Alajouanine *et al.*, 1959b; Ardito and Meloni, 1960; Bacher *et al.*, 1960; Vallat *et al.*, 1961).

We also tried to use electroencephalography to see how it can be applied in the overall system of care for alcoholic patients (Hudolin, Vi., 1967). Our material consisted of 391 unselected alcoholics (348 men and 43 women) subjected to EEG investigation and routine activation by hyperventilation and occasionally also by photostimulation. All our cases fell into four groups: those in the first group (264 patients) showed no serious neurological or mental disorders; those in the second group (46 patients) had some neurological disorders, showing in particular symptoms of polyneuritis; the third group (21 patients) were with psychopathic personality traits. The analysis of EEG findings concentrated upon the following:

(1)   alpha-rhythm voltage;
(2)   alpha-rhythm frequency;
(3)   alpha-rhythm blockage;
(4)   reaction to hyperventilation;
(5)   frequency of appearance of medium-fast beta activities;
(6)   possible anomalies in EEG findings;
(7)   pathological activities.

Our findings can be summarised as follows:

In most alcoholics, findings were normal. The number of normal findings dropped when alcoholism was accompanied by some other lesions in the nervous system or by epileptic fits.

The relationship between the frequency of pathological changes in the electroencephalogram and age was such that pathological findings were more frequent in older patients.

Low voltage findings in 28 per cent of alcoholic patients should be seen as an important characteristic of the electroencephalograms of alcoholics. No significant variations in voltage were recorded in different age groups.

Disturbances in the blocking of alpha rhythm were also found to be characteristic of alcoholic patients' electroencephalograms.

Alcoholics with epileptic seizures had electroencephalograms showing a relatively high percentage of changes in the course of hyperventilation and were thus similar to alcoholics with other organic lesions.

An increased amount of fast cerebral activities should be seen as another characteristic of electroencephalograms of alcoholics. This phenomenon is most probably due to an atrophic process in the brain, mostly in the cortical region.

Among the characteristic EEG findings in alcoholics, mention should also be made of theta activities in the fronto-temporal section in amounts greater than in the normal electroencephalogram.

Pathological changes in the electroencephalogram are not characteristic of EEG findings in alcoholics.

Pneumoencephalography and gamma encephalography, like electroencephalography, are important for the diagnosis and understanding of cerebral processes in alcoholism.

Echoencephalographic Studies of Alcoholics

As far back as 1965, when echography was first introduced in our Department, attempts were made to determine the state of the brain by measuring the width of the third ventricle and later also of other brain structures. Subsequent measurements were made on the lateral ventricles, and the so-called *index cellae mediae* was determined. Finally, successful measurements were made of the temporal lobe, and the so-called *brain mantle index* was determined.

A large number of echographic examinations have been made in our Department involving a considerable number of patients (Hudolin, Vi. and Kryanovski, 1977). Our echographic findings agreed, in principle, with the results of our earlier or parallel pneumoencephalographic examinations.

Compared with the results obtained by pneumoencephalography, echographic findings showed smaller values, by about 30 per cent, for the third ventricle, and generally a somewhat smaller number of atrophic processes. This can be explained by the different characteristics of patients within the fifteen years during which observations were made, as well as by differences resulting from the technical characteristics of the echographic and radiological methods.

Computerised Axial Tomography (CT) of the Brain

Recently we confirmed the results of our earlier investigations, using

CT in over 80 unselected patients. As CT investigations are also considered elsewhere in this volume, here we give just two pictures (Figures 9.1 and 9.2).

Figure 9.1: CT Picture of the Brain of an Alcoholic with Advanced Cortical and Subcortical Atrophy of the Brain

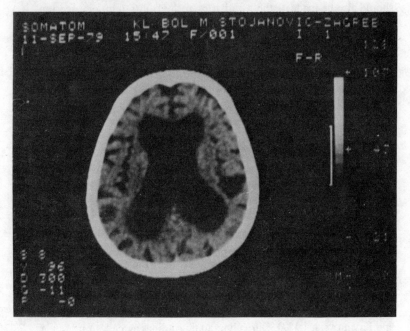

Statistics of Treatment of Alcoholics in the Department for Neurology, Psychiatry, Alcohology and other Addictions in Zagreb in 1978

Large numbers of alcoholics are treated in our Department, both as inpatients and as outpatients. The total number of inpatient alcoholics in 1978 was 2,218. In order to obtain a better evaluation of our programmes of treatment, we initiated a research project to study the characteristics of alcoholics undergoing treatment. This project is still running, but some data are already available and are presented below in Tables 9.1-9.7.

In some of the tables which follow two variables are given. The total number of cases may vary slightly, because only those cases are included in the survey for which both variables are known. As already noted, the total number of patients was 2,218.

Figure 9.2: **CT Picture of the Brain of an Alcoholic with Advanced Cortical Atrophy (in this case also, enlargement of the ventricles was present)**

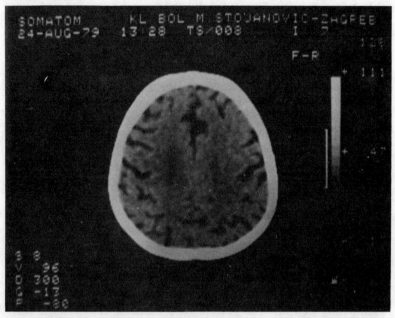

Table 9.1: **Treated Alcoholics According to Sex and Age**

Sex		−19	20-29	30-39	40-49	50-59	60-69	70+	Total
M	f	39	320	493	628	236	94	34	1844
	a	1.76	14.46	22.28	28.38	10.66	4.25	1.54	83.33
	b	90.70	87.91	82.72	81.35	81.94	86.24	82.93	
	c	2.11	17.35	26.06	12.80	5.10	5.10	1.84	100.0
F	f	4	44	103	144	52	15	7	369
	a	0.18	1.99	4.65	6.51	2.35	0.68	0.32	16.67
	b	9.30	12.09	17.28	18.65	18.06	13.76	17.07	
	c	1.08	11.92	27.91	39.02	14.09	4.07	1.96	100.0
Total		43	364	596	772	288	109	41	2213
		1.94	16.45	26.93	34.88	13.01	4.93	1.85	100.0

f = frequency (number in age group)
a = percentage of the total
b = vertical percentages
c = borizontal percentages

Exact age was unknown for five patients and these were not included in the survey. However, since the total number of patients was 2,218, the exclusion of five patients can have no statistical significance. It can be seen from Table 9.1 that the survey covered 1,844 men (83.33 per cent) and 369 women (16.67 per cent). The number of women admitted for treatment is on the increase in absolute and relative terms. At present, the ratio between men and women among alcoholic patients is 6:1, while some ten years ago the ratio stood at 8:1. This fact may be due to a number of medical and nonmedical factors; but it shows how difficult it is to conduct comparative investigations, not only between different countries but also within one and the same country at different points in time.

A total of 1,480 men and 295 women were under 50 years old, which represents 80.26 per cent of all men and 79.93 per cent of all women covered by the survey. These figures are particularly significant, because they show that alcoholics who come for treatment tend to be younger and younger. Until recently the majority of alcoholics undergoing treatment were between 40 and 60 years old. Age is particularly important in the study of cerebral atrophic processes, because there have been attempts to ascribe cerebral atrophy in alcoholics to age rather than to the alcoholic disease.

It is noteworthy that 2.11 per cent of all men and 1.08 per cent of all women were under 20 years of age at the moment of admission to hospital. This finding agrees with the observations of other authors who report that excessive drinking recently is appearing among children and adolescents and that alcoholic disease may develop at a very early age.

Of the total number of patients of both sexes, only 19.79 per cent were over 50 years of age when they were hospitalised for alcoholism.

Epilepsy and Alcoholism

In some cases alcoholism is accompanied by serious neurological or psychiatric complications. Among these complications, a certain number of seizures or true alcoholic epilepsy have always attracted the attention of researchers.

A convulsive fit is the clearest indication of a more or less serious organic lesion in the brain. Table 9.2 gives data about those of our patients for whom epilepsy was entered as an additional diagnosis. The statistics do not include patients with suspected convulsions at the time of admission or who had only an isolated seizure due to heavy intoxication, but in whom no epileptic clinical manifestations were recorded in the clinical history or while under subsequent clinical observation.

Table 9.2: Alcoholics with Diagnosed Epilepsy Treated in 1978, by Sex

Sex		With epilepsy	Without epilepsy	Total
M	f	168	1,680	1,848
	a	7.57	75.74	83.32
	b	85.28	83.13	
	c	9.09	90.91	100.0
F	f	29	341	370
	a	1.31	15.37	16.68
	b	14.72	16.87	
	c	7.84	92.16	100.0
Total		197	2,021	2,218
		8.88	91.12	100.0

It follows from Table 9.2 that epilepsy was diagnosed in 197 (8.9 per cent of total patients) alcoholic patients – 168 men (9.09 per cent of all men) and 29 women (7.84 per cent of all females). With respect to sex, there is a statistically significant relationship between the variables of sex and epilepsy. Epilepsy was more often diagnosed in men (9.1 per cent) than in women (7.8 per cent). Data on the incidence of alcoholic epilepsy given in the literature vary so widely that comparisons are very difficult to make. It can only be said that the number with clear epileptic symptoms is relatively high (we refer to clear clinical, not merely EEG, manifestations).

Alcoholic Psychosis

Alcoholic psychosis is another important indicator of organic lesions in the brain, regardless of whether the psychotic picture is acute or chronic (see Table 9.3).

In our population, 107 male patients (5.79 per cent of all men) and 11 female patients (2.97 per cent of all women) had the diagnosis of alcoholic psychosis. The relationship between alcoholic psychosis and

Table 9.3: Of the Total Number of Alcoholics Undergoing Treatment in the Clinic in 1978, 5.32 per cent were with Alcoholic Psychosis

Sex		With alcoholic psychosis	Without alcoholic psychosis	Total
	f	107	1,747	1,848
M	a	4.82	78.49	
	b	90.68	82.90	
	c	5.79	94.21	100.0
	f	11	359	370
F	a	0.5	16.19	
	b	9.32	17.10	
	c	2.97	97.03	100.0
		118	2,021	2,218
Total		5.32	94.68	100.0

sex was found to be statistically significant, in that a significantly greater proportion of men than women were affected. The total number of cases of alcoholic psychosis in our population (both sexes) was 118 or 5.32 per cent of the total number of patients.

Polyneuropathy

Degeneration of peripheral nerves in alcoholics has been known for a long time and is well described. Milder forms of alcoholic polyneuritis usually go unnoticed and are therefore not recorded in the patient's history. Sometimes they are not at all easy to diagnose, especially in the early stages when there may be parallel slight spinal damage. Milder forms of spinal damage are more frequent in alcoholics than is commonly thought (see Table 9.4).

The relationship between sex and polyneuropathy was not statistically significant.

The proportion of patients with diagnosed polyneuropathy among the alcoholics was found to be 11.09 per cent.

Degeneration of peripheral nerves is very frequent in alcoholics. Using sufficiently detailed diagnostic, or microdiagnostic, procedures, damaged peripheral nerves are found in practically every alcoholic patient. In the case of the patients covered by this survey, the diagnosis of polyneuropathy was entered only when damage to peripheral nerves

Table 9.4: Alcoholics with Diagnosed Polyneuropathy Treated in 1978, by Sex

Sex		Polyneuropathy With	Without	Total
	f	212	1,636	1,848
	a	9.56	73.76	
M	b	86.18	82.96	
	c	11.47	88.53	100.0
	f	34	336	370
	a	1.53	15.15	
F	b	13.82	17.04	
	c	9.19	90.81	100.0
		246	1,972	2,218
Total		11.09	88.91	100.0

was the main clinical symptom apart from alcoholism. Polyneuropathy was diagnosed in 212 (11.47 per cent) of our male patients and in 34 (9.19 per cent) of our female patients. The relationship between sex and polyneuropathy was not found to be statistically significant.

The Chronic Psycho-organic Syndrome

The chronic psycho-organic syndrome with more or less developed dementia is a typical consequence of cerebral damage caused by alcohol (See Table 9.5).

A total of 207 (11.20 per cent) of our male patients and 43 (11.6 per cent) of our female patients had the diagnosis of chronic psycho-organic syndrome. The total number of patients of both sexes displaying the clinical picture of chronic psycho-organic syndrome was 250 (11.27 per cent). The difference between male and female alcoholics with respect to this disease was not statistically significant.

Electroencephalographic Findings

A total of 405 patients were examined electroencephalographically, and a completely normal EEG was recorded in 198 cases (48.09 per cent).

Table 9.5: Alcoholics with Diagnosed Chronic Psycho-organic Syndrome

Sex		Chronic psycho-organic syndrome With	Without	Total
M	f	207	1,641	1,848
	a	9.33	73.99	
	b	82.80	83.38	
	c	11.20	88.80	100.0
F	f	43	327	370
	a	1.94	14.74	
	b	17.20	16.62	
	c	11.62	88.38	100.0
Total		250	1,968	2,218
		11.27	88.73	100.0

Cerebral Apoplexy and Alcoholism

The number of deaths in our population was 45 (2.03 per cent). of whom 36 were men and 9 women. Those who died were mainly patients admitted to the Nuerological Department with symptoms of cerebrovascular insult accompanying alcoholism. We were particularly interested in the possible effects of alcohol on cerebral vascular damage, which has been a subject of special study in our clinic.

One of the aspects of our research was the study of the incidence of alcoholism among the patients treated in our Department for cerebral apoplexy in the course of 1978 (see Table 9.6).

Table 9.6: Incidence of Alcoholism Among the Patients Treated in our Department for Cerebral Apoplexy in 1978, by Sex

Alcoholism	M	%	F	%	Total	%
Not recorded	207	70	262	96	469	82.6
Recorded	88	30	11	4	99	17.4
Total	295	100.0	273	100.0	568	100.0

Data in Table 9.6 show that the incidence of alcoholism among those treated for cerebral apoplexy is twice as high as in the total population of persons over eighteen years of age. This points to a mutual interdependence between the two diseases. It can be seen that 30 per cent of the male apoplectic patients and 4 per cent of the female apoplectic patients treated at our clinic in 1978 were alcoholics.

While the ratio between male and female alcoholics in the entire group covered by the survey was 6:1, among those treated for cerebral apoplexy the ratio was 8:1. This would seem to point to the presence of some other risk factors in men, or to the fact that the relative increase of women alcoholics has not yet become manifest in this age group. We have focused our attention on smoking as a risk factor which is considerably more often seen in men.

Table 9.7: Incidence of Alcoholism in Different Age Groups of Patients Treated for Cerebral Apoplexy

Age group	Alcoholism Without	%	With	%	Total	%
Under 40	15	65	8	35	23	100.0
41-50	50	76	16	24	66	100.0
51-60	84	77	25	23	109	100.0
61 and over	331	87	50	13	381	100.0
Total	469	83	99	17	568	100.0

Data in Table 9.7 show that the relative proportion of alcoholics among apoplectic patients is distinctly greater in younger age groups. In the group of patients under 40, the ratio between alcoholics and nonalcoholics among apoplectic patients was 1:1.9, which meant that there were 35 per cent of alcoholics in that age group (in many cases cerebral hemorrhage was involved). (It is interesting to note that mortality was lower in alcoholics than in nonalcoholics.)

Data from the Croatian Register of Alcoholics

In 1965 we introduced a scheme which enabled us to follow up all inpatient alcoholics in Croatia after their release from hospital. This was intended to give us a better insight into the nature of the alcoholic disease and to facilitate the evaluation and continuous improvement of practical procedures for the solution of alcohol-related problems.

Since 1 January 1965 we have kept a register of inpatient alcoholics in Croatia (the treatment is done mainly in psychiatric institutions). Below in Table 9.8 we analyse data for the years 1965-76.

Table 9.8: Registered Alcoholics in the Period 1965-76, by Age and Sex (only first Hospitalizations were Recorded)

Age group	M	%	F	%	Total	%
under 19	591	1.3	114	1.6	705	1.3
20-29	5,777	12.4	537	7.7	6,314	11.6
30-39	14,899	31.9	1,755	25.2	16,654	31.0
40-49	14,248	30.5	2,179	31.3	16,427	30.6
50-59	6,599	14.1	1,328	19.1	7,927	14.6
60-69	3,462	7.4	723	10.4	4,185	7.8
70 and over	622	1.3	227	3.3	849	1.6
unknown	565	1.2	108	1.6	673	1.3
Total	46,763	100.0	6,971	100.0	53,734	100.0

The number of first hospitalisations of alcoholics in Croatia in the 1965-76 period was 53,734, over 70 per cent of whom were under 50 years old. The difference with respect to sex is statistically significant, but the relative proportion of women is greater in all age groups over 50. In other words, women either come for treatment later or (more probably) become alcoholics later in life. It is interesting to note that the relative share of women is somewhat greater in the youngest age group. Our data seem to indicate that more attention should be paid to female alcoholism in the future (even though this problem is not in the focus of our attention in this chapter).

Epilepsy was diagnosed in 5 per cent of all treated and registered alcoholics (see Table 9.11). There is a statistically significant relationship between the variables of alcoholism and epilepsy with regard to sex, in that epilepsy is somewhat more frequent among male alcoholics.

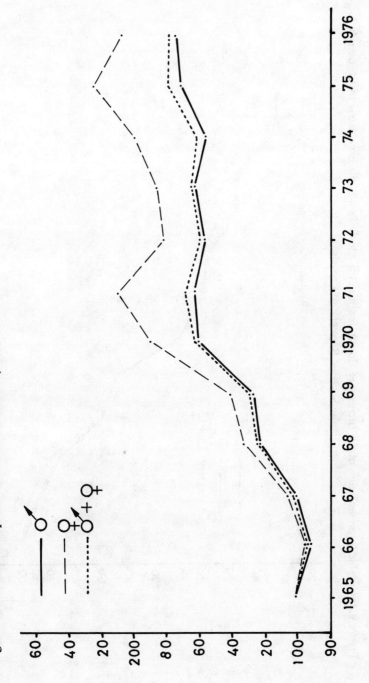

Figure 9.3: Increase in Inpatient Alcoholics in Croatia, 1965-76

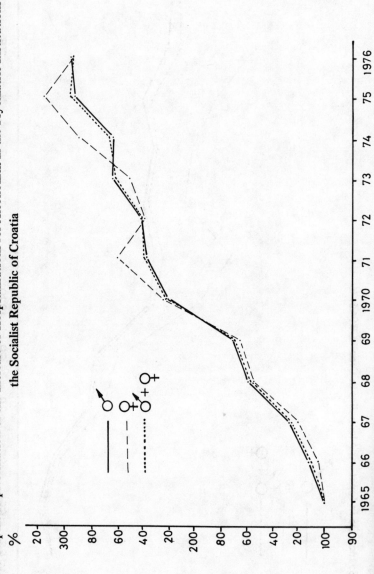

Figure 9.4: Graphic Representation of the Increase of Hospitalisations for Alcoholism in the Psychiatric Institutions in the Socialist Republic of Croatia

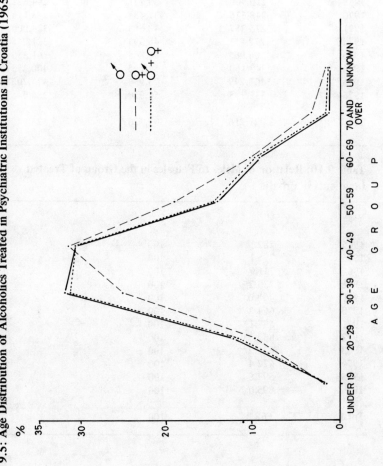

Figure 9.5: Age Distribution of Alcoholics Treated in Psychiatric Institutions in Croatia (1965-76)

Figure 9.9: Days Alcoholics Spent in Hospitals in Croatia in the Period Period 1965-1976 for Treatment of Alcoholism

Year	Days spent in Hospital M	F	Total
1965	131,829	19,509	151,338
1966	142,643	23,458	166,101
1967	166,763	28,230	194,993
1968	183,068	27,006	210,074
1969	210,900	33,721	244,621
1970	248,676	37,438	286,114
1971	275,387	48,613	324,000
1972	272,851	48,397	321,248
1973	306,965	54,885	361,850
1974	343,160	57,193	400,353
1975	403,249	73,956	477,205
1976	335,725	50,320	386,045
Total	3,021,216	502,726	3,523,942

Table 9.10: Relation of Males to Females in the Group of Treated Inpatients in Croatia

Year	M	F
1965	782.1	100
1966	795.1	100
1967	741.7	100
1968	730.2	100
1969	708.0	100
1970	664.7	100
1971	597.1	100
1972	662.3	100
1973	676.2	100
1974	622.4	100
1975	597.6	100
1976	695.0	100
Total	668.8	100

Table 9.11: Incidence of Epilepsy Among the Alcoholics Included in the Register of Treated Alcoholics in Croatia, by Sex

Sex	With	%	Without	%	Total	%
			Epilepsy			
M	2,372	5.1	44,391	94.9	46,763	100.0
F	286	4.1	6,685	95.9	6,971	100.0
Total	2,658	5.0	51,076	95.0	53,734	100.0

Table 9.12: Incidence of Alcoholic Psychosis (with Acute or Chronic Psychotic Symptoms) among Registered Alcoholics – All Hospitalisations

Sex	With	%	Without	%	Total	%
		Diagnosed alcoholic psychosis				
M	14,353	30.7	32,410	69.3	46,763	100.0
F	2,010	28.8	4,961	71.2	6,971	100.0
Total	16,363	30.5	37,371	69.5	53,734	100.0

Table 9.12 shows that the proportion of alcoholics with diagnosed alcoholic psychosis is very high. As many as 30.5 per cent of the registered alcoholics have so far been in an alcoholic psychosis. The incidence of alcoholic psychosis among employed male alcoholics is 24.6 per cent, and among employed female alcoholics 18.4 per cent. Among male alcoholics who are already retired, it is 35.5 per cent and among retired women 30.4 per cent. The percentage is highest among socially insured farmers (about 50 per cent), which can be explained by the inadequate system of health care for this part of the population in earlier periods. The relationship between the variables of sex and alcoholic psychosis is not statistically significant.

Table 9.13: Incidence of Polyneuropathy among Registered Alcoholics – all Hospitalisations

Sex	With	%	Without	%	Total	%
		Diagnosed polyneuropathy				
M	5,172	11.1	41,591	88.9	46,763	100.0
F	628	9.0	6,343	91.0	6,971	100.0
Total	5,800	10.8	47,934	89.2	53,734	100.0

According to the data in the Register, about 11 per cent of registered alcoholics had polyneuropathy (see Table 9.13). The actual proportion of severe forms of polyneuropathy (as these are the only ones which are so diagnosed) is probably higher.

With respect to sex, there is a slight statistically significant difference between men and women, in that polyneuropathy is a little more frequent in men.

The Register records 8.0 per cent of cases of alcoholic dementia or chronic psychosis syndrome. It might have been expected that the percentage of such cases should be higher, but a certain number probably went unrecorded because some of the institutions participating in the project rarely bothered to add another diagnosis in addition to alcoholism.

Among the rest of the data, it might be mentioned that psychopathy was diagnosed in 7.1 per cent of alcoholic patients and tuberculosis in 2.4 per cent. 1.8 per cent of the alcoholics died during the first hospitalisation.

Conclusions

The data from different investigations done in our Department show clearly that brain atrophy is a constant lesion in alcoholics.

The results of our studies point to the conclusion that the interpretation and comparison of data presented by different researchers are still quite difficult. We have tried to overcome these difficulties within one of the Yugoslav constituent Republics by starting a uniform system of registration of alcoholics. We feel that such co-operation should in future extend and become international in scope.

Our research since 1960 indicates that cerebral impairments can be said to be always present in alcoholics, but they do not always go hand in hand with the clinical picture of alcoholism.

Clinically, brain damage often does not produce clear symptoms, and it appears from our investigations that it would be useful to work out techniques of psychological measurement to be used in clinical work.

Sometimes a mild clinical picture is found to be associated with severe cerebral atrophy, and vice versa. Also the prognosis in individual cases does not follow the degree of brain atrophy. We have seen severe atrophy in patients who made a good recovery and mild atrophy in cases which took a progressive, malignant clinical course.

Our recent research suggests the possibility that alcoholic vascular brain lesions may be the cause of the brain atrophy. Our data on this problem are still at a preliminary phase and we shall carry out further investigations in this direction.

References

Alajouanine, Th., Castaigne, P., Contamin, F. and Lebourges, J. (1959a), Sur six cas d'atrophie cérébelleuse du type cortical tardif, observés chez des alcooliques chroniques', *Rev. neurol. 100*, 411

Alajouanine, Th., Laplane, D. and Castaigne, P. (1959b), Les épilepsies alcooliques', *Rev. Prat.*, Paris, *9*, 13, 1401

Ardito, R. and Meloni, C. (1960), 'Considerazioni sulle manifestazioni epilettiche degli acoolist', *Rass. Stud. psichiat.*, *49*, 659

Bacher, F., Chanoit, P., Rouquette, J., Verdeaux, G. and Verdeaux, J. (1960), 'Epilepsie et alcoolisme, Études statistiques de critères electro-encéphalographiques', *Rev. Neurol.*, *103*, 228

Beaussart, B. (1963), 'Contribution à l'étude électro-encéphalographique d'alcoliques chroniques', *Thèse*, Paris

Benedek, L. and Juba, S. (1944), 'Beiträge für Pathologie des Diencephalon, III. Histologische Befunde beim chronisch-alkoholischen Korsakoff-Syndrom', *Z. ges. Neurol. Psychiat.*, *177*, 282

Bleuler, M. (1955), 'A comparative study of the constitutions of Swiss and American alcoholic patients', in Diethelm, O. (ed.), *Etiology of Chronic Alcoholism*, Charles Thomas, Springfield, Illinois, 167-78

Bonetti, U. (1961), 'Sulle alterazioni elettroencefalografiche negli alcolisti cronici, prima e durante trattamento con tetraetiltiuram-disolfuro', *Cervello, 37*, 121

Boudin, G., Barbizet, J., Brion, S., Nivet, M. and Masson, S. (1959), 'Epilepsie subintrante et grande insuffisance hépatique. Etude clinique, electrique et anatomique de six cirrhoses alcooliques ascitiques avet état de mal', *Bull. Sox. Med.*, Paris, *75*, 301

Courjon, J. and Perrin, J. (1952a), 'Intérét du contrôle électroencéphalographique des alcooliques chroniques', *EEG Din. Neurophysiol. 4*, 248

——— (1952b), 'Intérét du contrôle électroencéphalographique des alcoholiques chroniques', *Rev. Neurol.*, *86*, 135

Courville, C.B. (1955), *Effects of Alcohol on the Nervous System of Man*, San Lucas Press, Los Angeles

Delay, J., Boudin, G., Brion, S. and Barbizet, J. (1956), 'Étude anatomo-clinique de huit encéphalopathies alcooliques (encéphalopathie de Gayet-Wernicke et syndromes voisins)', *Rev. neurol.*, *94*, 596

Delay, J., Brion, S., Escourolle, R. and Sanchez, A. (1959), 'Rapports entre la dégénérescence du corps calleux de Marchiafava-Bignami et la sclérose laminaire corticale de Morel', *Encéphale, 48*, 281

Delay, J., Verdeaux, J. and Chanoit, P.A. (1957), 'L'électroencéphalogramme des alcooliques chroniques', *Ann. méd. psychol.*, *115*, 427

Dréano, A. (1953), 'Epilepsie alcoolique', *Thèse*, Paris

Dyken, M., Grant, P. and Whitte, P. (1961), 'Evaluation of electroencephalographic changes associated with chronic alcoholism', *Dis. Nerv. Syst.*, *22*, 284

Enkin, M. (1957), 'Étude anatomo-clinique des encéphalopathies carentielles d'origine ethylique', *Thèse*, Paris

Fau, R. and Chateau, R. (1956), 'Encéphalopathies subaiguës alcooliques à prédominance amyotrophique et atrophie cérébelare', *Rev. Neurol., 94*, 616

Flügel, F.E. (1932), quoted from Santagati, F. and Ferazzi, D. (1954), 'L'indagine encefalografica nell alcoolismo cronico', *Neurone, 2,* 3

Funkhouser, J.B. (1953), 'Electroencephalographic studies in alcoholism', *EEG Clin. Neurophysiol., 5*, 130

Gamper, E. (1928), 'Zur Frage der Polioencephalitis hemorrhagica der chronischen Alkoholiker, Anatomische Befunde beim Alkoholischen Korsakow und ihre Beziehungen zum klinischen Bild', *Dtsch Z. Nervenheilk, 102,* 122

Greenblatt, M., Levin, S. and Di Cori, F. (1944), 'The electroencephalogram associated with chronic alcoholism, alcoholic psychosis and alcoholic convulsion', *Arch. Neurol. Psychiat., 52*, 290

Gioire, H., Charbonnel, A., Vercelletto and Trichet (1956), 'Remarques sur l'étiologie de 200 cas d'épilepsie généralisée à début tardif (importance du facteur alcoolique'), *Rev. Neurol., 94*, 634

Gudden, H. (1896), 'Klinische und anatomische Beiträge zur Kenntniss der multiplen Alkoholneuritis nbst Bemerkungen über die Regenerationsvorgänge in peripheren Nervensystem', *Arch. Psychiat. Nervenkr., 28*, 643

Guillain, G., Bertrand, I. and Guillain, J. (1939), 'Étude anatomoclinique d'un cas d'atrophie cérébelleuse corticale progressive', *Bull. Soc. Méd.*, Paris, *6*, 218

Gullotta, F. and Mazzoleni, G. (1959), 'Sulla demielinizzazione del corpo calloso negli alcoolisti (malattia di Marchiafava-Bignami)', *Archivio Italiano di patologia e clinica dei tumori, 3*, 1

Horsey, W.J. and Akert, K. (1953), 'Influence of alcohol on the electro-encephalogram of the cat', *EEG Clin. Neurophysiol., 5*, 318

Huber, G. (1954), 'Zur patologischen Anatomie des Delerium tremens', *Arch. Psych. Nervenkr., 192*, 356

Hudolin, Vl. (1962), 'Pneumoencefalografska slikda ostećenje mozga kod kroničnog alkoholizma', *Anali Bolnice 'Dr. M. Stojanović', 1*, supplement 1

Hudolin, Vi. (1967), 'Electroencephalographic characteristics in chronic alcoholism', *Alcoholism, 3,* supplement 1

Hudolin Vl. (1967), 'Alkoholizam', *Medicinska Enciklopedija*, I, II izd. Leksikografski zavod SFRJ, Zagreb

Hudolin, Vi. and Kryžanovski, J. (1977), 'Dijagnostika ultrazvukom u neurologiji i psihijatriji' in Kurjak, A., *Ultrazvuk u Klinickoj Medicini*, Medicinska naklada, Zagreb, 269-306

Hudolin, Vi. and Gubarev, N. (1965), 'Karakteristike alfa ritma kod kroničnih alkoholičara', *Anali Bolnice 'Dr. M. Stojanović', 4*, 206

Hudolin, Vi., Spaventi, Š., Gubarev, N., Gabelić, I. and Meztger, B. (1966), 'Correlation between gammaencephalographic and electroencephalographic findings in chronic alcoholism', *Alcoholism, 2*, 147

Hudolin, Vi. (1967), 'The characteristics of the alpha rhythm in chronic alcoholics', *Brit. J. Addict., 62*, 55

Jolliffe, N. (1940), 'The influence of alcohol on the adequacy of the B. vitamins in the American diet', *Quart. J. Stud. Alcohol., 1*, 74

Jolliffe, N., Bowman, K.M., Rosenblum, L.A. and Fein, H.D. (1940), 'Nicotinic acid deficiency encephalopathy', *J. Amer. Med. Ass., 114*, 307

Környey, St. and Saethre, H. (1937), 'Die Hypothalamische Lokalisation der histologischen Befunde in Korsakowfällen', *Acta psychiat. scand., 12*, 491

Lafon, R., Pages, P. *et al.* (1956a), 'Les données de la pneumoencephalographie et de l'électroencéphalographie au cours de l'alcoholisme chronique', *Rev. Neurol., 94*, 611

—— (1956b), 'L'épilepsie tardive de l'alcoholisme chronique', *Rev. Neurol., 94,* 62⊲

Lapresle, J. and Claz, R. (1959), 'Nécrose centrale du pied de la protubérance dans une encéphalopathie alcoolique avec lésions des corps mamillaires', *Rev. Neurol., 101*, 769

Lereboullet, J. (1957), 'Diskusija na referat o prehrani i alkoholizmu 1956 (S. Tara)', *Alcool ou Santé, 23*

Lereboullet, J. and Pluvinage, R. (1956), 'L'atrophie cérébrale des alcooliques. Les conséquences médico-sociales', *Bull. Acad. Nat. Méd.*, Paris, *21, 22* et *23*, 398

Lereboullet, J., Pluvinage, R. and Amstutz, Cl. (1956a), 'Aspects cliniques et électroencéphalographiques des atrophies cérébrales alcooliques', *Rev. neurol, 94*, 674

Lereboullet, J., Pluvinage, R. and Bonis, A. (1954), 'Les atrophies cérébrales', *Rev. Prat., 4*, 775

Lereboullet, J., Pluvinage, R., Delarue, R. and Prudent, F. (1956b), 'L'électroencéphalogramme chez l'alcoolique. Etude de 100 cas avant et après désintoxication', *Rev. Neurol., 94*, 638

Lereboullet, J., Pluvinage, J. and Levillain, R. (1959), 'Les lésions encéphaliques au cours des polynevrites alcooliques', *Rev. Alcool., 5*, 3

Levin, S. and Greenblatt, M. (1948), 'Electroencephalogram in cases with cortical atrophy and ventricular dilation', *Amer J. Psychiat., 105*, 22020

Limeno, A.L. (1958), 'Estudios pneumoencephalograficos en el alcoholismo', *Rev. clin. esp., 68*, 161

Little, S.C. and McAvoy, B. (1952), 'Electroencephalographic findings in chronic alcoholism', *EEG Clin. Neurophysiol., 4*, 245

Lundervold, A., Engeset, A. and Lönnum, A. (1962), 'The EEG in cerebral atrophy', *Wld Neurology, 3*, 226

Lynch, M.J.G. (1960), 'Brain lesions in chronic alcoholism', *Arch. Pathol., 69*, 342

Malmud, H. and Skillicorn, S.A. (1956), 'Relation between the Wernicke and the Korsakoff syndrome. A clinicopathologic study of seventy cases', *Arch. Neurol. Psychiat., 76*, 585

Marchiafava, E. and Bignami, A. (1903), 'Sopra un álterazione del corpo callos osservata in soggetti alcoolisti', *Riv. Pat. nerv. ment., 8*, 544

Marinacci, A.A. (1957), 'The electroencephalogram in forensic criminology: Alcoholism', *EEG Clin. Neurophysiol., 9*, 377

Marinacci, A.A. and Courville, C.B. (1958), 'Alcohol intoxication as a misleading element in convulsive episodes and unconscious states: Value of the EEG in the clarification of the diagnosis', *EEG Clin. Neorophysiol., 10*, 360

Menzi, W. (1955), 'Pathogenetische Untersuchungen über das Delirium tremens', *Mschr Psychiat. Neurol., 129*, 418

Meyer, E. (1930), 'Encephalographische Befunde aus neurologischem und psychiatrischem Gebiete', *Arch. Psychiat. Nervenkrankh., 89*, 177

Morel, F. (1939), 'Une forme anatomo-clinique particulière de l'alcoolisme cronique: Sclérose corticale laminaire alcoolique', *Rev. Neurol., 71*, 280

Morel, F. and Duman, R. (1940), 'Contribution à l'étude anatomo-clinique du syndrome de Korsakoff ethylique', *Mschr. Psychiat. Neurol., 103*, 1

Mukasa, H. (1962), 'A study on EEG during alcohol drinking', *Clin. Psychiat.*, Tokyo, *4/5*, 309

Müller, E. and Rutenfranz, J. (1960), 'Das EEG als Test der cerebralen Funktionsstörung nach Alkohol', *Dtsch Z. Ges. Gerichtl. Med. 50*, 54

Newman, W.H. (1956), 'The effect of alcohol on the electroencephalogram', *EEG Clin. Neurophysiol., 8*, 156

Perrin, J. (1951), 'Contribution à l'étude électro-encéphalographique des alcooliques psychiatriques à propos de 100 électro-éncéphalogrammes d'alcooliques', *Thèse*, Lyon

Pluvinage, R. (1954), 'Les atrophies cérébrales des alcooliques', *Bull. Soc. Med. Paris, 70*, 524

Postel, J. and Cossa, P. (1956), 'L'atrophie cérébelare des alcooliques chroniques', *Rev. Neurol., 94*, 604

Prudent (1956), 'Contribution à l'étude EEG de l'intoxication éthylique chronique', *Thèse*, Paris

Sisson, B.D. and Ellingson, R.J. (1956), 'The EEG in cerebral atrophy', *J. Nerv. Ment. Dis., 123*, 244

Streljčuk, I.V. and Melehova, A.M. (1962), 'Elektrofiziologičeskoe issledovanie kory golovnogo mozga zdorovih ljudjej i bolnyh hroničeskim alkogolizmom pri vozdejstvij čerez pervuju i vtoruju sistemu vo vremja gipnotičeskogo sostojanija', *Z. Nerv. i Psih. Korsakov, 62*, 428

Subbotnik, S.I. and Špilberg, P.I. (1959), 'Elektroencefalografičeskoe issledovanie pri hroničeskom alkogolizme', *Alkogolizam*, Moskva

Thompson, G.N. (1957), 'Further electroencephalographic correlation between pathological intoxication and psychomotor epilepsy', *EEG Clin. Neurophysiol., 9*, 378

Tumarkin, B., Wilson, J. and Snyder, G. (1955), 'Cerebral atrophy due to alcoholism in young adults', *US Armed Forces Medical Journal, 6*, 67

Vallat, J.N., Lepetit, J.M. and Demart, D. (1961), 'Étude du tracé immédiatement post-critique après crise convulsive "occasionnelle" chez certains éthyliques', *Rev. Neurol., 105*, 217

Vercelletto, P. (1952), 'Epilepsie, pubertaire et comitialité tardive apparue chez des éthyliques', *EEG Clin. Neurophysiol., 4*, 249

Wernicke, C. (1881), *Lehrbuch der Gehirnkrankheiten für Aerzte und Studierende, 2*, Verlag von Theodor Fischer, Kassel, 229-42

10 COMPUTED TOMOGRAPHY OF THE BRAIN AND NEUROPSYCHOLOGICAL ASSESSMENT OF MALE ALCOHOLIC PATIENTS

Hans Bergman, Stefan Borg, Tomas Hindmarsh,
Carl-Magnus Ideström and Sture Mützell

The aim of this study was to map the frequency and location of morphological cerebral changes in alcoholic patients by computed tomography of the brain and assess their functional state by neuropsychological tests, and then to relate the findings to their clinical characteristics.

Since our first report of computed tomography (CT scan) of the brain and neuropsychological assessment of a series of 20 alcoholic patients (Myrhed et al., 1976) several reports on the CT scans of alcoholic patients have been presented (e.g. Carlen et al., 1976; Fox et al., 1976; Epstein, 1977; Cala et al., 1978; Götze et al., 1978; Hill, 1978; Bergman et al., 1979). The frequency of pathological findings varies with respect to how often cortical changes and ventricular enlargement are reported. The variability might be due to the lack of common criteria for the evaluation of the CT scans or to the use of different patient selection criteria resulting in the investigation of alcoholics of different types.

To allow us to divide the patient sample into subgroups that were homogeneous with regard to pertinent patient characteristics, we aimed to collect a group of considerable size. In order to get well defined variables the investigation of each subject was to be carried out as uniformly as possible, with predefined criteria of the neuroradiological, neuropsychological and clinical conditions.

Material

The patient material comprised 148 consecutive male inpatient admissions out of 180 patients of both sexes. They fulfilled the criteria of being born on an uneven day of the month and of staying at least one week at the Alcohol Clinic at the Karolinska Hospital for voluntary treatment of alcohol problems. The clinic has a geographically defined catchment area at the north of Stockholm. The results of the 32 women who were also investigated are not presented. Because of drop-outs in the patient material, due to relapse into drinking and/or discharge from the hospital, it was only possible to carry out CT scans and psychological assessments on 130 patients. The clinical investigation, the CT scan and the neuropsychological assessment were performed during the patients' stay at the clinic.

Table 10.1: Some Medical Conditions at the Time of Admission of 148 Male Alcoholic Patients

Clinical conditions	Percentage distribution
Age, years	
20-29	12
30-39	29
40-49	23
50-59	30
60-65	6
Duration of alcohol abuse, years	
≤ 5	22
6-10	27
11-15	19
≥ 16	32
Type of drinking pattern	
Continuous	27
Periodic	51
Combined type	22
Maximum daily consumption, g abs. alcohol	
≤ 125	13
126-250	35
251-375	25
≥ 376	27
Blackouts	79
Epileptic fits	20
Delirious episodes	35
Hypnotic/sedative abuse	10
Previous medical care for alcohol problems	56
Head trauma with hospital care	18

Note: Data are lacking for ten patients.

Clinical Conditions

Clinical data were gathered by means of standardised questionnaires
with predefined response alternatives. The medical history of the
patient group is shown in Table 10.1. The median age was 44.2 years
(range: 20-65 years). About half of the group had a duration of alcohol
abuse of 10 years or more. About three quarters reported
'bender' type drinking. The median daily intake of alcohol when
drinking heavily was reported to be about 250 g of absolute alcohol,
equivalent to one bottle (75 cl) of hard liquor. More than three
quarters of the sample reported histories of blackouts and one third of
delirious episodes. Eighteen per cent reported previous hospital
treatment for head trauma. Somewhat more than half of the sample
had been treated for alcohol problems on an inpatient basis prior to
admission to the clinic. However, serious neuropsychiatric conditions,
such as the Wernicke-Korsakoff syndrome, were not diagnosed in any
of the cases.

**Table 10.2: Some Social Characteristics at the Time of Admission of
148 Male Alcoholic Patients**

Social conditions	Percentage distribution
Education	
Elementary school	80
Lower secondary school	9
Senior secondary or higher	11
Civil status	
Never married	30
Separated or divorced	48
Married	20
Widowed	2
Work status	
Pensioned	10
Unemployed	24
Employed	66
Development of working capacity	
Never occupationally adjusted	25
Normal occupational development	30
Occupational decline	45

Note: Data are lacking for six patients.

Table 10.2 shows some social characteristics at the time of admission. About three quarters of the patients had received elementary school education only. About half of the group were separated and about one quarter were unemployed at the time of admission to the clinic.

None were homeless. About one quarter had never established themselves on the common labour market and nearly half had declined occupationally. Summing up, this patient group was clinically rather heterogeneous and consisted mainly of moderate to severe cases with regard to their social and clinical conditions.

CT Scan and Morphological Cerebral Findings

The CT scans were performed in the Departments of Radiology and Neuroradiology at the Karolinska Hospital. A scanning of the brain consists of eight or nine horizontal sections, each 10-13 mm in depth. The CT scan is about 100 times more sensitive than conventional X-ray techniques but has considerably less resolution. The X-ray dose corresponds fairly well to that of an ordinary skull examination with two exposures ($\leq$ 2 rad) (see Axelsson and Bergström, 1978).

The tomographic pictures were evaluated according to a standardised procedure (Department of Neuroradiology, 1977). To assess cortical changes a 4-step scale was used, based on a general assessment of the tomographs by the radiologist with regard to observed widened sulci. On this scale: 1 = normal, i.e. no sulci visible or sulci less than 3 mm in the scale of 1:1; 2 = suspected degenerative changes, i.e. up to five sulci exceeding 3 mm in diameter; 3 = clear-cut changes, i.e. more than five sulci exceeding 3 mm in diameter; 4 = high-grade changes, i.e. marked widening of a great number of sulci. The inter-rater reliability of the 4-step scale was found to be 0.81 (Hindmarsh, 1979).

It was found that 62 per cent of the patients were rated to show clear-cut or high-grade changes by the radiologist, about half of the 20-29 year old patients and two thirds of the 50-59 year olds (see Figure 10.1). The central, subcortical parts of the brain were assessed by a number of direct measurements of the ventricular system. An anterior horn index was obtained by dividing the width of the anterior horns by the largest inner skull diameter.

It was found that 33 per cent of the patients had an anterior horn index above 0.31, 15 per cent in the age group 20-29 and 37 per cent

Figure 10.1: Percentages of Clear-cut or High-grade Cortical Changes, Anterior Horn Index > 0.31 and Width of 3rd Ventricle > 6 mm in 130 Male Alcoholic Patients by Age Groups

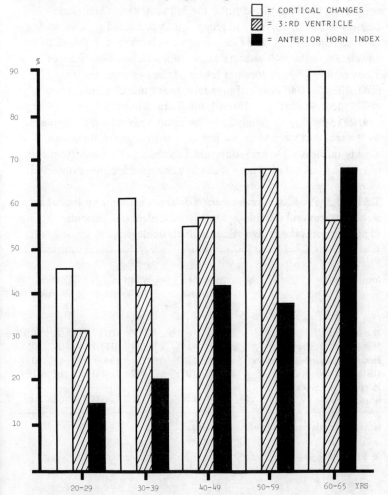

among those 50-59 years of age (Figure 10.1). Fifty-three per cent of the patients gave evidence of an enlarged 3rd ventricle according to the criterion of more than 6 mm maximal transverse diameter; they included 31 per cent of those of 20-29 years and 67 per cent of those in the 50-59 age group. Cerebellar changes were assessed by the presence of wide cisterns. The frequency varied from 15 per cent of those of 20-29 years to 20 per cent of those in the 50-59-year age group.

The product-moment correlation between the anterior horn index and the width of the 3rd ventricle in the present investigation was 0.46 (p<0.001). There was a low but statistically significant correlation between the width of the 3rd ventricle and cortical changes in the 20-39-year old group, which decreased with advancing age (see Figure 10.2). The same trend was observed with regard to the correlation between the anterior horn index and cortical changes. These findings do not speak in favour of the hypothesis of a generalised, overall effect of long-term heavy drinking on the brains of our alcoholic patients. Instead, the findings might suggest alternative courses of cerebral degeneration. This hypothesis is further supported by the fact that a tendency to high frequency of cortical changes already in the 20-29-year group, and a comparatively lower frequency of pathological anterior horn index and 3rd ventricle, were observed.

Table 10.3: Product-moment correlations between chronological age, medical status and CT findings in 130 male alcoholic patients. Figures in parenthesis give values with chronological age singled out.

Medical Status	Anterior Horn Index		CT Scan Width of 3rd Ventricle		Cortical Changes	
Chronological age	43[c]		36[c]		28[b]	
Duration of abuse in yrs.	13	(−02)	19[a]	(07)	06	(−04)
History of blackouts	01	(18)	02	(15)	−04	(05)
History of delirious episodes	−02	(20[a])	16	(24[b])	13	(02)
History of epileptic fits	04	(07)	−07	(−06)	17	(19[a])
Hospital treatment for head trauma	−15	(−06)	−11	(−03)	04	(10)

Note: Decimals omitted from correlations.

a: p <0.05
b: p <0.01
c: p <0.001

With the exception of chronological age and duration of abuse there were no significant correlations between the clinical findings and morphological cerebral changes (see Table 10.3). It should be noted that the correlation between duration of abuse and cerebral changes was low and only significant with regard to the width of the 3rd ventricle; it also tended to be lower than the correlation between age

Figure 10.2: Product-moment Correlations Between Cortical Changes and Anterior Horn Index and Between Cortical Changes and Width of 3rd Ventricle in 130 Male Alcoholic Patients in the Age Groups 20-39 and 50-65 years.

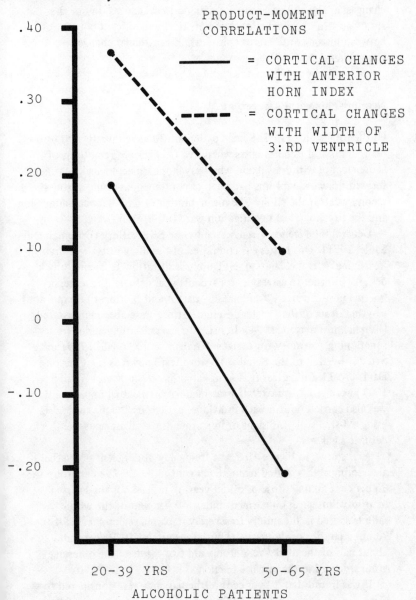

and cerebral changes. When chronological age was singled out from the correlations no relationship between duration of abuse and width of the 3rd ventricle was observed; but a history of delirious episodes showed a low but statistically significant correlation with ventricular changes, as also did epileptic fits with cortical changes. In our first study we also observed a low but statistically significant correlation between history of delirious episodes and ventricular changes (Bergman *et al.*, 1979).

Neuropsychological Assessment

Of the total sample of 148 male patients, 130 were investigated by a team of clinical psychologists when free from visible symptoms of acute alcohol withdrawal and when psychopharmacological treatment for withdrawal symptoms had been discontinued, as a rule during the second week at the clinic. The mean number of days between admission and the psychological investigation was 10.

General intelligence was assessed by the SRB battery (Dureman and Sälde, 1971). This battery is composed of the three tests: 'synonyms', 'reasoning' (i.e. the Thurstone Figure Classification Test) and 'block design'. In order to assess neuropsychological deficits, the 'category', 'tactual performance', 'trail making' part A and B, 'finger tapping' and 'rhythm' tests of the Halstead-Reitan battery were also administered (Reitan and Davison, 1974). In order to assess learning and memory functioning, 'memory-for-designs' (Graham and Kendall, 1960) and a Swedish version of the Schulze 10-word test known as the Claeson-Dahl verbal learning test (Claeson, Esbjörnsson, Carlé and Wahlbin, 1971) were given. An overall assessment of intellectual impairment was also carried out for each individual patient by the psychologists using a 3-step scale (no signs of impairment = 1, slight signs = 2, definite signs = 3).

As is shown in Figure 10.3, the frequency of deficient nonverbal abstracting ability varied from 38 per cent in the 20-29-year group to 76 per cent among those of 50-59 years of age. As for the Halstead neuropsychological impairment index, 49 per cent of the whole sample scored in the mildly to severely impaired region, i.e. 0.5-1.0. About a quarter of the patients in the age group 20-29 years, and about half of the 30-39-year group and two thirds of the older age groups, scored in the impaired region.

It was found that 22 per cent of the patients were considered to

Figure 10.3: Percentage of Deficient Nonverbal Abstracting Ability, Deficient Visual Short-term Memory and Neuropsychological Impairment According to Halstead Impairment Index (≥ 0.5) in 130 Male Alcoholic Patients of Different Age Groups

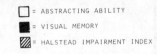

= ABSTRACTING ABILITY

= VISUAL MEMORY

= HALSTEAD IMPAIRMENT INDEX

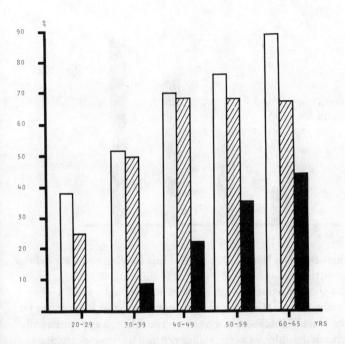

show definite signs of intellectual impairment according to the psychologist's overall assessment of test results (see Figure 10.4). Impairment was more often diagnosed in the older groups than in the younger. The correlation coefficients between age and results in individual tests of the battery were all highly significant ($p < 0.001$).

Figure 10.4: Definite Signs of Intellectual Impairment According to the Psychologist's Overall Assessment of Test Results in 130 Male Alcoholic Patients by Age Groups, in Percentages

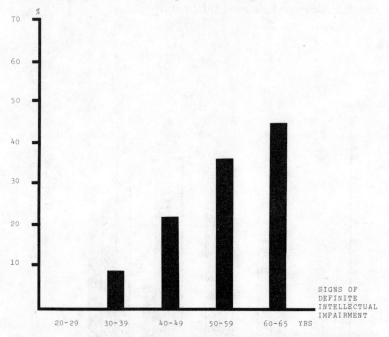

Correlations Between Neuropsychological Functioning and CT Findings

Table 10.4 shows product-moment correlations between the SRB measures of general intelligence and neuropsychological functioning on the one hand and CT scan results on the other. There was a statistically significant relationship between intelligence and the two ventricular measures, i.e. the anterior horn index and the width of the third ventricle. The correlation with cortical changes was low but significant, mainly due to the results in 'block design'. Learning and memory functioning as measured by the Claeson-Dahl and 'memory-for-designs' tests were also significantly correlated with the ventricular measures, but not with cortical changes. Thus, patients with ventricular enlargement tended to have lower general intelligence and inferior learning and memory abilities.

The 'category', 'tactual performance', 'tapping' and 'trail-making' tests of the Halstead-Reitan battery were also significantly correlated with the morphological cerebral status of our patient group. There was

Table 10.4: Product-moment correlations between general intelligence, neuropsychological functioning and CT findings in 130 male alcoholic patients. Figures in parenthesis give values with chronological age singled out.

Tests	CT Scan		
	Anterior Horn Index	Width of 3rd Ventricle	Cortical Changes
SRB, IQ	−34[c] (−27[b])	−32[b] (−25[b])	−21[a] (−15)
Synonyms, raw score	−26[c] (−17)	−31[b] (−18)	−12 (−06)
Reasoning, raw score	−37[c] (−21[a])	−20[a] (−18)	−16 (−04)
Block design, raw score	−41[c] (−25[b])	−30[b] (−15)	−25[b] (−14)
Halstead-Reitan Battery			
Category, errors	28[b] (11)	33[b] (19)	15 (03)
Tactual, total time	24[a] (09)	28[b] (17)	07 (−04)
Tactual, memory	−01 (20)	−03 (13)	−14[a] (−03)
Tactual, location	−05 (16)	−15 (06)	−24[b] (−10)
Trail making A+B, credits	−29[b] (−09)	−30[b] (−14)	−09 (06)
Tapping, dominant hand	−08 (03)	−35[b] (−29[b])	−27[b] (−22[a])
Rhythm, raw score	−15 (−02)	−04 (09)	−21[a] (−13)
Impairment index	14 (−10)	24[a] (06)	32[b] (22[a])
Learning and Memory			
Memory-for-designs, error score	39[c] (22[a])	27[b] (12)	14 (01)
Claeson-Dahl verbal learning, error score	40[c] (25[b])	27[b] (13)	06 (−08)
Overall assessment of intellectual impairment	27[b] (07)	22[a] (−05)	28[b] (17)

Note: Decimals omitted from correlations; data missed in 6 cases.

a: $p < 0.05$
b: $p < 0.01$
c: $p < 0.001$

a low but significant correlation between the Halstead Impairment Index, which summarises the neuropsychological test results, cortical changes and width of third ventricle. The findings with regard to 'category' and 'trail-making' are hardly surprising, since these particular tests seem to be sensitive in alcoholics (Kleinknecht and Goldstein, 1972). There was also a low but statistically significant correlation between the 3-step scale of overall assessment of intellectual impairment and the morphological cerebral status of the patient group.

In conclusion, the correlations between neuropsychological functioning and the morphological CT measures were generally low, but tended to fall into a specific pattern. The results indicate that learning and memory functioning in our alcoholic patients are correlated with the status of the subcortical parts of the brain, while the Halstead-Reitan battery and Index, and the psychologist's overall assessment of test results with regard to intellectual impairment, are to some degree predictive of cortical changes as well.

When chronological age was singled out — and thus also to a certain extent the effects of the duration of heavy drinking — the correlations between neuropsychological performance and brain morphology decreased. General intelligence and learning and memory were significantly correlated with central changes, while 'finger tapping' and Halstead Impairment Index were significantly correlated with cortical changes (see Table 10.4).

Implications

The results of this study are in agreement with our earlier reported findings (Bergman *et al.*, 1979) and show that cortical changes and an enlarged ventricular system can often be observed in a consecutive male patient population from an alcohol clinic. Cortical changes were often diagnosed already in many of the 20-29-year old patients. Thus, cortical changes might antedate heavy drinking or might occur rather early in the drinking career. The duration of abuse was only 5½ years on the average in this age group.

On the other hand, the frequency of ventricular enlargement was comparatively lower in the younger patients and then gradually increased with age. This might indicate a gradual increase in pathological changes during the whole drinking career.

Correlational analyses showed that the cortical and the ventricular changes were related in patients below 40 years of age, but not in older patients.

The correlation between cerebral changes and clinical factors, with the exception of age, was low. It should be pointed out that the correlation between duration of abuse and cerebral changes tended to be lower than that between age and cerebral changes.

Neuropsychological deficits were also observed in many patients, particularly in the area of abstracting ability. The correlations between neuropsychological functioning and the cerebral morphological status were generally low. However, the results suggest that learning and memory functioning are sensitive only to subcortical changes in the brains of alcoholic patients, while the Halstead-Reitan battery, the Halstead Impairment Index as a summary measure of neuropsychological deficits and an overall assessment of intellectual impairment, are also sensitive to cortical changes as well.

These findings support the view that different pathological CNS processes are involved in connection with alcohol abuse. To be able to interpret the significance of the cerebral morphological changes and neuropsychological deficits in this study we have collected a random sample of men from the general population (Bergman *et al.*, 1979). We are also collecting data in a follow-up programme for the patient group in order to assess the stability and prognostic significance of the cerebral morphological and neuropsychological findings.

Acknowledgements

This project was supported by grants from the Bank of Sweden Tercentenary Foundation (project no. 77/24).

References

Axelsson, B. and Bergström, H. (1978), 'Radiation doses related to collimator geometry in the first generation EMI Scanner', *Acta. Radiologica Oncology, 17*

Bergman, H., Borg, S., Hindmarsh, T., Ideström, C.-M. and Mützell, S. (1978), 'Computed tomography of the brain and neuropsychological assessment of alcoholic patients' in *Proceedings from the Fourth Biennial International Symposium on Biological Research in Alcoholism*, Zürich, Switzerland, June 1978, Begleiter, H. and Kissin, B. (eds.), Plenum Press, New York

——— (1979), 'Alcoholism and brain damage: A review' in preparation

——— (1980), 'Computed tomography of the brain and neuropsychological assessment of male alcoholic patients and a random male sample from the general population', Paper presented at the second Magnus Huss Symposium on Alcoholism in Stockholm, September 5-8, 1979, to be published in *Acta Psychiatrica Scandinavica*

Cala, L.A., Jones, B., Mastaglia, F.L. and Wiley, B. (1978), 'Brain atrophy and intellectual impairment in heavy drinkers – a clinical psychometric and computerized tomography study', *Australian and New Zealand Journal of Medicine, 8*, 147-53

Carlen, P.L., Wilkinson, A. and Kiraly, L.T. (1976), 'Dementia in alcoholics: A longitudinal study including some reversible aspects', *Neurology, 26*, 355

Claeson, L.-E., Esbjörnsson, E., Carlé, B.-M. and Wahlbin, M. (1971), 'Claeson-

214   *Computed Tomography and Neuropsychological Assessment*

Dahls inlärningstest för kliniskt bruk (Claeson-Dahl verbal learning test for clinical use)', *Skandinaviska Testförlaget*, Stockholm

Department of Neuroradiology, (1977), 'Alcohol EMI ^{X}f 427 questionnaire', *Karolinska sjukhuset*

Dureman, I. and Sälde, H. (1971), *DS-batteriet (The DS battery)*, Almqvist and Wiksell, Stockholm

Epstein, P.S., Pisani, V.D. and Fawcett, J.A. (1977), 'Alcoholism and cerebral atrophy', *Alcoholism: Clinical and Experimental Research, 1*, 61-5

Fox, J.H., Ramsey, R.G., Huckman, H.S. and Proske, A.E. (1976), 'Cerebral ventricular enlargement: Chronic alcoholics examined by computerized tomography', *JAMA, 236*, 365-8

Götze, P., Kuhne, D., Hansen, J. and Knipp, H.P. (1978), 'Hirnatrophische Veränderungen bei chronischen Alkoholismus', *Archiv für Psychiatrie und Nervenkrankheiten, 226*, 137-56

Graham, F.K. and Kendall, B.S. (1960), 'Memory-for-Designs Test: Revised general manual', *Perceptual and Motor Skills, 11*, 147-88

Hill, S.Y. (1978), 'Computerized transaxial tomography and neuropsychological impairment in alcoholics and opiate abusers: A comparison', Paper presented at the Ninth Annual NCA-AMSA-RSA Medical-Scientific Conference of the National Alcoholism Forum, USA, May 1978

Hindmarsh, T. (1979), 'Computed tomography of the brain in a group of industrial painters exposed to organic solvents', *Scandinavian Journal of Work and Environmental Health*, in press

Kleinknecht, R.A. and Goldstein, S.G. (1972), 'Neuropsychological deficits associated with alcoholism', *Quarterly Journal of Studies on Alcoh., 33*, 999-1019

Myrhed, M., Bergman, H., Borg, S., Hindmarsh, T. and Ideström, C.-M. (1976), 'Computer tomographic cerebral findings in a group of alcoholic patients', *Hygiea Acta Societas Medicorum Suecanae, 85*, 253

Reitan, R.M. and Davison, L.A. (1974), *Clinical Neuropsychology: Current Status and Applications*, Winston, New York

11 COMPUTED TOMOGRAPHY OF THE BRAIN AND PSYCHOMETRIC ASSESSMENT OF ALCOHOLIC PATIENTS — A BRITISH STUDY

W.A. Lishman, M. Ron and W. Acker

The new technique of computerised axial tomography has brought us to an interesting situation with regard to alcoholism. The older literature, which had often reported cerebral atrophy on air encephalography in small groups of alcoholics (e.g. Tumarkin *et al.*, 1955; Haug, 1968; Brewer and Perrett, 1971) has come into sharp focus. A number of groups of workers, including ourselves, have indeed confirmed a high incidence of cerebral changes in alcoholic patients using this non-invasive means of examining the brain (Carlen *et al.*, 1976; Fox *et al.*, 1976; Epstein *et al.*, 1977; Bergman *et al.*, 1978; Cala *et al.*, 1978; von Gall *et al.*, 1978; Ron *et al.*, 1979). The task must now be to interpret the meaning of such changes and attempt to discover their aetiological and prognostic significance. In particular we shall wish to discover to what extent the changes are permanent or reversible, and what bearing they may have on so-called 'alcoholic dementia'.

Alcoholism was selected as one of the first research projects to be undertaken with the EMI head scanner installed at the Maudsley Hospital. Not only was there the literature referred to above, sometimes suggesting atrophy in quite young subjects, but this had occasionally been confirmed at post-mortem examination (Courville, 1955; Lynch, 1960). Secondly, there was a growing body of information pointing to cognitive impairments in alcoholic subjects, often persisting well beyond the immediate 'drying-out' process (e.g: Fitzhugh *et al.*, 1960; Kleinknecht and Goldstein, 1972; Long and McLachlan, 1974; Clarke and Haughton, 1975; Tarter, 1975; Page and Schaub, 1977; Eckardt *et al.*, 1978). Finally there was the possibility, repeatedly raised but nowhere conclusively demonstrated, that alcoholics might eventually proceed more often than chance expectation to a state of 'accelerated cognitive decline', 'deterioration' or 'dementia' (Horvath, 1975; Cutting, 1978). A concerted attack on such problems by CAT scanning and psychometry seemed indicated. These investigations, by their non-invasive nature, should be readily applicable to 'unselected' groups of alcoholic subjects who would otherwise usually have escaped such comprehensive evaluation.

The investigation to be described has been a joint undertaking. Dr. Maria Ron, psychiatrist, and Dr. William Acker, psychologist, have been involved at every stage and carried out the field work. Dr. K. Shaw and his team at the Bexley Hospital Alcoholism Unit have collaborated throughout. Miss S. Aldridge has assisted greatly with the tracing and follow up of patients, and Dr. R.D. Hoare has put his radiographic facilities and expertise at our disposal.

The present account must be regarded as an interim report only. Further analysis of data is proceeding and further subjects are being recruited. It cannot be claimed that our present results have given clear answers to the problems mentioned above; indeed they are raising new and interesting problems of their own. But in conformity with studies proceeding in other centres we think they demonstrate that CAT scanning is adding a new and important dimension to our conceptions of the effects of alcohol on the brain.

The Maudsley Alcoholism Study

Our selection of patients for examination differs from that of most other series in that we have set out to include only those who were superficially 'intact'. We felt it important to establish whether or not radiographic and psychometric abnormalities would emerge in such a group, i.e. before clinical evidence of brain damage or deterioration had become immediately obvious, and if so to determine their associations.

The patients were recruited from the Bexley In patient Treatment Unit where they were undergoing a six-week course of therapy after completion of the drying-out process. Any patient with obvious mental impairment, or where there was reason to suspect brain damage (e.g. history of drug overdose or head injury with post-traumatic amnesia > 24 hours) was excluded. A detailed history and clinical examination was undertaken, with emphasis on key aspects of the drinking pattern, using a modified version of the Standardised Alcoholism Interview Schedule (Caetano *et al.*, 1978). One hundred such patients have been examined to date, all male. Ages range from 22-63 with a mean of 43.5. The average length of the drinking history was 17.3 years, and the average amount of alcohol consumed per day during a 'heavy' drinking period was 462.7g (slightly less than two bottles of spirits or equivalent). A point of some importance, as will emerge below, is that the patients had been abstinent for an average of 34 days prior to scanning and psychometric testing, with a range of from 12 to 120 days.

A group of 41 volunteer male control subjects was meanwhile recruited from local sources including the hospital staff, a Salvation Army Training Centre, and from among patients attending a nearby general practitioner with minor complaints unrelated to central nervous system disorder. Controls were screened for absence of neurological and psychiatric disorder, and to ensure as far as possible no more than a small alcohol intake. Most were abstemious and the rest had at all times drunk only in moderation. Their ages ranged from 29-61 with a mean of 40.0.

Alcoholic and control subjects were scanned in the same manner as one another and given an identical battery of psychometric tests. CAT scanning was carried out using a CT 1010 EMI scanner, 5-6 contiguous pairs of 'cuts' being made parallel to the orbitomeatal line, so as to encompass the whole ventricular system and display the cortical sulci in top-most cuts. Psychometric testing employed a battery of test procedures chosen to sample a broad spectrum of cognitive abilities. Details will emerge in the results that follow.

CAT Scan Findings

A number of ratings and measurements were made on the photographic records of the scans, the raters being unaware whether they were dealing with the scan of an alcoholic patient or a control subject.

Three ratings relevant to the cerebral cortex — of sulcal widening, Sylvian fissure widening and interhemispheric fissure widening — were made by simple visual inspection of the scans, two raters (M.R. and W.A.L.) working independently then comparing their results. Sulcal widening was rated on a 4 point scale (0-3), illustrated in Figure 11.1, judging each scan against pre-agreed 'norms', representing the transition from one grade to the next. Sylvian fissure widening was rated in a similar manner on a 3 point scale (0-2), and interhemispheric fissure widening on a 2 point scale (0-1). Ratings of 0 indicated a judgement of 'definite normality' on rather conservative criteria.

Agreement between raters was high, their final scores being identical in 80-90 per cent of cases and in no case differing by more than a single grade. When differences could not be resolved by re-inspection, the lower score prevailed.

Figure 11.1: Grades of sulcal atrophy: samples used for allocation to grades 0-3. The distribution of grades between alcoholics and controls is shown in Table 11.1.

SULCAL WIDENING

(GRADES 0 to 3)

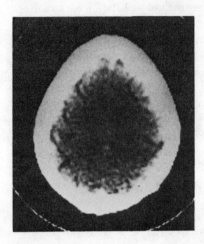

UPPER LIMIT of 0

UPPER LIMIT of 1

UPPER LIMIT of 2

Table 11.1: CAT Scan Findings in Alcoholics and Controls

	Alcoholics (N=100)	Controls (N=41)		
Sulcal widening				
Grade 0	32	32		
Grade 1	24	7	$x^2 = 27.5$	P < .0001
Grade 2	29	2		
Grade 3	14	0		
Sylvian fissure widening				
Grade 0	51	35		
Grade 1	35	6	$x^2 = 15.5$	P = .0004
Grade 2	14	0		
Interhemispheric fissure widening				
Grade 0	71	40	$x^2 = 10.7$	P < .001
Grade 1	29	1		
Ventricle/brain ratio				
Mean	9.5	6.1	$t = 6.7$	P < .0001
(S.D.)	(2.9)	(1.8)		

Ventricular size was measured by selecting the two consecutive slices showing the maximal amount of ventricle for each subject. Taking each of the slices in turn, a planimeter was used to trace around the margins of all ventricular elements in the slice, then around the inner margin of the skull. A 'ventricle/brain' ratio was thus computed for each subject; the higher the ratio, the larger the ventricles in proportion to total cranial volume. Measurements were again made independently by two raters (M.R. and W.A.) without knowing which were scans of alcoholics or controls (inter-rater agreement r = 0.87, P < .00001).

Table 11.1 shows comparisons between the alcoholics and controls on these various indices. On all three measures of cortical shrinkage, the alcoholics show highly significant differences from the controls, a large number having the more severe grades of shrinkage. Ventricular size is considerably larger in the alcoholics, being on average half as large again as in the controls.

When the alcoholics were subdivided into two age groups — above and below the mean age for the sample (43.5) — the younger alcoholics as well as the older remained significantly different from their age-matched controls on all radiographic indices. Indeed the younger alcoholic group had a larger mean ventricular size (V/B ratio 8.8) than the older group of controls (V/B ratio 7.3).

Thus we are clearly finding, like others, that the brains of alcoholics are markedly unusual, with evidence of both cortical shrinkage and ventricular enlargement. We are finding it in alcoholics who have superficially seemed intact, and without reason to suspect brain damage on clinical examination. What is its significance? And what is the aetiology? As a preliminary approach to such problems we have looked for correlates of the radiological changes in terms of detailed drinking history and in terms of behavioural abnormalities as revealed on psychometric testing.

CAT Scan Findings and Drinking History

In the analyses carried out to date no convincing evidence has emerged to relate the cortical or ventricular changes to length of drinking history. The current age of the patients is highly correlated with the amount of shrinkage observed (e.g. sulcal widening *vs* age, r = .43, P = .001; ventricle/brain ratio *vs* age, r = .28, P = .002); but when groups of patients of similar age but markedly different duration of drinking were compared the radiological measurements scarcely changed from one group to the next. Estimates of peak alcoholic consumption, while necessarily very approximate, have similarly failed to reveal clear associations with severity of the CAT scan changes.

The feature of the drinking history which does appear to be of importance is the number of days of abstinence prior to the CAT scan examination. Thus both sulcal widening and Sylvian fissure widening are negatively correlated with duration of abstinence (r = −0.20, P = .02; r = −0.24, P = .007 respectively); so is the ventricle/brain ratio (r = −0.13, P = .09). In other words, the shorter the period of abstinence before the scan, the greater has been the cortical shrinkage and the greater the ventricular enlargement. These relationships remained significant after controlling for the effects of age. On examining the situation in the younger and older groups of alcoholics the results shown in Table 11.2 emerged. It is only in the older group that noteworthy relationships to duration of abstinence appear. Moreover in the older group there is often a significant relationship between the severity of the CAT scan changes and a rough retrospective estimate of the number of weeks of abstinence during the preceding year.

Altogether the results strongly suggest that, apart from current age,

Table 11.2: CAT Scan Changes in Relation to Recent Drinking History in Younger and Older Alcoholic Groups

| | Alcoholics aged 43 or younger (N=48) | | Alcoholics aged 44 or older (N=52) | |
	Correl. Coeff.	*P*	*Correl. Coeff.*	*P*
Sulcal widening				
No. days abstinent prior to examination	.05	N.S.	−.36	.004
No. weeks abstinent previous year	.09	N.S.	−.08	N.S.
Sylvian fissure widening				
No. days abstinent prior to examination	−.08	N.S.	−.33	.008
No. weeks abstinent previous year	−.03	N.S.	−.26	.03
Ventricle/brain ratio				
No. days abstinent prior to examination	.15	N.S.	−.29	.016
No. weeks abstinent previous year	.06	N.S.	−.31	.011

the most substantial influence on the degree of the CAT scan abnormalities has been the duration of abstinence prior to scanning, and that this has itself been operative almost exclusively among the older alcoholics. A recent impact of alcohol on the brain would therefore appear to have been important in determining, at least in part, the degree of brain shrinkage observed. Two points deserve emphasis, however.

First it should be noted that this impact must last for a considerable period of time — none of the patients was scanned after less than 12 days of abstinence, and the majority after abstinence for several weeks (mean 34 days). Relationships have often emerged, moreover, between the severity of the radiographic changes and estimates of the number of weeks of abstinence over the preceding *year*. Whatever toxic or metabolic actions of alcohol are responsible must have considerably long-lasting effects.

The second point to note is that even among the younger alcoholics, in whom duration of abstinence was without apparent effect, CAT scan findings were markedly different from the controls. Thus, while we may have identified a contributory *factor* towards the severity of the radiographic changes we have by no means explained them *in toto*. A model suggests itself whereby brain changes are established quite early in the drinking careers of a substantial proportion of alcoholics and are at that stage largely uninfluenced by recent excess or abstinence. With increasing age, however, the brain becomes more vulnerable and reflects the recent drinking pattern quite closely.

Repeat Scanning at Follow-up

Follow-up after a considerable interval should clarify the position further. If a short- to medium-term impact of alcohol on the brain should be a principal *determinant* of the brain changes, in addition to influencing their severity, very substantial resolution of such changes might be expected after a prolonged period of total abstinence.

To date we have re-scanned 23 of the original sample of patients after intervals ranging from 30 to 91 weeks (mean 56.8 weeks). During that period 9 patients had remained totally abstinent or had had less than 4 periods of drinking of less than a week's duration. The remaining 14 patients had continued to drink as previously. The initial and repeat scans were examined and measured in the usual way, the raters being unaware of the interim drinking history and of which was the first and which the second scan.

In the abstinent group, either sulcal or Sylvian fissure ratings had improved in 4 patients, always by a single grade only. No improvements were observed among the continuing drinkers and in several of these the picture had worsened. At follow up the mean ventricle/brain ratio among the abstinent group was 9.8, compared to 11.0 at first examination, a decrease which approaches statistical significance ($P = 0.08$). No change was observed in ventricular size among the continuing drinkers.

So it appears from this preliminary analysis of a small group of patients that abstinence for approximately a year may sometimes allow partial resolution of both cortical and ventricular abnormalities. It should be noted, however, that even after such an interval the ventricular size (V/B ratio = 9.8) remains distinctly larger than normal (V/B ratio in controls = 6.1). Abstinence for a year clearly cannot ensure total resolution of the radiographic changes. Fortunately, however, a trend exists which suggests the possibility that with further prolonged abstinence there may yet be continuing improvement.

Psychometric Findings

The psychometric findings will only be presented in broad outline. Among the patients and controls tested to date there is a significant difference in educational attainment and a small but significant difference in estimate of premorbid intelligence as judged by the New Adult Reading Test (Nelson and McKenna, 1975). The alcoholics are inferior in both these respects. Detailed analysis of performance and firm interpretation of results must therefore await the recruitment of a larger and better balanced sample. Certain broad comparisons are, however, already worth attention.

To date, 93 of the alcoholics and 36 of the controls have been examined with the full battery of psychometric tests. This includes, in addition to the New Adult Reading Test, a shortened version of the Wechsler Adult Intelligence Scale (vocabulary, similarities and digit span subtests for verbal IQ, and digit symbol, picture completion and block design subtests for performance IQ); several tests of new learning ability – the Wechsler Logical Memory Test, recognition tests using Warrington and Weiskranktz's partially completed words and figures, Williams' Object Memory Test, and a face-name paired associate learning test; the Trail Making Test from the Halstead-Reitan battery; the Modified Wisconsin Card Sorting Test; and tests of verbal fluency.

Both verbal and performance WAIS IQ were significantly lower in the alcoholics than the controls (see Table 11.3). This persisted after controlling for age and premorbid IQ differences between the groups. Similar differences are seen to extend to several tests of new learning ability, to subtests measuring perceptual-motor skills and to abstracting tasks.

The alcoholics are thus clearly impaired in many areas of psychological functioning, despite being selected on the basis of having no obvious indications of brain damage and despite being tested only after a period of total abstinence. It should be added that, with the exception of the Object Memory Test, none of the tests listed in Table 11.3 showed any noteworthy relationship with the number of days abstinence at the time of testing.

We shall ultimately seek to determine how far these two sets of observations – CAT scan changes and psychological impairments –

Table 11.3: Psychometric Comparisons Between Alcoholics and Controls

	Alcoholics	Controls	P
Premorbid IQ estimate (New Adult Reading Test)	107	112	.05
WAIS IQ – verbal (3 subtests)	32.4	36.9	.01*
– non-verbal (3 subtests)	28.5	33.6	.01*
New learning ability			
Logical memory test – immediate	41%	53%	.01*
– delayed	32%	48%	.01*
Cued partial word recognition	55%	67%	.05*
Object memory test (errors)	14	11	.05*
Face-name paired associates (savings)	24	28	.05
Perceptual-motor tasks			
WAIS digit symbol	8.1	10.1	.01*
WAIS block design	8.0	10.0	.01*
Trail making test (part A)	48 secs.	41 secs.	.05
Abstracting tasks			
Card sorting – total errors	14.0	8.6	.01*
– perseverations	7.8	4.1	.05
WAIS similarities	10.8	11.9	.01

*Remains significantly different after controlling for age and premorbid IQ.

may march hand in hand with one another. Already it is clear, however, that the situation is complex, with interacting factors that will need to be controlled. Age effects and premorbid IQ effects appear likely often to confound one another in the interpretation of results.

When considering ventricular size, for example, we immediately encounter a paradoxical finding. The ventricles tend to be *larger* the *higher* the scores in premorbid IQ and present verbal IQ. This is probably accountable in terms of selection processes among the alcoholics we have studied so far. During selection for admission to the Bexley Hospital treatment programme it is likely that patients with poor verbal skills would tend to be excluded; and for a patient with substantial brain damage to be accepted for treatment, the greater would his premorbid endowment need to be, and the greater the relative preservation of his verbal abilities. Selection processes will almost certainly have operated on verbal skills rather than non-verbal skills.

Nevertheless there are other findings which proceed in the expected direction. The larger the ventricular size the larger is the verbal-performance discrepancy on the WAIS; and the poorer are certain tests of non-verbal memory. And when attention is restricted to alcoholics of only low or average premorbid intellectual endowment, we find that certain memory and perceptual tasks (name-face test and Trail Making Test) appear to be more impaired as sulcal atrophy worsens.

Altogether, however, the lack of extensive and systematic relationships between CAT scan and psychometric findings in the sample so far collected suggests that the morphological changes, observed so clearly in the brains of alcoholics, tell by no means the whole story of the cerebral disorder they suffer. Clearer patterns may emerge when a larger, better matched control group is collected, and when repeated follow up examinations help to separate reversible from permanent damage.

Conclusions

In conclusion it must be stressed again that this is an interim report. We are finding, however, that alcoholics are decisively abnormal on both radiographic and psychometric indices, and we are beginning to discern some of the factors that might have influence on such changes. We know that considerable brain shrinkage — both cortical and subcortical — can be evident in quite young alcoholics, that it can come to be influenced by the recent drinking history, and that some aspects at least can persist despite abstinence for approximately a year. Nevertheless a beginning improvement appears to be discernible after after abstinence of such duration and hopefully may continue for longer. Further studies will be required to tell whether it is ever completely reversible, and what in behavioural terms its effects on the individual may be. The precise nature and the aetiological significance of the brain changes are matters for present speculation and for future research.

Acknowledgement

This work was supported by a grant from the Medical Research Council.

References

Bergman, H., Borg, S., Hindmarsh, T., Indeström, C-M. and Mützell, S. (1978), 'Computed tomography of the brain and neuropsychological assessment of alcoholic patients', *Proceedings from the Fourth Biennial Symposium on Biological Research in Alcoholism, Zürich, Switzerland,* Begleiter, H. and Kissin, B. (eds.), Plenum Press, New York

Brewer, C. and Perrett, L. (1971), 'Brain damage due to alcohol consumption: An air encephalographic, psychometric and electroencephalographic study', *British Journal of Addiction, 66,* 170-82

Caetano, R., Edwards, G., Oppenheim, A.N. and Taylor, C. (1978), 'Building a standardized alcoholism interview schedule', *Drug and Alcohol Dependence, 3,* 185-97

Cala, L.A., Jones, B., Mastaglia, F.L. and Wiley, B. (1978), 'Brain atrophy and intellectual impairment in heavy drinkers: A clinical psychometric and computerized tomographic study', *Australia and New Zealand Journal of Medicine, 8,* 147-53

Carlen, P.L., Wilkinson, A. and Kiraly, L.T. (1976), 'Alcoholic dementia – a longitudinal study including some reversible aspects', *Neurology, 26,* 355

Clarke, J. and Haughton, H. (1975), 'A study of intellectual impairment and recovery rates in heavy drinkers in Ireland', *British Journal of Psychiatry, 126,* 178-84

Courville, C.B. (1955), *Effects of Alcohol on the Nervous System of Man,* San Lucas Press, Los Angeles

Cutting, J. (1978), 'The relationship between Korsakov's syndrome and "alcoholic dementia"', *British Journal of Psychiatry, 132,* 240-51

Eckardt, M.J., Parker, E.S., Noble, E.P., Feldman, D.J. and Gottschalk, L.A. (1978), 'Relationship between neuropsychological performance and alcohol consumption in alcoholics', *Biological Psychiatry, 13,* 551-65

Epstein, P.S., Pisani, V.D. and Fawcett, J.A. (1977), 'Alcoholism and cerebral atrophy', *Alcoholism: Clinical and Experimental Research, 1,* 61-65

Fitzhugh, L.C., Fitzhugh, K.B. and Reitan, R.M. (1960), 'Adaptive abilities and intellectual functioning in hospitalized alcoholics', *Quarterly Journal of Studies on Alcohol, 21,* 414-23

Fox, J.H., Ramsay, R.G., Huckman, M.S. and Proske, A.E. (1976), 'Cerebral ventricular enlargement in chronic alcoholics examined by computerized tomography', *Journal of the American Medical Association, 236,* 365-8

Gall, M. von, Becker, H., Artmann, H., Lerch, G. and Nemeth, N. (1978), 'Results of computer tomography on chronic alcoholics', *Neuroradiology, 16,* 329-31

Haug, J.O. (1968), 'Pneumoencephalographic evidence of brain damage in chronic alcoholics', *Acta Psychiatrica Scandinavica, Supplement, 203,* 135-43

Horvath, T.B. (1975), 'Clinical spectrum and epidemiological features of alcoholic dementia', in *Alcohol, Drugs and Brain Damage,* Rankin, J.G. (ed.), Addiction Research Foundation of Ontario, Toronto

Kleinknecht, R.A. and Goldstein, S.G. (1972), 'Neuropsychological deficits associated with alcoholism', *Quarterly Journal of Studies on Alcohol, 33,* 999-1019

Long, J.A. and McLachlan, J.F.C. (1974), 'Abstract reasoning and perceptual motor efficiency in alcoholics: Impairment and reversibility', *Quarterly Journal of Studies on Alcohol, 35,* 1220-29

Lynch, M.J.G. (1960), 'Brain lesions in chronic alcoholics', *Archives of Pathology, 69,* 342-53

Nelson, H.E. and McKenna, P. (1975), 'The use of current reading ability in the assessment of dementia', *British Journal of Social and Clinical Psychology*, *14*, 259-67

Page, R.D. and Schaub, L.H. (1977), 'Intellectual functioning in alcoholics during six months abstinence', *Journal of Studies on Alcohol*, *38*, 1240-6

Ron, M.A., Acker, W. and Lishman, W.A. (1979), 'Dementia in chronic alcoholism: A clinical psychological and computerized tomographic study' in *Biological Psychiatry Today*, Obiols, J., Ballus, C., Gonzalez Monclus, E. and Pujol, J. (eds.), Elsevier/North-Holland Biomedical Press, Amsterdam

Tarter, R.E. (1975), 'Psychological deficit in chronic alcoholics: A review', *International Journal of the Addictions*, *10*, 327-68

Tumarkin, B., Wilson, J.D. and Synder, G. (1955), 'Cerebral atrophy due to alcoholism in young adults', *U.S. Armed Forces Medical Journal*, *6*, 67-74

12 ACTIVITY OF MONOAMINE OXIDASE AND BRAIN LEVELS OF MONOAMINES IN ALCOHOLICS

C.G. Gottfries

It is believed that in some psychiatric disorders there is a changed activity in the pathways of the central nervous system which utilises the monoamines as transmitters. In affective disorders and schizophrenic pschoses as well as in the dementia disorders of old age this assumption is made. Chronic ethanol administration induces fluctuations in mood and can also cause a clinical syndrome characterised by dementia. From animal experiments it is known that short periods of ethanol administration may increase catecholamine metabolism in mice, but this system is unaffected in rats. When ethanol has been administered to mice for several months the dopamine levels are elevated and after the withdrawal of chronic ethanol administration there appears to be an increased activity in both central dopamine and noradrenaline neurons (Liljequist, 1979).

There are some indications of a correlation between monoamine turnover and monoamine oxidase (MAO) activity in the brain. In investigations by Adolfsson *et al.* (1978) significant positive correlations were found between the 5-hydroxytryptamine (5-HT) level and MAO activity when human brain material was investigated post mortem. Positive correlations were also found between concentrations of 5-hydroxyindoleacetic acid (5-HIAA) and MAO activity. Whether such a correlation also exists with monoamine transmitters other than 5-HT still needs to be investigated. In order to obtain further information about possible disturbances of monoamine metabolism in chronic alcoholics, monoamine levels in brain tissue were estimated and the MAO activity was determined in brain tissue and also in blood platelets. The results of these investigations are reported here.

MAO Activity in Brain Tissue

In a study of the brain tissue MAO in patients with affective disorders and in alcohol addicts, 15 patients who had committed suicide were studied and from each patient 13 parts of the brain were dissected out.

228

Selected as controls were 20 persons, matched for age and sex, who had died from accidents or somatic diseases and who had never suffered from neurological or psychiatric disorders (Gottfries *et al.*, 1975).

When the control series was compared with the suicide series, a lower MAO activity was found in the suicides in all parts of the brain. The age of the patient, the time the dead body was kept at room temperature and the time between death and autopsy were examined and did not appear to influence the results obtained. MAO exists in two forms, MAO-A and MAO-B. In our material the substrates used for estimating MAO-activity were tryptamine and β-phenylethylamine. It appears that the activity of both forms of MAO is reduced (see Table 12.1).

Table 12.1: Activity of Monoamine Oxidase in Brain Tissue from a Group of Suicides (N = 15) and Controls (N = 20)

Part of the Brain	MAO (Tryptamine- oxidising)		MAO (β-Phenyl- ethylamine- oxidising)	
	Controls	Suicides	Controls	Suicides
Nucleus Caudatus	100%	75%[c]	100%	75%[a]
Hippocampus	100%	66%[c]	100%	71%[b]
Cortex Gyrus Singuli	100%	78%[b]	100%	77%

a: $P < 0.05$
b: $P < 0.01$
c: $P < 0.005$

Of the 15 patients who had committed suicide, it was found that interviewing the relatives that eight had been alcoholics. When these eight alcoholic suicides were examined separately it was evident that this group had the lowest MAO activity. The non-alcoholic suicides had, however, also significantly lower MAO activity than the controls when the differences between the brains as a whole were tested by analysis of variance ($p < 0.01$) (see Table 12.2).

Table 12.2: Activity of Monoamine Oxidase in Brain Tissue from Alcoholic Dependent Suicides (N = 8) and Non-alcoholic Suicides (N = 7) Expressed as Percent of Controls (N = 20)

Part of the Brain	MAO (Tryptamine-oxidising)		MAO (β-Phenyl-ethylamine-oxidising)	
	Alcoholics	Non-alcoholics	Alcoholics	Non-alcoholics
Nucleus Caudatus	62%[c]	89%	62%[c]	90%
Hippocampus	58%[c]	75%	59%[b]	84%
Cortex Gyrus Cinguli	59%[c]	94%	61%[a]	90%

a: $P < 0.05$
b: $P < 0.01$
c: $P < 0.005$

The finding that all of the suicides had lower brain MAO activity is somewhat surprising since the group included patients in different diagnostic categories. There were a few who had suffered from affective disorders, one schizophrenic patient, some alcoholics but also six patients in whom there was no evidence of alcohol abuse. The probable explanation is that suicidal behaviour as such, rather than affective disorder, may be the crucial syndrome associated with low MAO activity.

It was, however, also obvious that the group including the alcoholic suicides had the lowest MAO activity, which may indicate that there was also some sort of relationship between alcohol abuse and low MAO activity.

MAO in Platelets

In another investigation (Wiberg *et al.*, 1977a), the platelet MAO activity was studied to see if platelet MAO activity is also low in patients with alcohol abuse. Twenty-four patients admitted to a psychiatric hospital were investigated: all were heavily addicted to alcohol and showing an active withdrawal syndrome. The blood samples were taken as soon as possible after admission and also later in the abstinence phase. The last day of alcohol consumption was determined as carefully as possible. Controls matched for age and sex and not including alcoholics were collected from the staff of the hospital. MAO was estimated with β-phenylethylamine and tryptamine as substrates.

Figure 12.1: Platelet MAO Activity in Human Alcoholics and Controls with Mean Values and Standard Deviation for the Two Substrates Used

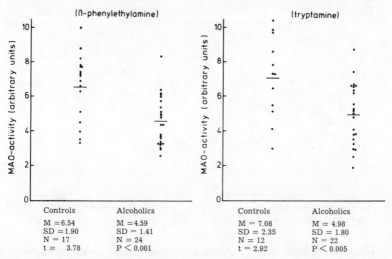

	Controls	Alcoholics		Controls	Alcoholics
	M = 6.54	M = 4.59		M = 7.08	M = 4.98
	SD = 1.90	SD = 1.41		SD = 2.35	SD = 1.80
	N = 17	N = 24		N = 12	N = 22
	t = 3.78	P < 0.001		t = 2.92	P < 0.005

Source: After Wiberg *et al.,* 1977a.

In all patients blood samples were taken on days 0-3 in the abstinence phase. As is evident from Figure 12.1, the platelet MAO activity in the alcoholics was significantly lower than in the controls at that time. This was true both with β-phenylethylamine and tryptamine as substrates. Blood samples were also taken later in the abstinence phase and, as is evident from Figure 12.2, there was a significant rise in the platelet MAO activity during the two first weeks of the abstinence phase. In only seven of the patients was it possible to get blood samples after more than two weeks, but in these seven patients the increase in MAO activity was followed by a decrease.

Figure 12.2: Platelet MAO Activity in Human Alcoholics at Various Times in the Abstinence (the Arrows Indicate the Start of Disulfiram Treatment)

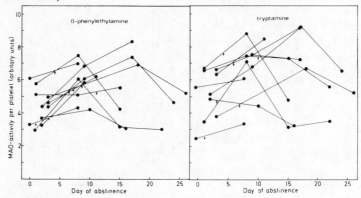

Source: After Wiberg *et al.*, 1977a.

Figure 12.3: MAO-activity (tryptamine-oxidising) in human alcoholics during their abstinence phase. Samples taken on nine consecutive occasions. Group differences are analysed with Student's t-test.

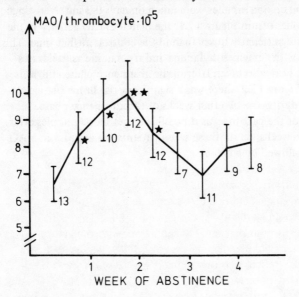

* $p < 0.05$
** $p < 0.01$

Source: After Wiberg, 1979.

As we assumed the occurrence of a constitutionally lower platelet MAO activity in individuals disposed to alcohol abuse, it was necessary to establish whether the increase of MAO in the first two weeks of the abstinence phase was transitory. If there was not a reduction to the originally low level, the low MAO activity observed early in the abstinence phase might be merely an effect of ethanol itself. In an investigation by Wiberg (1979), blood samples from chronic alcoholics newly admitted to a psychiatric hospital were collected twice every week for one month. In this investigation it could be shown that there was a significant increase in the platelet MAO activity during the fourth to the fourteenth day of the abstinence phase in comparison with the activity on the first day after the start of abstinence. It could, however, also be shown that the increase was temporary and the values returned to the original low levels three weeks after the start of abstinence (see Figure 12.3).

A possible explanation for the transitory increase during the abstinence phase is that this can be related to an increase in adrenergic activity which also takes place in the abstinence phase (Ahten *et al.*, 1977). It could, however, also be related to a changed turnover of platelets in the abstinence phase. In their investigation Major and Murphy (1978) found that the platelet count was significantly lower in chronic alcoholics studied up to eight days after the last period of drinking than in chronic alcoholics who had been abstinent for more than eight days. The reduced MAO activity in chronic alcoholics has been confirmed by others (Sullivan *et al.*, 1978a and b; Major and Murphy, 1978).

Before putting too much emphasis on the hypothesis that alcoholics have a constitutionally low MAO activity it is important to study the effect of chronic ethanol administration on MAO activity. In an animal investigation, Wiberg *et al.* (1977b) have tried to study the effect of ethanol on MAO. Rats were given chronic treatment with ethanol under different conditions for 7 to 34 weeks. In these animal experiments no change in brain monoamine oxidase activity was recorded that could be related to the ethanol intake. The result supports the hypothesis that the lowered monoamine oxidase activity found in the brain and platelets of alcoholics is not a direct effect of ethanol, but may reflect a constitutionally low enzyme activity.

The MAO activity seems to be, at least partly, genetically determined (Nies *et al.*, 1973). Both platelets and brain MAO activity thus appear to be rather stable characteristics of each individual. It therefore seems reasonable to conclude that the low MAO activity found in the brain

Figure 12.4: An Interpretation of Low MAO Activity

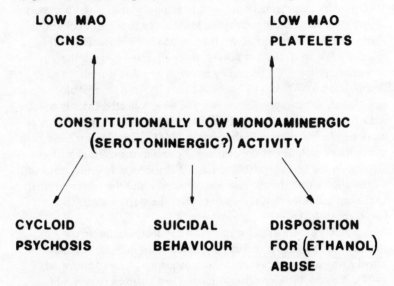

and platelets of alcoholics is a constitutional factor making the individual vulnerable to the alcohol abuse. According to our investigations, the same assumption can be made for suicidal behaviour and this hypothesis is supported by the observations of Buchsbaum *et al.* (1976) who found a significantly higher incidence of suicide attempts, psychosocial problems or criminality in probands with low platelet MAO activity. It seems that low MAO activity can also be related to other psychiatric illnesses such as schizophrenia (Murphy *et al.*, 1974) and affective disorders (Murphy and Weiss, 1972).

It appears to us improbable that it is the low MAO activity itself which makes the individual vulnerable to psychiatric disorders. However, as mentioned in the introduction, it appears that the MAO activity is positively related to monoaminergic activity in the brain. Changes in the metabolism of the monoamines are considered to be of great importance for mental health and for the pathogenesis of certain psychiatric disorders. We therefore conclude that the low MAO activity is an indicator of a weak monoaminergic system in the brain (see Figure 12.4). This weak monoaminergic system makes the individual vulnerable to affective disorders, suicidal behaviour and ethanol abuse.

Levels of Monamines in the Brains of Human Alcoholics

In dementia of the Alzheimer type several investigations have shown reduced activity in the metabolism of the neural transmitters acetylcholine, the catecholamines and serotonin (Gottfries, 1980). Drachman and Leavitt (1974) and Drachman (1977) have shown that anticholinergic drugs produce memory disturbances which resemble those seen in old age. Chronic alcohol abuse also often terminates in dementia. It is, however, evident from a clinical point of view that the impairment of mental functions caused by chronic administration of alcohol is not the same as that found in the dementia disorders of Alzheimer type. It is not easy to characterise the differences, but memory disturbances dominate the picture of Alzheimer dementia, whereas emotional bluntness or emotional rigidity characterise the picture of alcoholic dementia.

Table 12.3: Neurotransmitters in Caudate Nucleus

	Controls means ± S.E.M. N = 17	Senile Dementia % control N = 15	Alcoholism % control N = 13
Dopamine, nmoles/g	15.8 ± 0.90*	54[c]	45[c]
3-Methoxytyramine, nmoles/g	6.6 ± 0.34*	70[b]	43[c]
Homovanillic acid, nmoles/g	22.7 ± 1.37	67[b]	86
Noradrenaline, nmoles/g	0.16 ± 0.012	73[a]	65[a]
MHPG, nmoles/g	0.10 ± 0.019	183[a]	164
5-HT, nmoles/g	0.51 ± 0.043	49[c]	30[c]
5-HIAA, nmoles/g	1.4 ± 0.11	87	60[b]
MAO B	3390 ± 158	115[a]	85
d.p.m.			(120)**
Choline acetyltransferase, pkatal/1	17172 ± 1879	55[b]	90

a: $P < 0.05$.
b: $P < 0.01$.
c: $P < 0.001$ *vs* control.
* N = 54.
** Corrected for age.

Source: Carlsson *et al.*, 1979.

Table 12.4: Neurotransmitters in Hypothalamus

	Controls means ± S.E.M. N = 17	Senile Dementia % control N = 15	Alcoholism % control N = 14
Dopamine, nmoles/g	0.51 ± 0.079	56[a]	0[d]
Homovanillic acid, nmoles/g	5.9 ± 0.52	83	85
Noradrenaline, nmoles/g	6.6 ± 0.75	49[c]	66
Normetanephrine, nmoles/g	0.30 ± 0.044	58	80
MHPG, nmoles/g	0.75 ± 0.090	87	103
5-HT, nmoles/g	0.57 ± 0.078	46[c]	11[d]
5-HIAA, nmoles/g	2.1 ± 0.21	69[b]	4[d]
MAO B	4734 ± 229	110	827[b]
d.p.m.			(116)*
Choline acetyltransferase, pkatal/1	593 ± 77	74	113

a: $P < 0.1$.
b: $P < 0.05$.
c: $P < 0.01$.
d: $P < 0.001$.
*   Corrected for age.

Source: Carlsson *et al.*, 1979.

Table 12.5: Neurotransmitters in Hippocampus

	Controls means ± S.E.M. N = 17	Senile Dementia % control N = 14	Alcoholism % control N = 13
Homovanillic acid, nmoles/g	2.0 ± 0.15	101	53[b]
Noradrenaline, nmoles/g	0.11 ± 0.009	58[b]	70[a]
MHPG, nmoles/g	0.18 ± 0.021	128	111
5-HT, nmoles/g	0.13 ± 0.016	22[c]	47[b]
5-HIAA, nmoles/g	1.1 ± 0.08	64[b]	59[c]
MAO B	3266 ± 163	129[b]	84
d.p.m.			(117)*
Choline acetyltransferase, pkatal/1	1333 ± 115	57[b]	81

a: $P < 0.05$.
b: $P < 0.01$.
c: $P < 0.001$ *vs* control
*   Corrected for age.

Source: Carlsson *et al.*, 1979.

Table 12.6: Neurotransmitters in Cortex Gyrus Cinguli

	Controls means ± S.E.M. N = 17	Senile Dementia % control N = 15	Alcoholism % control N = 14
Noradrenaline, nmoles/g	0.15 ± 0.017	60[a]	49[b]
MHPG, nmoles/g	0.22 ± 0.021	140[a]	127
5-HT, nmoles/g	0.06 ± 0.010	37[b]	57
5-HIAA, nmoles/g	0.61 ± 0.051	93	91
MAO B	2337 ± 121	117[a]	80[a]
d.p.m.			(148)[b*]
Choline acetyltransferase, pkatal/1	776 ± 53	50[c]	76[a]

a: P < 0.05.
b: P < 0.01.
c: P < 0.001.
* Corrected for age.

Source: Carlsson *et al.*, 1979.

It is of interest to consider the activity of the neural transmitters in alcoholic dementia. In an ongoing Swedish investigation on which a preliminary report has been given by Carlsson *et al.* (1979), the brains of 13 alcoholics who died accidentally were investigated together with those of a group of patients with dementia disorders of Alzheimer type and a control group. As can be seen from Tables 12.3, 12.4, 12.5 and 12.6, the levels of catecholamines and serotonin were reduced in alcoholics almost to the same extent as in the group with Alzheimer dementia. Also the activity of choline acetyltransferase (CAT) was estimated. Interestingly enough there was no reduction in the CAT activity when the alcoholics were compared to the controls in three out of four of the regions investigated.

These findings may be interpreted on the basis that in dementia disorders of Alzheimer type there is a more general disturbance of the neural transmitters. In alcoholic dementia the disturbance of the neurotransmitters seems to be more selective, since only the monamine levels are reduced, while the activity in the acetylcholinergic system still is fairly normal. These biochemical changes may perhaps be of relevance for the syndromes of dementia and may explain the differences between the syndromes of Alzheimer and alcoholic dementia.

Summary

In alcoholics there is a low MAO activity in brain tissue and also in blood platelets. This indicates a weak monoaminergic system in these patients. The low MAO activity and the weak monoaminergic system is a constitutional factor and not the consequence of chronic ethanol administration. The weak monoaminergic system makes the individual vulnerable not only to abuse of alcohol but also to suicidal behaviour and to affective and schizophrenic disorders. Thus there may be a sub-group of alcoholics in which genetic factors have pathogenetic importance.

The chronic administration of alcohol causes an impairment of mental functions. The alcoholic dementia syndrome, which is rather characteristic, can be distinguished clinically from the dementia syndrome seen in Alzheimer dementia. Previous investigations have shown reduced activity both of acetylcholinergic and of monoaminergic systems in the human brain in dementia disorders of Alzheimer type. In alcoholic dementia the brains contain reduced levels of monoamines while the activity of cholinacetyltransferase is not reduced.

It may be concluded that in dementia of Alzheimer type there is a more general disturbance of neural transmitters in the brain causing clinical symptoms of intellectual as well as of emotional type. In alcoholic dementia there is a more selective disturbance and it is the catecholamines and the serotonin systems which are affected while the acetylcholinergic system is unaffected. This may explain the clinical picture seen in alcoholic dementia, in which emotional bluntness rather than memory disturbance is the dominating feature.

Acknowledgement

This investigation was supported by grants from Hjalmar Svensson's Foundation, Fredrik and Ingrid Thunberg's Foundation and from the Swedish Medical Research Council (Grant no. B80-21X-05002-04).

References

Adolfsson, R., Gottfries, C.G., Oreland, L., Roos, B-E., Wiberg, Å. and Winblad, B. (1978), 'Monoamine oxidase activity and serotoninergic turnover in human brain', in *Prog. Neuro-Psychopharmac., 2*, Pergamon Press Ltd., 225-30

Ahten, D., Beckmann, H., Ackenheil, M. and Markianos, M. (1977), 'Biochemical investigations into the alcoholic delirium: Alterations of biogenic amines', *Arch. Psychiat. Nervenkr., 224*, 129-40

Buchsbaum, M.S., Coursey, R.D. and Murphy, D.L. (1976), 'The biochemical high-risk paradigm: Behavioral and familial correlates of low platelet monoamine oxidase activity', *194*, 339

Carlsson, A., Adolfsson, R., Aquilonius, S.M., Gottfries, C.G., Oreland, L., Svennerholm, L. and Winblad, B. (1980), 'Biogenic amines in human brain in normal aging, senile dementia and chronic alcoholism', in Goldstein, Calne, Lieberman and Thorner (eds.), *Ergot Compounds and brain function*, Raven Press Books Ltd., 295-304

Drachman, D.A. (1977), 'Memory and cognitive function in man: Does the cholinergic system have a specific role?', *Neurology, 27*, 783-90

Drachman, D.A. and Leavitt, J. (1974), 'Human memory and the cholinergic system', *Arch. Neurol., 30*, 113-21

Gottfries, C.G. (1980), 'Biochemical determinants of dementia' in van Praag, H., Lader, M.H., Rafaelsen, C.J. and Sachar, E.J. (eds.), *Handbook of Biological Psychiatry, Brain Mechanisms and Abnormal Behaviour*, Marcel Dekker Inc., New York, in press

Gottfries, C.G., Oreland, L., Wiberg, Å. and Winblad, B. (1975), 'Lowered monoamine oxidase activity in brains from alcoholic suicides', *J. Neurochem., 25*, 667-73

Liljequist, S. (1979), *Behavioural and Biochemical Effects of Chronic Ethanol Administration*, Department of Pharmacology, University of Göteborg, Sweden

Major, L.F. and Murphy, D.L. (1978), 'Platelet and plasma amine oxidase activity in alcoholic individuals', *Brit. J. Psychiat., 132*, 548-54

Murphy, D.L., Belmaker, R. and Wyatt, R.J. (1974), 'Monoamine oxidase in schizophrenia and other behavioural disorders', *J. Psychiatric Research, 11*, 221-47

Murphy, D.L. and Weiss, R.(1972), 'Reduced monoamine oxidase activity in blood platelets from bipolar depressed patients', *Am. J. Psychiatry, 128*, 1351-7

Nies, A., Robinson, D.S., Lamborn, K.R. and Lampert, R.P. (1973), 'Genetic control of platelet and plasma monoamine oxidase activity', *Arch. Gen. Psychiatry, 28*, 834-8

Sullivan, J.L., Stanfield, C.N., Maltbie, A.A., Hammett, E. and Cavenar, Jr., J.O. (1978a), 'Stability of low blood platelet monoamine oxidase activity in human alcoholics', *Biol. Psychiatry, 13*, 391-7

Sullivan, J.L., Stanfield, C.N., Schanberg, S.S. and Cavenar, J. (1978b), 'Platelet monoamine oxidase and serum dopamine-β-hydroxylase activity in chronic alcoholics', *Arch. Gen. Psychiatry, 35,* 1209-12

Wiberg, A. (1979), 'Increase in platelet monoamine oxidase activity during controlled abstinence after alcoholic abuse', *Medical Biology, 57,* 133-4

Wiberg, A., Gottfries, C.G. and Oreland, L. (1977a), 'Low platelet monoamine oxidase activity in human alcoholics', *Med. Biol., 55*, 181-6

Wiberg, A., Wahlström, G. and Oreland, L. (1977b), 'Brain monoamine oxidase activity after chronic ethanol treatment of rats', *Psychopharmacology, 52*, 111-13

13 BIOCHEMICAL AND CEEG INVESTIGATION OF DRUG ADDICTS: PRELIMINARY FINDINGS

M. Del Vecchio, L. Vacca, F. Marciano, G. Nolfe,
G. Iorio, M. Maj and D. Kemali

Introduction

The causes of drug addiction are not yet clear. While some regard it as
a personality disorder resulting from social stresses, others attach
greater importance to biological factors affecting the basic biochemical
and neurophysiological mechanisms of the brain. Current disagreements
over the nature and causes of drug addiction extend to the practical
problem of the treatment and handling of the large numbers in every
country who are chronically disabled by drug abuse.

One approach to the study of drug addiction is to look for possible
biochemical and neurophysiological mechanisms underlying the addict's
behaviour. In trying to assess this biological contribution to the state of
chronic drug dependence, uncertainties about the drugs used,
impurities in the drugs and dosage variations undoubtedly create
problems.

A more serious difficulty, which does not arise in research of the
kind that can be done under controlled conditions, is the lack of
specific information on drug addicts under normal baseline conditions.
In view of these problems most current biological research on drug
dependence gives information about the pharmacological effects of
the common drugs of abuse rather than about the biological correlates
of addictive behaviour.

Morphine and its congeners have recently been shown to produce a
number of behavioural, endocrinological and neurochemical effects
that recall those elicited by neuroleptics and which suggest an
antidopaminergic activity (Lal, 1975; Pert, 1978). Among these effects,
particularly interesting from a clinical point of view appears to be the
enhancement of prolactin (PRL) release, which has been reported to be
induced by the acute administration of morphine, both in the rat
(Meites, 1966) and in man (Tolis et al., 1975). This enhancement is
reproduced in the rat by the intraventricular injection of methionine-
enkephalin as well as by β-endorphin (Dupont et al., 1977), and it is
antagonised by naloxone, which has also been found to inhibit stress-
induced and suckling-induced PRL release in the rat (Ferland et al.,
1978) and the nocturnal rise in serum PRL levels in man (Labrie et al.,

240

1978), suggesting a physiological role of endorphins in modulating the secretion of this hormone.

A mechanism which could account for the release of PRL induced by morphine and β-endorphin has recently been proposed by Labrie *et al.* (1978). This postulates that morphine and endorphins both act by impairing the release of dopamine, which is known to be a physiological inhibitor of PRL release (MacLeod, 1976) at the level of the hypothalamus.

This hypothesis is confirmed by the failure of haloperidol, even at high doses, to produce a further increase in PRL secretion in animals treated with morphine (Ferland *et al.*, 1978). A tolerance to morphine-induced enhancement of PRL release has been thought to develop after chronic administration. However, some cases of galactorrhea and some of gynecomastia, attributed to an increased release of this hormone, have been reported in chronic heroin addicts (Camiel *et al.*, 1967, quoted by Brambilla, 1976; Pelosi *et al.*, 1974). An increased incidence of gynecomastia has also been reported in chronic marihuana smokers by Harmon and Aliapoulios (1972), though other investigators failed to detec any difference between the plasma PRL levels of chronic marihuana users and those of non-marihuana smoking controls (Kolodny *et al.*, 1974; Lemberger *et al.*, 1975).

Recently, two enzymes involved in catecholamine metabolism, dopamine-β-hydroxylase (DBH) and monoamine oxidase (MAO), have been identified as possible genetic markers for vulnerability to a number of psychiatric disorders, including alcoholism and drug abuse. Platelet MAO activity was found to be significantly lower in a sample of chronic marihuana smokers in comparison with a group of non-marihuana smoking controls (Stillman *et al.*, 1978). Further, low platelet MAO and high serum DBH activities have been reported to be associated with vulnerability to alcoholism (Ewing and Rouse, 1974; Wieberg *et al.*, 1977; Sullivan *et al.*, 1978). Finally, several studies on college student volunteers have shown that subjects with low MAO have significantly higher sensation-seeking scores and use significantly more mood-altering drugs (Zuckerman, 1972; Murphy *et al.*, 1977; Coursey *et al.*, 1979).

There are also indications that opiates, marihuana, alcohol and many other drugs may induce neurophysiological changes in the central nervous system (CNS) (Kay *et al.*, 1969; Lewis *et al.*, 1970; Fink *et al.*, 1971; Deniker *et al.*, 1975; Alberti, 1976; Snyder *et al.*, 1977; Coger *et al.*, 1978). Grant and Judd (1976), on the basis of electroencephalographic studies, suggest that cerebral dysfunction in polydrug users might be 'the result of organic brain damage of intermediate duration'.

It is reported that marihuana and its derivatives (Deniker *et al.*, 1975) increase alpha and beta activity but decrease the frequency of the alpha peak (Fink, 1976). Stillman *et al.* (1977) suggest that this drug may produce differential effects on the right and left hemispheres.

Fink *et al.* (1971) found a decrease of alpha rhythm and an increase of slow frequencies as well as bursts of theta waves in chronic opiate users. A REM-suppressant effect of heroin was reported by Kay *et al.* (1969). Similarly Lewis *et al.* (1970) emphasised that morphine increases the frequency of shifts to the first stage of sleep. Moreover Alberti (1976) found spikes and slow wave bursts in the EEG of chronic opiate addicts.

The effects of alcohol, marihuana (Lewis *et al.*, 1977), opiates and their antagonists (Dafny and Burks, 1976; Snyder *et al.*, 1977) on the CNS have also been investigated by evaluating somatosensory and visual-evoked potentials (SEP, VEP). Furthermore, Coursey *et al.* (1979) emphasised the possible role of MAO and VEP as markers for the identification of subjects biologically at risk for psychiatric disorders.

The fragmentary and conflicting results regarding the long-term effects of chronic abuse of opiates and cannabis derivatives on brain functions stimulated our group to approach the problem by undertaking an integrated biological study. In this chapter we describe the preliminary results of PRL, DBH, MAO, CEEG and VEP investigations on a sample of 23 heroin addicts and 5 marihuana abusers, selected from 229 subjects attending the Drug Dependence Unit in Naples.

Methods

The 229 drug addicts (197 males and 32 females, age range 13-40 years) underwent a structured interview consisting of 33 items, which examined their family, medical, psychiatric and drug history. Since toxicological examination of body fluids was not feasible, very strict criteria were used for admission in our study. Only subjects with at least a one year reliable history of regular heroin or marihuana abuse (without use of any other drug) and with no physical disease were included.

Finally 23 heroin addicts (21 males and 2 females, age range 17-31 years, mean 23.7 ± 3.7) and 5 marihuana users (4 males and 1 female, age range 16-22 years, mean 18.4 ± 2.3) were selected. They were compared with a healthy volunteer group of 28 age- and sex-matched controls, with no history of drug abuse.

Females were in the follicular phase of their ovarian cycle. Both drug addicts and controls assured us that they had not taken any drug for at least 12 hours, but on clinical examination no relevant withdrawal symptoms were observed. Blood samples for platelet MAO, plasma DBH and PRL estimation were taken at 9.00 a.m.

Plasma levels were determined by a double-antibody radioimmunoassay (Hwang *et al.*, 1971). Plasma DBH activity was estimated by the spectrophotometric method of Nagatsu and Udenfriend (1972), using tyramine as substrate. Platelet MAO activity was determined by fluorimetric assay according to Wirz-Justice *et al.* (1975), using kynuramine as substrate.

EEGs were recorded on paper by means of a Nihon-Khoden EEG machine, and, at the same time, stored on analog tape (Analog 7 Philips) for computer analysis. The EEG channels were recorded by unipolar leads from symmetrical frontal, central and occipital areas. The records were visually screened and a position encoder was used to select 40-5 samples, each of 4 seconds, free from artifacts.

The selected EEG records were transferred for spectral analysis to a 2116 HP computer, as described in detail by Kemali *et al.* (1977). In the present investigation the raw spectral estimates, calculated by means of Fast Fourier Transform, were averaged for a total record time of 2.5-3 min. The EEG spectra were divided into frequency bands (delta 2.75-3.75 c/s; theta 3.75-7.75 c/s; alpha 7.75-13.25 c/s; beta 13.75-31.75 c/s).

For each frequency band the spectral properties were defined by evaluating the following parameters: (a) Relative Activity (relative mean power); (b) Barycentric Frequency (mean weighted frequency), which means the frequency measured at the barycentric point; (c) Barycentric Inertial Radius, which indicates the band width measured at the barycentric point (Kemali *et al.*, 1977).

The data for 15 healthy control subjects, age and sex matched, were compared with data for 15 chronically heroin addicted subjects. Inter-hemispheric comparisons were made in each group (drug users and controls). The spectral data were also compared in heroin addict and control subgroups with different MAO activities.

In the VEP investigation 7 heroin users were compared with 7 matched healthy controls. The VEPs were recorded from the scalp in both occipital areas (O_1 and O_2 according to the 10-20 International System) by means of silver disc electrodes. Bipolar leads were used with occipital electrodes and an electrode located at the vertex (C_z). Light flashes, each of 200 μsec duration and 0.3 Joule intensity, were used for stimulation at a frequency of one flash per second.

The cortical responses to the first hundred single flashes were averaged by means of NeuroAverager OTE 1172, and plotted on paper. Latencies and amplitudes (peak to peak) of the early and late components were evaluated and indicated, according to the nomenclature of Ciganek (1961), as I, II, III, etc. The evaluation depended mainly on the latencies and amplitudes of the second and third components.

Biochemical and VEP findings were analysed statistically by Student's t-test, and the CEEG data by the Mann-Whitney test. The correlated t-test was used for interhemispheric comparisons. The EEG data, because of the small sample size, were tested at a significance level $0.05 \leq P \leq 0.1$. Data from comparisons between MAO subgroups were evaluated by means of an independent sample statistical analysis.

Results

Figure 13.1 shows PRL levels determined in 27 subjects of our sample (22 heroin addicts and 5 marihuana abusers versus 27 normal controls). Since only minimal sex differences were observed, no separation of males and females was required. All values were found to be within the normal range. Plasma DBH activities were estimated in the whole sample of drug addicts and controls (see Figure 13.2). Also in this case males and females were included together in view of the lack of any significant sex difference in enzyme activity. Both in heroin and in marihuana abusers DBH activity was found to be lower than in controls, but this difference was not significant when statistical analysis was performed by Student's t-test.

The platelet MAO activities of drug addicts and controls given in Figure 13.3 are limited to male subjects, since according to previous reports (Wirz-Justice *et al.*, 1975; Schooler *et al.*, 1978), there is a significant sex difference, and our female sample appeared to be too small for a separate analysis. Data on 22 male drug addicts and 23 male controls were obtained and the MAO activity was found to be lower both in heroin and in marihuana addicts than in controls; but also in this case statistical analysis, performed by Student's t-test, did not show a significant difference.

Figure 13.1: Plasma Prolactin Levels

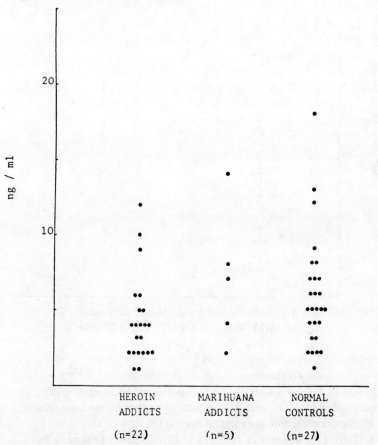

A very low MAO activity (less than 5 nmoles/mg protein/hr) was found in a sub-group of 10/18 heroin addicts (55.5 per cent), in comparison with 5/23 controls (21.7 per cent). This difference was found to be statistically significant when compared by means of an independent samples evaluation (P < 0.02). Some anomalies were found in the visual screening of the ink-written records of heroin addicts. They were seen in 4 subjects as bursts of theta waves,

Figure 13.2: Plasma Dopamine-β-hydroxylase Activity

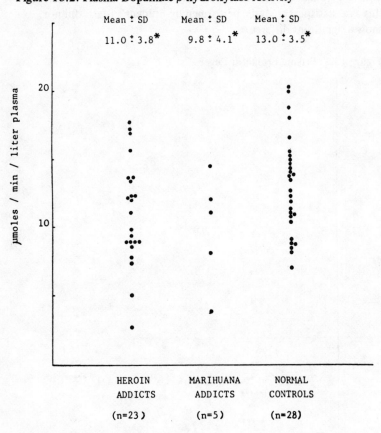

in 4 as spread theta activity and in 3 as low amplitude spikes, In these subjects neither epileptic seizures nor brain disease were present. All the other records were within normal limits.

Table 13.1 shows that the theta Relative Activity (relative mean power) of the heroin users was significantly higher than controls in all explored leads (frontal, central and occipital of both hemispheres). On the contrary the alpha Relative Activity was lower in the same leads. The delta and beta Relative Activity were on average higher in the heroin addicts, but not significantly.

The delta Barycentric Frequency was significantly higher in the heroin addicts in the right and left occipital areas only, whereas the beta Barycentric Frequency was significantly lower in both frontal

Figure 13.3: Platelet Monoamine-oxidase Activity

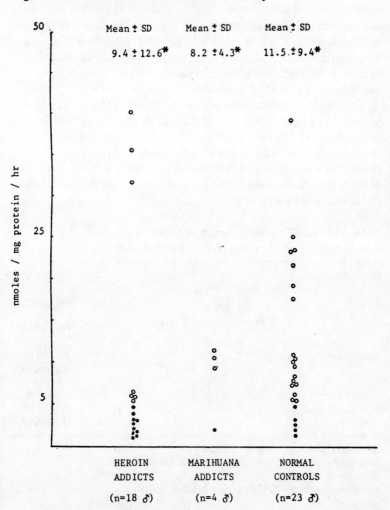

* *not* significant

● Low MAO subjects. Significant difference between hercin addicts and normal controls (p< 0.02)

leads of heroin users. The Barycentric Frequency of the theta and alpha bands were higher and lower respectively in the heroin users, but not significantly. The beta Barycentric Radius in the heroin addicts was smaller than in controls but mostly in the right hemisphere. The Barycentric Radius of all other bands did not show any significant difference. Few interhemispheric asymmetries were found either in heroin users or in control groups.

The comparisons among subjects with different MAO activities are presented in Tables 13.2, 13.3 and 13.4. Table 13.2 shows that there were significant differences (delta and beta Relative Activity) within the group of heroin addicts when subjects with MAO activity lower than 5 nmoles/mg protein/hr were compared with subjects with MAO activity higher than 5 nmoles/mg protein/hr. No difference was found within the group of normal controls.

Table 13.1: CEEG Spectral Parameter Differences,
Heroin Addicts (n=15) versus Normal Controls (n=15)

Spectral Parameters	δ	ϑ	α	β	EEG Leads
		>	<		Frontal RL
Relative Activity		>	<		Central RL
		>	<		Occipital RL
Barycentric Frequency				<	Frontal RL
	>				Occipital RL
				<	Frontal R
Barycentric Radius				<	Central RL
				<	Occipital R

Significant differences only are indicated ($0.05 \leq p \leq 0.1$).
> means higher values in the addicts; < means higher in controls.
R = right; L = left.
Greek letters indicate EEG frequency bands.

On the other hand significant differences occurred in all evaluated bands and in almost all explored leads when heroin addicts and normal controls, both with low MAO activities, were compared. The comparison between heroin users and controls, both with MAO activities higher than 5 nmoles/mg protein/hr, showed a significant difference in the frontal theta band only.

Table 13.2: EEG Relative Activity Differences, Comparisons among Subjects with Different MAO Activities

				EEG Leads
	MAO < 5 (n= 7)	δ	>	Frontal – Central – Occipital R
Heroin	*vs*	ϑ		
Addicts	MAO > 5 (n= 8)	α		
		β	>	Occipital RL
	MAO < 5 (n= 4)	δ		
Normal	*vs*	ϑ		
Controls	MAO > 5 (n=11)	α		
		β		
Heroin		δ	>	Frontal L – Central – Occipital R
Addicts	MAO < 5 (n= 7)	ϑ	>	Central – Occipital RL
	vs	α	<	Frontal – Central – Occipital RL
Normal	MAO < 5 (n= 4)	β	>	Occipital RL
Controls				
Heroin		δ		
Addicts	MAO > 5 (n= 8)	ϑ	>	Frontal RL
	vs	α		
Normal	MAO > 5 (n=11)	β		
Controls				

Significant differences only are indicated ($0.05 \leq p \leq 0.1$).
> means higher values in the low MAO group; < means higher values in the high MAO group.
R = right; L = left.
MAO = monoamine oxidase activity evalued in nmoles/mg protein/hr.
Greek letters indicate EEG frequency bands.

Table 13.3 shows that within the group of heroin addicts, as well as within the group of normal controls, when sub-groups with lower MAO activity were compared with sub-groups with higher MAO activity, significant differences of the Barycentric Frequencies were found only in the frontal beta and occipital alpha leads respectively. Theta, alpha and beta bands showed significant differences in most of the explored leads when low MAO heroin addicts and normal controls were compared, whereas only the beta band showed a significant difference between higher MAO heroin addicts versus higher MAO normal controls.

The Barycentric Radius did not show any significant difference when low MAO sub-groups were compared with higher MAO sub-groups either of heroin addicts or of controls. On the other hand, in the comparisons between heroin addicts and normal controls with low

Table 13.3: EEG Barycentric Frequency Differences, Comparisons Among Subjects with Different MAO Activities

				EEG Leads
Heroin Addicts	MAO <5 (n= 7) vs MAO >5 (n= 8)	δ ϑ α β	>	Frontal RL
Normal Controls	MAO <5 (n= 4) vs MAO >5 (n=11)	δ ϑ α β	>	Occipital RL
Heroin Addicts vs Normal Controls	MAO <5 (n= 7) MAO <5 (n= 4)	δ ϑ α β	> < >	Frontal – Central – Occipital RL / Frontal – Central – Occipital RL / Frontal RL
Heroin Addicts vs Normal Controls	MAO >5 (n= 8) MAO >5 (n=11)	δ ϑ α β	<	Frontal – Central RL – Occipital R

Significant differences only are indicated ($0.05 \leq p \leq 0.1$).
> means higher values in the low MAO group; < means the reverse.
R = right; L = left.
MAO = monoamine oxidase activity evaluated in nmoles/mg protein/hr.
Greek letters indicate EEG frequency bands.

MAO activity, the delta and alpha Barycentric Radius was significantly larger in the heroin sub-group. Within the group of subjects with MAO activity higher than 5 nmoles/mg protein/hr only the beta Barycentric Radius was lower in the heroin sub-group. The mean amplitude and the mean latencies of the VEP did not show any significant difference between heroin addicts and normal controls.

Discussion

Our finding of normal plasma PRL levels both in heroin and in marihuana addicts may be ascribed either to a lack of any effect of these drugs on PRL secretion or to the development of a tolerance to the stimulating effects of the drugs as a consequence of chronic administration.

So far as heroin addiction is concerned, the latter hypothesis should be preferred, since evidence has been reported both of an enhancement of plasma PRL levels in man after acute administration of morphine (Tolis *et al.*, 1975) to which heroin is hydrolysed *in vivo* (Way *et al.*, 1965), and of an adaptation of dopaminergic systems to the chronic presence of opiates in the brain (Clouet, 1977). However, further investigation is desirable.

On the other hand, in our opinion, clinical reports of gynecomastia and galactorrhea in chronic heroin addicts deserve attention. In fact, though these effects were not observed in any drug addicts in our sample, we found a considerable frequency of libido reduction in the male heroin addicts, which could very likely be regarded as a consequence of an impairment of hypothalamic functions. It would be informative if recent reports of an inhibition of PRL release in the rat after withdrawal from chronic morphine treatment (Lal *et al.*, 1977), suggesting a dopamine receptor hypersensitivity outlasting the period of drug-induced impairment of dopaminergic transmission, could be replicated in man, but that would present understandable methodological problems.

As regards our finding of normal plasma PRL levels in chronic marihuana addicts, confirming previous reports (Kolodny *et al.*, 1974; Lemberger *et al.*, 1975), neither of the above-mentioned hypotheses can be preferred. Although the interference of cannabinoids with biogenic amine functions at the level of the hypothalamus is well established (Truitt and Braude, 1974), the mechanisms are less clear than for opiates.

As to the plasma DBH activity, our study failed to establish its significance as a possible marker for vulnerability to drug addiction. Previous investigations on alcoholics have also given conflicting results (Sullivan *et al.*, 1978), and reports of an involvement of this enzymic activity as a predictor of vulnerability to alcoholism have come mostly from observations on normal subjects during ethanol ingestion (Ewing and Rouse, 1974).

As regards platelet MAO activity, the significant concentration of subjects with very low MAO activity in our sample of heroin addicts seems to us of some interest. However, the significance of this finding is difficult to explain. In fact, low MAO activity could be regarded either as a biological correlate of psychological vulnerability to drug addiction or as a consequence of chronic heroin administration.

Recent reports (Murphy *et al.*, 1977; Schooler *et al.*, 1978; Coursey *et al.*, 1979) of low MAO activity in normal drug-free subjects with high sensation-seeking scores speak in favour of the first hypothesis, since high drug usage among high sensation seekers is well known (Zuckerman, 1972). On the other hand, though experimental studies have failed to show any effect of common drugs of abuse on platelet MAO activity (Coursey *et al.*, 1979), the possibility of an enzyme inhibition after chronic assumption cannot be excluded. Brown's (1977) report of a reduction of platelet MAO activity in chronic alcoholics followed by a return to levels similar to those of normal subjects after six months of abstinence appears to corroborate this last hypothesis.

A similar problem arose in connexion with the investigation of MAO activity in schizophrenic patients. Wyatt and Murphy (1976) reported the absence of any effect of neuroleptics upon platelet MAO activity and regarded the lower MAO activity in schizophrenics compared with normal controls as a marker of their vulnerability to the disease. However, Friedhoff *et al.* (1978) found a significant decrease in MAO levels only in schizophrenics chronically treated with neuroleptics.

Clearly, in the case of drug addicts the problem is complicated by the difficulty of obtaining normal baseline values. It is evident that the evaluation of the results of MAO studies is a difficult problem and the large variability of the activity of this enzyme in the general population also contributes to the difficulty.

Our results on the visual screening of the EEGs confirm the presence of low amplitude spikes, bursts of theta waves and diffuse theta activity in the heroin addicts, as already reported by Alberti (1976). These anomalies are indicative of cerebral impairment. We agree with other investigators (Grant and Judd, 1976; Judd *et al.*, 1978) that this cerebral dysfunction is very likely related to chronic drug abuse. However, without drug-free normal baseline EEG data, it is impossible to assert this definitely.

The computerised spectral EEG analysis data obtained by our methods (Kemali *et al.*, 1977), indicate that in frontal, central and occipital areas the power values of the heroin addicts' theta activity is higher than in controls, whereas the alpha Relative Activity and the beta Barycentric Frequency and Barycentric Radius are lower. These findings are in line with previous reports (Fink *et al.*, 1971), and may be indicative of a state of hypovigilance in chronic heroin addicts. The occipital delta Barycentric Frequency was higher in the heroin addicts, and this last finding, together with the above mentioned power data, may be indicative of a depressant effect of heroin on CNS functions, as reported by Judd *et al.* (1978).

Within both groups, heroin addicts and controls, few EEG

differences among subjects with lower and higher MAO activity were found. On the other hand many differences were seen when the low MAO heroin addict sub-group was compared with the low MAO control sub-group. These differences were larger than those observed between sub-groups with higher MAO activity, but the size of the sample was too small to allow us to draw any conclusions about a possible relationship between MAO activity and EEG parameters.

Finally, despite the EEG differences found also in the occipital leads, the VEP mean amplitudes and latencies did not show any significant differences between heroin addicts and normal controls. It may be concluded that a result of some interest that has emerged from our investigation is the significant concentration of subjects with low MAO activity in the group of heroin addicts. Moreover in these individuals the CEEG showed a larger number of significant anomalies than in normal controls. However, a difficulty in establishing a relationship between MAO activity and EEG parameters was also observed. It should also be mentioned that the differences that were found might be attributable to withdrawal (12 hours from the last intake) even though no clinical withdrawal symptoms were observed when the addicts were examined. It would appear that further integrated biological investigations could make a useful contribution to the advance of research in this field.

Acknowledgements

The authors wish to thank Mr. C. D'Angelo, F. Di Franco and N. Milici for their technical assistance.

References

Alberti, G.G. (1976) in *Le Tossicomanie Giovanili*, De Maio, D. (ed.), Il Pensiero Scientifico Editore, Roma, 203-16

Brambilla, F. (1976) in *Le Tossicomanie Giovanili*, De Maio, D. (ed.), Il Pensiero Scientifico Editore, Roma, 159-201

Brown, J.B. (1977), 'Platelet MAO and alcoholism', *Am. J. Psychiat., 134*, 206-7

Ciganek, L. (1961), 'The EEG response (E.P.) to light stimulus in man', *Electroencephal. Clin. Neurophysiol., 13*, 165-72

Clouet, D.H. (1977) in *Neurotoxicology*, Roizin, L., Shiraki, H. and Gzcevic, N. (eds.), Raven Press, New York, 63-70

Coger, R.W., Dymond, A.M., Sezafetimioles, E.A., Lowenstam, J. and Pearson, D. (1978), 'EEG signs of brain impairment in alcoholism', *Biol. Psychiat., 13*, 729-39

Coursey, R.D., Buchsbaum, M.S. and Murphy, D.L. (1979), 'Platelet MAO activity and evoked potentials in the identification of subjects biologically at risk for psychiatric disorders', *Brit. J. Psychiat., 134*, 372-81

Dafny, N. and Burks, T.F. (1976), 'Opiate-independent effects of naloxone on the central nervous system. Neurophysiological approach', *Experiment. Neurol., 53*, 633-45

Deniker, P., Ginestet, D., Etevenon, P. and Peron-Magnan, P. (1975), 'Comparison des effects cliniques du △9 tetrahydrocannabinol avec les actions classiques du hashish', *Encephale I*, 33-41

Dupont, A., Cusan, L., Garon, M., Labrie, F. and Li, C.H. (1977), 'Beta-endorphin-stimulation of growth hormone release in vivo', *Proc. Natl. Acad. Sci., 74*, 358-9

Ewing, J.A. and Rouse, B.A. (1974), 'Alcohol susceptibility and plasma dopamine-β-hydroxylase activity', *Res. Commun. Chem. Pathol. Pharmacol., 8*, 551-4

Ferland, L., Kelly, P.A., Denizeau, F. and Labrie, F. (1978) in *Characteristics and Function of Opioids*, Van Ree, J.M. and Terenius, L. (eds.), Elsevier/North Holland Biomedical Press, Amsterdam, 353-4

Fink, M. (1976), 'Effects of acute and chronic inhalations of hashish, marijuana and △9-tetrahydrocannabinol on brain electrical activity in man. Evidence for tissue tolerance', *Am. N.Y. Acad. Sci., 282*, 387-98

Fink, M., Zaks, A., Volavka, J. and Roubucek, J. (1971) in *Narcotic Drugs, Biochemical Pharmacology*, Clouet, D. (ed.), Plenum Press, New York, 452-67

Friedhoff, A.J., Miller, J.C. and Weisenfreund, J. (1978), 'Human platelet MAO in drug-free and medicated schizophrenic patients', *Am. J. Psychiat., 135*, 952-5

Grant, I. and Judd, L. (1976), 'Neurophysiological and EEG disturbances in polydrug users', *Am. J. Psychiat., 133*, 1039-42

Harmon, J. and Aliapoulios, M.A. (1972), 'Gynecomastia and marihuana', *New Engl. J. Med., 287*, 936

Hwang, P., Guyda, H. and Friesen, H. (1971), 'A radioimmunoassay for human prolactin', *Proc. Natl. Acad. Sci. USA, 68*, 1902-6

Judd, L.L., Grant, I., Bickford, R.G. and Lee, W.G. (1978) in *Polydrug Abuse: The Results of a National Collaborative Study*, Wesson, D.R., Carlin, A.S., Adams, K.M. and Beschner, G. (eds.), Academic Press, New York, 273-97

Kay, D.C., Eisenstein, R.B. and Jasinski, D.R. (1969), 'Morphine effects on human REM, waking state and non REM sleep', *Psychopharmacol., 14*, 404-16

Kemali, D., Vacca, L., Marciano, F., Nolfe, G., Celani, T. and Iorio, G. (1977) in *Atti del XXXIII Congresso Nazionale della Società Italiana di Psichiatria*, Giordano, P.L., Kemali, D. and Tansella, M. (eds.), Cooperativa Libraria Universitaria Editrice Democratica, Verona, 264-73

Kolodny, R.C., Masters, W.H., Kolodner, M.R. and Toro, G. (1974), 'Depression of plasma testosterone levels after chronic intensive marijuana use', *New Engl. J. Med., 290*, 872-4

Labrie, F., Cusan, L., Dupont, A., Ferland, L. (1978) in *Characteristics and Function of Opioids*, Van Ree, J.M. and Terenius, L. (eds.), Elsevier/North Holland Biomedical Press, Amsterdam, 333-44

Lal, H. (1975), 'Narcotic dependence, narcotic action and dopamine receptors', *Life Sci., 17*, 483-96

Lal, H., Brown, W., Drawbaugh, R., Hynes, M. and Brown, G. (1977), 'Enhanced prolactin inhibition following chronic treatment with haloperidol and morphine', *Life Sci., 17*, 483-96

Lemberger, L., Crabtree, R., Rowe, H. and Clemens, J. (1975), 'Tetrahydrocannabinols and serum prolactin levels in man', *Life Sci., 16*, 1339-43

Lewis, E.G., Dustman, R.E. and Beck, E.C. (1977) in *Auditory Evoked Potentials in Man*, Desmedt, J.E. (ed.), *2*, Karger, Basel, 160-74

Lewis, S.A., Oswald, I., Evans, S.I., Akindale, M. and Tompset, S.L. (1970), 'Heroin and human sleep', *Electroencephal. Clin. Neurophysiol.*, *28*, 374-81

MacLeod, R.M. (1976) in *Frontiers in Neuroendocrinology*, Martini, L. and Ganong, W.F. (eds.), Raven Press, New York, 169-94

Meites, J. (1966) in *Neuroendocrinology*, Martini, L. and Ganong, W.F. (eds.), Academic Press, New York, 669-707

Murphy, D.L., Belmaker, R.H., Buchsbaum, M.S., Wyatt, R.J., Martin, N.F. and Ciaranello, R. (1977), 'Biogenic amine-related enzymes and personality variation in normals', *Psychol. Med.*, *7*, 149-57

Nagatsu, I. and Udenfriend, S. (1972), 'Photometric assay of dopamine-β-hydroxylase activity in human blood', *Clin. Chem.*, *18*, 980-3

Pelosi, M., Sama, J., Caterini, H. and Kaminetzky, H. (1974), 'Galactorrhea-amenorrhea syndrome associated with heroin addiction', *Am. J. Obst. Gyn.*, *118*, 966-70

Pert, A. (1978) in *Characteristics and Function of Opioids*, Van Ree, J.M. and Terenius, L. (eds.), Elsevier/North-Holland Biomedical Press, Amsterdam, 389-401

Schooler, C., Zahn, T.P., Murphy, D.L. and Buchsbaum, M.S. (1978), 'Psychological correlates of monoamine oxidase activity in normals', *J. Nerv. Ment. Dis.*, *166*, 177-86

Snyder, E.W., Dustman, R.E., Straight, R.C., Wayne, A.W. and Beck, E.C. (1977), 'Sudden toxicity of methadone in monkeys: Behavioral and electrophysiological evidence', *Pharm. Bioch. Behav.*, *6*, 87-92

Stillman, R., Wolkowitz, O., Weingartner, H., Waldman, I., De Renzo, E. and Wyatt, R. (1977), 'Marijuana: Differential effects on right and left hemisphere functions in man', *Life Sci.*, *21*, 1793-800

Stillman, R.C., Wyatt, R.J., Murphy, D.L. and Rauscher, F.P. (1978), 'Low platelet monoamine oxidase activity and chronic marijuana use', *Life Sci.*, *23*, 1577-82

Sullivan, J.L., Stanfield, C.N., Schanberg, S. and Cavenar, J. (1978), 'Platelet monoamine oxidase and serum dopamine-β-hydroxylase activity in chronic alcoholics', *Arch. Gen. Psychiat.*, *35*, 1209-12

Tolis, G., Hickey, J. and Guyda, H. (1975), 'Effects of morphine on serum growth hormone, cortisol, prolactin and thyroid stimulating hormone in man', *J. Clin. Endocrinol. Metab.*, *41*, 797-800

Truitt, E.B. and Braude, M.C. (1974) in *Research Advances in Alcohol and Drug Problems, 1*, Gibbins, R.J., Israel, Y., Kalant, H., Popham, R.E., Schmidt, W. and Smart, R.G. (eds.), John Wiley and Sons Inc., New York, 199-242

Way, E.L., Young, J.M. and Kemp, J.W. (1965), 'Metabolism of heroin and its pharmacologic implications', *Bull. Narc.*, *17*, 25-33

Wieberg, A., Gottfries, C.G. and Oreland, L. (1977), 'Low platelet monoamine oxidase activity in human alcoholics', *Folia Psychiat. Neurol.*, *30*, 453-62

Wirz-Justice, A., Pühringer, W., Hole, G. and Menzi, R. (1975), 'Monoamine oxidase and free tryptophan in human plasma: Normal variations and their implications for biochemical research in affective disorders', *Pharmakopsychiat.*, *8*, 310-17

Wyatt, R.J. and Murphy, D.L. (1976), 'Low platelet monoamine oxidase and schizophrenia', *Schiz. Bull.*, *2*, 77-89

Zuckerman, M. (1972), *Manual and Research Report for the Sensation Seeking Scale*, University of Delaware, USA

14 VITAMIN STATUS IN BRAIN-DAMAGED CHRONIC ALCOHOLICS

Allan D. Thomson, S.A. Rae and A. Rowe

A chronic organic brain syndrome that limits rehabilitation and often results in long-term hospitalisation is a common consequence of the chronic abuse of alcohol (Ron, 1977). Older studies demonstrating cortical atrophy and ventricular enlargement by air-encephalographic techniques have been confirmed by recent studies such as those reported by Bergman *et al.* and Lishman *et al.* in Chapters 10 and 11 of this volume, making use of the modern radiographic procedure, computerised axial tomography. The severity of the syndrome ranges from the easily recognisable classical Wernicke-Korsakoff psychosis to milder states characterised by affective changes of an apathetic or euphoric type, a diminished ability to analyse information and make discriminating judgements, and impairments of memory of mild Korsakoff type. Cutting (1978) has suggested that this milder syndrome is more likely to arise insidiously in the older drinker, particularly the female drinker, with a long drinking history.

In line with this observation is Harper's (1979) finding, that of 51 cases of Wernicke's encephalopathy found at autopsy only 7 had been diagnosed during life. He also found the pathological lesions of Wernicke's encephalopathy present in 1.7 per cent of all neuropathological autopsies carried out in Perth, Australia, between 1973 and 1976. Since Wernicke's encephalopathy is known to be caused by thiamine (B_1) deficiency, this suggests the possibility that vitamin deficiency may be a common cause of brain damage in alcoholics, who have often been found to be malnourished (for review, see Thomson, 1978). In support of this view it is well established that in both prisoner-of-war populations and in human volunteers taking deficient diets, altered psychological states may be found (for review, see Lishman, 1978). The psychological changes associated with specific vitamin deficiencies are displayed graphically in Figure 14.1.

Finally the pathological changes, both macroscopic and microscopic, which have been described in chronic drinkers have much in common with the changes described in the brains of thiamine-deficient drinkers. Figure 14.2 shows brain changes found in human and animal studies of thiamine deficient subjects with and without the complicating factor

Figure 14.1: Psychological Symptoms of Vitamin Deficiency Reported by Various Authors

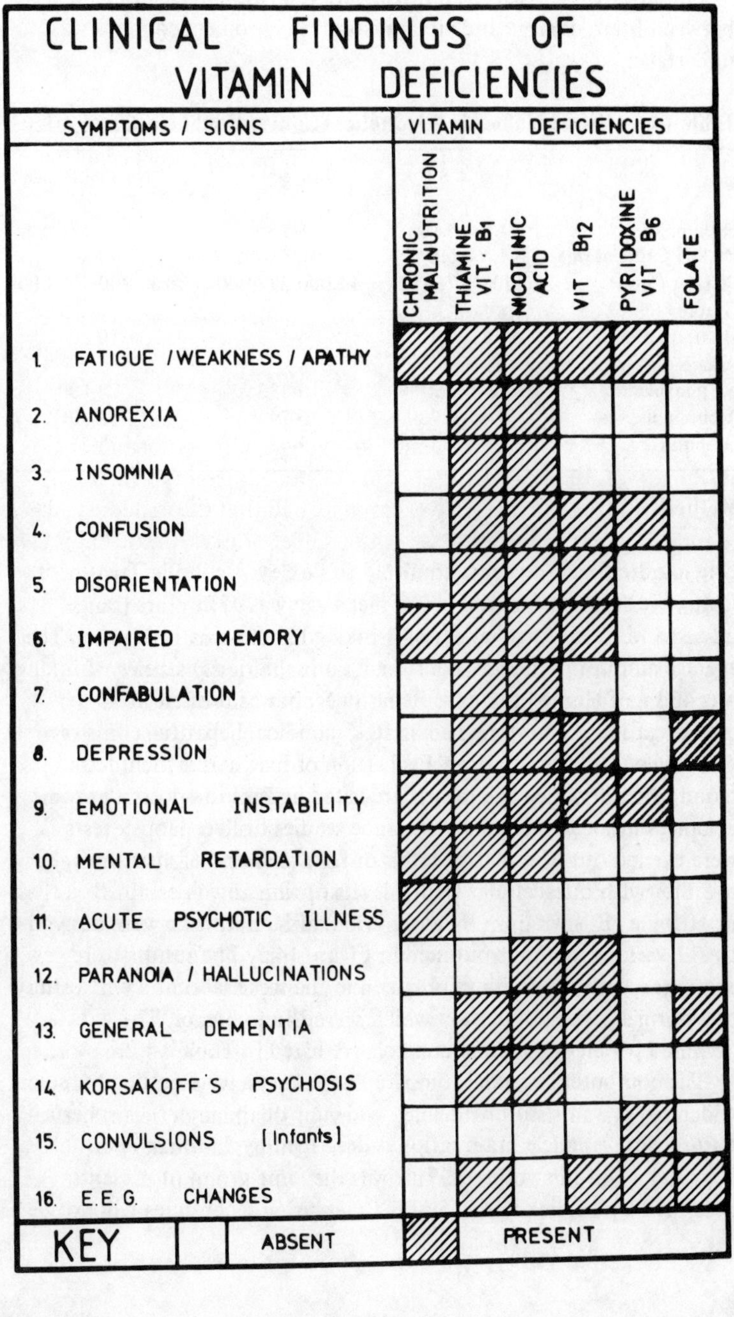

CLINICAL FINDINGS OF VITAMIN DEFICIENCIES

SYMPTOMS / SIGNS	VITAMIN DEFICIENCIES					
	CHRONIC MALNUTRITION	THIAMINE VIT. B_1	NICOTINIC ACID	VIT B_{12}	PYRIDOXINE VIT B_6	FOLATE
1. FATIGUE / WEAKNESS / APATHY	PRESENT	PRESENT	PRESENT	PRESENT	PRESENT	
2. ANOREXIA		PRESENT	PRESENT			
3. INSOMNIA		PRESENT	PRESENT			
4. CONFUSION		PRESENT	PRESENT			
5. DISORIENTATION		PRESENT	PRESENT	PRESENT		
6. IMPAIRED MEMORY	PRESENT	PRESENT	PRESENT			
7. CONFABULATION		PRESENT	PRESENT			
8. DEPRESSION		PRESENT	PRESENT	PRESENT	PRESENT	PRESENT
9. EMOTIONAL INSTABILITY	PRESENT	PRESENT	PRESENT	PRESENT	PRESENT	
10. MENTAL RETARDATION	PRESENT	PRESENT	PRESENT			
11. ACUTE PSYCHOTIC ILLNESS	PRESENT					
12. PARANOIA / HALLUCINATIONS		PRESENT	PRESENT			
13. GENERAL DEMENTIA		PRESENT	PRESENT	PRESENT		PRESENT
14. KORSAKOFF'S PSYCHOSIS		PRESENT	PRESENT			
15. CONVULSIONS [Infants]					PRESENT	
16. E.E.G. CHANGES		PRESENT		PRESENT	PRESENT	PRESENT

KEY		ABSENT	PRESENT

of chronic alcohol abuse. In the case of deficiencies of other vitamins, adequate brain studies are lacking.

For all of these reasons an investigation of the interrelationship between brain damage and vitamin status in chronic alcoholics was undertaken.

Table 14.1: Blood Values in Alcoholics (Conventional Units)

	Mean ± S E	Range	Normal Range
Haemoglobin	14.9 ± 0.16	16.8-18.1	13-18
Packed Cell Volume	44.4 ± 0.8	33-56	40-54
Platelet Count	190,000 ± 720	42,000-332,000	150,000-400,000
Glutamate transaminase	48.8 ± 7.6	4-446	10-30
Alkaline phosphatase	75.6 ± 4.6	19-433	20-100
Albumin	46.4 ± 0.73	30-79	35-50
Globulin	27.6 ± 0.5	19-42	23-37

Methods

One hundred male patients admitted to Bexley Alcoholic Treatment Unit were selected for study. The mean age was 43.5 years (range 22-63) and the average length of drinking history was 17.3 years. The average amount of alcohol consumed during periods of heavy drinking was 463 g of alcohol per day. Hepatomegaly was present in 50 per cent of patients, but none had ascites, jaundice, hepatitis, coma or bleeding oesophageal varices. Evaluation of liver status included blood tests, of which the results are listed in Table 14.1, and in some instances indocyanine green clearance studies or liver biopsy tests were carried out. Circulating levels of folic acid and of vitamin B_{12}, together with intracellular (RBC) levels of thiamine (vitamin B_1), riboflavine (B_2), vitamin B_6 and pyridoxal-5-phosphate were assayed by the various methods outlined in Figure 14.3. The results were compared with the findings obtained in the same laboratory in a study of a normal Swiss population which served as a control. The data obtained for alcoholics and controls are listed in Table 14.2.

The computerised axial tomographic pictures were graded for sulcal widening, sylvan fissure widening, widening of the interhemispheric fissure, and ventricle brain ratios as described by Lishman *et al.* (Chapter 11 in this volume). This was the same group of patients described by Lishman *et al.* and the measuring techniques will not be

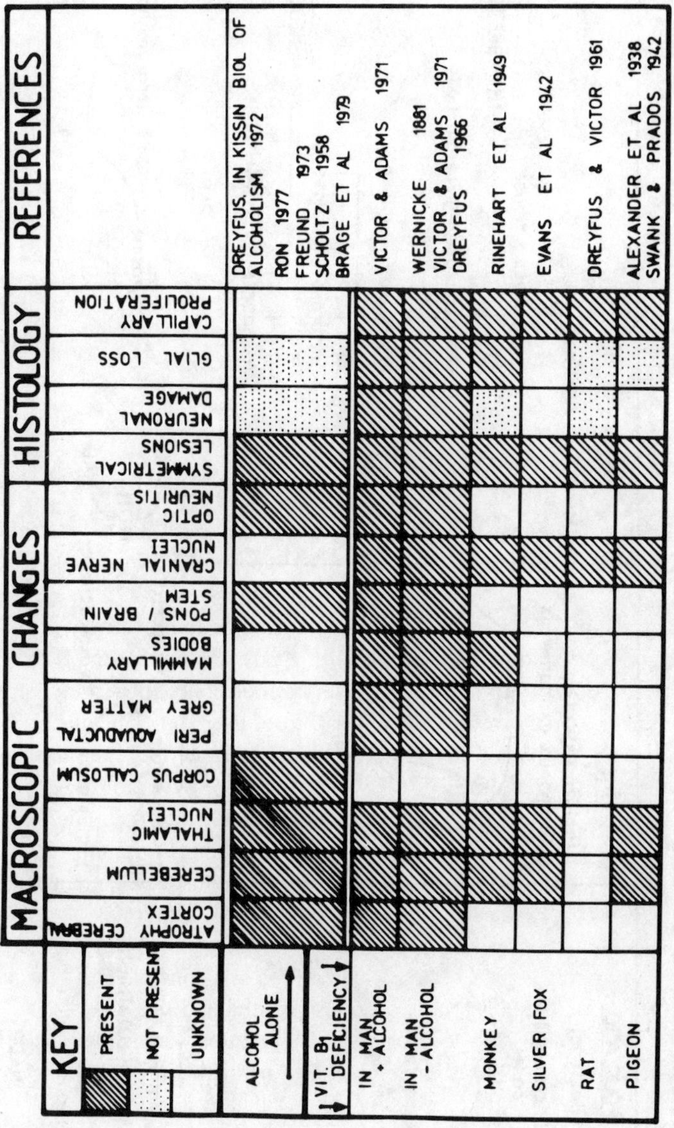

Figure 14.2: Macroscopic and Microscopic Changes in Alcoholics and Following Thiamine Deficiency in Man and Animals

Figure 14.3: Methods of Vitamin Assay Used in this Study

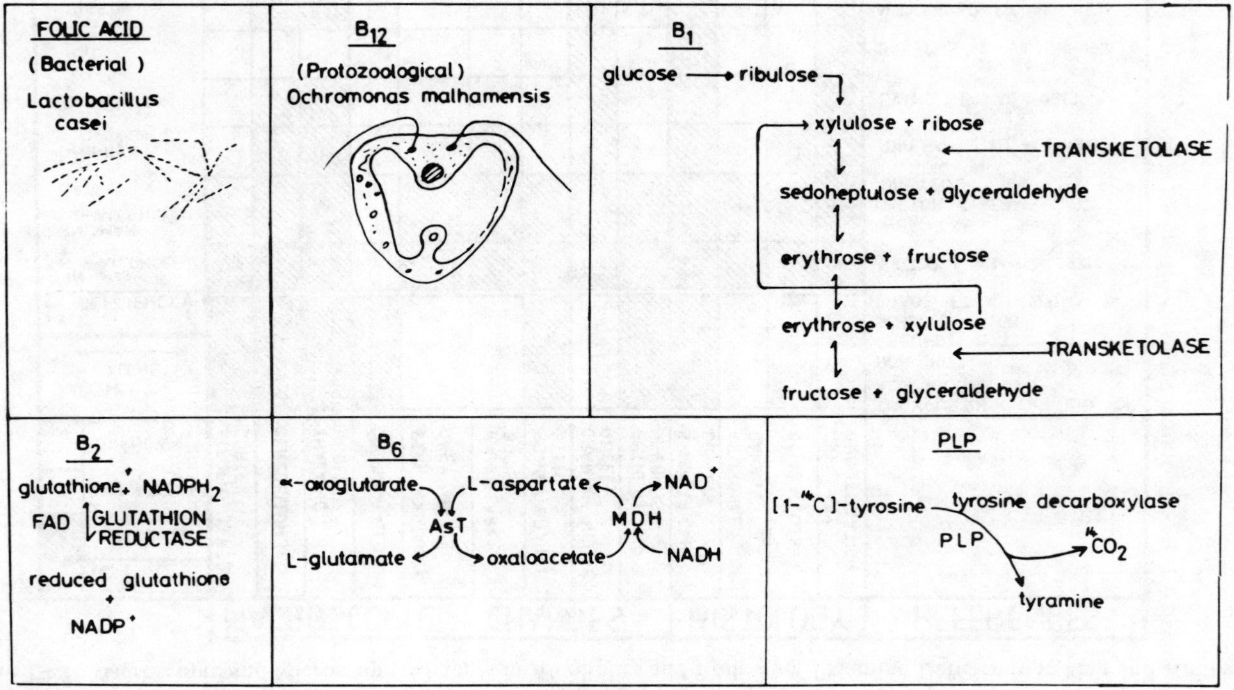

FOLIC ACID
(Bacterial)
Lactobacillus casei

B₁₂
(Protozoological)
Ochromonas malhamensis

B₁
glucose ⟶ ribulose → xylulose + ribose → sedoheptulose + glyceraldehyde — TRANSKETOLASE
erythrose + fructose
erythrose + xylulose → fructose + glyceraldehyde — TRANSKETOLASE

B₂
$glutathione + NADPH_2$
$FAD \downarrow GLUTATHION \ REDUCTASE$
reduced glutathione + $NADP^+$

B₆
$\alpha-oxoglutarate \rightleftharpoons L-aspartate \rightarrow NAD^+$
AsT MDH
$L-glutamate \leftarrow oxaloacetate \rightarrow NADH$

PLP
$[1-^{14}C]-tyrosine$ tyrosine decarboxylase
PLP → CO_2
tyramine

described again. As indicated, there was decisive evidence of abnormal radiological findings in this group of alcoholic patients.

Table 14.2: Blood Vitamin Status in Alcoholics and a Normal Swiss Population

No.	Vitamin	Test (α = Activation Coefficient)	Alcoholics (mean ± S.D.)	Controls (mean ± S.D.)
1.	Thiamine (B_1)	ETK_0 μmol/1 (N > 70)	62.1 ± 17.8	89.7 ± 15.0
		αETK (N $\leqslant$ 1.15)	1.18 ± 0.19	1.11 ± 0.06
2.	Riboflavin (B_2)	αEGR (N $\leqslant$ 1.20)	1.15 ± 0.19	1.02 ± 0.09
3.	Pyridoxine (B_6)			
	(a)	$EGOT_0$ (μg/1)	470 ± 128	355.7 ± 86.9
		αEGOT (N $\leqslant$ 2.0)	1.3 ± 0.26	1.79 ± 0.23
	(b)	5-PLP (Pyridoxal-5-phosphate) (N = 10-20 ng/ml)	7.97 ± 3.6	12.0 ± 3.0
4.	Folate	L. Casei		
		Serum	6.2 ± 4.2	(N = 5-21 μg/l)
		Red Blood Cell	314 ± 184	(N = 160-640 μg/l)
5.	Vitamin B_{12}	O.Malhamensis	501 ± 273	(N = 160-960 ng/l)

ETK = erythrocyte transketolase
ETK_0 = enzyme activity without added co-enzyme.
EGOT = erythrocyte glutamate-oxaloacetate transaminase.
$EGOT_0$ = enzyme activity without added co-enzyme.
EGR = erythrocyte glutathione-reductase.
αETK
αEGR] ratio of enzyme activity with added co-enzyme to that without it —
αEGOT a high ratio indicates deficiency of that particular vitamin.
N = normal values.

Relationship Between Brain Damage and Hepatic Status

A search was made for correlations between all parameters of brain damage and all indices of liver status including blood data (Table 14.1). The only correlation of significance to emerge was a positive relationship between ventricular size and liver damage. Thus cirrhotic patients were found to have ventricles which were significantly larger than those of non-cirrhotic patients. Cirrhotic patients, however, tended to be older than other patients and it will be recalled that ventricle size increases with increasing age in the normal population. Further work is therefore required to evaluate the significance of this finding. What clearly emerged, however, was that brain changes of an advanced kind are at times observed in those in whom no significant liver damage is discernible, implying that different mechanisms of injury are involved.

Brain Damage and Vitamin Status

Alcoholic patients were found to have significantly lower levels of thiamine (B_1), riboflavine (B_2), pyridoxal-5-phosphate and serum folate than normal controls. Furthermore, many patients had multiple vitamin deficiencies, most commonly two or three.

A previous history of heavy drinking correlated with low levels of vitamin B_1 and vitamin B_2 and there was a highly significant ($p < 0.01$) association between low levels of thiamine (B_1) and parameters of brain damage.

Our finding of low levels of pyridoxal-5-phosphate, the active form of vitamin B_6, is in keeping with previous reports of vitamin B_6 deficiency in alcoholics (Luming and Li, 1974; Mitchell *et al.*, 1976), but measurements of vitamin B_6 by estimation of erythrocyte glutamate oxaloacetate transaminase (EGOT) activity gave unexpectedly high results. Our observations relate a high EGOT activity to the amount of alcohol consumed, suggesting that a high intake of alcohol is followed by increased activity of this enzyme system.

Reduced circulating levels of vitamin B_6 in alcoholics have been reported consistently, and a shift in the breakdown of tryptophan via the kynurenine pathway, giving increased levels of urinary xanthurenic acid following a tryptophan load, confirms vitamin B_6 deficiency.

As shown in Figure 14.4 ethanol or acetaldehyde may interfere with

Figure 14.4: Interference in Absorption, Conversion and Breakdown of Vitamin B_6 by Alcohol or Acetaldehyde

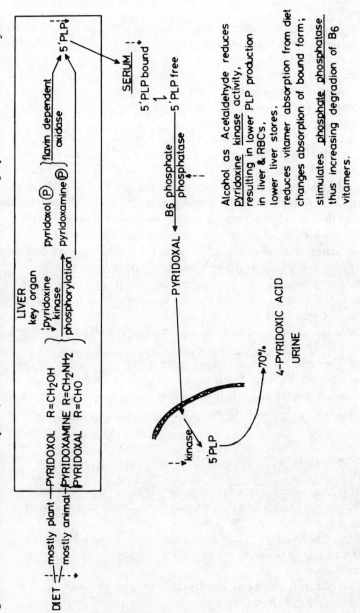

the intracellular availability of pyridoxal-5-phosphate by reducing pyridoxine kinase activity and by stimulating phosphate phosphatase activity.

An unexpected situation was found in alcoholic patients. The rate of the initial erythrocyte transamination reaction ($EGOT_0$) was elevated in alcoholics ($470 \pm 18 : 356 \pm 87$ micrograms/litre) and the addition of the co-enzyme pyridoxal-5-phosphate produced proportionately less increase in enzyme activity in the alcoholic group than in normal controls, and very much less than would be expected in a deficient population.

Figure 14.5 shows the initial rates of reaction in alcoholics and controls ($EGOT_0$), the rate of reaction after adding the coenzyme pyridoxal-5-phosphate ($EGOT_+$) and the ratio of the second reaction to the first ($\alpha EGOT$). It will be understood that the higher the ratio $\alpha EGOT$ the more deficient the subject. On the surface this would imply that the control group were more deficient than the alcoholic group, but the high initial rate of reaction in the alcoholics and the low circulating levels of pyridoxal-5-phosphate suggest, however, that this enzyme system is induced by ethanol and that it preferentially attracts pyridoxal-5-phosphate, thus diverting it from other reactions such as decarboxylations in which it also acts as a coenzyme. It will be recalled that decarboxylation is an essential step in the synthesis of neurotransmitters and this could be an important effect of vitamin B_6 deficiency.

The evolution of non-invasive techniques for assessing brain damage and the availability of highly sensitive enzymatic methods of vitamin assay allow more accurate investigation of the role of malnutrition in the aetiology of brain damage.

Conclusions

(1)   Parameters of brain damage are related to recent drinking history but do not parallel liver damage, suggesting different mechanisms of injury.

(2)   The histology of alcoholic brain damage is not adequately documented and our knowledge of the mechanisms of damage is limited.

(3)   There is a well-established relationship between vitamin deficiency and altered brain function. In the case of thiamine deficiency, there is frequently a significant degree of cerebral atrophy

Figure 14.5: Transamination Activity Before and After Adding 5' PLP in an Alcoholic Group (A) and a Control Group (C)

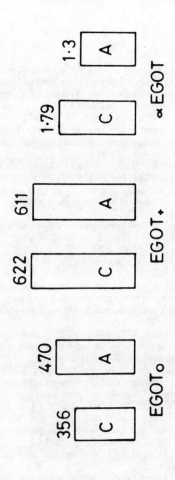

1. Reduction in available intracellular coenzyme 5'PLP

2. Elevated transamination activity ($EGOT_O$) leaving insufficient 5'PLP for carboxylation necessary for the synthesis of neurotransmitters (serotonin, GABA etc).

associated with Wernicke's encephalopathy and Korsakov's psychosis.
(4)   This study suggests that ethanol causes:

a reduced availability of thiamine, correlated with measures of brain damage,

a reduction in the availability of intracellular pyridoxal-5-phosphate, and

increased transamination activity ($EGOT_0$), perhaps reducing the availability of pyridoxal-5-phosphate for decarboxylation processes necessary for neurotransmitter synthesis.

References

Alexander, L., Pijoan, M., Myerson, A. and Keane, H.M. (1938), 'Beriberi and scurvy: an experimental survey', *Trans. Amer. Neurol. Assoc., 64,* 135-9

Brage, D. (1974), 'Alcohol and the nervous system', *Int. J. Neurol., 9,* 173-83

Cutting, J. (1978), 'The relationship between Korsakov's syndrome and "alcoholic dementia" ', *Brit. J. Psychiat., 132,* 240-51

Dreyfus, P.M. (1972), 'Diseases of the nervous system in chronic alcoholics' in *The Biology of Alcoholism,* Kissin, B. and Begleiter, H. (eds.), Plenum Press, New York and London, 265-89

Dreyfus, P.M. and Victor, M. (1961), 'On the aetiology of alcoholic neurological diseases', *Amer. J. Clin. Nutr., 9,* 379-431

Evans, C.A. (1942), 'The pathology of paralysis in foxes', *Amer. J. Path., 18,* 79-91

Freund, G. (1973), 'Chronic central nervous system toxicity of alcoholism', *Ann. Rev. Pharmacol., 13,* 217-27

Harper, C. (1979), 'Wernicke's encephalopathy: a more common disease than realised. A neuropathological study of 51 cases', *Journal of Neurology, Neurosurgery and Psychiatry, 42,* 226-31

Lishman, W.A. (1978) *Organic Psychiatry,* Blackwell Scientific Publications, Oxford

Lumeng, L. and Li, T-K. (1974), 'Vitamin B6 metabolism in chronic alcohol abuse. Pyridoxal phosphate levels in plasma and the effects of acetaldehyde on pyridoxal phosphate synthesis and degradation in human erythrocytes', *J. Clin. Invest., 53,* 693-704

Mitchell, D., Wagner, C., Stone, W.J., Wilkinson, G.R. and Schenker, S. (1976), 'Abnormal regulation of plasma pyridoxal-5-phosphate in patients with liver disease', *Gastroenterology, 71,* 1043-9

Rinehart, J.F., Friedman, M. and Greenberg, L.D. (1949), 'Effect of experimental thiamine deficiency on the nervous system of the Rhesus monkey', *Arch. Pathol., 48,* 129-39

Ron, M.A. (1977), 'Brain damage in chronic alcoholism: A neuropathological, neuroradiological and psychological review', *Psychol. Md, 7,* 103-12

Scholtz, W. (1958) *Handbuch der Speziellen Pathologischen Anatomie und Histologie,* Springer, Berlin and Heidelberg, 2214-69

Swank, R.L. and Prados, M. (1942), 'Avian thiamine deficiency II, *Arch. Neurol. and Psychiat., 47,* 97

Thomson, A.D. (1978), 'Alcohol and Nutrition', *Clinics in Endocrinology and Metabolism, 7,* 405-28

Victor, M. and Adams, R.D. (1971) *The Wernicke-Korsakoff Syndrome,* FA Davis Company, Philadelphia

15 BRAIN DAMAGE IN CHRONIC ALCOHOLICS: A REVIEW OF THE PSYCHOLOGICAL EVIDENCE

Ralph E. Tarter

There is mounting evidence from both neurological and psychological research that the chronic consumption of alcohol places the individual at risk for incurring cerebral pathology. However, the precise nature and progress of the cerebral pathology is, at this time, poorly understood. Moreover, the potential deleterious role of other contributing factors to the neurological and psychological disturbance is unknown. Thus, the age of onset of excessive drinking, nutrition, liver pathology, sex differences, congeners in the alcoholic beverage, and other extrinsic factors may be interacting with the alcohol to produce the observed deficits so far reported in the literature.

This chapter will focus on the major areas of neuropsychological research pertaining to the existence and extent of cerebral pathology in chronic alcoholics. The specific topics of discussion will consider: (1) characteristics of the psychological deficits; (2) neuropsychological interpretations of the disturbances; (3) the reversibility of the deficits; (4) complicating factors of liver pathology, nutrition and age; (5) the role of subject and methodological factors; and (6) future interdisciplinary research directions.

The Nature of the Psychological Deficit

Intellectual Competence

Previous comprehensive reviews of the literature (Tarter, 1975; Tarter, 1976) have led this author to the conclusion that alcoholics do not exhibit a global or generalised intellectual impairment. On psychometric measures of intelligence such as the Wechsler-Bellevue or Wechsler Adult Intelligence Scale, alcoholics typically obtain full scale intelligence quotients in the average to bright normal ranges. Investigations with these intelligence scales, however, do reveal a small but generally consistent superiority of verbal over non-verbal capacities. More specialised testing has tended to confirm the finding of a deficit on non-verbal tasks. Jones and Parsons (1972) reported that alcoholics performed more poorly than a matched group of normal controls on the Ravens Progressive Matrices Test, a non-verbal measure of intelligence requiring perceptual organisation in the formation of concepts. Thus, while overall IQ is intact, components of intelligence that tap visual spatial capacities are associated with impaired performance in alcoholics.

While most psychometric measures of intelligence do not reveal evidence for a generalised impairment, there are indications that tests of 'biological intelligence' (Halstead, 1947), as measured by the Halstead-Reitan Neuropsychological Battery, do elicit impaired performance in chronic alcoholics. The Halstead-Reitan Neuropsychological Battery consists of seven measures that are sensitive to neurological integrity. Alcoholics have been shown, in a number of studies, to perform poorly on this battery, with overall performance lying between normal and acutely brain damaged individuals (Fitzhugh *et al.*, 1960, 1965; Vivian *et al.*, 1973).

Measures of intellectual deterioration have not proven useful in distinguishing alcoholics from non-alcoholics. Tarter and Jones (1971a) found no difference between alcoholics, normals, and psychiatric patients on the Shipley-Hartford Institute of Living Scale, a test which measures vocabulary knowledge and verbal-logical abstracting ability. A derived conceptual quotient, an index of intellectual deterioration, did not discriminate these three groups. Nor have alcoholics been found to be impaired on a battery of 23 factorially pure tests of intellectual capacity (Tarter *et al.*, 1975). However, on the General Aptitude Test Battery, Kish (1970) observed that alcoholics performed more poorly than would be expected from the standardised norms on several of the subtests, these being numerical aptitude, motor co-ordination, and finger and manual dexterity.

In conclusion, alcoholics do not exhibit a global intellectual disturbance as revealed by psychometric tests. Utilising the more sensitive measures of biological intelligence, there are indications that alcoholics are neuropsychologically impaired. However, it is important to point out that the deficits appear to be selective and not generalised to all tasks. Below are summarised the various areas of psychological competency that have been examined in chronic alcoholics.

Cognition

Alcoholics have been demonstrated to perform poorly on a number of different cognitive tasks. The early studies revealed a disturbance in non-verbal abstracting ability, as measured by the Category Test of the Halstead-Reitan Neuropsychological Battery (Fitzhugh *et al.*, 1960, 1965; Jones and Parsons, 1971). Lovibond and Holloway (1968) found that on a modified form of the Goldstein Object Sorting Test alcoholics exhibited more concrete abstractions than a group of normal controls.

Verbal abstracting deficits have been reported as well. For example, Jonsson *et al.* (1962) found that alcoholics were impaired in comprehending the abstract meanings of proverbs. Alcoholics were also limited in their capacity to provide alternative responses to homonyms. On other verbal tasks no deficits have been detected. In the capacity to identify synonyms from groups of unrelated words, no disturbances have been observed (Claeson and Carlsson, 1970; Jonsson *et al.*, 1962; Tarter and Jones, 1971a). Also, inductive reasoning has been found to be intact, as measured by the Thurstone Figure Classification Test (Claeson and Carlsson, 1970).

In a series of experiments in concept identification, Tarter (1971, 1973; Tarter and Parsons, 1971) administered the Wisconsin Card Sorting Test, a task which requires the subject to identify simple concepts, such as colour, shape, or number, and, once having achieved the criterion, to be able to shift to a new concept (e.g. from colour to shape). In the first study (Tarter and Parsons, 1971), it was found that alcoholics were not impaired in simple abstracting but did have a relatively greater difficulty in shifting to new concepts and abandoning a previously learned concept. Thus, once the concept would shift, without their awareness, they tended to sustain a perseverative pattern of responding. In a subsequent study (Tarter, 1973) it was found that drinking history was related to the magnitude of the cognitive deficit. Alcoholics who had been drinking excessively for ten years or more exhibited a greater decrement in cognitive capacity than alcoholics with a lesser history of abusive drinking. Besides making more perseverative errors, the longer-term alcoholics were inclined to interrupt a correct pattern of responding, signifying attentional lapses or a breakdown of temporal integration in mediating ongoing behaviour. In addition, it was observed that the alcoholics were less capable of utilising the information contained in an erroneous response to achieve a subsequently correct mode of responding. However, the most significant finding from these studies was that chronicity of drinking was found to be related to magnitude of performance deficit.

Congruent with this finding was the observation by Jones and Parsons (1971b) that it was the older alcoholics who exhibited the most pronounced abstracting impairment on the Category Test of the Halstead-Reitan Neuropsychological Battery. An additional finding in the Jones and Parsons (1971b) study was that the deficit on this test was most dramatic on that portion that involved acquisition and utilisation of a visual spatial concept. Thus, there is some evidence to suggest that chronic alcoholics are impaired on certain types of abstracting tasks, even though conceptual capacity *per se* may be intact (Pishkin *et al.*, 1972). Relevant to this finding is the report by Parker and Noble (1977) who observed that social drinkers, without evidence of addiction or manifesting the quantity and frequency of consumption of alcohol typically found in alcoholics, were also impaired on the Wisconsin Card Sorting Test. From these results, it appears that alcoholics and heavy social drinkers are deficient in some aspects of abstracting. The deficits appear to be more pronounced on visual spatial tasks, although impairments have been observed on some verbal abstracting tasks as well.

Perceptual and Spatial Capacities

As just noted, the most pronounced deficits were found on tasks that involved a visual spatial requirement. Given these findings, the question is raised as to whether or not alcoholics suffer from a basic perceptual deficit or incapacity. With respect to perceptual and spatial tests, the results to date suggest a high degree of task specificity in which alcoholics are likely to be impaired. Goldstein and Chotlos (1965) administered the Stroop Test and found that alcoholics were not deficient at speed reading a list of words, but were relatively impaired on speed colour-naming and an interference aspect of the test where the words and colours are incongruent. However, when the effects of colour were partialed out of the interference task, no perceptual speed disturbance was noted. On the Street Gestalt Test, a task in which the subject must synthesise a complete figure from its fragmented components, there is no evidence that alcoholics are impaired (Claeson and Carlsson, 1970).

On tests of perceptual motor coordination the findings are less consistent. Bender (1938) administered the Bender Gestalt Test to a group of chronic alcoholics who were also psychotic. She reported that alcoholics suffer from deficits in integration and are impaired in spatial synthetic capacity. Other investigators, however, have not been able to replicate this finding, and overall the available evidence points to normal performance of alcoholics on this test (Hirschenfang *et al.*, 1967, 1968; Kates and Schmolke, 1953; Silber *et al.*, 1968). Tarter and Jones (1971b) reported a deficit level of performance on the Purdue Pegboard Test, but the initial impairments disappeared after a three-month-period of abstinence from alcohol. Vivian *et al.* (1973)

observed that alcoholics were impaired on a star-tracing task, suggesting eye-hand co-ordination problems in alcoholics, but this has yet to be confirmed by other investigators.

Spatial synthetic abilities appear to be disturbed in alcoholics. Fitzhugh *et al.* (1965) reported that the Kohs Block Design Subtest of the Wechsler-Bellevue Intelligence Scale was the only measure which significantly discriminated alcoholics from normals. Goldstein *et al.* (1970) also reported that alcoholics were impaired on the WAIS Block Design Test. This test was found to be the best measure for distinguishing alcoholics from normals by O'Leary *et al.* (1979), who used a refined discriminant analysis procedure. Claeson and Carlsson (1979) reported that chronic alcoholics obtained a mean stanine transformed score of five on the Kohs Block Design Test, where the theoretical average for the population is between six and seven. In an analogous type of test, Grassi (1953) observed a modest impairment on the Grassi Block Substitution Test in a group of deteriorated alcoholics, a finding which was subsequently replicated by Gordan (1957) and Jonsson *et al.* (1962).

Utilising another spatial test, Fitzhugh *et al.* (1965) found that alcoholics were impaired on the Tactual Performance Test of the Halstead-Reitan Neuropsychological Battery. This test requires the blindfolded subject to place ten geometrically shaped blocks into a formboard as quickly as possible. He found that the alcoholics were impaired in their speed of performance as well as subsequent recollection of the locations of the various blocks in the formboard.

One task which has received a large amount of experimental analysis is the Rod and Frame Test. This task requires the subject to adjust a luminous rod to its true vertical position, despite the distracting background of a frame in varying degrees of tilt. The closer the subject can adjust the rod to its true vertical position, the better is the performance. Witkin *et al.* (1954) dichotomised alcoholics as either perceptually field independent, in which case they could perform this task without any disrupting effects from the background distraction of the frame, or field dependent, in which case they tended to adjust the rod more in line with the orientation of the background frame than to the true vertical axis. There is a substantial amount of evidence which indicates that there is a significantly larger proportion of chronic alcoholics who react in a perceptually field dependent fashion than normal controls (Bailey *et al.*, 1961; Goldstein and Chotlos, 1965; Karp *et al.*, 1965a, 1965b; Witkin *et al.*, 1959). It is not certain as to whether this is a predisposing trait prior to alcohol consumption or whether this perceptual style is a consequence of chronic alcoholism. There is some evidence that anterior frontal damage, particularly in the area of the frontal eyefields, results in perceptual field dependency (Teuber, 1964). However, duration of drinking history was not found to be correlated with severity of field dependency (Karp and Konstadt, 1965), and neither was length of sobriety related to performance on this measure (Karp *et al.*, 1965a). On the other hand, alcoholics performed more like brain damaged subjects than any other psychiatric group, suggesting that a possible organic factor may be responsible for the deficit.

On other tests of perceptual orientation, alcoholics have been found to be impaired as well. Claeson and Carlsson (1970) reported that 70 per cent of their alcoholic sample were impaired on the Thurstone Figure Turning Test. On this test, the subject must be able to match correctly one of an array of seven geometric figures which, upon orientation, would be identical to a stimulus figure. Thus, there may be some difficulty in the chronic alcoholic population to perform tasks requiring orientation skills.

An instrument which correlates highly with the Rod and Frame Test is the Embedded Figures Test. This task requires the subject to identify a simple geometric figure that is hidden or embedded in a complex stimulus array. From a factor analytic standpoint, this test measures speed and strength of perceptual closure and secondarily taps an individual's capacity to process perceptual information under changing gestalts. Alcoholics generally perform as well as normal subjects on this test (Jones and Parsons, 1971a; Rudin and Stagner, 1958; Rhodes *et al.*, 1968). Claeson and Carlsson (1970) found that alcoholics performed as well as normals on Thurstone's Gottschaldt Test. On the Copying Test, Tarter (1971) found no evidence for a performance deficit in alcoholics where the subject must draw an identical geometric picture from a sample figure onto a grid of dots.

In conclusion, on tests of spatial and perceptual capacity, alcoholics exhibit impairments on certain tasks, most notably those that require a synthetic ability and, secondly, where perceptual orientation is involved. Perceptual speed and perceptual motor co-ordination are intact, as is performance on tasks measuring closure.

Memory

The evidence for a permanent memory disturbance in chronic alcoholics is equivocal. Jonsson *et al.* (1962) reported that alcoholics were deficient at remembering a display of common objects but could perform as competently as normals on a paired associative learning task. Claeson and Carlsson found that 65 per cent of their alcoholics performed in the impaired ranges on the Benton Visual Retention Test. Weingartner *et al.* (1970) observed that alcoholics learned more slowly than controls in a serial learning and recall paradigm. Fitzhugh *et al.* (1965) found no difference in the memory measure of the Tactual Performance Test. Other investigators have noted impairments in alcoholics on the Benton Visual Retention Test (Brewer and Perrett, 1971; Berglund and Sonesson, 1976; Page and Linden, 1974). Thus, there may be some signs for a memory disturbance for figural information.

However, on another measure, the Graham-Kendall Memory for Designs Test, there does not appear to be a significant memory disorder. Donovan *et al.* (1976) and May *et al.* (1970) found intact performance by alcoholics on this test. While this latter test also taps figural memory, it is important to point out that in the usually administered procedure it does not require delayed recall, as does the Benton Visual Retention Test. Therefore, there are certain procedural differences between these two tests that could account for the differences in the results. Inconsistencies in the findings also exist in verbal learning and memory. For example, alcoholics demonstrate an impairment in the number of words recalled in a serial learning task (Allen, Faillace and Reynolds, 1971; Weingartner and Faillace, 1971; Weingartner, Faillace and Markley, 1971) but do not demonstrate an overall disturbance in paired associate learning (Jonsson *et al.*, 1962; Berglund and Sonesson, 1976).

In summary, the results of memory testing are equivocal. The type of task appears to be a crucial factor in whether or not a deficit will be demonstrated. For non-verbal or figural information, it appears that an impairment is observed only where delayed recall is required. In verbal learning, the evidence is more equivocal, but presently indicates that alcoholics have a relatively greater difficulty in serial learning and recall than in paired associate learning. Again, like the findings on perceptual spatial capacity, the presence or absence of an observed impairment is, to a great extent, task dependent.

Motor Capacity

Alcoholics have frequently been observed to suffer from muscle atrophy, along with peripheral neuropathy of both large and small nerve fibres. Given this pathology, it is not surprising that alcoholics are impaired on tasks of motor speed and dexterity. Tarter and Jones

(1971b) reported that alcoholics were deficient in simple tapping speed of a telegraph key. Kish and Cheney (1969) observed that on the General Aptitude Test Battery alcoholics were deficient in finger and manual dexterity as well as motor co-ordination. These results are at variance with other findings inasmuch as Vivian *et al.* (1973) noted that there were no impairments in motor speed in their sample of alcoholics. Reaction time has also been tested, but with mixed results. Talland (1963) observed that alcoholics in comparison to normals exhibited slower reaction times. Johnson *et al.* (1963), on the other hand, found no impairment in reaction time when tested in a continuous performance paradigm. Nor have alcoholics been observed to be more susceptible to the effects of distraction in a reaction time paradigm (Callan *et al.*, 1972). Contrary to the above findings, Vivian *et al.* (1973) were able to detect an impairment in reaction time in their alcoholic sample.

Motor regulation may be disturbed in alcoholics. Parsons *et al.* (1972) found that alcoholics were less controlled in turning a knob through a 180° arc when requested to do so as slowly as possible. The alcoholics performed the task faster than normals, suggesting that they may be motorically disinhibited. Using psychophysiological measurements, Coopersmith (1964) and Coopersmith and Woodrow (1967) also found that alcoholics were inclined to be disinhibited relative to normals. Generally, the results at this time indicate that alcoholics, when contrasted to a normal population, exhibit muscle weakness and possibly reduced motor speed and impaired motor regulation as well. However, the research conducted to date is far from conclusive. Hopefully, further research will be conducted that can elucidate the nature and extent of any motor impairment as a sequela of chronic alcohol consumption.

Neuropsychological Interpretation

Neuroradiological Findings

From the above literature review, it is clear that alcoholics exhibit a number of psychological deficits. One interpretation of these findings is that the disturbances are manifestations of a neurological pathology; although motivational, personality, and situational factors cannot be ruled out entirely. To strengthen the neurological hypothesis, it is important to examine the evidence for brain damage from the neuroradiological research, and if possible to determine whether there is congruence between the neurological and psychological findings.

There is increasing evidence from direct and indirect observation that alcoholics suffer from cerebral pathology. Examinations conducted by Courville (1955) of brains at autopsies led him to conclude that older alcoholics, particularly those in the fifth and sixth decades of life, suffer from cortical atrophy that is most apparent in the dorsolateral surface of the frontal lobes. He also reported a number of other pathological changes ranging from ventricular enlargement to cell loss and proliferation of neuroglia. Since these findings were reported, a number of other investigators have also observed cerebral pathology that is accentuated in the anterior regions (Lynch, 1960; Mancall, 1961).

Radiological techniques confirm the presence of cerebral pathology. The pneumoencephalogram has been applied to an alcoholic population with positive findings. Tumarkin *et al.* (1955) reported that in a group of eleven alcoholic military men diffuse bilateral atrophy was present in six subjects and frontal atrophy extant in four of these six. They also described ventricular dilatation in three of the subjects. The EEG tracings were found to be abnormal in six of the subjects, and where abnormality was present, it was most pronounced in the frontal regions. These abnormalities were also demonstrated to be correlated with performance competency on psychological tests. As such, a correlation was observed between the existence of clinical pathology and performance on the Digit Symbol subtest and Digit Span subtest of Wechsler-Bellevue Intelligence Scale.

In another investigation, Brewer and Perrett (1971) administered the electroencephalogram and pneumoencephalogram to a group of alcoholics and, in addition, conducted a psychological assessment employing the Wechsler Adult Intelligence Scale and Benton Visual Retention Test. They found clinical atrophy in 30 of 33 cases, with ventricular dilatation in 24 of the subjects. The location of the atrophy in 19 of the subjects was found to be primarily in the frontal-parietal regions. Where atrophy was identified, it was noted as clinically significant in 70 per cent of the subjects. Thus, not all drinkers exhibited neuropathology, but where it was recorded, it appeared to be of a significant degree and in concordance with psychological findings in 50 per cent of the cases.

In another important study, Haug (1968) administered the pneumoencephalogram to 60 alcoholics and observed a positive correlation between length of drinking history, psychometric performance, and cerebral atrophy. Ventricular size was found to be negatively related to abstracting ability. In addition to the above studies, other investigators have also reported cerebral atrophy in alcoholics upon pneumoencephalographic examination (Aguirre, 1970; Iivanainen, 1975; Skillicorn, 1955).

In an interesting study, Berglund and Ingvar (1976) investigated regional cerebral blood flow in a group of alcoholics. They observed that relative to other regions of the brain, there is a marked reduction of cerebral blood flow in the anterior temporal and frontal regions in older alcoholics. Another technique which has recently been found to be extremely useful in directly observing neurological pathology involves the use of computerised tomography. In one study, Fox *et al.* (1976) found that 75 per cent of their alcoholics (N = 12) exhibited ventricular dilatation, while two demonstrated enlarged sulci, which they concluded reflected cerebral atrophy.

In another study, Carlen *et al.* (1978) investigated a group of eight medically intact alcoholics who had been drinking, on the average, for almost two decades. They observed both cortical atrophy and ventricular enlargement. One peculiar finding in this study was that upon re-examination after at least a six-month interval there was a decrease in atrophy in half (N = 4) of the subjects, and this in turn was associated with clinical improvement as well as abstinence. The authors theorise that alcohol abuse can lead to neurological damage, but that upon maintenance of sobriety there can be glial or vascular tissue regrowth.

Considering these studies in total, it is apparent from this brief review of the neuroradiological literature that a substantial proportion of alcoholics suffer from cerebral pathology, even though there is inconsistency between the various studies as to its severity, pervasiveness and localisation.

Neuropsychological Hypotheses

Tarter (1976) summarised four contemporary hypotheses regarding the nature of the neuropsychological disturbance in chronic alcoholics. This section will review each of the hypotheses, its current status, and capacity to explain the pattern of the observed impairments.

Hypothesis 1: Chronic Alcohol Consumption Leads to Diffuse or Generalised Cerebral Damage. By definition, this hypothesis implies that the effects of long-standing alcohol abuse are not focalised to any specific brain site or system. Evidence for diffuse cerebral atrophy has not been forthcoming as revealed by the electrophysiological studies of Lereboullet *et al.* (1956), neuropsychological studies of Fitzhugh *et al.*

(1960, 1965) and neuropathological studies of Courville (1955).
However, there are a number of other studies which point to a
regionalised general impairment extending from the parietal to frontal
regions as suggested from several of the neurological investigations
reviewed above. There is, as yet, no evidence to implicate occipital or
posterior temporal disturbance from either the psychological or
neurological research. Brosin (1967) described the symptoms of
generalised cerebral atrophy as memory impairment, poor judgement,
reduced intellectual competence, reduced clarity of consciousness,
and disorientation. From the psychological research, it is quite clear
at this time that alcoholics do not exhibit, to any marked degree,
these disturbances.

Hypothesis 2: Alcoholics Are Relatively More Disrupted in the Right
than Left Hemisphere of the Brain (Jones and Parsons, 1971a).
Evidence in favour of this hypothesis comes primarily from the
psychological research, inasmuch as no direct evidence for differential
lateralised pathology has been reported from the neurological or
pathological research. Support is derived from the finding that the
majority of deficits in alcoholics appear to involve non-verbal types of
task demands. Thus, on the Wechsler Scales, alcoholics demonstrate a
small but consistent inferiority of performance IQ relative to verbal
IQ. Spatial capacities are generally thought to be observed by the
right hemisphere and, as described previously, this is a major source of
impairment in alcoholics. Deficits have been observed in alcoholics on
the Block Design Test of the WAIS which, according to O'Leary *et al.*
(1979), is the most potent discriminator between alcoholics and non-
alcoholics.

Similarly, non-verbal memory has been reported to be more
impaired in alcoholics than verbal memory. Miglioli *et al.* (1979)
administered a battery of verbal and non-verbal tests to a group of
alcoholics and found that it was the non-verbal measures that most
discriminated alcoholics from controls, leading them to interpret the
results as supporting a right hemisphere dysfunction. Ryan and Butters
(1979) have similarly reported that the largest deficits emerge where
the alcoholics must learn unfamiliar non-verbal information.

Another source of evidence in support of the right hemisphere
hypothesis has accrued from the finding that alcoholics are inclined to
exhibit a greater degree of impairment with the use of the left hand
than with the right. An inferiority in performance with the non-
preferred hand relative to the preferred hand is expected, and this is the

left hand for the majority of people. But it has been found that the non-preferred hand is relatively less efficient when comparing alcoholics to normals, while right hand performance has been found to be equivalent on a task of motor regulation (Parsons *et al.*, 1972). Tarter and Jones (1971b) observed a trend in this direction as well, on tasks of speed and co-ordination. Goodglass and Peck (1972) found that, in a dichotic memory task, only items presented to the left ear were recalled less well by alcoholics when compared to normals.

Thus, there is some psychological test evidence which supports the hypothesis of a greater impairment in those functions that are subserved by the right hemisphere. However, it is not clear at this time whether these impairments are due to a lateralisation of cerebral pathology or whether the threshold for the observed impairment is lower for visual spatial than verbal tasks. Thus, because verbal processes are so automatic and overlearned in the habits of everyday living, they may be less susceptible to the effects of cerebral pathology of the nature induced by alcohol consumption. Consequently, hypothetically equal atrophy in each hemisphere may reveal psychological deficits in only the visual spatial modality. In conclusion, it is not clear at this time whether the observed deficits reflect the relative vulnerability of verbal versus non-verbal capacities, or if they, in fact, relate to differential lateralisation of cerebral pathology.

Hypothesis 3: The Chronic Consumption of Alcohol Causes an Acceleration of the Ageing Process (Kleinknecht and Goldstein, 1972).
The evidence that alcohol use in its chronic form can lead to accelerated ageing, and that the psychological manifestations are similar to that seen in older patients, is derived from a number of studies. Jones and Parsons (1971b) observed that young alcoholics performed as well as young normal controls on a battery of neuropsychological tests, but that the older alcoholics performed much more poorly than their age-matched controls. Similar results have been obtained in a hypothesis testing task (Klisz and Parsons, 1977). This led the authors to conclude that alcohol interacts with the ageing process in that there is immunity from deficit during the early years of abusive drinking, after which there is an accelerated rate of deterioration as drinking and ageing conjointly proceed. In another study, Schau and O'Leary (1977) found that the brain-age quotient of alcoholics was significantly lower than that of a group of normal subjects. The brain-age quotient is a composite index derived from scores on several of the Halstead-Reitan tests, such as the Category

Test and Tactual Performance Test, along with the Trail Making Test, and Block Design and Digit Symbol subtests of the Wechsler-Bellevue Scale. Performance on these tests is contrasted with a reference group of other psychological tests that are presumably insensitive to brain lesions but sensitive to educational level. These other measures include several of the Wechsler-Bellevue subtests, such as Information, Comprehension, Similarities, and Vocabulary.

Upon deriving this index in a group of 38 alcoholics, Schau and O'Leary (1977) found that indeed their alcoholic subjects had a mean brain-age quotient lower than what would be expected from the general population. The alcoholics obtained a mean score of 88, which is 12 below the expected population norm for their age, and 14 lower than a non-alcoholic control group. Moreover, on the problem solving variables, they found that the alcoholics performed comparably to the non-alcoholics on only the localisation measure on the Tactual Performance Test. On the education measures, the alcoholics performed equally well on three of the four tests, with the exception of the Comprehension subtest of the Wechsler-Bellevue Intelligence Scale.

Using experimental instead of clinical techniques, Ryan and Butters (1980a) found that alcoholics who had been sober for several months still exhibited impairments on several learning and memory tasks that are more demanding than the usual clinical instruments typically employed. Of particular interest was the demonstration that alcoholics between 34-49 years old performed almost identically with a normal control group ranging between 50-59 years of age. Alcoholics whose age range was between 50-59 years performed most closely to controls whose age range was between 60-65 years. This study provides a strong and clear experimental demonstration that alcoholics perform comparably to normals only when the latter group is about a decade older than themselves. Unlike the studies by Parsons and his colleagues, the findings by Ryan and Butters illustrate that even young alcoholics are impaired relative to their age-matched controls, suggesting an earlier insidious adverse effect from their drinking than has been previously realised. These two sets of experiments also indicate that different tests may elicit deficits at specific stages of the drinking history, a factor that needs to be considered especially when studies fail to reveal a neuropsychological impairment. In another study, Williams *et al.* (1973) analysed the WAIS profiles of 158 alcoholics and reported independent dual processes of accelerated mental ageing and organicity.

Thus, there are some indications that the performance of alcoholics on neuropsychological tests is analogous to a premature ageing process. However, it should be pointed out that the evidence in this regard is very limited and that a much more extensive research effort is required before this hypothesis can be further tested. In addition, it is important to emphasise that even if alcoholics exhibit a pattern of deficits similar to that of a premature ageing process, it does not necessarily mean that alcoholism causes an acceleration of ageing; and secondly does not, by itself, inform us about the mechanism or underlying substrate at the neurological level that is responsible for the process. However, as an analogy, the notion that ageing and alcohol use may interact is indeed a very important issue, particularly insofar as treatment prognosis may be concerned.

Hypothesis 4: Alcoholics Suffer from Frontal-limbic-diencephalic Pathology (Tarter, 1973, 1975, 1976). There is a large body of evidence demonstrating that these brain regions are morphologically and functionally integrated (Fulton, 1952; Nauta, 1964; Pribram, 1958). Lesions in various locations within this system have been shown to produce similar behavioural deficits (Brutkowski, 1965). The evidence that alcoholics suffer from pathology of the anterior basal regions of the brain is derived from several different sources. First, it has been demonstrated that individuals suffering from the Wernicke-Korsakoff syndrome have neurological pathology in the limbic and diencephalic regions (Meissner, 1967; Talland, 1965). It is therefore plausible that alcoholics have a similar disturbance, but in a less advanced stage that is nonetheless detectable upon psychological measurement.

Another source of information is derived from clinical neurological studies. Segal *et al.* (1970) presented a detailed description as to how alcoholics during detoxification manifest symptoms that are quite similar to non-alcoholics suffering from lesions in the diencephalon. There are also a number of studies, as previously discussed, in which the pneumoencephalogram and CAT scan have revealed ventricular dilatation in alcoholics, causing obvious disruptions of limbic and diencephalic circuits. It is therefore possible that the atrophy of neuronal tissue adjacent to the ventricles may be creating a disruption of the frontal-basal neuronal connections.

In addition to direct physical evidence for diencephalic pathology, there is also information to suggest that there is a frontal pathology as well. Lereboullet *et al.* (1956) observed that the EEG tracings in alcoholics indicated frontal lobe atrophy. In another important study,

Berglund and Ingvar (1976) found differences in regional cerebral blood flow in alcoholics that were most pronounced in the anterior regions of the brain. And finally, Courville's (1955) observations of frontal lobe atrophy upon dissection adds weight to this hypothesis. Tarter (1976) reviewed the literature and described a variety of characteristics exhibited by alcoholics that are also found in individuals with focal lesions and animals with surgically induced lesions. Among the similarities between the alcoholics and these other groups are their qualitatively comparable performance on a number of cognitive tasks.

The similarities include difficulties in shifting cognitive sets (Tarter and Parsons, 1971), utilising an error response to achieve subsequently a correct response in a concept identification task (Tarter, 1973), and inability to persist with a cognitive set to sustain a correct mode of responding (Tarter, 1973). Another common characteristic found in lesioned humans and animals with anterior basal damage is spatial perseveration. This is behaviourally manifested as a tendency on the part of the subject to respond to the particular physical location during a cognitive task, regardless of the stimulus characteristics or task demands at the time. Such a tendency has also been observed in alcoholics (Tarter, 1971). Similarly, spatial scanning, as measured by maze tests, has been observed on a number of occasions to be deficient in alcoholics (Fitzhugh *et al.*, 1965; Goldstein and Chotlos, 1965; Tarter, 1971), and this too is frequently seen in humans and animals with acute frontal lesions. The spatial deficits in turn may be related to a more fundamental disorder in visual searching abilities (Bertera and Parsons, 1978).

There is accumulating empirical evidence demonstrating the important role of the frontal lobes in behavioural regulation. Luria (1966) has emphasised how this region of the brain is involved in the verbal mediation and evaluation of ongoing behaviour. Zangwill (1966) has similarly discussed the important role of the frontal lobes in sustaining behavioural persistence. He described the absence of this capacity in lesioned individuals who symptomatically exhibited what he referred to as *antrieb*, or the inability to sustain a motor act in a modulated manner regardless of the time required for completion. Alcoholics in this regard have been reported to have a reduction in initiative (Mallerstein, 1969). Similarly, behavioural impersistence in sustaining a cognitive set has been reported by Tarter (1973).

Another measure of frontal lobe disturbance has been derived from Rod and Frame Test performance. Teuber (1964) observed that it is this region of the brain which results in the greatest behavioural deficits on this task, a factor which he attributed to a disruption of the frontal eyefields. Alcoholics have been found to respond consistently in a deficient manner on this test (Bailey *et al.*, 1961; Goldstein and Chotlos, 1965; Karp *et al.*, 1963, 1965a, 1965b). While an impairment in alcoholics' performance on this test has been frequently reported, it is yet not totally clear whether it is due to personality factors or reflective of a neuropsychological disturbance. Attempts to correlate this perceptual deficit with personality factors have failed (Goldstein *et al.*, 1968), but attempts to relate this performance to drinking history and other neurological findings have also not been successful; although Tarter *et al.* (1975) found that it did correlate with a number of capacities such as general reasoning, perceptual capacity, and speed of closure.

Another source of neuropsychological evidence concordant with the hypothesis of an anterior basal pathology in alcoholics has accrued from performance on clinical neuropsychological tests. For example, Halstead (1964) observed that 75 per cent of his patients with frontal lobe damage performed in the impaired ranges on the Category Test and Tactual Performance Test. It is precisely on these two measures that Fitzhugh *et al.* (1965) observed a deficit. Porteus (1959) reported that his maze tests were selectively capable of identifying anterior lesions, and in this regard similar deficits have been noted in alcoholics on other maze-types of tests (Jonsson *et al.*, 1962; Fitzhugh *et al.*, 1965; Goldstein and Chotlos, 1965; Tarter, 1971). Thus, there is some evidence at this time to implicate an anterior basal disruption in chronic alcoholics and, on some of the measures, the degree of deficit appears to be correlated with chronicity of alcoholism history (Tarter, 1973).

Unlike the other neuropsychological hypotheses pertaining to the nature of the neuropathology in alcoholics, the anterior basal position invokes a functional system and not simply a brain region or structure. As previously discussed, there is ample evidence which demonstrates a structural and functional connection between the frontal and basal regions of the brain. Pribram (1958) has speculated that the prefrontal region serves as the association area for the limbic system. Lesions in either the anterior or basal brain regions have been known to produce similar behavioural deficits (Fulton, 1952; Pribram, 1958). Nauta (1964) observed upon histological analysis that fibres from the dorsal lateral region project to the superior temporal gyrus, while those of the orbital regions project to the middle and inferior temporal gyri.

There is also evidence to indicate the existence of a frontal hypothalamic tract. W. LeGros Clark (1948) theorised that the hypothalamus has projections to and from the anterior regions of the brain, synapsing first in the dorsal medial nucleus of the thalamus, and then projecting to the lateral and orbital prefrontal regions. Three tracts were identified that emanate from the dorsomedial nucleus of the thalamus that project to the prefrontal regions, these being the *pars paramellaris* to the frontal eyefields, the *pars magnocellularis* to the orbital region, and the *pars parvocellularis* to the lateral surface. Thus, there appear to be reciprocal connections between the anterior and basal structures of the brain. Whether a chronic history of alcohol abuse disrupts all of these systems, or results in a selective pathology to any one or more tracts, remains to be determined.

Considering the combined evidence from the neuropsychological, neuroradiological, and pathological findings, the most viable hypothesis at this time seems to favour an anterior basal focus of disturbance. Nonetheless, there are still a number of questions and inconsistencies in the literature which prevent a conclusive statement at this time (Tarter, 1971). Perhaps further research can focus on neurochemical mechanisms that might be involved, particularly as they might shed some light on a particular neuronal system or neurotransmitter that may be deficient within a specified brain region. Nonetheless, the above review of the literature suggests that alcoholics, soon after a period of detoxication, exhibit impairments on a variety of psychological tests and performance measures which can be parsimoniously explained from a neuropsychological perspective. Personality and motivational factors cannot account for the range and diversity of the observed deficits. Because some of the observed impairments are associated with chronicity of drinking history (Tarter, 1976), it appears safe to conclude that a progressive neuropathological deterioration does take place that is ultimately expressed as psychological incompetence in specific areas of functioning.

Reversibility of Impairment

One vital topic which has not received sufficient attention among investigators concerns the degree to which the observed deficits are permanent or are ameliorated after extended sobriety. Dramatic improvement in overall functioning is seen in the alcoholic as he passes through withdrawal and detoxifies, but as yet there is insufficient information as to whether or not there is additional recovery of capacity after abstinence has been achieved and maintained. In one of the first studies conducted, McLachlan and Levinson (1974) observed that the WAIS Block Design performance subtest score increased after a year of abstinence to the point where there was no significant difference between alcoholics and a control sample. In a similar investigation, Long and McLachlan (1974) reported a significant improvement on several of the Halstead-Reitan and Wechsler Adult Intelligence Scale subtests.

Finger tapping speed and abstracting ability, measured by the Category Test, likewise improved. Tarter and Jones (1971b) observed that alcoholics with a less than ten-year-history of excessive drinking increased their finger tapping speed and perceptual motor co-ordination as well as muscle strength during three months of sobriety. Page and Linden (1974) administered a number of psychological tests and found that after two weeks of sobriety there was major improvement in functioning, but that further changes did not occur after an additional two months of abstinence. Clarke and Houghton (1975) administered a battery of intellectual and memory tests and found that alcoholics were still deficient on a visual spatial and visual motor co-ordination task after ten weeks of abstinence. Memory was also somewhat impaired. Smith *et al.* (1971) observed that their alcoholics improved upon retesting on a number of perceptual and intellectual tasks. Allen *et al.* (1971) reported that in serial and free recall memory tasks, it took up to two weeks of recovery time for these capacities to recover to a level comparable to a control group. In addition to learning ability, it has also been found by Weingartner *et al.* (1971) that retentive capacities recover after about three weeks of hospitalisation and sobriety.

Other investigators have not observed such marked improvements. Carlsson *et al.* (1973) found that on a battery of perceptual and cognitive tests substantial improvement did not occur after two weeks of sobriety. Freund and Walker (1971) found that, in an animal study using mice, the performance impairment persisted after four months of sobriety in an avoidance learning task. In another study, they found that timing behaviour was also impaired after a 30 day interval of sobriety, even when nutritional and liver pathology factors were controlled (Walker and Freund, 1973). Miglioli *et al.* (1979) observed that alcoholics were initially more impaired than controls on several perceptual and memory tasks. However, after a two-month period of sobriety, there were significant improvements on several of the verbal measures, but only marginal increments in visuospatial competency. These results are important inasmuch as they reveal a greater disturbance of visual spatial as opposed to verbal skills, and that these former disturbances seem to be more resistant to improvement after sobriety has been achieved.

In another study, O'Leary *et al.* (1977) found that upon administering the Trail Making Test at the beginning and end of one year of sobriety there remained a persistent impairment in alcoholics relative to normal controls. The alcoholics did show some improvement in their performance after one year, but their level of competency was still in the clinically impaired ranges. In another investigation, Ornstein (1977) administered the Hooper Visual Organisation Test and the Shipley Institute of Living Scale to a group of detoxified alcoholics upon admission to a treatment programme, and again approximately three months later. There was some improvement on the Hooper Test for Visual Organisation, suggesting recovery of perceptual and spatial capacities. On the Shipley Institute of Living Scale there was a slight improvement on the vocabulary measure in the alcoholics who were eventually to become abstainers. A general improvement in the conceptual quotient was also noted between admission and discharge. The improvements in the conceptual quotient and Hooper score were insufficient, however, after three months of abstinence, to bring the alcoholics up to the normal population level. Thus, despite the benefit of practice from test to retest on the measures, the alcoholics, though improving, still did not fully recover from their initial deficits.

In conclusion, it appears that alcoholics do demonstrate some recovery of capacities with sobriety. What is not clear is the degree to which these functions can continue to improve beyond the limited time scope of the investigations conducted to date. Thus, it may take several years for full recovery. The present studies, which find only limited improvement after several months to a year, do not completely portray the potential for reversibility of the deficits. Moreover, it is quite feasible that the rate of recovery of some functions may proceed more quickly than for other capacities. Thus, for example, the improvements may take on a different recovery course for verbal than for non-verbal processes. This aspect of reversibility has not been investigated other than by a recent study of Miglioli *et al.* (1979).

The rate at which reversibility of the deficits can be enhanced through nutrition and cognitive therapy also needs to be investigated. And finally, it is also unclear what role is played by psychopathological factors in the observed deficits. Thus, an individual who has remained abstinent but is still very anxious or depressed, would be expected to exhibit more residual psychological deficits than a normal person, especially when timed tests are involved. Perhaps future investigations should consider the inclusion of a functional psychopathology sample that is matched for clinical status with an alcoholic group when assessing for competency of cognitive and intellectual functions.

Complicating Factors

While the weight of the empirical evidence points to a neuropsychological deficit, there is still little known about the causal mechanisms that produce the observed impairments and the reasons for the large variability in performance capacities in alcoholics. A number of factors could be contributing indirectly to the deficits and variability. The presence of hepatic pathology may be one such contributing variable.

Smith and Smith (1977) compared alcoholics with and without a history of cirrhosis with a group of normal controls. They found that alcoholics suffering from cirrhosis performed more poorly than non-cirrhotic alcoholics on the measures of verbal intelligence, performance intelligence, and full scale IQ of the WAIS. There was an average of four points difference between the two alcoholic groups on the verbal scale, but a ten point inferiority of the cirrhotic group on the performance scale. The full scale intelligence quotient of the cirrhotic group was 93.7, while the non-cirrhotic alcoholic group had an IQ of 101. However, both of these two groups were inferior to the control sample, who obtained a full scale IQ of 112, which is somewhat higher than the population mean of 100.

In the context of population norms, the non-cirrhotic group performed within the normal ranges while the cirrhotic group performed in the low average ranges. Interestingly, the cirrhotic group performed poorest on those subtests that measured attention and spatial synthesis, obtaining their lowest scores on the Digit Symbol, Block Design, and Object Assembly subtests. Moreover, it was found that the deterioration quotient of the cirrhotic group was lower than that of the controls and non-cirrhotic alcoholics, while the latter two groups did not differ from each other. From these findings, it appears that cirrhosis in alcoholics is a contributing factor to intellectual impairment.

The intriguing possibility that liver pathology may interact with psychological competency needs to be further researched in the light of these findings, and possibly controlled for in subsequent investigations examining alcoholism history and neuropsychological capacity.

Another factor which has been largely neglected concerns sex differences. Almost all of the studies conducted on neuropsychological competency have studied men, with very little attention paid to women. The one study that has been published, which specifically examined neuropsychological competency in female alcoholics, Hatcher *et al.* (1977), found impairments on both a spatial and verbal abstracting test when they were compared to a control group. These investigators observed that on the Shipley-Hartford Institute of Living Scale, the alcoholic women obtained a lower abstracting score and lower conceptual quotient than the normals. On the Raven Progressive Matrices, a test which measures general intelligence and perceptual organisation, they found that the alcoholic women were also impaired.

Thus, unlike the studies with male alcoholics, this report presents evidence for a verbal abstracting deficit in women that has not been typically found in men suffering from alcoholism. Also interesting in this regard was the finding that, even though the women of this study had an average age of 44 years, which is comparable to most studies with men, their drinking history extended about eight years, which is less than that usually found in men of that age range. In previous studies of alcoholics with such a drinking history, deficits have not been noted on most neuropsychological tests. It is therefore quite possible that a neuropsychological impairment occurs at a progressively faster rate in female than male alcoholics. Needless to say, one cannot conclude this unequivocally on the basis of one study, but the magnitude of the impairments reported by Hatcher *et al.* (1977) is significant and deserves further follow-up research. Furthermore, the above investigation found an association between cognitive capacity and menstrual factors.

Menstruating alcoholics performed more poorly than controls on the Shipley abstracting measure as well as the Raven Progressive Matrices. Non-menstruating alcoholics performed more poorly than controls on only the latter test. Within groups comparisons revealed that the menstruating alcoholics did not differ from non-menstruating alcoholics, but the menstruating controls were adversely affected by this factor on cognitive performance. Thus, the possibility of endocrinological mechanisms interacting with drinking history is raised, and although the results of this study are tentative and somewhat unclear, they do indicate that the cognitive impairments may not be simply due to alcohol toxicity.

Another factor which has not received sufficient attention concerns nutrition. Fleming and Guthrie (in press) observed that alcoholics exhibited an initial disturbance on EEG and psychometric measures after detoxication but improved after a one-year period of abstinence. The initial EEG disturbance was correlated with indices of malnutrition and folate deficiency. Reversal of the EEG abnormalities tended to occur with the restoration of nutrition. Psychometric competency was also found to correlate with the EEG abnormalities, but it was not clear whether the latter disturbances were due to nutritional factors or alcoholism history, or both of these variables.

In another investigation, Guthrie and Elliott (1977) found that malnutrition was correlated with cerebral impairment as inferred from psychological assessment. The greatest initial improvement after detoxification was found in those alcoholics suffering from malnutrition, folate deficiency and peripheral neuropathy. This finding leads to the engaging hypothesis that the initial recovery of psychological function after withdrawal may be related to the restoration of nutritional balance, but that the more long-standing deficits that have been reported even after a year or more of sobriety may be tied to the toxic effects of alcohol itself.

In another investigation, Guthrie (unpublished) reported that while the malnourished group improved the most from two to four weeks after withdrawal, the nourished alcoholics showed the greatest degree of recovery beginning from six months to a year later, and to a lesser extent, this was also found in the malnourished group. Thus, there may exist multiple factors contributing to the recovery of psychological function. Initial recovery may be related to nutritional mechanisms, but the more long-standing improvements, which appear from previous studies to be less than complete, may be due to the recovery from the chronic toxic effects of the alcohol.

Subject and Methodological Factors

There is less than unanimous agreement on the nature of the psychological deficit in alcoholics. This stems in large part from a lack of consistency in empirical methods employed. This discrepancy between findings can be attributed to sampling differences, tests utilised, and subject characteristics that are either uncontrolled or unspecified. Unfortunately, there are too many published reports that have not assessed for concomitant neurological conditions, such as trauma or seizures, and the role that these factors play in the psychological deficits. Nutritional factors and type of beverage are also often neglected in describing the alcoholic sample. If the chronic consumption of alcohol produces a progressive deterioration in functional capacity, then one would expect this variable to be correlated with psychological performance.

Tarter and Jones (1971b) and Tarter (1973) have found differences between short- and long-term alcoholics on cognitive capacities as well as the potential for recovery of motor and perceptual motor deficits. Thus, alcoholics of a similar age, but with divergent drinking histories, may exhibit differential patterns of neuropsychological deficit. Such a delineation of the alcoholism population based on drinking history would therefore seem to have both research and clinical significance.

A number of other variables also merit consideration, but as yet have received little, if any, attention in the research literature. The degree to which the congeners contribute to psychological impairment in the acute and long-term effects has yet to be systematically investigated. Further clarification as to the progressive nature of the deficits is required, particularly as the research may reveal a picture of neuropsychological dysfunction unique to chronic alcoholism or alternatively resembling features of other clinical pathologies, such as the Wernicke-Korsakoff syndrome, dementia, Alzheimer's disease, and so forth.

To date the only research programme that has been directed toward elucidating the relationship between alcoholism and the Korsakoff psychosis has been conducted by Dr. Nelson Butters and his colleagues at the Boston Veterans Administration Hospital. While the results are too extensive to describe in detail here, their research has revealed a surprising similarity of deficits in alcoholics and Korsakoff patients (Ryan and Butters, 1980b). These investigators thus provide strong support for a continuity of impairment that is observable first in heavy social drinkers (Parker and Noble, 1977) which then becomes increasingly severe during alcoholism (Tarter, 1976) and culminates in a 'borderline Korsakoff' disorder (Ryan and Butters, 1980b).

If excessive drinking continues unabated, and along with it there exists poor nutrition and a genetic vulnerability, then the person is at risk for eventual deterioration into a florid Korsakoff psychosis. Thus, systematic neuropsychological research affords an opportunity to investigate the progressive nature of impairments. Hopefully, future research will delineate in a precise and quantitative fashion the rate and quality of impairment that could then yield a reliable index of clinical neuropsychological status as a function of drinking history and pattern.

However, for the purposes of this discussion, it is important to point out that the above objective can be realised only if demonstrations of deficit can be related to the best levels (normals) and worst levels (Korsakoff) of performance. This would enable a scaled reference of severity of impairment to be derived for a given capacity. In turn, such an index, as for example the brain-age quotient, could then provide useful information about treatment prognosis and drinking pattern (O'Leary *et al.*, 1979).

Predrinking pathology may also need to be assessed. Tarter *et al.* (1977) identified a subgroup from the population of alcoholics who report a history of hyperactivity in childhood. Given this constitutional disturbance, it is not unreasonable to theorise that the cognitive deficits, to some extent, may be influenced by factors unrelated to the alcoholism history, but rather may reflect a fundamental antecedent neurological condition. The degree to which functional psychopathological considerations, such as anxiety, depression, and sociopathy also contribute to the observed deficits, needs to be examined in more detail and controlled for in subsequent research. Alcoholism usually occurs with a clinical overlay, and thus comparison with a normal control group prevents separation of pathological status from alcoholism history, rendering the interpretation of the results extremely difficult if not impossible.

The complexity of human psychological functioning demands consideration of a multitude of factors and processes. The effects of a chronic history of alcohol usage are expected to be complex and producing organismic changes at all levels of biological organisation. Complicating the situation is the fact that alcohol beverages are impure and are metabolised in a complicated way with much interindividual variation. Therefore, to understand the end-point of alcohol abuse, that is, its effects on psychological competency, one must inevitably take into account and control for basic characteristics such as age of onset, duration and pattern of consumption, evidence of functional psychopathology, prealcoholic predisposing factors, and neurological as well as nutritional history. For a comprehensive understanding of the effects of alcohol consumption ever to emerge, further research must be more specific in identifying subject and beverage characteristics, to enable more meaningful comparisons of results between investigations.

Future Research Directions

At this stage of research development into the neuropsychological consequences of alcohol abuse, it has been assumed that alcoholism is itself a homogeneous clinical entity and that the pattern of effects of alcohol on the organism are universal. Both of these assumptions are open to question. The clinical literature, for example, is replete with reports of alcoholic subtypes that have been derived along a number of different empirical criteria such as personality traits, psychosocial history, drinking style, and genetic-familial relationships. From a clinical psychological standpoint, alcohol addiction may constitute several disorders, of which drinking excess is but one unifying common characteristic. With such an emerging picture of alcoholism categories, it is quite possible that differential vulnerability to the effects of alcohol may be a crucial factor in the eventual manifestation and progression of cerebral pathology.

In this context, it is quite understandable that almost all neuropsychological studies have observed sharp variation in levels of competency in alcoholics. In one large-scale investigation, Goldstein and Shelly (in Press) evaluated 100 alcoholics and found that 22 per cent of them could not be classified as brain damaged. Thus, a substantial proportion of the alcoholic population, despite a history of long-standing excesses, does not present evidence for a neuropsychological disorder. The question is therefore raised as to what could be contributing to this dichotomy among alcoholics, since these results seemingly suggest that the consumption of alcohol may not be the only factor responsible for the deficits. Drawing from the research on the Wernicke-Korsakoff syndrome, it has recently been demonstrated that the development of this disorder depends on two factors: thiamine deficiency and a genetically determined deficiency of the enzyme transketolase (Blass and Gibson, 1977). Thus, if the chronic alcoholic is at risk for evolving into the Korsakoff state, complete with clinical and neuropsychological sequelae, there are factors at play such as diet and genetic predisposition that contribute to this vulnerability. On the other hand, it has yet to be established for certain that alcoholics inevitably evolve into a Korsakoff psychosis. It is indeed possible that there are a number of different organic consequences of alcohol abuse, with the Korsakoff disorder being only one of a number of different end points.

Thus, the neuropsychological sequelae may be variable and comprise several different syndromes. In this regard, it is important to note that in the study by Goldstein and Shelly (in Press), in which alcoholics were compared to anterior, posterior, and diffusely lesioned patients, 37.5 per cent of the alcoholics were classified as diffusely brain damaged from the psychological tests, 19 per cent exhibited a pattern of deficits analogous to left hemisphere pathology, and 21.5 per cent presented a picture similar to a right hemisphere disturbance. Hence, comparing the alcoholics to a verified reference group of neurological patients did not reveal a single pattern of neuropsychological deficits.

Future research must take into consideration the variability inherent in the alcohol abusing population, and strive to identify typologies that could be predictive of the type of cerebral pathology that is reflected in a specified form of neuropsychological disturbance. Approaching the problem from the other end, neuropsychological deficits need to be systematised and classified into syndromes and, if possible, related to specific alcoholic subtypes based on genetic, nutritional, psychological and clinical information.

With the identification of homogeneous neuropsychologically impaired subgroups of alcoholics, the next step would involve the development of a comprehensive picture of the consequences of abusive drinking that incorporates neurological, radiological, psychological, nutritional and biochemical information. This information could then be applied to the derivation of clinical subtypes. Viewed in this context, the elucidation of impairments in alcoholics would not only be important in simply describing the effects of alcoholism, but could also potentially add to our awareness of its causes, processes, and multiple modes of expression, as well as facilitate specifically structured treatment modalities that are tailored to individual needs.

References

Aguirre, A. (1970), 'Cerebral atrophy in delerium tremens', *Archivos de Neurobiologia, 33*, 423-30

Allen, R., Faillace, L. and Reynolds, D. (1971), 'Recovery of memory functioning in alcoholics following prolonged alcohol intoxification', *Jrnl. of Nervous and Mental Diseases, 153* 417-23

Bailey, W., Hustmyer, F. and Kristofferson, A. (1961), 'Alcoholism, brain damge, and perceptual dependence', *Quarterly Jrnl. Studies Alc., 22*, 387-93

Bender, L. (1938), 'A visual motor Gestalt test and its clinical uses', *Amer. Orthopsychiat. Assoc. Res. Mgr., 3*

Berglund, M. and Ingvar, D. (1976), 'Cerebral blood flow and its regional distribution in alcoholism and Korsakoff's psychosis', *Jrnl. of Studies of*

Alcohol, 37, 586-97

Berglund, M. and Sonesson, B. (1976), 'Personality impairment in alcoholism; its relation to regional cerebral blood flow and psychometric performance', *Quarterly Jrnl. of Studies on Alcohol, 37*, 298-310

Bertera, J.H. and Parsons, O.A. (1978), 'Impaired visual search in alcoholics', *Alcoholism: Clin. Exp. Res., 2*, 9-14

Blass, J.P. and Gibson, G.E. (1977), 'Abnormality of a thiamine-requiring enzyme in patients with Wernicke-Korsakoff syndrome', *New England Jrnl. of Medicine, 297*, 1367-70

Brewer, C. and Perrett, L. (1971), 'Brain damage due to alcohol consumption: An air-encephalographic study', *British Jrnl. of Addiction, 66*, 170-82

Brosin, H. (1967), 'Acute and chronic brain syndromes' in Freedman, A. and Kaplan, H. (eds.), *Comprehensive Textbook of Psychiatry*, Williams and Wilkins, Baltimore

Brutkowski, S. (1965), 'Functions of prefrontal cortex in animals', *Physiol. Rev., 45*, 721-46

Callan, J., Holloway, F. and Bruhn, P. (1972), 'Effects of distraction upon reaction time performance in brain damaged and alcoholic patients', *Neuropsychologia, 10*, 363-70

Carlen, P.L., Wortzman, G., Holgate, R.C., Wilkinson, D.A. and Rankin, J.G. (1978), 'Reversible cerebral atrophy in recently abstinent chronic alcoholics measured by computed tomography scans', *Science, 200*, 1076-8

Carlsson, C., Claeson, L. and Pettersson, L. (1973), 'Psychometric signs of cerebral dysfunction in alcoholics', *British Jrnl. of Addictions, 68*, 83-6

Claeson, L. and Carlsson, C. (1970), 'Cerebral dysfunction in alcoholics; a psychometric investigation', *Quarterly Jrnl. of Studies on Alcohol, 31*, 317-23

Clark, W. le Gros, (1948), 'The connections of the frontal lobes of the brain', *Lancet, 254*, 353-6

Clarke, J. and Houghton, H. (1975), 'A study of intellectual impairment and recovery rates in heavy drinkers in Ireland', *The British Jrnl. of Psychiatry, 126*, 178-84

Coopersmith, S. (1964), 'Adaptive reactions of alcoholics and nonalcoholics', *Quarterly Jrnl. of Studies on Alcohol, 25*, 262-78

Coopersmith, S. and Woodrow, K. (1967), 'Basal conductance levels of normals and alcoholics', *Quarterly Jrnl. of Studies on Alcohol, 28*, 27-32

Courville, C. (1955), *Effects of Alcohol on the Central Nervous System*, San Lucas Press, Los Angeles

Donovan, D., Queisser, H. and O'Leary, M. (1976), 'Group embedded figures test performance as a predictor of cognitive impairment among alcoholics', *The International Jrnl. of the Addictions, 11*, 725-39

Fitzhugh, L., Fitzhugh, K. and Reitan, R. (1960), 'Adaptive abilities and intellectual functioning in hospitalized alcoholics', *Quarterly Jrnl. of Studies on Alcohol, 21*, 414-23

—— (1965), 'Adaptive abilities and intellectual functioning in hospitalized alcoholics: Further considerations', *Quarterly Jrnl. of Studies on Alcohol, 26*, 402-11

Fleming, A.M.M. and Guthrie, A. 'The electroencephalogram, psychological testing, and other investigations in abstinent alcoholics: A longitudinal study', in press.

Fox, J.H., Ramsey, R.G., Huckman, M.S. and Proske, A.E. (1976), 'Cerebral ventricular enlargement; chronic alcoholics examined by computerized tomography', *Jrnl. of the American Medical Association, 236*, 365-8

Freund, G. and Walker, D. (1971), 'Impairment of avoidance learning by prolonged ethanol consumption in mice', *Jrnl. of Pharmacology and*

Experimental Therapeutics, 179, 284-92

Fulton, J. (1952), *The Frontal Lobes and Human Behaviors: The Sherrington Lectures,* Liverpool University Press, Liverpool

Goldstein, G. and Chotlos, J. (1965), 'Dependency and brain damage in alcoholics', *Percept. Motor Skills, 21,* 135-50

Goldstein, G., Neuringer, C. and Klappersack, B. (1970), 'Cognitive, perceptual and motor aspects of field dependency in alcoholics', *Jrnl. Genet. Psychol., 117,* 253-66

Goldstein, G., Neuringer, C., Reiff, C. and Shelly, C. (1968), 'Generalizability of field dependency in alcoholics', *Jrnl. Consult. Clin. Psychol., 32,* 560-4

Goldstein, G. and Shelly, C., 'Neuropsychological investigation of brain lesion localization in alcoholism', in press

Goodglass, H. and Peck, E. (1972), 'Dichotic ear order effects in Korsakoff and normal subjects', *Neuropsychologia, 10,* 211-17

Gordan, K. (1957), 'Grassis Kubsubstitutiontest (Grassi's Substitution Test)', Unpublished dissertation, Stockholm

Grassi, J. (1953) *The Grassi Block Substitution Test for Measuring Organic Brain Pathology,* Charles C. Thomas, Springfield, Illinois

Guthrie, A. 'The first year after treatment: factors affecting time course of reversibility of memory and learning deficits in alcoholism', Unpublished

Guthrie, A. and Elliott, W.A. (1977), 'The nature and reversibility of cerebral impairment in alcoholism: Treatment implications', Paper given at the NATO Conference, Experimental and Behavioural Approaches to Alcoholism, Bergen, Norway

Halstead, W. (1947) *Brain and Intelligence,* University of Chicago Press, Chicago
——— (1964), Unpublished communication to Ackerly, S. cited by Ackerly, S. in Warren, J. and Akert, K. (eds.), *The Frontal Granular Cortex and Behavior,* McGraw-Hill, New York, 208

Hatcher, E.M., Jones, M.K. and Jones, B.M. (October 1977), 'Cognitive deficits in alcoholic women', *Alcohol: Clin. and Exper. Res., 1(4),* 371-7

Haug, J. (1968), 'Pneumoencephalographic evidence of brain damage in chronic alcoholics', *Acta Psychiatrica Scandinavica, 203,* 135-45

Hirschenfang, S., Silber, M. and Benton, J. (1967), 'Comparison of Bender-Gestalt reproductions in patients with peripheral neuropathy', *Perceptual and Motor Skills, 24,* 1317-18
——— (1968), 'Personality patterns in peripheral neuropathy', *Diseases of the Nervous System, 29,* 46-50

Iivanainen, M. (1975), 'Pneumoencephalographic and clinical characteristics of diffuse cerebral atrophy', *Acta Neurological Scandinavica, 51,* 310-27

Johnson, G., Parsons, O., Holloway, F. and Bruhn, P. (1973), 'Intradimensional reversal shift performance in brain damaged and chronic alcoholic patients', *Jrnl. Consult. Clin. Psychol., 40,* 253-8

Jones, B. and Parsons, O. (1972), 'Specific vs. generalized deficits of abstracting ability in chronic alcoholics', *Archives of General Psychiatry, 26,* 380-4
———(1971), 'Impaired abstracting ability in chronic alcoholics', *Archives of General Psychiatry, 24,* 71-5

Jonsson, C., Cronholm, B. and Izikowitz, S. (1962), 'Intellectual changes in alcoholics', *Quarterly Jrnl. of Studies on Alcohol, 23,* 221-42

Karp, S. and Konstadt, N. (1965), 'Alcoholism and psychological differentiation: long range effects of heavy drinking of field dependence', *Jrnl. of Nervous and Mental Disease, 140,* 412-16

Karp, S., Poster, D. and Goodman, A. (1963), 'Differentiation in alcoholic women', *Jrnl. of Personality, 31,* 386-93

Karp, S., Witkin, H. and Goodenough, D. (1965a), 'Alcoholism and psychological differentiation: Effect of achievement of sobriety on field dependence', *Quarterly Jrnl. of Studies on Alcohol, 26,* 580-5
────── (1965b), 'Alcoholism and psychological differentiation: Effect of alcohol on field dependence', *Jrnl. of Abnormal Psychology, 70,* 262-5
Kates, S. and Schmolke, M. (1953), 'Self-related and parent-related verbalizations and Bender-Gestalt performances of alcoholics', *Quarterly Jrnl. for Studies on Alcohol, 14,* 38-48
Kish, G. (1970), 'Alcoholics GATB and Shipley profiles and their interrelationships', *Jrnl. Clin. Psychol., 26,* 482-4
Kish, G. and Cheney, T. (1969), 'Impaired abilities in alcoholism measured by the General Aptitude Test Battery', *Quarterly Jrnl. for Studies on Alcohol, 30,* 384-8
Kleinknecht, R. and Goldstein, S. (1972), 'Neuropsychological deficits associated with alcoholism: A review and discussion', *Quarterly Jrnl. of Studies on Alcohol, 33,* 999-1019
Klisz, D.K. and Parsons, Q.A. (1977), 'Hypothesis testing in younger and older alcoholics', *Jrnl. for Studies on Alcohol, 38,* 1718-29
Lereboullet, J., Pluvinage, R. and Anstutz, D. (1956), 'Aspects cliniques et electroencephalographiques des atrophies cerebrales alcoliques', *Revue neurologique, 94,* 674-782
Long, J. and McLachlan, J. (1979), 'Abstract reasoning and perceptual motor efficiency in alcoholics; impairment and reversibility', *Quarterly Jrnl. of Studies on Alcohol, 35,* 1220-9
Lovibond, S. and Holloway, I. (1968), 'Differential sorting behavior of schizophrenics and organics', *Jrnl. Clin. Psychol., 24,* 307-11
Luria, A. (1966) *Human Brain and Psychological Processes,* Harper and Row, New York
Lynch, M. (1960), 'Brain lesions in chronic alcoholics', *Archives of Pathology, 69,* 342-53
Mallerstein, A. (1969), 'Korsakoff's syndrome and resumption of an interrupted task as an index of initiative', *Jrnl. Nervous Mental Diseases, 248,* 506-14
Mancall, E. (1961), 'Some unusual neurological diseases complicating chronic alcoholism', *American Jrnl. of Clinical Nutrition, 9,* 404-13
May, A., Urquhart, A. and Watts, R. (1970), 'Memory for designs test – a follow-up study', *Perceptual and Motor Skills, 30,* 753-4
McLachlan, J.F. and Levinson, T. (1974), 'Improvement in WAIS block design performance as a function of recovery from alcoholism', *Jrnl. of Clin. Psychology, 30,* 65-6
Meissner, W. (1967), 'Memory functions in the Korsakoff's syndrome', *Jrnl. Nerv. Mental Disease, 145,* 106-22
Miglioli, M., Buchtel, H.A., Campanini, T. and De Risio, C. (1979), 'Cerebral hemispheric lateralization of cognitive deficits due to alcoholism', *Jrnl. of Nerv. and Ment. Disease, 167(4),* 212-17
Nauta, W. (1964), 'Some efferent connections of the prefrontal cortex in monkeys' in Warren, J. and Akert, K. (eds.), *The Frontal Granular Cortex and Behavior,* McGraw-Hill, New York, 397-409
O'Leary, M., Donovan, D.M., Chaney, E.F. and Walker, R.D. (1979), 'Cognitive impairment and treatment outcome with alcoholics: Preliminary findings', *Jrnl. of Clinical Psychiatry, 56,* 397-8
O'Leary, M.R., Donovan, D.M., Chaney, E.F., Walker, R.D. and Schau, E.J. (January 1979), 'Application of discriminant analysis to level of performance of alcoholics and nonalcoholics on Wechsler-Bellevue and Halstead-Reitan Subtests', *Jrnl. of Clin. Psychol., 35(1),* 204-8

O'Leary, M.R., Radford, L.M., Chaney, E.F. and Schau, E.J. (April 1977), 'Assessment of cognitive recovery in alcoholics by use of the Trail Making Test', *Jrnl. of Clin. Psychol., 33(2)*, 579-82

Ornstein, P. (1977), 'Cognitive deficits in chronic alcoholics', *Psychological Reports, 40*, 719-24

Page, R. and Linden, J. (1974), ' "Reversible" organic brain syndrome in alcoholics', *Quarterly Jrnl. of Studies on Alcohol, 35*, 98-107

Parker, E.S. and Noble, E.P. (1977), 'Alcohol consumption and cognitive functioning in social drinkers', *Jrnl. of Studies on Alcohol, 38(7)*, 1224-32

Parsons, O., Tarter, R. and Edelberg, R. (1972), 'Altered motor control in chronic alcoholics', *Jrnl. of Abnormal Psychology, 80*, 308-14

Pishkin, V., Fishkin, S. and Stahl, M. (1972), 'Concept learning in chronic alcoholics: Psychological and set functions', *Jrnl. Clin. Psychol., 28*, 328-34

Porteus, S. (1959) *The Maze Test and Clinical Psychology*, Pacific Books, Palo Alto, California

Pribram, K. (1958), 'Comparative neurology and the evolution of behavior' in Roe, A. and Simpson, G. (eds.), *Behavior and Evolution*, Yale University Press, New Haven, Connecticut

Rhodes, R., Carr, J. and Jurji, E. (1968), 'Interpersonal differentiation and perceptual field differentiation', *Perceptual and Motor Skills, 27*, 172-4

Rudin, S. and Stagner, R. (1958), 'Figure-ground phenomena in the perception of physical and social stimuli', *Jrnl. Psychol., 45*, 213-25

Ryan, C. and Butters, N. (1979), 'Accelerated aging in chronic alcoholics: Evidence from tests of learning and memory', Paper presented at 10th Annual NCA/ANSA/RSA Medical-Scientific Conference, Washington, D.C.

———— (1980a), 'Learning and Memory impairments in young and old alcoholics: Evidence for the premature-aging by hypothesis', *Alcoholism: Clin. Ex. Res., 4,* in press

———— (1980b), 'Further evidence of a continuum-of-impairment encompassing alcoholic Korsakoff patients and chronic alcoholics', *Alcoholism: Clin. Ex. Res., 4,* 190-8

Schau, E.J. and O'Leary, M.R. (1977), 'A comparison of adaptive abilities of hospitalized alcoholics and matched controls using the brain-age quotient', *Jrnl. of Studies on Alcohol, 38*, 403-9

Segal, B., Kushnarev, V., Urakov, I. and Misionzhnik, E. (1970), 'Alcoholism and disruption of the activity of deep cerebral structures: Clinical-laboratory research', *Quart. J. Studies Alc., 31*, 587-601

Silber, M., Hirschenfang, S. and Benton, J. (1968), 'Psychological factors and prognosis in peripheral neuropathy', *Diseases of the Nervous System, 29*, 688-92

Skillicorn, S. (1955), 'Presenile cerebellar ataxia in chronic alcoholics', *Neurology, 5*, 527-34

Smith, H.H. and Smith, L.S. (January 1977), 'WAIS functioning of cirrhotic and noncirrhotic alcoholics', *Jrnl. of Clin. Psych., 33(1)*, 309-13

Smith, J., Johnson, L. and Burdick, J. (1971), 'Sleep, psychological and clinical change during alcohol withdrawal in NAS-treated alcoholics', *Quart. Jrnl. of Studies on Alcohol, 32*, 982-4

Talland, G. (1963), 'Alcoholism and reaction time', *Quart. Jrnl. Studies on Alcohol, 24*, 610-21

———— (1965) *Deranged Memory: A Psychonomic Study of the Amnestic Syndrome*, Academic, New York

Tarter, R. (1971), 'Neuropsychological examination of cognition and perceptual capacities in chronic alcoholics', Unpublished doctoral dissertation, University of Oklahoma

———— (1973), 'Analysis of cognitive deficits in chronic alcoholics', *Jrnl. of*

Nervous and Mental Diseases, 157, 138-47

―――― (1975), 'Psychological deficits in chronic alcoholics: A review', *The International Jrnl. of Addictions, 10(2),* 327-68

―――― (1976), 'Empirical investigations of psychological deficit' in Tarter, R. and Sugerman, A. (eds.), *Alcoholism; Interdisciplinary Approaches to an Enduring Problem,* Addison-Wesley Publishing Company, Massachusetts

Tarter, R., Buonpane, N. and Wynant, C. (1975), 'Intellectual competence of alcoholics', *Quarterly Jrnl. of Studies on Alcohol, 36,* 381-6

Tarter, R. and Jones, B. (1971a), 'Absence of intellectual deterioration in chronic alcoholics', *Jrnl. Clin. Psychol., 27,* 453-4

―――― (1971b), 'Motor impairment in chronic alcoholics', *Jrnl. Nervous Diseases, 32,* 632-3

Tarter, R., McBride, H., Buonpane, N. and Schneider, D. (July 1977), 'Differentiation of alcoholics: childhood history of minimal brain dysfunction, family history, and drinking pattern', *Archives of General Psychiatry, 43,* 761-8

Tarter, R. and Parsons, O. (1971), 'Conceptual shifting in chronic alcoholics', *Jrnl. of Abnormal Psychology, 77,* 71-5

Teuber, H.L. (1964), 'The riddle of frontal lobe function in man', in Warren, J. and Akert, K. (eds.), *The Frontal Granular Cortex and Behavior,* McGraw-Hill, New York, 410-44

Tumarkin, G., Wilson, J. and Snyder, G. (1955), 'Cerebral atrophy due to alcoholism in young adults', *U.S. Armed Forces Medical Jrnl., 6,* 57-74

Vivian, T., Goldstein, G. and Shelly, C. (1973), 'Reaction time and motor speed in chronic alcoholics', *Perceptual and Motor Skills, 36,* 136-8

Walker, D. and Freund, G. (1973), 'Impairment of timing behavior after prolonged alcohol consumption in rats', *Science, 182,* 597-8

Weingartner, H. and Faillace, L. (1971), 'Alcohol state-dependent learning in man', *Jrnl. of Nervous and Mental Diseases, 153,* 395-406

Weingartner, H., Faillace, L. and Markley, H. (1970), 'Verbal information retention in alcoholics', *Quarterly Jrnl. of Studies on Alcohol, 4,* 983, prepublication abstract

―――― (1971), 'Verbal information retention in alcoholics', *Quarterly Jrnl. of Studies on Alcohol, 32,* 293-303

Williams, J.D., Ray, C.G. and Overall, J.E. (1973), 'Mental aging and organicity in an alcoholic population', *Jrnl. Consulting and Clin. Psych., 41(3),* 392-6

Witkin, H., Karp, S. and Goodenough, D. (1959), 'Dependence in alcoholics', *Quarterly Jrnl. on Studies on Alcohol, 20,* 493-504

Witkin, H., Lewis, H., Hertzman, M., Machover, K., Meissner, P. and Wapner, S. (1954) *Personality Through Perception: An Experiment and Clinical Study,* Harper and Row, New York

Zangwill, O. (1966), 'Psychological deficits associated with frontal lobe lesions', *Intern. Jrnl. Neurolog., 5,* 395-402

16 CONCLUSION

G.K. Shaw

The Helping Hand Organisation treats and rehabilitates alcoholics and drug dependents, so that its concerns are of a practical kind. When therefore, they decided to bring together basic scientists and clinicians active in the field of dependency for a symposium to mark their fifteenth anniversary, two themes of practical importance for the field workers were chosen for study. Dependence, which by depriving the individual of choice, makes the attainment of abstinence difficult, and brain damage, which limits the individual's capacity for co-operation and his ability to benefit from rehabilitative measures.

It is not my intention to review individual chapters of this book, but I would like to comment on some themes which seem central. In his opening chapter, Sir Hans Krebs talked of that important human attribute, the ability to adapt to changing circumstances. He reminded us that, in biochemical terms, much of this adaptability rests on the capacity of the liver to synthesise enzymes appropriate to the needs of the moment. Alcohol's ability to impair that adaptability by, *inter alia*, inhibiting protein synthesis, was a theme to which many speakers returned during the course of the symposium. Albert Hertz, for example, when reviewing the similarity of effects of ethanol and opiates on the endorphin system, pointed out that opiates, and possibly alcohol, may act by blocking the uptake of specific amino-acids, thereby inhibiting the synthesis of endorphin precursors.

The debate over the role of acetaldehyde remains unresolved. Cogent arguments supporting the view that condensation products of acetaldehyde and catecholamines can produce long-lasting changes in alcohol preference in laboratory animals have been advanced. Doubts that acetaldehyde was formed in the brain in sufficient quantity to play a part in dependence or brain damage in humans have also been repeatedly expressed.

Interesting animal studies distinguishing between the related but not identical states of tolerance and dependence were described, as was the careful description of changes in the synaptic membrane following exposure to alcohol. The intriguing possibility of manipulating tolerance and dependence in the human has now been opened up.

The second part of the book has focused on clinical investigations of brain damage. Older clinical studies have now been amply confirmed by the new techniques of computerised tomography. It can no longer be doubted that chronic exposure to alcohol is followed by brain changes in an alarmingly high proportion of cases. That these brain changes are important is attested to by the careful psychological measurements carried out in the reported studies and in the studies reviewed by Ralph Tarter. It is a matter of considerable surprise that recent drinking history is more highly predictive of damage than length or quantity of drinking, as is the encouraging finding that some improvement in the brain picture occurs after a lengthy period of abstinence. It will clearly be important to know how far this damage syndrome is reversible with abstinence and whether there is any way by which recovery can be expedited.

The question of constitutional vulnerability to dependence and brain damage has been touched upon in a number of chapters and there were suggestions supporting this thesis from animal studies on the cell membrane and the studies on neurotransmitters.

It is likely that there are many routes to alcoholic brain damage, and a number of possible mechanisms have been discussed. Changes in the endocrine system perhaps operating via hypoglycaemia, the role of vitamin deficiency, toxic and nutritional disorders secondary to liver damage, and the possibility that an imbalance in the availability of amino acids might result in deprivation or intoxication of the nerve cell were all suggested as possible mechanisms. A theme to which many authors have alluded, however, is interference of transport of nutrients across the cell membrane, and many different ways in which this might be affected have been suggested. Changes in lipo-protein structure of the cell membrane itself, blockade of carrier systems by unwanted amino acids, alterations in calcium ion concentration and deficiency of thiamine were all commented on in terms of their ability to impair transport into the cell.

It is clear that much research and much speculation is required before exact mechanisms can be fully understood. The gravity of the situation has, however, been so patently demonstrated that one must hope that researchers and grant-giving bodies will be willing to explore these areas as a matter of urgency.

Finally, I would wish to pay tribute to the chairmen of the individual sessions, Dr Derek Richter, Dr Brian Hoare, Dr Max Glatt and Dr D.L. Davies for their significant contribution to the success of the symposium upon which this book is based.

NOTES ON CONTRIBUTORS

Derek Richter, former Director, MRC Neuropsychiatry Unit, Epsom and Carshalton, England, and former Secretary-General, International Brain Research Organisation.

Hans Krebs, Metabolic Research Laboratory, Nuffield Department of Clinical Medicine, Radcliffe Infirmary, Oxford, England.

Virginia E. Davis, Director, Neurochemistry and Addiction Research Laboratory, Veterans Administration Medical Center, and Research Associate Professor of Biochemistry, Department of Biochemistry and Medicine, Baylor College of Medicine, Houston, Texas, USA.

Jesse L. Cashaw, Research Chemist, Neurochemistry and Addiction Research Laboratory, Veterans Administration Medical Center, Houston, Texas, USA.

Kenneth D. McMurtrey, Research Chemist, Veterans Administration Medical Center; Research Associate, Department of Biochemistry, Baylor College of Medicine, Houston, Texas, USA.

John M. Littleton, Department of Pharmacology, King's College, London.

Marie E. Bardsley and *Keith F. Tipton*, Department of Biochemistry, Trinity College, Dublin, Eire.

Oliver E. Pratt, Institute of Psychiatry, London.

Boris Takaboff, S. Urwyler and *P.L. Hoffman,* Department of Physiology and Biophysics, University of Illinois Medical Center, Chicago, USA.

Albert Herz, Department of Neuropharmacology, Max-Planck Institute for Psychiatry, Munich.

Vincent Marks, Department of Biochemistry, University of Surrey, Guildford, England.

Vladimir Hudolin, University Department for Neurology, Psychiatry, Alcoholism and other Dependencies, Zagreb, Yugoslavia.

Hans Bergman, Stefan Borg, Carl-Magnus Ideström and *Sture Mützell*, Department of Clinical Alcohol and Drug Research, Karolinska Institute, Stockholm, Sweden.

Thomas Hindmarsh, Department of Neuroradiology, Karolinska Sjukhuset, Stockholm, Sweden.

W.A. Lishman, M. Ron and *W. Acker*, Institute of Psychiatry, London.

C.G. Gottfries, University of Göteborg Psychiatric Research Centre, St. Jörgen's Hospital, Hisings Backa, Sweden.

M. Del Vecchio, L. Vacca, G. Iorio, M. Maj and *D. Kemali,* Prima Clinica Psichiatrica, Centro Medico e di Assistenza Sociale per le Tossicodipendenze, Policlinico Universitario, Naples, Italy.

F. Marciano and *G. Nolfe*, Consiglio Nazionale delle Richerche, Laboratori di Cibernetica, Sezione Bioelettronica, Arco Felice, Naples, Italy.

Allan D. Thomson, S.A. Rae and *A. Rowe*, Greenwich District Hospital, London.

Ralph E. Tarter, Associate Director and Chief, Clinical Neuropsychology, Neurobehaviour Research and Clinical Centre, Western Psychiatric Institute and Clinics, University of Pittsburg Medical School, USA.

G.K. Shaw, Bexley Hospital, Bexley, Kent, England.

INDEX